Reasoning from Evidence

Reasoning From Evidence

INDUCTIVE LOGIC

William Gustason

PURDUE UNIVERSITY

Macmillan College Publishing Company
NEW YORK

Maxwell Macmillan Canada
TORONTO

Maxwell Macmillan International
NEW YORK   OXFORD   SINGAPORE   SYDNEY

Editor: Maggie Barbieri
Production Supervisor: Bert Yaeger
Production Manager: Su Levine
Text Designer: Tash Sylvester
Cover Designer: Lauren Cohn

This book was set in Century Schoolbook by Carlisle Communications
and was printed and bound by Book Press.
The cover was printed by New England Book Components.

Macmillan College Publishing Company
866 Third Avenue, New York, New York 10022

Macmillan College Publishing Company is part of
the Maxwell Communication Group of Companies.

Maxwell Macmillan Canada, Inc.
1200 Eglinton Avenue East
Suite 200
Don Mills, Ontario M3C 3NI

Library of Congress Cataloging-in-Publication Data
Gustason, William.
    Reasoning from evidence : inductive logic / William Gustason.
        p.   cm.
    Includes index.
    ISBN 0-02-348533-7 (paper)
    1. Induction (Logic)   I. Title.
    BC91.G87   1994
    161—dc20   93–7501
                                                                    CIP

Printing: 1 2 3 4 5 6 7   Year: 4 5 6 7 8 9 0

Preface

This book grew out of notes used for a one-semester undergraduate course in inductive logic. Its aim is to provide a general introduction to the principles and problems of inductive inference. Topics found in elementary, general-purpose logic texts are covered in greater depth, and there is extensive coverage of subjects typically not found in them at all. No previous training in logic is required; the elements of deductive logic (specifically sentential logic) necessary for studying some of the topics covered are introduced in the last section of the first chapter. Beyond that, a familiarity with some very basic high school algebra will be helpful in a few places, and even in those contexts assistance for readers without a technical background is often provided.

At present, few colleges and universities are offering one-semester courses on induction, but their number is slowly growing. Inductive logic surely is as worthy of a full-semester introductory treatment as deductive logic, and because it focuses on such topics as chance, decision making, and scientific method, many students find it more appealing than the sometimes dry formalities (at least from their viewpoint) of sentential and quantificational logic. Ideally, those faculty contemplating the addition of an inductive logic course to their curriculum will find this text to be one that suits their needs. It is also hoped that students and interested readers will find the issues discussed here stimulating and worthy of further investigation (many references for further reading are provided throughout and a bibliography is provided at the end of the last chapter).

Of course, there are other applications, too. This book can serve as a useful reference source for undergraduate and graduate-level philosophy courses in subjects such as the philosophy of science and epistemology. Those in other fields, such as statistics and decision theory, should find it a useful supplement as well. Naturally, the book would fail in its purpose if it could not be read with profit by an interested reader having no formal academic commitment.

It is widely agreed that inductive logic has made less progress in the twentieth century than deductive logic, so it is not surprising that there is less of a consensus on what are the "standard" topics for an introductory discussion. Moreover, controversial issues arise more frequently concerning even the most elementary material in the field. I have tried to select topics based, first, on what consensus there appears to be, and second, on what is important and can be readily absorbed by students with a minimal background in logic and philosophy. Included in the discussion of topics that historically have been much debated is coverage of widely differing points of view. On the problem of justification, for example, several well-known approaches are covered in the fifth and seventh chapters. However, considerations of space and continuity preclude such coverage for all topics on which controversy exists (for example, the Dutch Book approach to justifying the calculus). In such cases, though, the instructor should be able to easily supplement the discussion with his or her own material if desired.

The text also provides some flexibility in order of coverage. Chapters Two and Three (on basic forms of induction and probability, respectively) could be covered in reverse order; Chapter Six (on hypotheses and problems in confirmation) could then be taken up directly following coverage of the second chapter. Because the text probably offers more material than would be covered in a one-semester (or certainly in a one-quarter) course, all or parts of Chapters Four and Seven can be omitted if coverage of technical matters is not a high priority (the last section of Chapter Five could be ignored, too). However, if such coverage is desired, all or parts of Chapters Two and Six could be omitted.

The final chapter (on the basic theories of inductive probability) offers more challenging material than the preceding ones, and an understanding of the third, fourth, and fifth chapters is essential. Instructors should expect to spend more than the usual amount of class time covering it. However, it will be time well spent for those who want a more than cursory examination of the work of Carnap, Reichenbach, and Bayesian theorists.

Anyone who writes a book owes many debts. The publisher's reviewers provided some valuable suggestions and corrections, as did my friends and colleagues, Rod Bertolet, Howard Kenreuther, Annie Pirruccello, and Ted Ulrich. Thanks go also to the many students who have used this material in one form or another in the past; their advice was especially helpful. Finally, I must thank Arthur Burks of the University of Michigan, from whom I first learned about induction and probability. That he has made many important contributions to these fields is well known; that he has been a guiding influence and inspiration to his many students is not.

Contents

CHAPTER 1

Inductive and Deductive Logic

Section 1. The Appraisal of Arguments _____

Logic is an area of philosophy, but it is also a science. Like mathematics it is a formal (or *a priori*) science whose problems can be dealt with in a study rather than a laboratory. It is sometimes described as the science of "reasoning" or "inference," and sometimes as the study of the "laws of thought"; but although these characterizations can be initially helpful, they can also be misleading. Reasoning (inferring, thinking) is a mental process and as such is the province of the empirical sciences of psychology and physiology. Logic does not study mental or brain activity and hence is not concerned with the actual process of reasoning. But the beginning and end points of the process are of prime interest. That is, we reason *from* certain items of information *to* another such item. The former are the **premises** of the inference, the latter its **conclusion.** And the question to be asked is: Do the premises *warrant* or *justify* the conclusion? Do they provide adequate grounds for accepting it?

These questions make clear that reasoning can be done well or badly, according to whether the premises do or do not warrant the conclusion. So we can rephrase our question in two parts: Is the inference of the conclusion from the premises a correct (or "good") one, and if so, on what basis do we judge it to be correct? One of the major tasks of logic is determining what good reasoning consists in and developing methods that will enable us to distinguish good inferences from bad ones. Logic is thus a normative science as well as a descriptive one; it not only studies the mechanisms underlying good reasoning, but in doing so it provides us with standards by which we *should* reason.

We express our thoughts—and hence the inferences in which they occur—in language. When we reason, we attempt to show that the conclusion is *true* given the premises, and truths are communicated through the use of sentences. Therefore premises and conclusions may be represented by the sentences of a given language, but not all sentences may serve in this capacity. Interrogative sentences ("Is the door closed?") and imperative sentences ("Close the door!") are not used to say something true or false, but rather to express questions and commands, respectively. Our main concern is with *indicative* sentences ("The door is closed."), for it is chiefly through them that we make claims that are judged true or false, and hence that may serve as premises and conclusions.

However, the matter is a bit more complicated. We cannot simply ascribe truth and falsehood to indicative sentences per se. The very same sentence can be used on different occasions to express different items of information, some true and some false. The sentence, "Jones was in Chicago yesterday" might be true when said by someone on May 14 of Sam Jones but false when said on June 22 of Betty Jones. Conversely, different sentences may in different contexts be used to express the same item of information; for example, "Jones was in Chicago yesterday" and "Sam Jones was in Chicago on May 13, 1992." We must therefore distinguish between the sentence itself and the information it expresses in a particular context of its use (either spoken or written), and only the latter may be said to be true or false.

Let us use the term 'statement' to mean what a sentence expresses in a given context of use. It is then statements rather than the sentences used to express them that are properly the bearers of truth and falsehood, and hereafter when we write down a sentence and call it a "statement" we will mean that piece of (true-or-false) information the sentence was used to express on a given occasion. The premises and conclusions of our reasoning may be regarded as **statements** in this sense.

A particular instance of reasoning may thus be represented in language as a list of statements, and we now introduce a special term for such lists:

> An **argument** is a set of statements, one of which is marked off as the conclusion of the argument, the rest serving as its premises.

The conclusion states the claim being argued whereas the premises provide the grounds being offered in support of the conclusion. Of course 'argument' is used in many ways in everyday speech; we speak of two people "having an argument" for example, and in mathematics we often talk of a certain quantity as an "argument" of a function, but hereafter, unless otherwise noted, we will use 'argument' only in the technical sense just mentioned.

Arguments are formulated in ordinary language in many ways. Usually the conclusion is signalled by a word such as 'therefore,' 'hence,' 'so,' 'thus,' and so forth, as in "The sky is clouding up, the temperature is falling, and the barometer is dropping rapidly; hence it will rain soon." Sometimes the conclusion is stated first with the premises following a word like 'since' or 'for,' as in "Jones will be defeated in the next election, for he supports higher taxes and most voters are opposed to a tax increase." And very often we do not explicitly state all the premises, presuming that those left out can easily be supplied by our listeners. If someone says, "Mrs. Lopez is a U.S. citizen over the age of 65, so she's eligible for Medicare," the missing premise is that all U.S. citizens over 65 are eligible for Medicare.

At its most elementary level, logic is concerned with the analysis and evaluation of arguments. Arguments come in many varieties, from the simple examples just mentioned to highly complex ones found in almost every human endeavor from theoretical physics to jury trials. A mathematical proof is a chain of arguments, the conclusion of one serving as a premise of a subsequent one. The logician's task is to find methods for appraising arguments: for developing a basis for classifying arguments according to whether their premises warrant the conclusion (the "good" ones) or whether they do not (the "bad" or "fallacious" ones). We will now look at two types of appraisal; they divide our subject into its two basic subareas: deductive logic and inductive logic.

Section 2. Deductive Logic: Validity and Form _____

It may seem strange to begin a study of inductive logic by first looking at deductive logic, but there is a good reason for this: the fundamental concepts of the former are more readily grasped when contrasted with those of the latter. Thus far, we have described arguments simply as being good or bad, correct or incorrect. These vague and not very helpful terms will now be replaced by more precise ones, and in deductive logic the terms we need are 'valid' and 'invalid.' When an argument is assessed from the standpoint of deductive logic, these are the terms that express the evaluation.

We begin with a simple example. Your car's fuel system is acting up, and from your account of the symptoms the mechanic tells you that either the carburetor or the fuel pump is at fault. An inspection of the former shows that everything is in order; the conclusion drawn is that the pump is the culprit.

We have here a simple argument that is undeniably a good—or valid—one

I.   Either the carburetor or the fuel pump is at fault
The carburetor is not at fault
∴ The fuel pump is at fault

(Words for the conclusion will hereafter be replaced by the three-dot sign.)

In a valid argument like (I), the conclusion *follows from* the premises; in an invalid one, it does not. But what does 'follow from' mean here? Notice that if both premises are true, the conclusion cannot fail to be true as well. That is, the truth of the premises *guarantees* a true conclusion. The attempt to suppose that the premises are both true but the conclusion false lands us in an outright contradiction. In argument (I), if the second premise is true then the carburetor is not at fault, and if the conclusion is false then the fuel pump is not at fault; hence *neither* of them is at fault. But the first premise tells us that it is *either* one *or* the other! There is hence no way the conclusion can be false if both premises are true. More fully,

> An argument is **valid** if and only if it is impossible for all of its premises to be true but its conclusion false.

Of course in many cases not all of the premises *are* true. Yet the argument can still be valid; it is important to realize that validity is a conditional notion: *if* we have true premises we thereby have a true conclusion as well. Each of the following arguments has a false premise, and in one of them the conclusion is false too. Both, however, are still valid; were the premises all true, the conclusion's truth would be guaranteed:

If 3 is even, then 3 is a multiple of 2   Either 3 or 5 is odd
3 is even   3 is not odd
∴ 3 is a multiple of 2   ∴ 5 is odd

To repeat, in many valid arguments not all premises are true, but what makes them valid is that *if* all premises were true the conclusion could not possibly be false. Valid arguments are, so to speak, "truth preserving."

It is an important fact that we can argue validly from false premises as well as true ones. In the empirical sciences, as we shall see later, scientists typically formulate hypotheses to explain various phenomena, and many of them are eventually shown to be false. This is often done by validly deducing from them a testable consequence. If experimental tests show the consequence to be false, then the hypothesis from which they were deduced is disconfirmed.

The upshot is that in evaluating an argument, there are at least two quite distinct questions to be asked:

Is the argument valid?
Are all of its premises in fact true?

The questions are equally important but only the first one falls within the province of logic. If the premises are about subatomic particles or the mating habits of polar bears or Napoleon's military prowess, then to determine their truth the persons to be consulted are (respectively) a physicist, zoologist, or historian, certainly not a logician. To establish definitively the truth of the conclusion, a "yes" answer to both questions is required, but a logician's expertise is relevant only to answering the first of them.

The following argument admits of a "yes" answer to the second question but not to the first:

II. If dogs are mammals, then they are vertebrates
    Dogs are vertebrates
    ∴ Dogs are mammals

All three statements are true, but the trouble is that the conclusion *does not follow from* the premises. If we rely on just the information provided by the premises, there is no reason for us to rule out dogs falling into the category of nonmammalian vertebrate. So although the conclusion is true along with the premises being true, its truth is not established by those premises—they do not guarantee its truth. Argument (II) is thus **invalid**—*it is possible for its conclusion to be false when all of its premises are true.*

So an invalid argument need not actually have true premises and a false conclusion; argument (II) shows that it is the possibility of such that makes it invalid. Of course, many invalid arguments do in fact have true premises and false conclusions, and they provide a means of showing that arguments like (II) are invalid as well. That is, if someone were to propose argument (II), we could show that person the error of his or her ways by comparing it to the following argument where the reasoning takes exactly the same form but has an obviously false conclusion accompanying true premises:

III. If whales are fish, then they are aquatic animals
    Whales are aquatic animals
    ∴ Whales are fish

The truth that dogs are mammals no more follows from the premises of (II) than the falsehood that whales are fish follows from the premises of (III).

More needs to be said about how the word *impossible* is being used in our definition of validity. In one common sense, it is impossible for a human being to lift a 4,000-pound object or for an unsupported object near the earth not to fall to the ground or for litmus paper not to turn red when dipped in acid. This is called *physical* (or sometimes *causal*) impossibility, but in saying that it is impossible to have true premises accompanying a false conclusion, we are using 'impossible' in an even stronger sense. We would indeed be astounded if, for example, a baseball did not fall to the ground when released from my hand, but we can still entertain the supposition of such an event occurring, no matter how farfetched or miraculous it would be. On the other hand, we cannot suppose there to be an object that is both round and not round at the same time; no such miraculous situation can be entertained here, for roundness and nonroundness *logically* exclude one another whereas being-released-from-my-hand and not-falling-to-the-ground do not. Although we can consider the possibility of an unsupported object not falling, there is no "possibility" of an object being round and not round simultaneously. The latter is a *logical* impossibility, and to revert to argument (I), the supposition that its conclusion is false when its premises are true is impossible in this sense. To suppose the fuel pump is not at fault flatly contradicts the premises, just as 'this is not round' contradicts 'this is round.' In valid inference it is logically impossible for a false conclusion and true premises to occur together.[1]

As a result the following argument is invalid as it stands:

IV. Bert Jones is a 70-year-old human being
Bert Jones's car weighs 3,500 pounds
∴ Bert Jones cannot lift his car

The supposition that the conclusion is false does not logically contradict the premises. Of course, if we added a further, well-confirmed premise—namely, that no 70-year-old human being can lift a 3,500 pound automobile—we would *then* have a valid argument.

The following argument has exactly the same form as argument (I):

V. Either Alice missed her train or else the train was late
Alice did not miss her train
∴ The train was late

Both arguments of course are valid, but what is important here is that they are valid *because* of the form they share; their content or subject matter has no bearing on their assessment as valid inferences. Validity depends only on the meanings of purely logical terms like 'either-or' and 'not'; those of the other constituent expressions can be ignored. Using the letters 'p' and 'q' to represent any pair of statements whatever, the common form of (I) and (V) is expressed

   a.   either p or q
            not-p
            $\therefore q$

Any argument of this form is valid. If this point is not already clear, we need only ask: Can there be an argument of form (a) with a false conclusion and true premises? The conclusion being false means that q is false. Now can we find a statement p such that both premises are true? No, because

   i. if we pick a statement for p that is true then the second premise is false
   ii. if we pick a statement for p that is false then the first premise is false (a disjunction or "either-or" statement is false whenever both component statements are false).

So in no case are there statements p and q that will give us true premises and false conclusion, and to show this, we did not need to specify particular statements for p and q. The point holds quite generally: *arguments are valid solely in virtue of their form.*

   Now let us return to arguments (II) and (III). We saw that both are invalid and that they also share a common form:

   b.   if p then q
            q
            $\therefore p$

Unlike form (a), we can obtain arguments with true premises and false conclusions from form (b) by finding appropriate statements for p and q. Argument (III) is a perfect example, where 'Whales are fish' replaces p and 'Whales are aquatic animals' replaces q. Not all arguments produced from form (b) will be like this; argument (II), which fallaciously inferred the truth that dogs are mammals, illustrates that. But the fact that there are any at all with true premises and false conclusion means that (b) is an *invalid argument form*; if we reason according to it, we can be led to false conclusions even if we begin with true premises. Such forms illuminate the sense of 'possible' used in our definition of invalidity: of all the specific arguments derivable from such a form, some will lead us from truths to a falsehood. In a *valid argument form* like (a), this can never happen no matter what specific statements are substituted for p and q.

Corresponding to every argument form is a *rule of inference*. A rule is by the nature of the case general; it must be applicable to a number of similar instances. For argument form (a) we have the following rule:

> *From*: a statement of the form *either p or q* and one of the form
> *not-p*
> *To infer*: the statement q

This rule "governs" instances like arguments (I) and (V). Since arguments are valid solely in virtue of their form, the notion of validity should be regarded as applying primarily to rules of inference. The specific arguments derivable by substitution from the associated argument form are valid in virtue of being governed by the rule. Our primary definition of validity is thus:

> A rule of inference is **valid** if and only if no argument derivable from its associated argument form has all true premises and a false conclusion. Otherwise, it is **invalid.**

(However, we shall continue to employ the earlier definition too.) At its most basic level, then, deductive logic is concerned with developing methods that will enable us to distinguish valid from invalid rules of inference.

Exercises

1. Construct two arguments whose premises and conclusion are all false, one of which is valid and the other invalid.

2. Show that the following argument forms are invalid by finding statements for p and for q that yield true premises and a false conclusion.

  a. either p or q **b.** if p then q
  $\therefore p$ not-p
                                             $\therefore$ not-q

3. Give an informal proof or explanation of why the following forms are valid.

  a. p **b.** if p then q
  $\therefore$ either p or q not-q
                                             $\therefore$ not-p

Section 3. Inductive Logic: Evidence and Probability _____

Arguments (II) and (III) of the previous section were invalid, and once seen to be invalid they are of little further interest. However argument (IV)—about Bert Jones lifting his car—was in *some* sense a "good" one even though invalid. Many arguments are like this; although invalid by the standards of deductive logic, they are still worthwhile and important. Here are some further cases:

   I.   95 percent of all native Italians are Roman Catholics.
        Angela is a native Italian.
   ∴ Angela is a Roman Catholic.

   II.   Smith was killed in his home by a .38 caliber revolver
          belonging to Jones.
        Jones badly needed money to pay off a large gambling debt.
        Jones has hated Smith for years.
        Jones was having an affair with Smith's wife, who would
          collect on Smith's life insurance policy in case of death.
        Two reliable witnesses saw Jones leave Smith's house about
          10 minutes after the estimated time of death.
        Jones's fingerprints were found on the murder weapon.
        Smith's wife testifies that she conspired with Jones to
          murder her husband.
   ∴ Jones murdered Smith.

   III.   [Shortly after the invention of the microscope,
        microorganisms were discovered in "fermentable" liquids
        such as meat broth and sugared yeast water. Some
        theorists claimed they arose through "spontaneous
        generation," but Louis Pasteur hypothesized that they
        entered the liquids from the air using as their vehicles
        airborne dust particles that came in contact with the
        liquids.]

Premise: Earlier experiments conducted by Pasteur had shown, first, that the dust particles carry with them microorganisms and, second, that sterilized fermentable liquids exposed only to purified air do not develop microorganisms. Pasteur then had special flasks made with long, very thin goosenecks. When meat broth was poured in and sterilized, the moisture that collected in the necks allowed air to pass through but blocked the dust particles. Broth was also placed in standard, wide-necked flasks and sterilized. In a short time, the liquids in these flasks developed microorganisms but those in the thin-necked flasks never did. In the former case, everything in the air entered the flask and microorganisms were found; in the latter, everything in the air *except* the dust entered and microorganisms were *not* found. Only when the thin-necked flasks were shaken vigorously enough to dislodge the dust that had collected in the neck were microorganisms detected in the broth.

Conclusion: Microorganisms enter fermentable liquids from the air by means of airborne dust particles.

All three arguments are invalid: Angela might be one of the few Italians who is not Roman Catholic; Jones conceivably is the victim of an elaborate and cunning frame-up; and it is barely possible that some component of the air other than the dust was blocked in the goose-necks or that some slip-up in the laboratory skewed the results of the experiment (in fact, of course, Pasteur's experiment was repeated many times with the same results).

But although it is *possible* in all three instances to have a false conclusion when the premises are true, it is *highly improbable* that this is the case. The premises provide strong evidence for the conclusion, and it is thus very likely the conclusion is true given the truth of the premises. In argument (II) the evidence contained in the premises makes the conclusion so probable that a jury would perhaps consider its truth to be "beyond reasonable doubt."

In deductive logic arguments are appraised as valid or invalid. Invalid arguments like the preceding three are still good ones when appraised in terms of how much *evidence* the premises provide for the conclusion. This kind of appraisal is the province of inductive logic, and we can now define the inductive counterpart of the term 'valid':

> An argument is **inductively strong** if and only if, first, it is invalid, but second, the evidence supplied by its premises makes it highly improbable that its conclusion is false when all premises are true.

In valid inferences, true premises guarantee a true conclusion; in inductively strong ones, true premises make it highly probable that the conclusion is true. Moreover, whereas arguments are valid by virtue of their form, arguments are inductively strong by virtue of the strength of the evidence they contain.

Validity is an all-or-nothing affair: an argument cannot be "partly valid" or "two-thirds valid." Inductive strength, however, is a matter of degree according to *how much* evidence is provided by the premises and therefore *how probable* the conclusion is. In argument (III) the degree of inductive strength is increased if a description of Pasteur's later work is included in the premise; it is decreased if the claim that dust particles carry microorganisms is deleted. In the following argument, the first four premises are the same as those of argument II but the last three are quite different. Here, we have an argument that, although it makes the conclusion probable, does not confer upon it as high a probability as does argument (II). In other words, it is a weaker argument—one with a lower degree of inductive strength:

> Smith was killed in his home with a .38-caliber revolver belonging to Jones.
> Jones badly needed money to pay off a large gambling debt.
> Jones has hated Smith for years.
> Jones was having an affair with Smith's wife, who would collect on his life insurance in case of death.
> A friend of Smith's who dislikes Jones claims he saw Jones leave Smith's house about 10 minutes after the estimated time of death.
> No fingerprints were found on the murder weapon.
> Smith's wife admits an affair with Jones but denies any murder plot.
> ∴ Jones murdered Smith.

While the evidence here would perhaps justify *indicting* Jones, it is doubtful a trial jury would consider it sufficient for conviction. The truth of the conclusion would not be regarded as being beyond reasonable doubt.

An **inductively weak** argument is simply one with a low degree of inductive strength—the premises offer some evidence for the conclusion but not enough to make the conclusion highly probable. In other words, there is a significant chance that the conclusion is false when the premises are true.[2] If we tinker further with the premises of (II) we obtain an inductively weak argument:

> Smith was killed in his home by a .38-caliber revolver.
> Jones has hated Smith for years.
> Jones was having an affair with Smith's wife, who would collect on his life insurance in case of death.
> Jones has no serious financial problems.
> No one was observed at Smith's house the night he died, and a bartender at the Kit Kat Cafe testifies that Jones was there during the estimated time of death.
> No fingerprints were found on the murder weapon.

Smith's wife admits to an affair with Jones but denies any
   murder plot.
∴ Jones murdered Smith.

Some of the evidence here might initially make Jones a *suspect,* but by
itself it is surely not sufficient to warrant indictment, much less
conviction.

We saw in the last section that a valid argument can have false
premises and a false conclusion, and the same holds for inductively
strong ones. The premises and conclusion of the following argument
are all false:

98 percent of all Republican politicians are liberals
John's 5-year-old daughter is a Republican politician
∴ John's 5-year-old daughter is a liberal

Yet the argument is inductively strong, for *if* the premises were true
they would make the conclusion's truth highly probable. Inductive
strength depends on the evidential relation between the premises and
conclusion, and here the information in the premises provides strong
evidence for the conclusion. The fact that the premises are undoubt-
edly false does not in any way affect the point that, were they true, the
conclusion's truth would be highly probable.

In light of this, what are we to say about the following argument?

Al's Buick gets at least 75 miles to the gallon
∴ Al's Buick gets over 200 miles to the gallon

The argument is inductively weak since the premise does not confer a
high probability on the conclusion. Notice however that, if we had
defined inductive strength as follows,

it is highly improbable that the conclusion is false *and* the
   premises are all true

then we would be forced to say that the argument was inductively
strong. For given the present state of development of internal combustion engines, it is very unlikely Al's Buick (or any standard production
car) gets at least 75 mpg. But this means that it is highly improbable
to have *both* a true premise and a false conclusion for the simple
reason that it is highly improbable that the premise is true to begin
with. Put another way, if it is improbable that the premise is true,
then the combination true-premise–false-conclusion must be improbable too.

In fact, however, we did not define inductive strength in this way. Instead, we said that the evidence makes it highly improbable for the conclusion to be false *when* the premises are all true, and the force of 'when' is not that of 'and' but of 'if' or 'given that.' The preceding argument is inductively weak because, even if the premise were true, it does not supply evidence that would make the conclusion's truth highly probable.

The contrast between validity and inductive strength can be set out in another way. The following argument is valid, it is impossible—not just improbable—for the conclusion to be false when the premise is true:

John is a bachelor
∴ John is unmarried

Since the term 'bachelor' is defined as 'adult unmarried male person,' the premise in effect tells us that John is such a person, and hence the information in the conclusion is already contained in the premise. Every valid argument is like this (but usually not in such a transparent way); that is, the content of its conclusion is present at least implicitly in that of the premise(s). This is but a consequence of the thesis, discussed earlier, that the denial of the conclusion of a valid argument logically contradicts its premises. Just as 'this is not round' contradicts 'this is both round and red,' so but in a somewhat less obvious way does 'John is not unmarried' contradict 'John is a bachelor.' The fact that he is a bachelor must include the fact of his being unmarried; otherwise, it would be logically possible to deny that he is unmarried while upholding his bachelorhood. In a valid inference, then, the information expressed in the premises includes the claim made by the conclusion.

This is not to say that all valid arguments are trivial or uninformative. From a psychological standpoint, they can yield conclusions that are surprising and unexpected—they can provide us with information of which we were not previously aware in any explicit form. Many people were surprised when it was proved that there is no greatest prime number, and the proof consisted of a chain of valid arguments whose first premises were well-known mathematical principles. The claim that no greatest prime exists is logically part of the content of those principles, but given the complexity of the content, discerning that fact is anything but easy.

An inductively strong argument, however, *can* have a false conclusion with true premises, and so denying the conclusion does not logically contradict the premises. The possibility of describing a situation in which the conclusion is false when the premises are true means that the conclusion supplies information that "goes beyond" the claims made by the premises. The conclusion makes a further claim distinct from those in the premises and is related to them by the key notion of inductive logic, that of *evidence*. The conclusion's content is not contained in that of the premises, but rather stakes out new ground that is *evidentially supported* by the data the premises provide. Inductively strong inference is by nature probable inference; there is always some risk, however small, that the evidence will lead us from truths to a falsehood. But it is by such inference that we incorporate "new" items into our accepted body of knowledge—information that was not even implicitly present before.

To this point, we have not used the terms 'inductive argument' and 'deductive argument.' Such terms can be misleading—suggesting that there are two sharply defined categories of argument. Rather, the contrast is not between arguments themselves, but in the criteria for appraising them. From the perspective of deductive logic, we may classify arguments as valid or invalid according to the form they exhibit. From that of inductive logic, we may classify them according to their degree of inductive strength, the prime consideration here being the amount of evidence the premises provide for the conclusion. Hereafter, when terms like *inductive argument* or *inductive inference* are used we shall mean the following: an invalid argument to be appraised in terms of the degree of evidential support the premises provide for the conclusion.

It might seem natural at this point to proceed as we did in our discussion of deductive logic; there, we talked about argument forms and the related concept of rules of inference. We can readily formulate some simple forms of argument that are studied by inductive logic. For example, where the italicized capital letters 'F' and 'G' abbreviate expressions for properties of individuals (such as "being a native Italian"), and the small letter 'x' serves as a variable ranging over individuals and 'n' ranges over real numbers from zero to 100, we can lay out the form of argument (I) as follows:

n% of all individuals that are F are also G
x is F
$\therefore$ x is G

This form of inference is simple enough—and used often enough—to have earned a name: *Statistical Syllogism*. The corresponding rule of inference would be this:

From: statements of the forms 'n% of all observed F's are G' and 'x is F'
To infer: a statement of the form 'x is G'

But a rule such as this is of limited practical interest. We saw that, if a rule of inference in deductive logic is appraised as valid, all arguments of its associated form are likewise valid. Here, however, some arguments derivable from the preceding form will be inductively strong but others will be inductively weak; it all depends on what specific choices we make for F, G, n, and x. In inductive logic we usually focus on other rules governing argument forms—rules that enable us to make judgments about the degree of inductive strength possessed by specific arguments of those forms. Stated very simply, one such rule for the above form would be this:

The closer n is to 100, the stronger is the argument.

Most rules of this sort, however, are anything but simple. In general, argument forms studied by inductive logic are much more complex and intractable than those of deductive logic; and this is perhaps the chief reason why inductive logic is the less advanced discipline of the two. It is very difficult to formulate general rules of inference governing arguments like (II) and (III), and we will not even try to do this. The Pasteur argument, for example, is much more resistant to formal treatment than those studied by deductive logic. Historically, attempts have been made to identify simple inductive argument forms and to formulate rules governing them, yet even in these simple cases the rules are not as easily applied as those of deductive logic. We shall take a closer look at these matters in Chapter Two.

Several problems arise when we attempt to state such rules formally and in general terms. For one thing, many inferences argue from an observed "sample" to a general population, and the degree of inductive strength of such inferences is influenced by whether the sample is a "fair" one—whether the data are gathered by an unbiased procedure. For another, general "background information" is often assumed in inductive inference, information in addition to the stated premises but not explicitly formulated (for example, in argument (II) such information would include the fact that many people who have been deeply in debt have resorted to foul play). Both background information and methods of data acquisition affect an argument's inductive strength and must somehow be factored into a general formulation of inductive rules. Still another reason has to do with arguments that, like Pasteur's, have a conclusion stating a cause-to-effect relation. Rules governing such arguments must be formulated in such a way that genuine causal connections can be distinguished from accidental correlations.

These are important matters and we shall address them more fully later on. For now, let it suffice to say that given the relatively primitive state of inductive logic, only the simplest forms of inductive inference will be given a formal treatment in this book, and only the most elementary inductive rules will be formulated. Even so, there is still much we can do to shed light on arguments appraisable in terms of the concept of inductive strength.

Addendum: How not to draw the inductive/deductive distinction: It is nothing short of amazing that in the 1990s a long discredited view about the difference between deduction and induction can still be found in some textbooks. This view attempts to draw the deductive/inductive distinction in terms of kinds of arguments instead of the kinds of criteria for evaluating them. The view is that in a "deductive argument" we infer from a general premise to a specific conclusion, whereas in an "inductive argument" we infer from specific premises to a general conclusion.

On this view, then, the following argument must be considered "deductive":

All ravens ever observed have been black
∴ The next raven to be observed will be black

Yet the argument is invalid and the premise offers strong evidence for the conclusion. Hence such an argument in fact belongs to *inductive* logic even though it moves from general to specific instead of the other way around.

Perhaps then we should amend the definition to read "a deductive argument is a *valid* argument that moves from general to specific." But the trouble now is that many valid arguments proceed from general to general or from specific to specific; for example,

All terriers are dogs   Rover is either a terrier or a spaniel
All dogs are mammals   Rover is not a terrier
∴ All terriers are mammals   ∴ Rover is a spaniel

and it is ludicrous to suppose that arguments like these fall outside the scope of deductive logic.

More important, there are valid arguments that proceed from the specific to the general. According to the view in question, they should be classified as inductive, though being valid, they clearly belong to deductive logic. For example,

Detroit is a large city
∴ Everyone who lives near Detroit lives near a large city

The premise's truth does not merely make the conclusion's truth probable, it guarantees it. There are thus arguments from the specific to the general that properly fall within deductive logic and, as we saw earlier, arguments from the general to the specific that properly qualify as inductive inferences.

Exercises

1. The following argument has five additional premises suggested for it. For each of them, decide whether its addition would increase or decrease the argument's inductive strength. If all five were added, how would you appraise the argument's strength?

> The Podunk State basketball team has won its last five games, and its opponent has won only half of its games thus far. Therefore, Podunk will win its next game.
>
> Suppose that Podunk has won all five of the games by a margin of 20 or more points.
>
> Suppose four of the last five games Podunk has played were on its home court and the next game is on the road.
>
> Suppose that in their last practice Podunk's leading scorer sprained his ankle.
>
> Suppose that the opposing team has played most of their games against teams rated in the top twenty.
>
> Suppose that the Podunk team is especially motivated for the game because of some negative remarks made by players on the opposing team.

2. Which of the following arguments are valid? Which are inductively strong? Do any of them fall into neither category?

a. All circles are figures. Therefore, all who draw circles draw figures.

b. The sky is clouding up, the wind is increasing, and the barometer is falling rapidly. Therefore, it will rain soon.

c. Every item we have ever observed that was made of copper conducted electricity. Therefore, the next copper item we examine will conduct electricity.

d. Everything made of copper conducts electricity. This wire is made of copper. Therefore, this wire conducts electricity.

e. Everyone who likes hard rock music likes to listen at high volume levels. Therefore, everyone who dislikes hard rock likes to listen at low volume levels.

f. If the earth is round, then a person on the moon's surface would see it as a large disk in the sky. People who have been on the moon's surface have seen it as a large disk in the sky. Therefore, the earth is round.

g. Every piece of paper ever examined has conducted electricity. This page is a piece of paper. Therefore, this page will conduct electricity.

h. Of the 1,100 registered voters who were interviewed, 60% said they would vote for the Republican candidate. All of the 1,100 were randomly selected from pedestrians in the financial district. Therefore, the Republican candidate will be elected.

3. Supply one or more additional premises that would make the following argument inductively strong.

Of 150,000 registered voters, 1,100 were interviewed and 60 percent said that they would vote for the Republican candidate. Therefore, the Republican candidate will be elected.

Section 4. Inductive Probability _____

The concept of inductive strength is essentially linked to the notion of probability: in an inductively strong argument there is a high probability that the conclusion is true if the premises are. There are many senses of the word 'probable' (and its cognates like 'chance,' 'likely,' 'plausible,' etc.), but we are here interested only in a probability concept directly related to reasoning or inference. More fully, we will explore the concept of *probability as a measure of an argument's inductive strength*. It is a concept employed widely in the empirical sciences, in law, and in our day-to-day affairs. Following the usual practice, we shall call it **inductive probability** (though sometimes "logical probability" is used), and again, it is probability in the sense of *degree of evidential support* or *degree of confirmation*. Along with that of inductive strength, it is among the most important concepts of inductive logic, and the two are intimately connected. The following statement is true by definition: an argument is inductively strong only if its conclusion has a high inductive probability relative to its premises.

Probability of course is a matter of degree and so is inductive strength. The conclusion's degree of inductive probability (and therefore the argument's degree of inductive strength) is conditional upon the evidence supplied by the premises. Now consider again the Pasteur argument from the preceding section. Let us represent its rather lengthy premise by the letter 'A' and its conclusion by C. The claim that the argument

III. A
        $\therefore$ C

is inductively strong can be reexpressed in the form of a certain probability statement; namely,

1. The (inductive) probability that C given that A is high.

Therefore talk of arguments and their degrees of inductive strength can be replaced by talk of certain probability statements and whether they are true. A probability claim of this sort is called an **inductive probability statement,** and they typically (though, as we shall see, not always) express an appraisal of a corresponding argument's degree of inductive strength—a true statement thus giving us a correct or accurate appraisal. Inductive probability statements are very important for us, since most of the questions that may be raised concerning inductive inference can be framed in terms of them.

Let us rewrite statement (1) more succinctly. Where p and q are any statements, we will introduce the expression 'Pr(p/q)' to mean "the (inductive) probability that p given that q." Now (1) becomes

1'. Pr(C/A) is high.

Alternately, an expression of the form 'Pr(p/q)' can be put in English as "the probability of p *on condition* (or *relative to*) q." It must be kept in mind that inductive probability is a conditional concept. Some varieties of probability are unconditional and can be expressed by a locution like 'Pr(p)', but inductive probability applies to *pairs* of statements: one the conclusion, and the other the premise (or conjunction of premises), of an inductive argument. We sometimes loosely talk of the probability of a statement per se, but if the concept being employed is that of inductive probability, there is always at least implicitly a second statement involved that supplies the evidence for the one mentioned explicitly. When someone says, "Very probably, there is no life on Mars," there is at least a tacit reference to the evidence available to the speaker on the subject.

Now consider the following argument:

This coin appears to be symmetrical and well-balanced, and when such coins have been tossed repeatedly in the past they have come up heads about half the time.
∴ This coin will show heads on the next toss.

Here, it seems reasonable to assign an exact numerical probability value. Using 'E' to represent the premise and 'H' the conclusion, the corresponding true inductive probability statement is

2. Pr (H/E) = 0.5

that is, the value 0.5 represents the degree to which the data in E support the conclusion H. Care must be taken here to distinguish between the entire probability statement—(2) in the present instance—and the conclusion, H, of the argument that corresponds to it. Although (2) is true, H might well not be (indeed, there is a 0.5 chance that it is not).

So an assessment of evidential support can either be qualitative ("high," "very low," etc.) or quantitative. Now suppose the coin in question is tossed many times with the result:

In 1,000 tosses of this coin, heads appeared 750 times.

Let us label this result 'R.' Obviously we would be very surprised to learn that R were true, and no doubt this new knowledge would change our expectations about the coin. If for example we were to wager on the outcome of toss 1,001, we would be foolish to bet on tails at even money.

But the fact that R is true does *not* show that statement (2) is false. Rather, it is true because the evidence in E supports H to the degree 0.5. Only now we have more information available to us in the form of R, and hence although (2) is true it is also a dead issue for us. At *this* point the relevant inductive probability statement to be considered is something like this:

3. $\Pr(H/E \text{ and } R) = 0.75$

(whether the value is exactly 0.75 here is debatable but it does not affect the point under discussion). Having learned that R is true, our beliefs and expectations concerning the coin should now be based on (3) rather than (2). A basic procedural rule known as the *Rule of Total Evidence* says that we should use *all* the information or evidence available to us in making an inductive judgment, and in the present instance the rule tells us that (even though (2) is true) we should use (3) as our basis for determining the likelihood with which the event described by H will occur. There is no inconsistency in supposing that (2) and (3) are both true even though they ascribe different probability values to H; the former tells us that E alone confirms H to the degree 0.5 whereas the latter tells us that E and R together confirm H to a different degree.

This point is important and brings out a crucial fact about inductive inference. Consider again argument (I) of the preceding section, and suppose that both of its premises are true: that 95 percent of all native Italians are Roman Catholics and that Angela is a native Italian. The conclusion that she is Roman Catholic is highly probable given those premises. But now consider another argument; we will suppose that its premises are also true:

IV.   95 percent of all people who reside in Israel are not Roman Catholic.

> Angela is a person who resides in Israel.
> ∴ Angela is not a Roman Catholic.

We here have an unusual but possible circumstance: there are two arguments of the same form, both with true premises, whose conclusions contradict one another. And yet, considered independently, *both* are inductively strong. If all Smith knows about Angela is that she is Italian, he will conclude by argument (I) that she is Catholic, but if Jones knows only that she lives in Israel, he will conclude just the opposite using (IV). One set of true premises makes it highly probable that Angela is a member of the Catholic faith, another set makes it highly probable that she is not. This can never happen in deductive logic; if two *valid* arguments of the same form are such that both have true premises, their conclusions *cannot* contradict one another. Being valid, if both sets of premises are true, the two conclusions must both be true as well, and thus it is impossible for one to logically contradict the other.

But in inductive logic we can have two conclusions, each with a high probability of being true, that are contradictory. Of course only one of these conclusions is *in fact* true, and this means that the other conclusion is false even though the premises confer upon it a high probability. That much should not be surprising; we have already seen that a highly probable conclusion could still turn out to be false. But what seems wrong here is that two statements that contradict each other can both have a high probability of being true. For, as we will see in Chapter Three, it is a basic probability principle that the probability of a statement p and that of its negation, not-p, should sum to 1, and hence if one of them has a high probability, the other should have a low one (if there is a 0.8 chance of rain tomorrow, there is a only 0.2 chance that it will not). So how can both p and not-p be highly probable?

Do we have a paradox here? Not at all. We must remember that inductive probability—or degree of evidential support—is a conditional notion; it expresses a *relation* between the conclusion and the premises of an argument rather than applying to the conclusion by itself. The term 'highly probable' when used with respect to inductive probability does not qualify a single statement but instead expresses a relation between statements. Therefore, we are not to think of the contrast in these terms:

> It is highly probable that Angela is a Roman Catholic.
> It is highly probable that Angela is not a Roman Catholic.

but rather like this:

> The statement 'Angela is a Roman Catholic' is highly probable relative to the evidence supplied by the premises of argument (I).

The statement 'Angela is not a Roman Catholic' is highly probable
relative to the evidence supplied by the premises of argument
(IV).

There is no inconsistency in supposing that the statements *p* and not-*p*
are both highly probable if the probability values are conditional upon
different sets of evidence statements. Only when the same evidence is
used for both *p* and for not-*p* must the probability values sum to 1,
thus precluding a situation where both are highly probable. As it
applies to inductive inference, then, probability must be construed as
a relation between statements, not as a qualifier of a single statement.[3]

A burning question remains of course: since arguments (I) and (IV)
are both inductively strong and both have true premises, which of
their conclusions should we accept or at least be prepared to act upon?
(If Angela is being invited for dinner, serving roast pork might not be
a good idea.) If we know no more about Angela than what both sets of
premises tell us (and are thus aware of the unlikely truth that she is
both a native Italian and an Israeli resident), there are some rules to
which we can appeal but a discussion of them is more appropriate for
Chapter Two. On the other hand, if we should acquire further information about Angela that is relevant to one's religious orientation,
then by the Rule of Total Evidence that information should be brought
to bear. If we were to learn that she went about her usual business on
Good Friday, for example, that would strengthen somewhat the conclusion of argument (IV). The total evidence, consisting of the Good
Friday information and the premises of *both* (I) and (IV), would now
increase the chance that she is not Roman Catholic.

A further consequence can be drawn from our discussion: if a weather
forecaster claims there is an "80 percent chance" of rain tomorrow on
the basis of the meterological information available and nothing but
sunshine and blue skies occur on that day, we are sometimes inclined
to complain that the forecaster was "wrong"—that what she said was
false. However, if the meteorological evidence supports the claim of rain
tomorrow to the degree 0.8 (or thereabouts), then what she said was
true. *The improbable sometimes happens*; it is after all improbable, not
impossible. Again, if there is a 0.8 chance of rain, then given the same
evidence, there is a 0.2 chance of no rain. The fact of its not raining does
not show that she said something false. If the available evidence
strongly *supports* a forecast of rain, then the forecaster was quite correct in predicting it (the inductive probability statement implicit in the
forecast is true) even though—as it turned out—no rain occurred.

We have seen that every inductively strong argument is one whose
conclusion has a high inductive probability relative to its premises;

indeed this is true by definition. But there are arguments whose conclusions have high probability relative to their premises that are *not* inductively strong (nor of course are they inductively weak). These are the *valid* arguments of deductive logic, for if their premises are true, there is no possibility (and hence no nonzero probability) that their conclusions are false. Since true premises guarantee a true conclusion in a valid inference, the probability that the conclusion is true when the premises are equals 1, the highest probability value.

But valid arguments are not inductively strong, for the definition of inductive strength given in the preceding section contained as one condition that the argument be *in*valid. And it seemed reasonable to do this as a way of emphasizing the contrast between the different kinds of appraisal in deductive and inductive logic. Hence valid arguments have conclusions with high (indeed the highest) probability relative to their premises, but do not qualify as inductively strong. Should this sort of probability be considered *inductive* probability? This notion was introduced at the outset as a "measure of inductive strength," but we will now expand it slightly to include deductive validity as a limiting case. Therefore, since the "evidence" in the premises of a valid argument guarantees the conclusion, we will say that the conclusion has an inductive probability of 1 relative to those premises.

So far, inductive strength has been defined in terms of the improbability of a false conclusion given true premises, and inductive probability was characterized as a measure of inductive strength. Obviously these definitions are vague, informal, and taken together, circular. They, along with the examples used, were designed only to give the reader an initial understanding—an intuitive grasp—of the two concepts. Our discussion has relied on examples and the reader's intuition. It was left to common sense and intuition to see that arguments (I), (II) and (III) were inductively strong and that some of the later examples were of lower inductive strength. Rarely was any exact or quantitative degree of strength specified, and no method for determining such degrees—exact or otherwise—was mentioned.

Indeed, nothing has been done thus far toward providing a means by which we can precisely measure an argument's inductive strength (or, in other words, measure the inductive probability of its conclusion). If such a method can be given, we would then have an exact means of determining whether a given inductive probability statement is true or false, and we would also be in a much better position to formulate precise and general rules governing inductive arguments, rules that would enable us to determine degree of inductive strength and that could serve as a guide for constructing inductively strong arguments.

The reason for omitting these topics here is not simply that they are too complex to be covered in an introductory discussion, but also that progress on these matters has been slow in coming. Again, inductive logic is a less advanced subject than deductive logic. Many basic concepts of the latter have been clarified, and their proper analysis is no longer a matter of debate. Also, highly sophisticated systems of inference have been fully developed. But for inductive logic, the results obtained thus far in answering the following questions are incomplete and controversial:

Can a precise account be given of the inductive probability concept (hence of what inductive strength consists in), and if so, what is it?
Can a comprehensive and systematic method be developed for measuring the inductive probability of an argument's conclusion, and if so, what is it?

Although solutions have been offered—at least in outline—to such questions, there is no widespread agreement as yet on which of them is correct or offers the most promising prospects.[4] Thus **a system of inductive logic,** in which an explication of the inductive probability concept is provided and in which methods of probability measurement as well as general rules governing inductive inference are formulated, remains a goal whose achievement is not yet in sight. Naturally, such a system, if it were developed, would be expected to uphold and endorse our most basic commonsense judgments of inductive strength, and it would exhibit the basis for such judgments by stating inductive rules in exact rigorous form and by organizing them into a unified body of principles in which the more complex elements are derived as theorems from the fundamental ones. We shall take a closer look at the problem of developing an adequate system of inductive logic in Chapters Five and Seven.

Section 5. An Important Distinction _____

It will be highly useful for us to distinguish between two different types of statements found in both ordinary and scientific discourse. This distinction parallels the one briefly noted at the beginning of this chapter between the formal and the empirical sciences. **Logically true-or-false statements** are employed and studied primarily in the formal sciences of deductive logic and pure mathematics. **Factually true-or-false statements** occur chiefly in the empirical (or experimental) sciences, where this includes the physical sciences (physics, chemistry), life sciences (such as zoology and botany), and social sciences (psychology, anthropology). In general, a given statement may be classified as logically true-or-false or as factually true-or-false without first knowing whether it is in fact true or in fact false.

As with the concept of inductive probability, the goal here is to provide only an intuitive understanding of the distinction rather than a full analysis of it, which in any case is still a controversial matter.[5] We simply want to be able to use the distinction here, not to explore its philosophical basis; the latter task would take us beyond inductive logic into other areas of philosophy such as epistemology (or "the theory of knowledge") and the philosophy of language. So we shall settle here for a rough and ready formulation.

The following are examples of *logically true* statements:[6]

1. Either it is now raining in Dubuque, Iowa, or it is not.
2. All unmarried men are unmarried.
3. All bachelors are unmarried.
4. $46 \times 38 = 1{,}748$.
5. For any real number x, $x^2 + 2x + 1 = (x + 1)^2$.
6. Every composite integer has a unique decomposition into prime factors.
7. If all premises of a valid argument are logically true, then its conclusion is also logically true.

Logically false statements would include "The earth is both round and not round," "Some bipeds are four legged," "$7 + 5 = 26$," and "There is a greatest prime number."

The category of logically true statements thus includes statements that are true on purely formal or logical grounds (more on this later) like (1) and (2); statements true by definition, for example, (3); mathematical principles like (4) and (5); and theoretical statements of mathematics and logic, such as (6) and (7). Logically false statements can be grouped similarly.

It will help our discussion to introduce a commonly used expression in logic. The **truth value** of a statement is simply the circumstance of its being true or that of its being false—whichever it happens to be. That is, there are just two truth values; truth and falsehood. A given statement will have one or the other of these values, but no statement has both.

Now there are two basic characteristics in virtue of which a statement qualifies as logically true-or-false. First, no observation or experience of the world around us is required for determining what its truth value is. We do not need to study the weather in Dubuque to see that (1) is true, nor do we need to observe any bachelors to conclude that (3) is true—we need only know what 'bachelor' means. For the mathematical statements, while reasoning, calculation and/or reflection is required for determining their truth, no observation or experiment is needed.

Such statements are said to be *a priori*; they are verified or falsified independent of our experience of the world. More fully, the truth value of an a priori statement can be established without the use of observation or experiment, relying instead solely on intuition, reflection, reasoning, or calculation.

An important qualification needs to be made here. It is through experience that we learn the meanings of our words; for example, one way in which we develop linguistic competence is by observing the linguistic behavior of others. Hence experience is necessary for *understanding* the statements in the previous list but it is not required for their verification or falsification. The term 'a priori' applies only to the means by which we come to learn a statement's truth value, not to the process that enables us to grasp its meaning.

But another characteristic is shared by all seven statements. Unlike a true statement such as, "The Twins defeated the Braves in the 1991 World Series," they are not true as a matter of fact, with the implication that things might have been otherwise. Rather, they are *necessarily* true; we cannot entertain a possible situation or state of affairs under which they would be counted as false. That is, it is *logically impossible* for them to be false—just as it is impossible for the conclusion of a valid argument to be false when its premises are true. We cannot entertain a situation in which it is both raining and not raining at the same time and in the same place, nor can we contemplate the existence of a bachelor who is married. It is equally impossible for a number other than 1728 to be the product of 46 and 38 (we can mistakely believe that another number is the product, but not because it is possible for it to be so, but simply because we calculated incorrectly).

The necessity that applies to all seven statements on our list arises from two sources. Statements (1) and (2) are true solely because of their respective forms; *any* statement of the form 'Either p or not-p' and of the form 'All (things that are both) F and G are F' is and must be true regardless of what statement we take p to be or what properties we suppose the letters F and G to represent. Statements (3)–(7), however, are true in virtue of the meanings of their component expressions; once the meanings of terms like 'bachelor' and 'unmarried' have been fixed in standard fashion, there is no possibility of (3) saying something false. The same holds for (4)–(7), though here calculation and reasoning are needed to discover their truth.

We shall thus describe statements (1) through (7) as *logically necessary*. Such statements are true (or false) either because of their logical form alone or else in virtue of the meanings of their component expressions. We can now define one of our key terms:

> A **logically true-or-false statement** is one which is both a priori and logically necessary.

The following statements, on the other hand, are *factually true*:

8. The litmus paper turned red [when it actually did].
9. All ravens are black.
10. The United States defeated Britain in the War of 1812.
11. It rained in Dubuque, Iowa, during April of 1972.
12. A U.S. citizen must be 65 years old to receive Medicare benefits.
13. Sodium salts burn with a yellow flame.
14. Every particle of matter attracts every other with a force inversely proportional to the square of the distance between them.

Our list includes observation statements (direct reports of our experience) such as (8), ordinary generalizations, e.g., (9), statements reporting facts of many different kinds such as (10), (11) and (12), descriptive laws like (13) and theoretical laws as in (14). Factually false statements (such as 'Lincoln was the third U.S. president', 'Salt is not soluble in water' and 'All swans are white') may be categorized in similar fashion.

Factually true-or-false statements are not a priori. Rather, they are *empirical* statements in that they must be confirmed—or disconfirmed—through experience and observation, and in many instances by resorting to experiment. However, reflection, calculation and reasoning is required in some cases as well (statement (14) is a good example).

Nor are these statements logically necessary. Instead, each is a *contingent* statement in that if true, it is nonetheless possible to specify a situation which, had it occurred, would have made it a false statement; and if false, a possible situation which, had it occurred, would have made it a true statement. That is, it is logically possible for a contingent statement to have a truth value other than the one it actually has, and *which* truth value it has depends on what the facts happen to be. So the truth value of such a statement is not due solely to its form nor to the meanings of its component expressions; rather it is true—or false—because of the facts that constitute the universe. We now have:

> A **factually true-or-false statement** is one which is both empirical and contingent.

The necessary/contingent distinction deserves more comment. Logically true-or-false statements are devoid of factual content. Statement (1) conveys no information about actual weather conditions in Dubuque (though of course (11) does). Because they lack factual import, they are true (or false) regardless of what the facts are. With a little imagination, we can envisage a possible universe comprised of a quite different set of facts from those that actually obtain and in which (8)–(14) are all false. Yet in such a case (1)–(7) will still be true. Even (14) can be supposed false since there are possible alternatives to it. It is not easy to say in detail what a universe would be like where force is inversely proportional, say, to the *cube* of the distance, but it is nonetheless an alternative that, logically speaking, *could* have occurred.

The a priori/empirical distinction also needs amplification. It was said that an a priori statement's truth value "can be" determined independently of observation, not that it must be. The reason is simple: some problems in logic and mathematics can be dealt with by empirical methods. Aeronautical engineers, for example, have used wind tunnels to solve mathematical equations. Furthermore, 'empirical' was defined using the words 'confirm' and 'disconfirm' rather than employing stronger language such as 'determining' or 'establishing' the truth value of such statements. Many empirical statements cannot be shown to be true (or false) with certainty but only with a high probability.

Logically true-or-false statements are established or refuted primarily through valid argument (as we just saw, they can sometimes be investigated empirically, but this is only an auxiliary mode of confirmation). A proof in mathematics or in theoretical areas of logic is a chain of valid arguments whose conclusion is a logical truth established through the use of other logical truths as premises.[7] As statement (7) above tells us, the only statements *validly* deducible from logical truths are themselves logically true. An argument with logically true premises and a factually true conclusion must be invalid; its premises are true under all possible conditions but the conclusion is not—hence the possibility of true premises and a false conclusion.

Factually true-or-false statements like (8) typically are not established through inference but by direct observation. However, (9)–(14) are also factual statements and are established by inductive reasoning from other factual statements as premises. In many instances, especially theoretical ones like (14), valid (or "deductive") inference may also be used, but ultimately the confirmation or disconfirmation of a factually true-or-false statement must trace back to other such statements which provide the evidence for (or against) it. Hence, factually true-or-false statements cannot be established by deductive reasoning alone; observation and inductive inference on the basis of those observations is required. These are the statements we shall focus on hereafter, for while they often occur in deductive inference (as many of the examples used in Section 2 attest), it is through inductively strong arguments that we come at last to accept or reject them.

We shall leave open here the question of whether there are statements which are neither logically true-or-false nor factually true-or-false. Some philosophers have argued that there are logically necessary statements which are not a priori (some have even argued that there are a priori statements that are not logically necessary).[8] We will not delve into this matter here; suffice to say that in the standard case the premises and conclusion of an inductive inference are factually true-or-false statements. Inductive logic thus studies arguments which reflect our empirical knowledge of a universe of contingent facts and events.

Section 6. Argument and Inquiry _____

We must distinguish between how a science develops through the discovery of new laws and how those laws are best organized to display their grounds or justification. Geometry provides a good example. The ancient Egyptians and Greeks had discovered many important geometric laws which enabled them to do such things as survey land, build imposing structures like the pyramids and the Parthenon and make rudimentary discoveries in astronomy. But until about 300 B.C. geometry was nothing more than a haphazardly collected group of principles. It was then that the Greek mathematician Euclid collected together the known principles of the subject and organized them into a systematic body of knowledge—into a *science.* He did this by formulating very fundamental principles called *axioms* which he claimed were self-evident and hence needed no proof. From the axioms, he then deduced as *theorems* the known principles of plane geometry. From very simple axioms like, "Between two points exactly one straight line can be drawn," Euclid constructed deductive proofs of well-known but complex laws such as the Pythagorean Theorem, thus exhibiting the logical grounds for them. While such theorems were widely known and used at the time, it is probably correct that before Euclid no one had ever explicitly entertained many of his axioms. We must therefore distinguish between the *order of discovery* and the *order of justification*; the Pythagorean law was discovered earlier than many of the axioms, but it is the latter statements that, logically considered, are more fundamental to the subject.

Examples like this abound in the history of science. Kepler's laws of planetary motion and Galileo's law of falling bodies were both discovered prior to Newton's formulation of his laws of gravity and motion. Yet Newton was able to deductively derive the principles of Galileo and Kepler from his own, thus bringing laws of celestial and terrestial motion under one umbrella. While the principles of Galileo and Kepler were prior in terms of discovery, Newton's were prior in terms of justification.

This distinction parallels another. We have seen that all reasoning proceeds according to rules, and logic studies and assesses the most general rules of reasoning. The **logic of inquiry** (or the "logic of discovery") studies rules of discovery—rules that are useful in solving problems and arriving at important results. It evaluates such rules in terms of their usefulness and applicability. The **logic of argument,** however, studies rules of inference; that is, it focuses on rules for deriving conclusions from premises, and appraises such rules as valid or invalid, inductively strong or weak. Inductive logic is thus a species of the logic of argument.

Historically, inductive logic and the logic of inquiry—where the latter is concerned with the discovery of factual truths—have been closely intertwined, often to the point of obscuring the distinction between them. We shall note some examples of this later on, but for now it will be worthwhile for us to take a brief look at the logic of inquiry and its relation to inductive logic proper. Below are some examples of rules of discovery:

> Given a complex problem, formulate in precise terms simpler problems whose solution will probably contribute to the solution of the original one.
> Search related fields for analogies that may be useful in solving the problem.
> The complex situation from which investigation begins must be analyzed into constituent conditions (or "factors").
> In an experimental situation, conditions believed to be relevant to the solution must be varied one at a time wherever possible.
> If the evidence for each of two competing hypotheses are otherwise equal, choose the simpler hypothesis.

Many people will no doubt respond that these "rules" are nothing more than common-sense guidelines; they certainly differ from precise rules such as algorithms and rules for translating numerical expressions into binary form. They cannot be applied in a purely mechanical fashion nor can our use of them guarantee success. They are more like the rules found in a cooking recipe; ingenuity and experience are needed for applying them and success is not assured. And just as following recipe rules will usually not produce the same results as that of a great chef, so employing the above rules will not turn one into the next Louis Pasteur. Scientific achievement requires creativity, insight, persistence and meticulous preparation, and hence it has sometimes been claimed that a "logic" of inquiry is too much to expect.

But this is far from being the whole story. Like inductive logic itself, the logic of inquiry is still in its early stages of development (this is one reason why the two subjects have often been run together), and the loosely formulated rules above reflect this fact. Yet progress has been made over the years. In some instances, scientific work that in the past had been considered creative has now been reduced to rule-governed activity, and in our own day a new instrument for mechanizing scientific inquiry has appeared: the computer. It is to be expected that research in "artificial intelligence" and related areas will some day enable us to reduce discovery in many scientific contexts to computer programs consisting of exact algorithmic rules. So while there will always be a place for insight, creativity and other intangibles, very probably a great deal of future scientific investigation will be mechanized through the use of precisely formulated rules of discovery.

An illustration of the interplay between the logic of argument and the logic of inquiry is provided by the dispute between Galileo and the Roman Catholic Church in the early seventeenth century. Galileo upheld the "heliocentric" theory developed earlier by Copernicus, according to which the earth and other planets moved around the sun, which was regarded as fixed in place. The church on the other hand endorsed the "geocentric" theory developed by the Greek astronomer Ptolemy and which was the prevailing theory of the day. According to it, the earth was motionless and the center of the universe, with the sun, planets, and stars revolving about it. The mathematical machinery of both theories enabled them to plot with good accuracy the paths of the known planets through the sky, but determining which of the theories came closest to the truth was not an easy matter given what was known at the time. The dispute is a complex one which cannot be fully discussed here, but we can say this much: the evidence available at the time of the debate on balance appeared to support the geocentric theory, while considerations of simplicity favored its opponent.

An example of the first point: if the heliocentric theory is true, then a given star should appear in different positions of the sky at different periods of the year. Since our planet moves in its orbit around the sun yearly, the theory requires, for example, that the star exhibit a shift in position from January to July when the earth is at opposite extremes in its orbit. However, no such shift was observed. Of course, we know

now why astronomers of that day could not observe the shift: their instruments were primitive and the stars were much farther away than anyone back then had supposed. But while the heliocentric theory could explain the star's seemingly constant position by claiming that it was too far from the earth, the explanation was *ad hoc* and unconvincing at the time. For there were no independent grounds on which to base that claim; none of the evidence and data then available supported the thesis that stars were literally light years away. The lack of any observed change in the position of a star obviously weakens the heliocentric thesis, but it was just what one should expect given the geocentric theory. Moreover, other evidence then available counted against the heliocentric view as well, and it seems fair to say that from the standpoint of inductive logic, the geocentric theory had at the time a higher inductive probability, given all the information then available, than the heliocentric theory.

However, considerations from the logic of inquiry put the dispute in a different light. One of the rules of discovery cited earlier tells us to choose the simpler of two competing hypotheses all other things being equal. Now of course they were not equal as we have just seen; the evidence does appear to favor the geocentric view. But the factor of simplicity nonetheless worked strongly in the opposite direction. For while the geocentric machinery predicted the paths of the planets with reasonable accuracy, it had to postulate a complex system of "epicycles" and "equant points" to account for the retrograde motion the planets appeared to exhibit: a planet would seem to halt in its motion and go into reverse, then halt once more and proceed "forward" again. But Copernicus discovered that if it is assumed that the earth itself is in motion, then it is possible to give all the planets including the earth a simpler and more straightforward motion that could more easily account for the apparent retrogradations. When taken all together, the paths of the planets are simpler using the sun as our reference point, and as a result the heliocentric theory was much easier and more convenient to use, as well as requiring fewer questionable assumptions about celestial motion. The importance of this development may be underscored by noting that Kepler would not have discovered his laws of planetary motion had he used the geocentric machinery.

Thus the logic of argument and the logic of inquiry give conflicting opinions in this instance; rules of evidence favoring the geocentric theory but rules of inquiry pointing to the heliocentric theory as the more promising approach. Of course from the perspective of evidence and inductive logic, the picture changes entirely when we include in our body of evidence later astronomical observations, the work of Kepler and Newton, and so forth; the heliocentric theory (or at least the modern day descendent of it) is decisively confirmed.[9] This illustration from the history of science helps us see that rules of discovery are just as important for scientific progress as rules of inference, but it is important to keep in mind that they are a different species of rule altogether.

Section 7. Elementary Deductive Logic _____

A familiarity with the simplest and most basic area of deductive logic will be highly useful to us in our study of inductive logic. We will therefore examine here what is often known as sentential (or "propositional") logic: the study of arguments whose premises and conclusions consist mainly of various kinds of **compound statements**— statements containing one or more other statements as parts. Some readers may already be acquainted with this material, but they should look it over nonetheless, since the terminology and symbolic notation may differ from their original sources.

We begin by examining three of the most common types of compound statements. Where p and q are any statements, **conjunctions** are statements of the form 'p and q' and will be abbreviated as 'p & q'. Both the English 'and' and the symbol '&' are **logical connectives,** they link together statements to form larger statements. The component statements here indicated by the variables 'p' and 'q' are called **conjuncts.** The conjunction:

Kennedy was a Democrat and Lincoln was a Republican

may be symbolized as 'K & L' where 'K' represents the conjunct 'Kennedy was a Democrat' and 'L' the conjunct 'Lincoln was a Republican'. Conjunctions are sometimes formulated in abbreviated form in English and other natural languages. The statement, 'Kennedy was both a Democrat and a liberal' is also a conjunction, as is, 'Lincoln and Nixon were both Republicans'.

To understand or grasp the meaning of a conjunction is to know the conditions under which it will be true. The conjunction just displayed is true because in fact both of its component statements are true. But if one or both of those components had been false, the entire conjunction would be counted as false as well. We thus have the following:

A conjunction is true if and only if both of its conjuncts are true, and false otherwise.

A **disjunction** is a compound statement of the form, 'either p or q,' where this has the force of *one or the other or both*. We will express it

in symbols as 'p v q'. The component statements are called **disjuncts.**
The disjunction

Either the carburetor is at fault or the fuel pump is at fault

has as its disjuncts the statements 'The carburetor is at fault' and 'The
fuel pump is at fault.' Representing these as 'C' and 'F' respectively, we
may express the disjunction more succinctly as, 'C v F'. As with
conjunctions, disjunctions often occur in English in abbreviated forms.

We can set out the meaning of the connectives 'either-or' and 'v' as
follows, again focusing on the conditions under which statements
containing them will be true:

A disjunction is true if and only if at least one of its disjuncts is
true, and false otherwise.

Hence our sample disjunction will be true if 'C' is true and 'F' is false or
vice versa, and it will also count as true if both 'C' and 'F' are true.
Only when both component disjuncts are false will we consider the
entire disjunction to be false.

Many either-or statements have disjuncts that mutually exclude
one another; that is, they cannot both be true. An example would be:
'Either the next card drawn will be a heart or it will be a diamond'. We
will consider such statements to be disjunctions even though the "or
both" condition is a dead issue. For our purposes, it is convenient (and
will not lead us astray) to translate them using the connective 'v'. The
statement thus becomes, using obvious notation, 'H v D'.

A **negation** is a statement of the form 'It is not the case that p' (or
just 'not-p') and will be abbreviated as '$\sim p$'. Unlike '&' and 'v' the curl
sign '$\sim$' attaches to single statements rather than linking a pair of
them. Many negations in English do not at first glance seem to be
compound at all; for example, 'Alice is not a politician'. But notice that
this statement is equivalently expressed:

It is not the case that Alice is a politician,

which makes clear that the sentence 'Alice is a politician' is a
component of the negation. Setting out the meaning of negations is an
easy matter:

A negation is true if and only if the statement negated is false,
and vice versa.

The definitions just given for the three connectives, '&,' 'v' and '$\sim$'
can be reexpressed in tabular form by enumerating all possible

assignments of truth values to the component statements in each compound. The result is a **truth table,** which literally displays the meanings of the connectives. For compounds of two components, there are exactly four possible truth value assignments, and each is displayed as a row of the truth table.

Table I.

p	q	$p \& q$
T	T	T
T	F	F
F	T	F
F	F	F

Table II.

p	q	$p \vee q$
T	T	T
T	F	T
F	T	T
F	F	F

The column under '$p \& q$' shows us that such statements are true in only one case: where both conjuncts are true (first row).[10] The fact that a **T** occurs in the first three rows of the column under '$p \vee q$' tells us that disjunctions are true whenever at least one disjunct is true. Since '~' attaches to single statements, there are just two truth value assignments: the component statement is either true or false. So we need only a two-row truth table to display the meaning of '~'.

Table III.

p	$\sim p$
T	F
F	T

For any compound statement containing one or more of '&', 'v' and '~', we can construct a truth table exhibiting its truth conditions using Tables (I), (II) and (III) as our guide. Consider the statement '~A v (B & A)', or in partial English, 'Either not-A or both B and A'. It is a disjunction whose left disjunct is a negation and whose right disjunct is a conjunction. Table (III) enables us to determine the truth value for the component '~A' and Table (I) does the same for 'B & A'. The truth value assignments for the entire disjunction are then obtained using Table (II). They are displayed directly underneath the 'v' which, since it gives the overall form of the compound, is called the *main connective* of the statement.

A	B	~A	v	(B & A)
T	T	F	T	T
T	F	F	F	F
F	T	T	T	F
F	F	T	T	F
			^	

Compound statements with exactly three distinct components require an eight-row table, since there are eight assignments of truth values that can be made to a triad of statements. To make sure the table has all eight assignments (that none has been omitted or duplicated), assign **T**s to the first four rows beneath the first component and **F**s to the last four. Then alternate two rows of **T**s and two of **F**s beneath the second component; finally alternate **T**s and **F**s in each row for the last one. A four-component compound requires a truth table of 16 rows, and in general, if there are n components, the number of truth table rows needed is 2^n. The following is an eight-row table for three forms of statement, each with three components:

p	q	r	p & $(q \lor r)$		$(p$ & $q) \lor r$		$(p$ & $q) \lor (p$ & $r)$		
T	T	T	T	T	T	T	T	T	T
T	T	F	T	T	T	T	T	T	F
T	F	T	T	T	F	T	F	T	T
T	F	F	F	F	F	F	F	F	F
F	T	T	F	T	F	T	F	F	F
F	T	F	F	T	F	F	F	F	F
F	F	T	F	T	F	T	F	F	F
F	F	F	F	F	F	F	F	F	F
			^		^		^		

Now compare the columns for 'p & $(q \lor r)$' (in English, 'p and either q or r') and '$(p$ & $q) \lor r$' ('either both p and q or else r'). Statements of these two forms differ only in the placement of parentheses, but they convey quite different information. Hence the parentheses are needed here to resolve ambiguity. That they make different claims is evident from the truth table itself, for the two forms have different columns of **T**s and **F**s. Specifically, one has an **F** and the other a **T** in the fifth and seventh rows. Using the seventh row as an example, when the statements represented by p and q are false but the one represented by r is true, then 'p & $(q \lor r)$' says something false but '$(p$ & $q) \lor r$' says something true.

On the other hand, 'p & $(q \lor r)$' and the third form, '$(p$ & $q) \lor (p$ & $r)$', say the same thing since their truth table columns are exactly alike (**T**s only in the first three rows). They are true under the same conditions and hence are just two different ways of making the same point.

Such statements are said to be **equivalent.** They convey the same information and typically will have identical truth table columns. For the compound statements of sentential logic we may therefore say that a pair of such statements is equivalent if and only if for each assignment of truth values to their component statements, both receive the same truth value.[11]

The equivalence just noted, together with a second one in which the occurrences of '&' and 'v' are interchanged, are known as "distribution" principles. The second one, like the first, is easily verified by constructing an appropriate eight row truth table. That task is left as an exercise. Meanwhile, we will state the principles as follows:

> ***Distribution:*** p & (q v r) is equivalent to (p & q) v (p & r)
> p v (q & r) is equivalent to (p v q) & (p v r)

Now compare statements of the forms '$\sim p$ & q' and '$\sim(p$ & $q)$'. Again, the parentheses are crucial since the two are not equivalent. The first is a conjunction whose left conjunct is a negation whereas the second is the negation of an entire conjunction. If the statement for q is false, then so is '$\sim p$ & q' since it has a false conjunct. But '$\sim(p$ & $q)$' is true in such a case, since the conjunction 'p & q' is false and negating it yields a truth. On the other hand, a little reflection shows that '$\sim(p$ & $q)$' *is* equivalent to the form '$\sim p$ v $\sim q$'—in English, 'not both p and q' says the same as 'either not-p or not-q' (compare 'Not both Kennedy and Lincoln were Republicans' with 'Either Kennedy was not a Republican or else Lincoln wasn't').

By the same token, 'neither p nor q' is equivalent to 'not-p and not-q' where the expression 'neither-nor' conveys the notion of negating a disjunction ('not' plus 'either' gives 'neither'). So the neither-nor statement may be expressed in symbols as '$\sim(p$ v $q)$'. The statement, 'Neither Lincoln nor Nixon was a Democrat' makes the very same claim as, 'Lincoln was not a Democrat and Nixon was not a Democrat'. Hence '$\sim(p$ v $q)$' and '$\sim p$ & $\sim q$' are equivalent.

To verify these equivalence claims, all we need is a four row truth table:

p	q	$\sim(p$ & $q)$		$\sim p$	v	$\sim q$	$\sim(p$ v $q)$		$\sim p$	&	$\sim q$
T	T	F	T	F	F	F	F	T	F	F	F
T	F	T	F	F	T	T	F	T	F	F	T
F	T	T	F	T	T	F	F	T	T	F	F
F	F	T	F	T	T	T	T	F	T	T	T
		^			^		^			^	

The truth table shows that '$\sim(p$ & $q)$' and '$\sim p$ v $\sim q$' are true under precisely the same conditions: when at least one of p and q is false. It does the same for '$\sim(p$ v $q)$' and '$\sim p$ & $\sim q$': they will be true just in case p and q are both false. These principles, named after their discoverer, will be useful to us later on.

> ***DeMorgan's laws***: $\sim(p$ & $q)$ is equivalent to $\sim p$ v $\sim q$
> $\sim(p$ v $q)$ is equivalent to $\sim p$ & $\sim q$

These hold also for conjunctions and disjunctions with more than two components.

It will also be worth our while to take note of some further—and quite obvious—equivalences. If we transpose the component statements of a conjunction or a disjunction, the result is equivalent to what we had before; '*p* & *q*' is equivalent to '*q* & *p*' and similarly for 'v'. Moreover, placement of parentheses in extended conjunctions and disjunctions does not affect the meaning or truth conditions of the whole: '*p* v (*q* v *r*)' is equivalent to '(*p* v *q*) v *r*' and the same holds for '&'. Because of this, we shall drop parentheses in such contexts. Finally, any statement *p* is obviously equivalent to its double negation, '~~*p*'. Any lingering doubts about these equivalences may be quickly dispelled by constructing a truth table.

We have been "translating" compound statements of English into a symbolic notation (or "formal language"), and we need to specify its vocabulary. The language contains the three logical connectives: '&', 'v' and '~'. (Two more will be introduced shortly.) Of course it also has parentheses (and brackets too for complex formulas). The capital letters 'A', 'B', and so forth are **statement letters,** they abbreviate particular statements of English. The small letters '*p*', '*q*', and so on are **statement variables,** which range over the statements represented by statement letters and over compounds of them as well. The relation between 'A' and '*p*' is very similar to that between '3' and '*x*' in arithmetic. Just as '3' designates a particular number, so 'A' represents a particular English statement; and just as '*x*' enables us to talk about any arbitrarily selected number, so '*p*' does the same for statements. When we wish to discuss disjunctions in general, without having a specific one in mind, we can use the **statement form** '*p* v *q*' rather than 'A v B', which represents a particular disjunction once the statements for 'A' and 'B' have been fixed.

It is an important fact for us that compound statements are *derivable by substitution* from statement forms, for as we saw earlier an argument is valid in virtue of its form, and hence of the forms of its component statements. 'A v B' is derivable by substitution from '*p* v *q*' by substituting 'A' for '*p*' and 'B' for '*q*'. But '~C v (A & B)' is also derivable from it, substituting '~C' for '*p*' and 'A & B' for '*q*'. Moreover, in a form like '*p* v (*q* & *p*)', the *same* statement, simple or compound, must replace '*p*' in both occurrences. Thus '~C v (A & ~C)' is derivable from it, but '~C v (A & B)' is not (the latter *is* derivable of course from '*p* v (*q* & *r*)' as well as from '*p* v *q*'). The same statement may also replace different variables: 'A v A' is derivable from '*p* v *q*' just as '3 + 3' may be obtained from '*x* + *y*'.

It will be useful for us to introduce two further logical connectives, though we will not need to call upon them as often as our basic three. An English statement of the form 'if *p* then *q*' is called a **conditional.** The component, *p,* on the left is its **antecedent** whereas *q* is the **consequent.** There are several varieties of conditionals, but the only ones of interest to us here are those that convey the same information as statements of the form 'either not-*p* or *q*' (in symbols, '~*p* v *q*'). In saying, "Either the Cubs won't win or I'll eat my hat," one could have made the same point more succinctly by saying, "*If* the Cubs win, then I'll eat my hat." We will use the "horseshoe" sign, '⊃', to represent the English 'if-then', and hence '*p* ⊃ *q*' will have the same truth table column as '~*p* v *q*'. The following table, then, formally defines '⊃':

p	*q*	*p* ⊃ *q*	~*p* v *q*
T	**T**	**T**	**F** **T**
T	**F**	**F**	**F** **F**
F	**T**	**T**	**T** **T**
F	**F**	**T**	**T** **T**
		^	^

The match-up in meaning between 'if-then' and '⊃' is not nearly as close as that between 'and' and '&', but for the range of arguments with which we are concerned, it is adequate for our purposes. Moreover, the truth table (in its second row) expresses an important point about a conditional: it will be false when its antecedent is true and its consequent is false. Should the Cubs win but my hat remain uneaten, then I have said something false. On all other truth value assignments, however, '*p* ⊃ *q*' will take the value **T.**[12]

'If-then' and '⊃' share several important logical properties as well. For example, 'if *p* then *q*' makes the same point as 'if not-*q* then not-*p*'. The statement "if it rained, the game was postponed" says the same as "if the game was not postponed, then it didn't rain." However, the negations are crucial, for 'if *p* then *q*' and its converse 'if *q* then *p*' convey quite different information. If on a sunny day the opposing team fails to show up, it will still be true that if it rained, the game was postponed, but it will be false to say that, if the game was postponed, then it rained (the antecedent is true but the consequent is false). The horseshoe has these same features, and they can be verified by a truth table (left as an exercise). So we have two more principles:

p ⊃ *q* is equivalent to ~*q* ⊃ ~*p*
p ⊃ *q* is not equivalent to *q* ⊃ *p*

An English statement of the form '*p* if and only if *q*' is a **biconditional.** As the name suggests, it is equivalent to the conjunction of two conditionals, specifically, 'if *p* then *q*' and its converse 'if *q* then *p*'. Suppose it is true that if it rained then the game was postponed, and that it is *also* true that if the game was postponed then it rained. It will then be true to say that the game was postponed if and only if it rained. We shall use the triple bar '≡' for 'if and only if' and the following truth table defines this connective as well as displaying the equivalence just cited:

p	*q*	*p* ≡ *q*	(*p* ⊃ *q*)	&	(*q* ⊃ *p*)
T	**T**	**T**	**T**	**T**	**T**
T	**F**	**F**	**F**	**F**	**T**
F	**T**	**F**	**T**	**F**	**F**
F	**F**	**T**	**T**	**T**	**T**
		^		^	

Thus '*p* ≡ *q*' is true just in case *p* and *q* have the same truth value; that is, when they are both true or when they are both false.[13]

Let us finally turn to arguments. We have seen that truth tables define the logical connectives and justify equivalence principles like DeMorgan's laws. However, their importance does not end there: they also provide us with a purely mechanical method of testing arguments containing compound statements for validity and invalidity. To see this, let us suppose that we have translated an argument from English with the result

$$A \lor B$$
$$A \supset (\sim C \,\&\, \sim B)$$
$$\therefore B \lor \sim C$$

We saw earlier that, if an argument is valid, it is impossible for the conclusion to be false when the premises are all true. Moreover, a truth table enables us to determine the truth values of the premises and the conclusion once we assign truth values to the components 'A', 'B' and 'C'. Hence if we run through *all* possible assignments of truth values to these letters and *no* such assignment yields a true-premises–false-conclusion combination, the argument must be valid. For arguments like this, the impossibility of a false conclusion accompanying true premises comes down to there being no assignment of truth values—that is, *no truth table row*—in which all premises are assigned **T** and the conclusion assigned **F.**

Now look carefully at the truth table for the premises and conclusion:

A	B	C	A v B	A ⊃ (~C & ~B)	B v ~C
T	T	T	T	F F F F	T F
T	T	F	T	F T F F	T T
T	F	T	T	F F F T	F F
T	F	F	T	T T T T	T T
F	T	T	T	T F F F	T F
F	T	F	T	T T F F	T T
F	F	T	F	T F F T	F F
F	F	F	F	T T T T	T T
			^	^	^

This truth table thus shows our argument to be valid, for there is no row with **T**s for both premises and an **F** for the conclusion. In each of the three rows in which the premises are both assigned **T** (the fourth, fifth, and sixth rows), the conclusion is also assigned **T.** Had the conclusion been assigned an **F** in just one such row, the argument would have been invalid. Thus if we interchange the conclusion and the second premise, this new argument has a **T** for both premises and an **F** for the conclusion in the first and second rows, making it invalid.

Truth tables thus provide an easy, mechanical routine for testing validity and invalidity with respect to arguments containing compound statements. But the preceding truth table does not just test our sample argument, it tests all arguments of the same form. *Any* argument with premises of the forms '*p* v *q*' and '*p* ⊃ (~*r* & ~*q*)' and a conclusion of the form '*q* v ~*r*' has been shown valid too. Truth tables also show us that there are statements true in virtue of their form alone. We have already noted some examples in Section 5, such as "Either it is now raining in Dubuque or it is not." We may not know the truth value of statement 'A' but we know that the statement 'A v ~A' is true and the same holds for *all* compounds of the form '*p* v ~*p*'—like '~A v ~~A', '(A & B) v ~(A & B)', and so forth. Such statements are true no matter what truth values we may suppose their component statements to have, and we will give them a special name:

A compound statement is a **tautology** if and only if it is true for every assignment of truth values to its component statements.

Such statements thus take a **T** in every row of their truth table column. The following truth table gives us three examples:

A B	A v ~A	A v ~(A & B)	(A & ~B) ⊃ A
T T	**T F**	**T F T**	**F F T**
T F	**T F**	**T F F**	**T T T**
F T	**T T**	**T F F**	**F F T**
F F	**T T**	**T T F**	**F T T**
	^	^	^

Tautologies are the simplest and most transparent examples of logically true statements. That they are necessarily true is evident from their having nothing but **T**s in their truth table columns, and the fact that their truth may be determined solely through truth table calculation demonstrates that they are a priori. They have no factual content, though of course their component statements are often factually true or false; empirical investigation may be needed for determining whether 'A' is true, but only a truth table is required for 'A v ~A'.

A **contradiction** is a compound statement that is false for all truth value assignments to its components and thus has an **F** in every row of its truth table column. A truth table will quickly show that 'A & ~A' and '~(A v ~A)' are examples.[14] The negation of a contradiction is a tautology and vice versa; they are thus a priori and necessarily false. Compound statements with at least one **T** and at least one **F** in their truth table columns are factually true-or-false statements.

Because they lack factual content, tautologies may well seem to be "trivial" truths; there is little point in uttering, "Either it is now raining in Dubuque or it is not," regardless of context. Yet their standing as logical truths gives them a theoretical importance in logic, as we will now see.

Let us say that the **corresponding conditional** of an argument is a conditional whose antecedent is the conjunction of the argument's premises and whose consequent is its conclusion. The corresponding conditional of the argument considered earlier would thus be

[(A v B) & (A ⊃ (~C & ~B))] ⊃ (B v ~C)

where the two premises are conjoined in the antecedent and the conclusion serves as the consequent. Since the argument itself was valid, we saw that there is no row of its truth table where both premises are assigned **T** and the conclusion **F**.

But this means that the corresponding conditional cannot have an **F** in its truth table column, and we do not need to construct the table to see this. For we saw earlier that a conditional takes an **F** only when its antecedent is assigned a **T** and its consequent an **F**; and for that to happen in the present case, both premises would have to be true (making the conjunction in the antecedent true) and the conclusion (here the consequent of the conditional) would have to be false. So if there is no row in which the premises are true and the conclusion false, there can be no row where the conditional has a true antecedent and false consequent. In other words, the argument is *valid* just in case its corresponding conditional is a *tautology*. The corresponding conditional of an invalid argument will thus have at least one **F** in its column (for the row(s) where all premises are true and the conclusion false).

This point holds generally, not just for arguments consisting of compound statements nor for logical truths that are tautologies:

> An argument is **valid** if and only if its corresponding conditional is a logical truth. Otherwise, it is **invalid.**

In Section 4 we saw that talk of arguments and their inductive strength can be replaced by talk of inductive probability statements and whether they are true. Similary, in deductive logic, questions about arguments and validity can be rephrased in terms of certain conditional statements and whether they are *logically* true.

Biconditionals stand to equivalence as conditionals stand to validity. The **corresponding biconditional** of a pair of statements, p and q, is a statement of the form '$p \equiv q$'. An equivalent pair of statements, such as '$\sim(A \& B)$' and '$\sim A \vee \sim B$' will be true under exactly the same conditions and hence have identical truth table columns. Since a biconditional is true only when both components have the same truth value, the statement '$\sim(A \& B) \equiv (\sim A \vee \sim B)$' must take a **T** in every row of its truth table column—it must be a tautology. More generally, then

> Two statements are **equivalent** if and only if their corresponding biconditional is logically true.

Exercises

1. Let 'A' be true, 'B' be false, and 'C' be a statement whose truth value is unknown. Which of the following are true and which false? Which cannot be determined?

a. A v (B & C)	**b.** A & (~B v C)
c. (~A & B) v (A & ~C)	**d.** (~A v B) & [~B v (C & A)]
e. C v ~C	**f.** (B & C) v ~(A & C)

2. Translate the following into our symbolic notation:

> **a.** Either the battery is weak or both the distributor and the starter need repair. (B, D, S)

b. Either the tax bill will be vetoed or else it will pass neither the House nor the Senate. (T, H, S)

c. If the carburetor is not at fault, then the problem lies with either the fuel pump or the gas line. (C, F, G)

d. If either the Mets or the Yanks do not win the pennant, it will not come as a surprise to anyone. (M, Y, S)

e. Jones and Smith are athletes, and at least one of them plays golf. (J, S, O, M)

f. No shoes, no shirt, no service. (O, I, V)

3. Using truth tables, determine which of the following are tautologies:

a. ~(C & D) v C

b. (E v F) ⊃ (F & E)

c. (A ≡ ~B) v (A & B)

d. (G & ~H) & [~G v (H & G)]

4. Using truth tables, show that the following pairs are equivalent:

a. *p* and ~~*p*

b. *p* ⊃ *q* and ~*q* ⊃ ~*p*

c. *p* and *p* v (*q* & ~*q*)

d. (*p* & *q*) ⊃ *r* and *p* ⊃ (*q* ⊃ *r*)

e. *p* v (*q* & *r*) and (*p* v *q*) & (*p* v *r*)

5. Which of the following arguments are valid? Use truth tables to decide.

a. ~A v (B & A)
   ~B
∴ ~A

b. ~B v (D & ~R)
   R v ~B
∴ ~B

c. C ⊃ (D v G)
   G ⊃ ~C
∴ D v C

d. A ≡ ~B
   B v (~A & C)
∴ ~A

Notes

1. This point will be discussed in more detail in Section 5 of this chapter.

2. There are still further invalid arguments that offer *no* evidence for the conclusion and indeed in many cases actually undermine it. The argument whose premise is, "All observed emeralds are green" and whose conclusion is, "The next emerald observed will be red" is such an example. Such arguments will simply be classified (and herewith dismissed) as *worthless*.

3. A few philosophers would still deny this. Space precludes any further discussion, except to say that it is hard to see how they could handle the contrast between arguments (I) and (IV). Perhaps the most prominent exponent of the qualifier-of-single-statements view is Stephen Toulmin; see his *The Uses of Argument* (Cambridge: Cambridge University Press, 1958). For a penetrating critique of Toulmin, and for more on inductively strong arguments with contradictory conclusions, see Carl Hempel, "Inductive Inconsistencies," in *Aspects of Scientific Explanation* (New York: Macmillan, 1965).

4. Concerning the second of these questions, there are differences among philosophers as to whether, if such a comprehensive method were developed, all inductive probability values would be expressed quantitatively. It is easy to accept the idea that probabilities like a coin falling heads or drawing a spade from a bridge deck are quantitative, but at the common-sense level at least, it seems unrealistic—or just wrong—to assign an exact numerical value to the claim that (given the relevant evidence) Einstein's general theory of relativity is true or that General Motors's common stock will rise sharply in the next six months. Whether such probabilities can ultimately be expressed quantitatively is a question we cannot address here, and hence we will allow that x in an expression of the form '$\Pr(p\,/\,q) = x$' ranges over qualitative values like "high" and "low" as well as quantitative ones such as "0.5" and "1/4."

5. So much so that some philosophers even deny that there is a hard and fast distinction to be drawn. But even these writers often use the distinction (or something very close to it) in an elementary, prima facie manner.

6. The term 'logically true' is often used in a more restricted manner that would include only statements (1) and (2) in the following list. However, we shall use it more broadly here to include all logically necessary statements.

7. Proofs by "mathematical induction" fall into this category. Despite the name, this form of inference is a valid one and hence is a species of deductive reasoning.

8. To further complicate matters, there are philosophers such as Kant who hold that some of the statements we have classified as logically true-or-false (for example, mathematical statements like (4), (5) and (6)) have factual content even though they are a priori and necessary. If there are such statements, however, that content is of a markedly different variety than what has been described here, and what we have said about logically true-or-false statements will in general apply to these statements as well.

9. For more on this example, see Arthur Burks, *Cause, Chance and Reason* (Chicago: University of Chicago Press, 1977), Chapter 1.

10. The term 'p & q' also translates such locutions as 'p but q', 'although p, q,' and 'p yet q'. Despite the difference in nuance or connotation, English statements of these forms will be true under the same conditions as 'p and q'; namely, when both components are true and only then.

11. However, we will apply the notion of equivalence in cases where just one of the statements is a compound; thus, A and A v A are equivalent.

12. A closer inspection of the truth table for '⊃' reveals the following formulation of its truth conditions: A conditional is true if and only if either its antecedent is false or its consequent true.

13. Like '&' and 'v' (and unlike '⊃') the sign '≡' is such that '$p \equiv q$' is equivalent to '$q \equiv p$'. Also, placement of parentheses in three-component compounds does not affect their meanings.

14. It was said back in Section 2 that the denial of the conclusion of a valid argument logically contradicts its premises. In present terms, this means that the conjunction consisting of the premises and the *negation* of the conclusion is a contradiction—it has nothing but **F**s in its truth table column.

Some Basic Forms of Inductive Inference

An examination of elementary general-purpose logic textbooks reveals wide variations in their coverage of inductive forms of inference, whereas deductive logic is handled in a more standardized fashion. This lack of consensus is perhaps a reflection of the fact that inductive logic is in an early stage of development and also that even relatively simple forms of inductive inference are more resistant to formal treatment than deductive forms. Our coverage here also reflects these things, and it is neither comprehensive nor can it be said to be in depth. To make it so would take us too far afield into subjects like statistics and the philosophy of science.

Section 1. Enumerative Inferences

The simplest of inductive argument forms consist of premises that itemize a set of observations that exhibit a pattern or uniformity, and the objects specified in these observations form a **sample.** The conclusion may be a generalization or else a claim about a further unobserved sample (or as a special case, about a single individual). In the former, we have a **sample-to-population** inference and in the latter a **sample-to-sample** one. We will use italicized capital letters, like F, G, to abbreviate predicate expressions expressing properties (or conditions) an object may or may not have, such as 'is a swan', 'is white', 'is heated to $t°C$', 'boils at $t°C$'; and we will use a, b, and so on to designate the observed objects. The premises are

a is F & a is G
b is F & b is G
c is F & c is G
   .   .
   .   .
   .   .

for however many objects have been observed. The premises are thus an enumeration of observed instances and for brevity may be replaced by the single premise: *all observed* Fs *are* G (e.g., 'all observed swans are white'). Although this, unlike the preceding list, does not tell us how many instances were observed, that information can of course be added yielding: '*n* Fs were observed and all were *G*' ('103 swans were observed and all were white'). Hereafter, this will be left understood unless the context requires its explicit inclusion.

An argument whose premise takes the form, 'all observed *F*s are *G*', is an *induction by simple enumeration,*[1] and traditionally two forms have been recognized. In the first, the conclusion is the unqualified generalization obtained by excising the word 'observed':

**Simple Enumeration to a
Generalization** (GSE): All observed   *F*s are *G*
                          ∴ All *F*s are *G*

Hence the observed instances in which the *F*s are uniformly *G* are taken as evidence for (confirmation of) the conclusion, and the probability of the conclusion—and thereby the inductive strength of the inference—will vary with the number of instances observed: the more instances there are, the stronger the inference. Later we will see that in actual practice further factors affect the strength of an enumerative inference, but in the pure and simple form just shown, the quantity of confirming instances is all that influences the conclusion's probability. Here, and in what follows, it is assumed that the properties represented by *F* and *G* are *logically independent* in the sense that an object's having one of them neither logically requires nor precludes its having the other (thus ruling out logically true-or-false statements as conclusions).

GSE arguments have historically been considered to be the most fundamental in inductive logic, but they may be regarded as a special case of a more general form of inference from a sample to a population:

Statistical Generalization (SG): n% of all *F*s observed are *G*
                          ∴ m% of all *F*s are *G*

In typical cases $m = n$, and where $m = n = 100$, we have GSE as the special case. Also, when we infer that no swans are red on the basis of none of the observed swans being red, we have $m = n = 0$.

In GSE and SG the conclusion drawn is about an entire population (about all *F*s), whether it be that each has *G* or that a certain percentage of them do. But there are other forms of enumerative inference, with the following often being regarded as just as basic as GSE:

**Simple Enumeration to
an Instance** (ISE): All observed *F*s are *G*
                          ∴ The next *F* to be observed will be *G*

In this simple form the conclusion's probability increases as the number of observed instances covered by the premise increases. And as before, ISE arguments may be construed as a special case of a more general form of sample-to-sample inferences, specifically by setting $k = 1$ and $m = n = 100$:

Statistical Inference to a Sample (SIS): $n\%$ of all observed Fs are G
∴ In a sample of size k, $m\%$ of all the Fs are G

Two points are worth noting about enumerative arguments. First, the word 'observed' should not be taken too literally. The information contained in the premise does not always come from direct visual sighting, as for example in inferences about force fields or neutrinos. Second, GSE and SG arguments often draw conclusions about unobserved Fs in the past as well as the future, so it should not be thought that they are always a projection from the one to the other. If we conclude from a partial study of French history that all French monarchs have been male, no future events are involved.

Although not enumerative inferences, inductive logic includes population-to-sample arguments too, and the simplest involves a sample of just one object (note the conspicuous absence of 'observed' in the first premise):

Statistical Syllogism (SS): $n\%$ of all Fs are G
a is F
∴ a is G

SS is a common form of inductive inference (though sometimes we use terms like "most of" instead of an exact figure). We might not know whether John passed his history exam, but we infer that he did upon hearing that 90 percent of the students passed. The class of Fs is said to be the *reference class,* here the class of students enrolled in the history course. Obviously the closer n is to 100, the stronger the inference; however when n is exactly 100, we obtain a *valid* argument that properly belongs to deductive logic. Also, the *farther n* is from 100, the stronger the inference whose conclusion is that a is *not* G.

But closeness to 100 percent is not the only basis for evaluating the strength of an SS argument. To see this, suppose John is majoring in English and we obtain the further information that only 10 percent of the English majors in the course passed the exam. We now have two arguments with conflicting conclusions:

90% of all enrolled students passed	10% of all enrolled English majors passed
John is an enrolled student	John is an enrolled English major
∴ John passed	∴ John did *not* pass

Which argument should we accept? The classes to which an individual belongs are countless, and to make a proper evaluation of an SS inference, we need a rule for determining which such class should be selected as the reference class for our inference. The Rule of Total Evidence discussed earlier tells us to use all available evidence in making the selection, and hence in this instance we should use the *most relevant* reference class for which information is available. What counts as "most relevant"? First, it is a class F whose defining properties are relevant to a's being $G,$ and second, it is the most *narrowly* specified of such classes (in our example, being an enrolled English major is more specific than being an enrolled student). So we now have two rules for judging the strength of an SS and a third governing applicability:

The closer n is to 100, the stronger the argument
The more relevant the reference class is to $G,$ the stronger the argument
Use the most relevant reference class for which information is available

More important, the second rule shows that SS arguments as they are used in practice should be given a more complex formulation, perhaps something like this:

$n\%$ of all Fs are G
a is F
Things that are F bear such-and-such relevance to property G
$\therefore a$ is G

Fill in the "such-and-such" with specific information and the third premise provides us with a more complete basis for determining how likely the conclusion is relative to the other premises. When someone puts forth an SS argument in an actual context, there is nearly always a presupposed premise concerning the relevance of F to $G,$ and it must be taken into account in assessing inductive strength. Such premises are rarely mentioned explicitly in everyday discourse but are instead *suppressed.* As such, they qualify as "background" information which must be ferreted out in order to make a proper evaluation.

Background information is at work in nearly all of the inductive inferences we draw, including the enumeration arguments specified earlier. Rarely if ever do we employ GSE, ISE, or SG without at least implicitly bringing suppressed data to bear, and that is why those argument forms in the neat and simple formulations given earlier are unrealistic as representations of our actual inductive reasoning. To illustrate, suppose an island in the the Pacific Ocean has just recently been discovered; no human being so far as we know has ever set foot on it before. Explorers soon notice a bird on the island unlike any previously catalogued, and because it looks like a cross between a swan and a goose, it is called a "swoose." Each swoose that is sighted is white and the explorers infer that swooses in general are white. This may superficially seem like an case of GSE but in fact the form of inference is more complex, taking into account known facts about birds and presuming that the observed sample of swooses is more or less representative of the entire population. When background information of this kind is included, the argument used by the explorers is more than a simple GSE:

> 85 swooses have been observed, and all of them are white
> Bird coloration tends to be uniform within species and sex
> The observed sample stands in such-and-such relation to the
>   population
> ∴ All swooses are white

The second premise provides relevant background information, in this case ornithological data that raises the conclusion's probability. Roughly put, the reason why we rarely use GSE in its pure form is because we know too much.

The third premise when fully spelled out will express the degree to which our explorers regard the observed sample as providing an accurate picture of the total population, and we shall call it *the sampling premise*. Such premises are most often suppressed but nonetheless are operative in nearly all inferences we draw from a sample. The inductive strength of such an inference, then, depends in part on what the sampling premise tells us concerning how representative the sample is of the entire population. In ordinary, everyday contexts of argument, determining this usually requires some work; we must reconstruct the argument in an attempt to see what the author had in mind. (Clues can often be found, as when, for example, the conclusion is hedged with language like "it is perhaps plausible to infer. . . .") An argument from a sample can be inductively strong only when the sampling premise specifies a strong resemblance between sample and population (it is then a further question as to whether the author is right in supposing such a resemblance—whether the sampling premise is indeed true).

So whereas the inductive strength of a GSE (or ISE or some other) argument in its pure form depends solely on the number of confirming instances (on how large the sample is), arguments based on samples that occur in practical affairs are such that their strength turns also on how representative the sample is of the whole population. In other words, for such an argument to be inductively strong, the sample, first, must be large enough and, second, must be varied enough so that it provides a reasonably accurate portrait of the variety present in the population itself. We will briefly elaborate on both points.

How large the sample should be depends on several factors; for instance, the nature of the background information available to us and whether acceptance of the conclusion would require us to reject certain statements that have already been confirmed. In general, we can say this much: the more homogeneous or uniform the population, the less the dependence of inductive strength on large samples. Thus, a metallurgist who develops a new alloy may conclude that all samples of it will melt at a certain temperature after just a few tests. To know the behavior of the tested items is to know pretty well how all of them will behave. On the other hand, it would be silly to conclude that a particular candidate will be the next president of the United States on the basis of polling just ten registered voters, all of whom indicated a preference for that candidate. Here, the population of registered voters in the United States is not only very large but far too diverse to warrant such an inference. An in-depth examination of how large a sample is needed for a given generalization is beyond our scope.

The more important consideration in determining inductive strength for arguments from samples is whether the variety in the sample comes close to matching the variety of the entire population, at least so far as we know it. That is, we must avoid "biased" samples. We would reach the wrong conclusion about American opinion on the abortion question if our sample consisted solely of Catholic clergy. To eliminate bias and obtain a high probability that the sample resembles the population we need a representative sample. But how can we be reasonably sure that we have one? In some cases we cannot, as in the swoose example. There, the explorers had to take what came their way, although perhaps a study of the island's climate and topography might be relevant in assessing the representativeness of the observed swooses. But in cases like polling opinion on abortion, we can set up our own sample and are constrained only by the time and expense involved. So how should we go about this?

When a population is known to be diverse but there is little information on just how it varies, we can try to obtain a **random sample,** in which each member of the population has an equal chance of being selected. Such samples tend to be large in order to better represent the variety in the total population. Random samples can be done in two ways: with replacement and without. If an urn contains one hundred balls of various colors, and we wish to determine the color composition but do not want to examine all one hundred, we may obtain a random sample by drawing just twenty balls. If after each draw the examined ball is returned to the urn, we have a random sample with replacement. But samples without replacement are usually preferred since the possibility of duplication is avoided. In a random sample *without replacement,* then, each member of the population has an equal chance of being chosen first, and for those members not selected before the nth choice, each has an equal chance of being the nth member chosen.

Political polling often involves random sampling, although more sophisticated kinds of samples are used as well. An example of the latter is *stratified* random sampling in which we attempt to "match the sample to the population" as closely as possible. Although a population might be diverse, in many cases we have enough information about it to know that it contains various subgroups (or "strata") and that these groups exhibit relevant differences concerning the subject under investigation. If we further know the proportions of these subgroups within the entire population, we can try to obtain a sample that exhibits those same proportions, and then select randomly from within each group. For example, if we are polling Podunk City to determine how many prospective voters prefer mayoral candidate Smith, we might stratify the sample according to race and ethnic background if that seems to be a relevant consideration and if we already know the percentages of such groups within the total population. Stratified sampling is more economical than the simple random variety in that it often allows us to obtain significant results with a smaller sample and avoids the need for an exhaustive census from which the sample is to be selected. Also, it is more efficient in reducing the kinds of error that can creep into the sampling process.

But regardless of whether the sampling is stratified or purely random, an *inference* from sample to population is basically a more sophisticated variety of the Statistical Generalization inference mentioned earlier. Here, as with GSE inferences, a sampling premise is added. Where the sampling is a simple random one (and we will focus on these hereafter) we have

Statistical Generalization II: *n%* of the *F*s in observed sample S
are *G*
S is of size *m* and was randomly selected without replacement from the entire population of *F*s
∴ *n%* of all *F*s are *G*

Clearly SG-II is a more potent and realistic inference than the simple SG. But further extensions are possible. In inductive inference, other things being equal, if we *weaken* the conclusion, we *strengthen* the inference. We thus have another common variation on SG:

Statistical Generalization III: *n*% of the *F*s in observed sample S
are *G*

S is of size *m* and was randomly
selected without replacement from
the entire population of *F*s

∴ *n* ± *k*% of all *F*s are *G*

Here instead of an exact figure, we have a certain percentage range, and of course it is more probable that the actual percentage of *F*s that are *G* in the total population falls within that range than that it is exactly *n*. For SG-III arguments then, we have another rule for judging inductive strength: the larger the value for *k*, the stronger the argument (though of course at some point the values of *k* will be so large—and hence the conclusion so weak—that the argument ceases to be of any interest).

The gathering and classification of evidence pertaining to the premises of SG-II and SG-III inferences properly belongs to the field of "descriptive" statistics, whereas our interest lies in the inferences drawn from such data, or "projective" statistics. However, the two fields are in practice so closely intertwined that it is worth mentioning some of the problems involved in arriving at true premises. "Nonsampling errors" will make the first premise of each inference pattern false; such errors concern the improper collection of statistical information, in particular mistakes made in observing or studying the sample. This can happen in many ways, and when it does the percentage figure of *F*s that are *G* is incorrect for the sample itself.

More important for our purposes are the "sampling errors" that could falsify the second (or sampling) premise. Here, as already noted, the sample selected is not representative either because it is not large enough or because it was not randomly chosen. A haphazardly collected sample, for example, is rarely a random one; if we fail to select members of the sample using some sort of randomizing process, the chance for a representative sample remains low. In some cases, as in drawing balls from an urn, this is a simple matter, but obtaining a truly random, 500-member sample of registered voters in Podunk City is something else again. Sometimes a sampling method may give the appearance of being random when it really is not, as when, for example, passersby are interviewed on a city street. If the street happens to be in the financial district, the sample obtained might well be unrepresentative of the voting population. Statisticians can try to remove bias of this kind by compiling an exhaustive list of the population and then using tables of random numbers to select the sample. In some cases a sample may be random but is inadvertently restricted to only a portion of the total population, as when names are

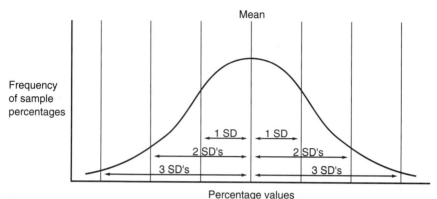

Figure 1. Frequency of sample percentages

randomly chosen from a phone directory but many residents have unlisted numbers.

However, no matter how well designed the sampling process might be, there will almost always be a difference between the actual percentage of *F*s that are *G* in the total population and the percentage in the observed sample of *F*s. It is rare indeed when the two figures are exactly the same, and the discrepancy that is usually present is called *random sampling error.* Fortunately, statisticians have developed powerful methods for accurately estimating the size of such errors, and in briefly looking at one of them we will discover yet another strengthened version of SG.

Random sampling error can be estimated by considering what we would obtain if we recorded the results of a long series of random samples where each such sample is of the same size. If we plot the percentage of *F*s that are *G* of all of these samples against the number of times we obtained a particular percentage figure, the result is a **sampling curve.** Now, for a very large number of repetitions, this curve tends to be *normally distributed,* and the greater the number the greater is the tendency. A normally distributed sampling curve assumes a bell-shaped form with the various percentage values lying on the horizontal axis and the observed frequencies for those percentages on the vertical (see Figure 1). Over the long run, most of the sample percentages cluster around the actual percentage, giving the curve its characteristic bell shape. The peak or central point of a normally distributed curve is called the *mean,* for it is the average value for all the sample percentage values. If we add up all the percentage values of the samples and divide by the number of samples, the resulting percentage value is the mean for all of them.

For illustration, suppose that the actual—though to us unknown—percentage of *F*s that are *G* for the total population is 55 percent. What we wish to know here is the probability that the percentage of *F*s that are *G* in any *single* sample of a given size (say, 100) will differ significantly from the actual percentage of the total population.

We can get an estimate of this probability if we know the **standard deviation** (for short, SD) of the sampling curve. Roughly, the SD is a unit of measurement that describes the spread of the distribution curve from the mean or central point. If we keep the mean fixed, then the larger the SD, the "flatter" will be the bell shape; the smaller the SD, the "steeper" will be the curve. A distance of one SD unit from the mean occurs where the upper, convex portion of the curve meets the lower, concave portion; thus the vertical grid lines in Figure 1 mark off SD areas for the curve. A full account of this concept may be obtained from any statistics textbook and is beyond our scope here.[2] For our purposes, it is sufficient to note that statisticians have formulated a rule (often called the "Empirical Rule") that they claim describes accurately the variability of bell-shaped distributions as found in nature (the justification for this rule is also well beyond our scope).

The Empirical Rule: For any normal distribution,

    a. 68 percent of all sample percentage values lie within one SD on either side of the mean

    b. 95 percent of all sample percentage values lie within two SDs on either side of the mean

    c. 99 percent of all sample percentage values lie within three SDs on either side of the mean

Suppose, then, that we have a 100-member random sample without replacement and the percentage of *F*s that are *G* is 52 (a random sampling error of 3 percent since the actual but unknown percentage is 55). A statistics text will also tell us that, for a 100-member sample, the SD of a normally distributed curve is about five units, or in effect 5 percent. That is, a single SD to the right of the mean (the first vertical grid line to its right) would be specified as 52 + 5%, and one SD to the left (the first grid line to the left) would be specified as 52 − 5%.

Given an SD of 5 percent, then by the Empirical Rule it follows that

    a. There is a 0.68 probability that the actual percentage of *F*s that are *G* in the entire population is within a range of 47 to 57 percent (that is, within one SD of 52 percent or 52 ± 5%).

    b. There is a 0.95 probability that the actual percentage of the population is within a range of 42 to 62 percent (within two SDs or 52 ± 10%).

c. There is a 0.99 probability that the actual percentage of the population is within a range of 37 to 67 percent (within three SDs or 52 ± 15%).

To spell this out a bit, the "true" sampling curve has a mean of 55 percent. Of course we do not know that its mean *is* 55 percent, but given that it is normally distributed and that its SD is 5 percent, then although we do not know exactly where the true curve lies on the graph's horizontal axis, its upper and lower limits may be determined according to the Empirical Rule. For example, clause (b) of the rule in effect tells us that *if* we desire a 0.95 chance that our estimate of the true value is correct—in statisticians' jargon, if we want a 95 percent "confidence level"—then the true curve cannot be any further to the left on the graph than a curve whose mean is 52 − 10 percent nor any further to the right than one whose mean is 52 + 10 percent. That is, there is only a 0.05 probability that it falls outside the range 52 ± 10 percent, so if the true curve were any further to the left, there would be less than a 0.025 chance that we would have obtained a 52 percent value in our sample, and similarly, a less than 0.025 chance if it were further to the right. And this falls outside the confidence level we have chosen to employ.

Therefore we can say that at the 95 percent confidence level, the true value is somewhere between 42 and 62 percent; that is, over the long run that value will be within this range in ninety-five cases out of one hundred.

Polling organizations usually report their results using the 95 percent confidence level. If we read in the newspaper that a recent poll shows public support for the president's policies to be 42 percent "with a margin of error of 3 percent" or "with an accuracy of plus-or-minus 3 percent," this generally means that there is a 0.95 probability that the correct value is within 39 to 45 percent. A probability of 0.95 provides us with a high degree of inductive strength. A higher confidence level would require that we either broaden the margin of error or else use much larger samples. We now have a very sophisticated upgrade of the SG inference.

Statistical Generalization IV: $n\%$ of the Fs in observed sample S are G

S is of size m and was randomly selected without replacement from the entire population of Fs

∴ At the $r\%$ confidence level, $n \pm k\%$ of all Fs are G

∴ $n \pm k\%$ of all Fs are G

We actually have here a two-step inference. The inference from the two premises to the first conclusion is a *deductive* one—at least when certain implicit premises are included (such as the Empirical Rule and that the sampling curve is normally distributed). The inference from the first conclusion to the second is inductive with a strength equal to the confidence level.

An important consequence to be drawn from our discussion of SG-IV is that the accuracy of a pollster's estimates depends on the absolute size of the sample, rather than its size relative to that of the entire population. It is worth noting that as sample size increases, a curve's SD decreases. For 1,000-member samples, the SD is just 1½ percent and hence the 95 percent confidence level (again, ± two SDs) provides an interval of ±3 percent instead of the ±10 percent for 100-member samples. A 1,500-member sample yields an SD of only 1 percent, thus at the 95 percent confidence level, the interval is but ±2 percent. Perhaps this gives us a glimpse of why political polling of a large population has acquired such a strong track record even though the samples employed are only a minute percentage of all registered voters.

Exercises

1. A produce distributor examines a carton of lettuce fresh off the train from California and finds every head to be in excellent condition. He decides to accept the entire load in the boxcar. Which form of inference is he using? What background premises might he plausibly be using? Do you think his inference is a strong one? Why or why not?

2. When a new drug is tested, it is often administered first to mice which have been bred to be genetically identical. What is the reason for doing this? Often in such testing, the drug is given to a group of mice randomly selected from the total population (the "experimental" group) but withheld from another randomly selected group (the "control" group). What is the point in doing this?

3. In 1936, during the Great Depression, the *Literary Digest* polled 2 million people randomly selected from lists of automobile and telephone owners concerning the upcoming presidential election of that year. The response overwhelmingly favored Alfred M. Landon over Franklin D. Roosevelt, and the *Literary Digest* confidently predicted a Landon victory. Yet when the election was held, Roosevelt won by a landslide. What went wrong?

4. Sally tosses a coin 100 times and heads comes up 42 times; she confidently asserts that this result shows the coin to be biased. Assuming that the tosses constitute a 100-member sample of all possible tosses of the coin (which we may suppose to be normally distributed), is Sally correct in her inference? Explain.

Section 2. Analogical Inferences _____

Analogical inference is perhaps the most common form of inductive reasoning. Wishing to see a suspense movie tonight, you rent an Alfred Hitchcock movie at the video store on the basis of having been entertained by other suspense films he has directed. You decide to purchase a Hacker modem because your Hacker computer, monitor, and printer have all performed reliably. Having taken and enjoyed, two astronomy courses, both taught by Professor Starr, you opt for another astronomy course he is offering. In each case, we infer something about an object or event on the basis of its resemblance to other objects or events; because the former is analogous in crucial respects to the latter, what holds for the latter will likely hold for the former as well.

Let us try to reconstruct the astronomy argument. We will use the predicate letters 'F_1' and 'F_2' to represent the properties of being an astronomy course and being taught by Professor Starr, respectively. These provide the resemblance that forms the basis for the inference, and they form the **positive analogy.** We will use 'G' for the property of being an enjoyable course to take, the **inferred property.** Where 'a_1' and 'a_2' designate the courses previously taken and 'b' the course under consideration, we thus have

a_1, a_2 and b all have F_1 and F_2
a_1 and a_2 also have G
∴ b has G as well

Here, we have the pattern of an analogical inference: The first premise states that several objects are similar in one or more respects, and the second states that some of them are similar in yet another respect. The conclusion is then drawn that the remaining object (or objects) has that property too.

Two points should be noted. First, although analogy occurs frequently in all forms of writing, it is not always used to draw an inference. Its use in poetry and literature is mostly confined to creating vivid or compelling imagery. In other discourse, analogy is used to explain or illuminate a point:

> The galaxies of our expanding universe are receding from one another, much as dots painted on a balloon grow further apart when it is inflated.

No inference is being drawn in either of these cases; in others it is not easy to tell whether the author's use of analogy is an argumentative one. Our focus hereafter will of course be on uses of analogy to draw a conclusion.

Second, an analogical inference is basically a sample-to-sample one, and as such it would appear to differ in no important respects from the form of argument described as a Simple Enumeration to an Instance (or ISE) in the preceding section. If we use F to abbreviate the conjunctive property of having F_1 and F_2 in the preceding example, then the inference proceeds from the fact that observed things having F also have G to the conclusion that the next thing to be observed having F (i.e., b) will also have G. We shall regard analogical arguments as a distinctive subclass of ISE since, as we will see shortly, they require more complex background premises than others of the ISE form and in addition place greater emphasis on the *resemblances* between the compared instances than on their *quantity*. Many analogical arguments have a high degree of inductive strength even though the number of objects involved is quite small.

Analogical inference is used extensively in legal reasoning where "precedent" is often the deciding factor in a judge's ruling. It is sometimes not sufficient for the judge to be guided by the relevant laws, which in many instances are formulated in rather general terms. Hence previous judicial decisions wherein the laws have already been interpreted and applied are taken into account. If there are previous rulings that favor the plaintiff's position, attorneys for the plaintiff will try to construct a positive analogy between those rulings and the present case. This applies especially if a previous ruling is a "controlling case"—one widely regarded as being of particular importance to the subject being litigated. Attorneys for the defendant will attempt to show relevant dissimilarities between such cases and the present one. If no controlling case is found, they will develop their own positive analogy by trying to find cases where the decision favored the defendant's position. Developing a positive analogy in legal matters is almost always less cut-and-dried than it is in scientific and everyday contexts, resulting in some highly imaginative argument that usually leaves plenty of room for dispute. Nonetheless, arguing from legal precedence is basically the same form of inference as our example about the astronomy course.

Evaluating the inductive strength of analogical arguments is a complex matter involving several criteria. In looking at these we will see that giving a reconstruction of such arguments as they occur in actual practice requires the inclusion of a great deal of background information. First, though, some sample inferences will help us in our discussion.

I. Like his father, his paternal grandfather, and two of his father's brothers, Jones has high blood pressure, eats a diet high in saturated fats, smokes heavily, and gets little exercise. Since his forebears died of heart disease while in their 50s, we infer that Jones will too.

II. The six Democratic senators who supported strong environmental laws, abortion rights, gun control, and sex education in public schools were opposed for reelection last year by the Committee for a Conservative America. Since Senator Brown supports these things and is up for reelection next year, we can expect the CCA to oppose her too.

III. An eighteenth-century writer, Thomas Reid,[3] argued that it is "not unreasonable" to suppose that life in some form exists on one or more of the other planets of the solar system. Each, he says, revolves around the sun and borrows its light from the sun just as the earth does. Like our planet, they rotate about their axes giving them a succession of day and night, and in their motions they are subject to the same physical laws.

IV. In laboratory tests, the experimental drug Herocaine was administered to rats, guinea pigs, and rabbits; in each case some animals suffered severe reactions. Hence, we can expect the same to happen with human beings.

By far the most important criterion in judging the strength of an analogical inference is the *relevance* of the properties in the positive analogy to the inferred property. The more relevant they are, the stronger is the resemblance between the inferring instances (in argument (I), Jones's relatives) and the inferred instance (Jones), and hence the greater the inductive strength. A property F is *positively relevant* to property G if the presence of F increases the probability that G is also present, and there are clear examples of this in the preceding arguments. A high-fat diet raises the risk of heart disease, receiving light from the sun increases the chance for development of life forms, and so forth. In arguments (I) and (III) the relevance is *causal:* the properties in the positive analogy are linked to the inferred property by laws or principles according to which they are causal agents (though a causal inference may proceed "backward" too, from effect to cause).

Argument (IV) calls for special comment, for unlike the others it is not clear exactly what the positive analogy is. For those of us who are not trained zoologists or physiologists, perhaps the most we can say is that the circulatory and nervous systems of rats, pigs, rabbits, and humans all share certain basic features in virtue of which it may be inferred that a substance which produces a particular physiological effect in the first three groups will likely produce a similar result in the fourth. To fully reconstruct argument (IV) for the purpose of assessing its strength, we must make explicit the points of resemblance that are implicit in the premises, and this demands more training in physiology than most of us possess. We simply lack the expertise necessary to state precisely the relevant similarities between experimental animals and human beings. In such cases, it is reasonable for us to rely on the experts that such similarities exist, but it must be kept in mind that an exact specification of the positive analogy would be needed for a proper evaluation.

But not every resemblance is a relevant one. Argument (I) would not be strengthened if the positive analogy were enlarged by noting that Jones and his relatives all attended the same high school or used the same brand of shaving cream. Any *striking* resemblance can form the basis for an analogical argument, as evidenced by an argument propounded by a sixteenth-century writer (who shall go nameless to spare his descendents any embarassment):

> There are seven windows in the head . . . from which and many other similar phenomena of nature such as the seven metals, etc., we gather that the number of planets is necessarily seven.

From the claim that head openings and the metals are seven in number it is inferred that another phenomenon, the planets, also numbers seven, though there is no relevance beyond the mere fact that all occur in the natural world. Moreover, the lack of relevance means that the argument's strength would not be significantly increased if more groups of seven were cited in the premises.

Another criterion is the *size of the positive analogy;* the greater the number of relevant properties in it, the stronger the argument. The strength of argument (I) is increased if it is added that Jones and his relatives were all at least 25 pounds overweight, and argument (II) yields a more probable conclusion if we include that Senator Brown like the others opposed by the CCA voted against the balanced budget amendment.

Let us say that a property F is *negatively* relevant to property G if the presence of F decreases the probability that G is present. The set of negatively relevant properties constitutes a **negative analogy,** and this provides us with yet another criterion: the *size of the negative analogy.* The larger it is, the weaker is the argument. Argument (I) is weakened if we add the information that, although his father, uncles, and grandfather all smoked cigarettes and suffered from rheumatic fever as children, Jones smokes only cigars and never had rheumatic fever. It is also less likely that the CCA will oppose Senator Brown if they find out that she—unlike the other Democratic senators—supports the school prayer amendment and favors a tax cut for capital gains. In argument (IV), although experimental animals and humans have similar nervous and circulatory systems, there are obviously differences in degree. The central nervous system of a rat or rabbit is less complex than that of a human being. They also differ in metabolic rate and other possibly relevant factors as well.

In argument (III) Reid himself is careful to point out some disanalogies. He notes that, although the other planets revolve about the sun as the earth does, they do so at different distances and in different periods. For this reason, his conclusion is hedged: "There is some probability in this conclusion by analogy." Of course astronomical research in the twentieth century has reduced this probability to near zero, but we must distinguish between the negative analogy that was known to Reid and the negative analogy known to us. The latter includes a great deal of information that Reid could not have known about, and consequently his probability estimate, although not high, was with justification significantly greater than zero.

A fourth criterion is the *variety and number of instances mentioned in the premises*. By itself, the sheer number of instances observed is not always an important consideration, as the seven-in-number argument shows. Doubling the number of groups of seven does not appreciably raise the conclusion's probability. On the other hand, the conclusion of Reid's argument has a higher probability even though it is an inference from only *one* instance, the planet earth. The stronger the relevance of the positive analogy to the inferred property, the less need is there for a large number of objects.

However, the variety of the observed instances is indeed a worthwhile consideration. The more dissimilar they are with regard to properties *not* in the positive analogy, the stronger is the argument. If the properties in the positive analogy occur together in a variety of otherwise dissimilar instances, the more likely it is that their relation to the inferred property is not coincidental or accidental. Thus the conclusion of argument (I) would be more probable with respect to the properties in the positive analogy if we found out that, although some of Jones's relatives worked in stressful occupations, others did not; and that some indulged in alcohol whereas others abstained. If our background information includes the fact that the positive analogy holds for a diverse sample, so much the better for the argument.[4]

We saw earlier that in general if the conclusion is weakened, the argument is strengthened. The reverse holds too, and analogical arguments are a good example of this. If the conclusion of Reid's argument is altered to assert the existence of *intelligent* life on other planets, its probability plunges. Therefore the stronger or more specific the conclusion, the weaker is the argument.

These five criteria for asssessing inductive strength may be formulated as inductive rules governing analogical argument—rules for gauging the probability of the conclusion given the information in the premises. Inductive logic is not yet to the point where they can be expressed with the precision and applicability of deductive rules, so we will settle for the rough form in which they have already been stated. We may now state the analogical form as follows; although not completely general, it is satisfactory for our purposes:

$a_1, \ldots, a_m$ and b all have $F_1, \ldots, F_n$
$a_1, \ldots, a_m$ also have G
$\therefore b$ has G

The object b is often a specific individual (Jones in argument (I)), but is sometimes a set of individuals (human beings in argument (IV)). The preceding schema is not completely general since the conclusion of Reid's argument says that *one or more* of the other planets supports life in some form.

More important, what holds for enumeration arguments holds here too, in fact even more so. A full reconstruction of an analogical argument presented in a given context would require the inclusion of additional premises spelling out the background information involved. One such premise would mention properties in the negative analogy:

$a_1, \ldots, a_m$ differ from b with respect to $H_1, \ldots, H_k$

Another needed premise would state the degree of variety or diversity of the observed instances, $a_1, \ldots, a_m$. Most important would be the relevance premise expressing the extent to which the positive analogy, $F_1, \ldots, F_n$, is relevant to the possession of the inferred property. In many cases, this premise would take the form of a long paragraph detailing information that if true would raise the conclusion's probability. Often this information includes causal laws that themselves have been confirmed through inductive reasoning. When such premises are included, reconstructing an analogical argument becomes a complex matter.

Exercises

1. Let $a_1, \ldots, a_4$ be Jones's relatives and b Jones himself, and let $F_1, \ldots, F_5$ be the properties in the positive analogy (having high blood pressure, for example, together with the property of family affiliation), and G be the inferred property. Then we may represent argument (I) as

$a_1, \ldots, a_4$ and b all have $F_1, \ldots, F_5$
$a_1, \ldots, a_4$ have G
$\therefore b$ also has G

Now do the same for arguments (II) and (III). Specify the properties and individuals involved.

2. For arguments (II) and (III), specify some properties (beyond those mentioned in the text) that if included in the positive analogy would strengthen them. Then specify some that if included in the negative analogy would weaken them.

3. Lay out the structure of the following argument and evaluate its strength.

> It is urged that motion pictures do not fall with the First Amendment's aegis because their production, distribution and exhibition is a large-scale business conducted for private profit. We cannot agree. That books, newspapers and magazines are published and sold for profit does not prevent them from being a form of expression whose liberty is safeguarded by the First Amendment. We fail to see why operation for profit should have any different effect in the case of motion pictures. (U.S. Supreme Court, *Burstyn* v. *Wilson,* 1952)

4. Lay out the structure of the following argument and evaluate its strength.

> If we found by chance a watch or other piece of intricate mechanism we should infer that it had been made by someone. But all around us we do find intricate pieces of natural mechanism, and the processes of the universe are seen to move together in complex relations; we should therefore infer that these too have a Maker. (From B. A. Williams, "Metaphysical Arguments," in D. F. Pears, ed., *The Nature of Metaphysics*)

5. Consumer decisions (like buying a Sony TV or a Buick Regal) are often the result of analogical reasoning based on experiences with other products from the same manufacturer, reports of friends about the same product, and so on. Give an example of one, spelling out both the positive and negative analogies.

6. A Gay and Lesbian Rights group applies for a permit to parade through a community with a heavy population of fundamentalists. The city denies the permit citing the possibility of violence and two previous judicial cases in which permits were refused. In one, Nazis had attempted to march through a predominantly Jewish community, and in the other, the Klan had wanted to parade through a black area. The rights group files suit claiming their First Amendment rights were violated. Construct an analogical argument supporting the city's position. Then specify a negative analogy that might be used by an attorney representing the rights group.

Section 3. Causal Inference:
Necessary and Sufficient Conditions _____

A great deal of scientific inquiry is focused on the discovery of causes. Knowing the cause of something beneficial or desirable will help us bring it about, and knowing the cause of something harmful or undesirable will help us prevent its occurrence. One of the chief concerns of inductive logic is with arguments whose conclusions state a relation of cause to effect between two kinds of phenomena, and we will look at some simple examples of such arguments in the next section. For now, however, we need to lay some groundwork.

The notion of causality is a complex one and many philosophers and scientists have wrestled with it over the centuries. A thorough discussion would quickly take us beyond inductive logic into epistemology and the philosophy of science. So we will settle here for a sketch of the "logic" of causality, and our starting point is a basic distinction that will shed light on various ways in which the word 'cause' is used in science and everyday affairs:

> A property C is a **sufficient condition** for E if and only if E always occurs in the presence of C; that is, whenever C is present E is present.
> A property C is a **necessary condition** for E if and only if E never occurs in the absence of C; that is, whenever E is present C is present.

The presence of oxygen is a necessary condition for combustion since the latter never occurs unless oxygen is present. But oxygen alone obviously is not sufficient for combustion; other ingredients are also required. For example, oxygen in combination with butane and a temperature of 200°C is sufficient for combustion; whenever these three occur together they ensure the occurrence of combustion. However, they are not necessary since there are many other ways of bringing about combustion (for example, oxygen, gasoline, and 250°C).[5] When we say that one event "causes" another, we sometimes mean a causally necessary condition, other times a causally sufficient one. Watering your plants causes them to grow because water is necessary for growth. A .30 caliber bullet to the temple causes death because it is sufficient for death to occur.

From these above definitions we may validly derive the following principles:

> C is sufficient for E if and only if whenever E is absent C is absent
> C is necessary for E if and only if whenever C is absent E is absent

If a bullet to the temple is sufficient for death, then the nonoccurrence of death ensures that no bullet struck; and if water is necessary for plant growth, lack of water guarantees lack of growth.

It must be noted here that the terms 'necessary condition' and 'sufficient condition' are often used without any association with the notion of causality. The following examples illustrate their *logical* use, according to which they express logical truths:

The truth of p is a sufficient condition for the truth of '$p \text{ v } q$'
Not being divisible by 3 is a necessary condition for being a prime
    number
Being a bachelor is a sufficient condition for being unmarried

These statements are not about "causes" but express a priori principles that are true on purely logical grounds or in virtue of the meanings of their component terms ('bachelor' is *defined* as 'unmarried adult male human being'). There are also "legalistic" uses that have nothing to do with causality:

Being a convicted felon is a sufficient condition for being ineligible
    to hold public office
Being at least 16 years of age is a necessary condition for
    obtaining a driver's license

In what follows, 'necessary condition' and 'sufficient condition' will be used *only* in the sense of *causal* condition, as in our examples about combustion and the like at the beginning of this section.

Two more points are worth making about necessary and sufficient condtions. First, 'cause' is often used in the sense of necessary condition when our concern is with eliminating a harmful or undesirable phenomenon. The bite of a certain variety of mosquito is a necessary condition for contracting yellow fever, so eliminating the mosquito through pest control measures will eliminate the disease. We typically use 'cause' in the sense of sufficient condition when we are concerned with producing something beneficial. An agronomist studies soybean plants to discover the precise cause (qua sufficient condition) of their growth patterns. Knowing this facilitates the breeding of better hybrids that can withstand drought and poor soil conditions.

Second, if we know that one event caused another in the sense of necessary condition, we can infer the cause upon observing the effect. Since oxygen is necessary for combustion, a continuously burning candle in a deep mine shaft assures us of the presence of oxygen. In the sense of sufficient condition, however, we infer the effect from an observation of the cause. We readily conclude that combustion is imminent if we see a tank of butane gas being heated by the approach of an uncontrolled fire.

But 'cause' is used in other ways as well. Suppose a forest ranger is trying to determine the cause of a particularly damaging forest fire. He is not looking for a necessary condition; he would hardly feel enlightened if he was told that the fire occurred because oxygen was present. Is he looking for a sufficient condition? In a case like this, there are typically many conditions that in combination bring about the fire, and he is not interested in compiling an exhaustive list of them (and some of them—e.g., dry weather conditions—he presumably already knows). However, if *one* of these conditions turns out to be that gasoline had been applied to some of the foliage and then ignited, the ranger would have found the cause he was looking for. Here, 'cause' means something like "precipitating factor." That is, it is that condition which in the presence of other causal conditions that generally accompany the effect (in this case, dry weather) was responsible for the event's occurrence rather than its nonoccurrence. We are not concerned with a full-blown sufficient condition but in a component that is of special interest for the investigator. When a coroner investigates "the cause" of death or an insurance adjustor "the cause" of an accident, this sense of 'cause' is operative.

Somewhat similar cases can be found in scientific contexts. It is sometimes said that the application of heat causes a gas to expand, meaning by this 'cause' in the sense of sufficient condition. But strictly it is heat together with gas pressure being within a certain range that constitutes the sufficient condition. To say that heat per se is the cause is to say that within the usual causal parameters it is the precipitating factor.

It is often claimed that smoking causes lung cancer, or perhaps more fully, heavy cigarette smoking over a prolonged period causes lung cancer. Is 'cause' here being used in the sense of necessary condition? Clearly not; many people who have developed lung cancer never smoked (e.g., those who inhaled asbestos fibers over a fairly long period). Is it then being used in the sense of sufficient condition? Once again the answer is no. Many smokers for whatever reason are resistant to the disease and live to a ripe old age, eventually dying of something other than lung cancer. What then do we mean when we say that smoking causes lung cancer? We mean that prolonged heavy smoking increases your risk; in other words, it *significantly raises the probability* that you will contract lung cancer. Here, we have yet a further sense of 'cause', the "probabilistic" sense. The causal agent does not invariably occur with the effect, but the occurrence of the latter is more likely given the presence of the former than it would be otherwise.

When 'cause' is used either in the sense of necessary condition or of sufficient condition, a given kind of event typically has a plurality of causes. For example, the combination of oxygen-butane-heat as well as that of oxygen-gasoline-heat are both "causes" of (sufficient conditions for) combustion. But in theoretical science especially, 'cause' is often used in the sense of *necessary-and-sufficient* condition, and here we may justly speak of *the* cause of an event; in this sense an event has a *unique* cause.

> C is a **necessary-and-sufficient condition** for E just in case E is present if
> C is present and vice versa; that is, E is present if and only if C is present.

Hence E cannot occur without the presence of C (necessary) and C's presence ensures the occurrence of E (sufficient). In such a case, C is the set of *all* necessary conditions that are, then, *jointly sufficient* to bring about E. In many cases, a necessary-and-sufficient condition is very complex—requiring for its comprehension more technical knowledge than most of us possess—but there are simple examples too. On the evidence available so far, the presence of the HIV virus in the human bloodstream is both necessary and sufficient for contracting AIDS: the disease will not develop unless the virus is present, and its presence would appear to ensure the eventual onset of the disease. And roughly speaking, for your plant seeds to germinate they need enough water, appropriate temperature, and suitable amounts of oxygen and light. When all of these necessary conditions occur together, they are sufficient for germination.

An underlying assumption of most scientific investigation is that for every specifiable kind of event, there is a unique cause—a set of necessary conditions jointly sufficient for its occurrence. This would appear to conflict with the more commonsense view that a given kind of event can admit of a plurality of causes. If your plants wilt, this could be due to insufficient water, not enough heat, insect infestation, and so on. But although wilting per se might be the result of a variety of different conditions, a specific type of wilt that perhaps only a trained botanist could identify will have a unique causal antecedent, lack of water, say, rather than insufficient heat. In such cases, then, a more precise specification of the effect removes the appearance of a plurality of causes.

Even so, obtaining a complete set of necessary conditions that are jointly sufficient can be a very arduous task. For example, research on laboratory animals has shown that the presence of certain micro-organisms in the mouth is necessary but not sufficient for tooth decay, and the same holds for the presence of food debris.[6] Is the presence of *both* of these necessary conditions *sufficient* for tooth decay? Not quite; some animals (and some humans) are more resistant to cavities than others. They will develop cavities at a much lower rate than others who have the same amounts (and kinds) of debris and germs in their mouths. We thus have a probabilistic cause at best; there are presumably further necessary conditions to be found, and finding them in a causal situation as complex as this one can be immensely difficult. The time and effort involved in exploring possibilities like genetic predisposition, impurities in drinking water, and so forth are enormous; and if our interest is in simply controlling the decay process, we may not be inclined to pursue the investigation with as much thoroughness as we would if we desired a complete theoretical understanding of the phenomenon in the form of necessary conditions jointly sufficient.

Does *every* phenomenon have a unique cause? That is, for each kind of event in the universe, is there a set of causal conditions such that when they are present—and only then—the event invariably occurs? This is a question whose discussion more properly belongs to the philosophy of science, metaphysics, and theoretical physics, but a word or two is in order here. It was said previously that scientific investigation appears to presuppose that a necessary-and-sufficient condition exists for any specifiable effect, and if this is so, then what we earlier called "probabilistic causes" are only an expression of our ignorance—a reflection of the complexity of many causal processes and of the presence of causal factors in these processes that we do not yet know about. Our lack of knowledge aside, then, the presupposition tells us that at the deepest or most fundamental level of scientific explanation, there are always necessary conditions jointly sufficient to be found.

However, it is worth noting that quantum physics recognizes probabilistic causal antecedents at this fundamental level; experimental findings (so we nonphysicists have been told) simply cannot be explained in terms of causal conditions that are invariably present when and only when an event occurs. At its present stage of development quantum physics cannot be adequately formulated in terms of necessary-and-sufficient causal conditions.

Exercises

1. Using the definitions at the beginning of this section and some elementary deductive logic, explain why the following principles are true:

    i. If C is sufficient for E, then $\sim E$ is sufficient for $\sim C$
    ii. If C is sufficient for E, then E is necessary for C
    iii. If C is sufficient for E, then $\sim C$ is necessary for $\sim E$

2. Here is an example of principle (ii) in the first question:

> If a bullet through the temple is a sufficient condition for death, then death is a necessary condition for (the occurrence of) a bullet through the temple.

But although a bullet through the temple *causes* death, death does not cause the occurrence of a bullet through the temple. Does this show that principle (ii) is false when the terms 'sufficient' and 'necessary' are interpreted to mean '*causally* sufficient' and '*causally* necessary?' Discuss.

Section 4. Causal Inference:
Eliminative Induction _____

When 'cause' is used in the sense of sufficient, necessary, or necessary-and-sufficient condition, it is presupposed, as we have seen, that cause and effect are *uniformly* connected. We would not say that a particular event *c* "caused" a particular effect *e* unless we are prepared to affirm in general that any instance of the same kind as *c* will in similar circumstances produce an effect of the same kind as *e*. Every occasion in which a cause produces an effect is thus an instance of a *causal law,* a generalization specifying a property or condition as causally necessary or sufficient or necessary-and-sufficient for given type of event. The claim that *C* is *sufficient* for *E* may be expressed by either of the forms:

All *C* are *E*
For every instance *x*, $Cx \supset Ex$

where '*Cx*' means '*x* is an instance of *C*'. Similarly, we may express the claim that *C* is *necessary* for *E* as

All *E* are *C*
For every instance *x*, $Ex \supset Cx$

Our concern is with inductive inferences whose conclusions state a causal law or an instance of one, so we need to ask how such laws are established. Since the GSE argument form from the first section has a generalization as its conclusion, it might be thought that simple enumeration is the relevant mode of inference, but in fact it is rarely used in such contexts. GSE inferences are sometimes suggestive of causal relationships but they are a poor means of confirming them. Reasoning by GSE will not enable us to distinguish between genuine causal laws and accidental correlations, and in using it we tend to overlook negative or disconfirming cases. A time-honored example illustrates both points. Two sophomores attempt to determine the cause of intoxication by consuming on successive nights bourbon and water, scotch and water, rum and water, and finally vodka and water (all, of course, purely in the interest of advancing human knowledge). In each case intoxication is the result, and our intrepid investigators conclude that water is the cause they are looking for. Their inference is a straightforward GSE but has a manifestly false conclusion (presumably stating a necessary condition) accompanying true premises. In their "tests" water/inebriation is a purely accidental, not a lawful, correlation.

One rule of causal investigation is that relevant factors should be varied one at a time, and this our sophomores failed to do. Yet by doing it properties that accompany but are causally unrelated to the effect can be eliminated from consideration. If they had tried bourbon alone one night, they would have eliminated water as a necessary condition, since intoxication would have been present in its absence. And if they had the slightest inclination to suppose that water was a sufficient condition, they could have (no doubt with less enthusiasm) tried orange juice and water or for that matter water alone, thus yielding a case where water was present in the absence of intoxication.

Causal investigation uses more sophisticated modes of inference than GSE, and most of them are *eliminative* inferences.[7] The premises of such inferences describe testing procedures aimed at determining which, if any, of a set of properties, $C_1, \ldots, C_n$, are causally related to a type of event E. These conditions are called **possible conditioning properties** (for short, PCPs), and prior to testing are considered plausible candidates for being a cause of E in either the sense of necessary condition, sufficient condition, or both. Through experiment and observation we then attempt to eliminate them as causal candidates, and any that resists our efforts at elimination is a probable cause of E. Any inquiry of this sort proceeds according to the following principles, and all specific forms of causal investigation and inference (including those in the next section) are but variations on these themes:

> *Necessary Condition:* Nothing that is absent when an event occurs is a cause of that event.
>
> *Sufficient Condition:* Nothing that is present when an event fails to occur is a cause of that event.

What we are testing in these procedures are generalizations, and it is easy to see in broad terms how to refute them. For sufficient conditions, the hypothesis 'all C are E' is falsified by producing an observed instance, a, in which C is present but E is absent; that is, where 'Ca' abbreviates 'a is an instance of C', that the statement 'Ca & $\sim Ea$' is true. For necessary conditions, the hypothesis 'all E are C' is falsified by producing an instance, b, where E is present but C is not, or in other words that 'Eb & $\sim Cb$' is true.

The studies on tooth decay noted earlier provide a good example of eliminating PCPs as sufficient conditions. There we had two PCPs: the presence of microorganisms in the mouth and the presence of food debris. Under normal everyday conditions, when both are present dental cavities generally occur. But when we experimentally withdraw one of them, cavities do not appear, thus showing that the *other* PCP is not sufficient (since it is present when the effect is not). Laboratory animals raised in a germ-free environment do not develop cavities, thus eliminating food debris. In a second test, animals raised in a normal environment but fed by tube directly to the stomach showed no evidence of cavities, thus eliminating the bacteria. Where C_1 is the presence of food, C_2 the presence of microorganisms, and E the occurrence of cavities, we can summarize the two experiments as follows (a "plus" means the property is present, a minus means that it is absent):

	C_1	C_2	E
a.	+	−	−
b.	−	+	−

Thus both PCPs are eliminated as sufficient conditions, but notice that *another* sufficient condition has not yet been ruled out: the presence of *both* C_1 and C_2. To eliminate it, we would need a third test (c):

	C_1	C_2	C_1 & C_2	E
a.	+	−	−	−
b.	−	+	−	−
c.	+	+	+	−

That is, to eliminate the complex condition C_1 & C_2, we would need an instance like $C_1 c$ & $C_2 c$ & $\sim Ec$. So a conjunction of two possible sufficient conditions is itself a third and distinct possible sufficient condition.[8] This is a direct consequence of the principle that

If C is a sufficient condition for E, so is C & D.

This principle is simply a reflection of the fact that the inference from 'all C are E' to 'all C and D are E' is deductively *valid* (from 'all humans are mortal' we may validly infer 'all humans over 6 feet tall are mortal'). So if we have a set of simple PCPs qua possible sufficient conditions, we thereby have a further set of complex PCPs that qualify as candidates for sufficient condition too. And as the tooth decay example shows, we can eliminate the former without eliminating the latter:

It is possible to eliminate C_1 alone and C_2 alone as sufficient conditions without thereby eliminating C_1 & C_2 as a sufficient condition.

If we are faced with three simple PCPs, then we have a grand total of seven possible sufficient conditions (though often in actual practice not all will be tested since some may be ruled out by evidence already available or they may be the conjunction of incompatible simple PCPs). Moreover, if all but one of the seven is eliminated, the remaining one is always the most complex condition:

	C_1	C_2	C_3	C_1 & C_2	C_1 & C_3	C_2 & C_3	C_1 & C_2 & C_3	E
a.	+	+	−	+	−	−	−	−
b.	+	−	+	−	+	−	−	−
c.	−	+	+	−	−	+	−	−

The only remaining live possibility is C_1 & C_2 & C_3, for it is the sole PCP not present in any of the three trials where E was absent. To eliminate it, all three of the simple PCPs must be present in a *single* trial, and that would rule out everything else as well. The same result holds of course not just for three PCPs but for any larger number as well.

There are complex necessary conditions as well. A change in pressure alone is not a necessary condition for a variation in the volume of a gas, since it expands when heat is applied while keeping pressure constant. However, what *is* necessary for a change in volume is a change in *either* pressure *or* temperature. Hence a disjunction of two possible necessary conditions is itself a third and distinct possible necessary condition. Here, the operative principle is

If C is a necessary condition for E, then so is C v D.

As in the case of sufficient condition, this principle is based on an elementary form of valid argument: from the premise 'all E are C' we may validly infer 'all E are either C or D'. Moreover, we can eliminate two simple PCPs as necessary conditions while their disjunction remains as a live candidate (note that in the following table E is *present* whereas in those for a sufficient condition it is absent):

	C_1	C_2	$C_1 \vee C_2$	E
a.	−	+	+	+
b.	+	−	+	+

In trial (a), C_1 is eliminated as a necessary condition since it is *absent* when E is present; similary, trial (b) eliminates C_2. However their disjunction has obviously not been eliminated; to do that we would need a trial (c) described by the sentence 'Ec & $\sim C_1c$ & $\sim C_2c$' (or equivalently '$\sim Ec$ & $\sim(C_1c \vee C_2c)$') wherein *both* of the simple PCPs are absent. As before, then, we have

> It is possible to eliminate C_1 alone and C_2 alone as necessary conditions without thereby eliminating $C_1 \vee C_2$ as a necessary condition.

And the following table shows for the case of three simple PCPs that, when all possible necessary conditions but one are eliminated, the remaining one is always the most complex:[9]

	C_1	C_2	C_3	$C_1 \vee C_2$	$C_1 \vee C_3$	$C_2 \vee C_3$	$C_1 \vee C_2 \vee C_3$	E
a.	−	−	+	−	+	+	+	+
b.	−	+	−	+	−	+	+	+
c.	+	−	−	+	+	−	+	+

On the other hand, suppose that experimental testing has eliminated C_2 alone and C_3 alone but C_1 has resisted our best efforts. If we conclude that C_1 is in fact a necessary condition for E, then as we have already seen the same conclusion must be drawn about $C_1 \vee C_2$, $C_1 \vee C_3$ and $C_1 \vee C_2 \vee C_3$ as well. As long as C_1 is not eliminated, neither will we eliminate any of the complex conditions of which C_1 is a disjunct. The same holds for sufficient conditions; if C_1 is sufficient, so is any complex condition of which it is a conjunct. So if testing has eliminated all but one PCP, the remaining one *cannot* be a simple PCP like C_1 alone; as we saw earlier it must be the most complex of the lot.

This is not an experimental impossibility but a logical one. If C_1 is always present when E is, then it follows on purely logical grounds that $C_1 \vee C_2$ is always present too. Moreover, the absence of C_1 similarly requires the absence of C_1 & C_2 as well. So it is logically impossible to eliminate the complex PCP while leaving C_1 as a live candidate. If in actual practice an investigator concludes that C_1 alone is the causally efficacious agent, this conclusion is based on reasoning that goes beyond eliminative induction.

In the tooth decay study noted earlier, the presence of food debris and the presence of bacteria were both eliminated as sufficient conditions, but the conjunction of them was absent in both tests, and hence was not eliminated. Yet we saw earlier that even this condition is not sufficient; some laboratory animals either do not develop cavities or else develop them at a much lower rate than the general populace even though they have plenty of food debris and bacteria in their mouths. The most we can conclude from the study is that this conjunctive condition is a *component* of a still more complex sufficient condition, one expressible in terms of three or more conjuncts.

It was also noted previously that, although neither food debris nor bacteria is sufficient for tooth decay, each is considered to be a necessary condition. However, it must be strongly emphasized that this conclusion was arrived at by other means; the study in question does *not* establish them as necessary conditions. Take for example the PCP of food debris: in one of the experiments it was absent when tooth decay was absent, and in the other it was present when decay was absent. But to show that it is a necessary condition in a series of eliminative tests, we must show that whenever cavities are *present,* food debris is also present—that is, that all attempts to find an instance where tooth decay was present but food debris absent were failures. The tooth decay experiment was not set up to show anything like this since there is no experimental instance in which the effect was indeed present.

The study does indirectly offer slight confirmation of a necessary condition. If food debris is necessary for tooth decay, then as we saw at the outset, when the debris is *absent* in a given case so will tooth decay be absent. And that is exactly what happened in one of the experiments (where rats were fed by tube to the stomach). However, this is a causal inference by *enumeration,* not by *elimination,* and as such yields the conclusion with a much lower probability. To see this, consider the following case. If we withdraw butane from the combination oxygen-butane-heat, combustion will not occur, so again we have a correlation of absence of PCP (butane) with absence of the effect (combustion). But even after observing many such instances, the inference by enumeration (by GSE) to the conclusion that butane is a necessary condition for combustion is a weak one. By eliminative inference, however, we can show that the conclusion is not just improbable but downright false. We need only produce an instance where combustion is *present* but butane is *absent.*

In addition to those expressed by conjunctions and disjunctions, there is yet another kind of complex condition. Negative properties will sometimes be included in a list of PCPs: not being exposed to bright sunlight is a necessary condition for growing a good crop of mushrooms. They may be represented in a plus/minus table using '~' if the corresponding "positive" property is also one of the PCPs (which can happen sometimes, but a conjunction and disjunction of the two does not qualify as a complex PCP); otherwise we can simply use a new predicate letter. Obviously, whenever a plus is assigned to $\sim C$, a minus must be assigned to C in the same row.

Let us now look briefly at complex necessary-and-sufficient conditions. In such a case E is present if C is and *only* then, so a causal law stating a necessary-and-sufficient condition may be expressed

For every instance x, $Cx \equiv Ex$

To eliminate C as necessary-and-sufficient, we can *either* produce an instance like 'Ca & $\sim Ea$' (which also eliminates it as sufficient) *or* one like 'Eb & $\sim Cb$' (thus eliminating it as necessary too). If we begin with three simple PCPs, C_1, C_2, and C_3, and our tests indicate that the complex property C_1 & C_3 is necessary-and-sufficient, then C_1 and C_3 are individually necessary for E.

We have already seen that three simple PCPs give rise to seven possible sufficient conditions and seven possible necessary ones. How many possible necessary-and-sufficient conditions are there in such a case? Each of the possible sufficient conditions is *also* a possible necessary-and-sufficient condition, and moreover *every disjunction* of two or more possible sufficient conditions also qualifies; for example, C_1 v (C_2 & C_3) v (C_1 & C_3). This yields in theory at least a grand total of 127 possible necessary-and-sufficient conditions![10] There are 127 distinct causal hypotheses arising from just three simple properties, and the numbers are gigantic for four or more. To attempt to eliminate all but one of these would be an enormous task, and in practice no scientific investigation proceeds like this. As noted earlier, there are always reasonable grounds for cutting down on the number of hypotheses to be tested; typically, many of them will be only formal possibilities that are implausible in light of our background knowledge. An investigator would usually be content with testing just five or six, and if all were eliminated others might then be considered. However, it is just as likely our investigator would instead turn to simple PCPs that were not on the original list but that might be regarded as plausible candidates when compared with our body of presupposed knowledge.

Exercises

1. a. Have all simple PCPs in the following table been eliminated as sufficient conditions? Explain.

	C_1	C_2	C_3	C_4	E
a.	+	−	+	−	−
b.	+	+	−	−	−
c.	−	−	−	+	−
d.	−	+	+	+	−

b. Which conjunctions of the simple PCPs have *not* been eliminated?

c. Have the following been eliminated as sufficient conditions? $\sim C_1$ & C_3? $\sim C_1$ & C_4?

2. a. Now replace the minuses with plusses in the column under E in the preceding table. Have all simple PCPs been eliminated as necessary conditions? Explain.

b. Which complex PCPs have not been eliminated as necessary conditions?

3. Suppose we alter the column for E in the table once more by putting minuses in the rows for (a) and (b) and plusses in the rows for (c) and (d). Which simple PCP has not been eliminated as necessary and sufficient? Has C_2 v C_3 been eliminated as necessary and sufficient? Why or why not?

4. Show that C v D is not a third distinct sufficient condition over and above C and D by proving:

If C v D is sufficient for E, then C is sufficient for E and so is D.

If C is sufficient for E and so is D, then C v D is sufficient for E.

5. It was stated earlier that when all sufficient conditions but one have been eliminated, the remaining one is the conjunction of all simple PCPs. However, this principle requires a qualification: the simple PCPs must be logically independent (see Section 1) of one another. Explain why.

Section 5. Causal Inference: Mill's Methods _____

The nineteenth-century philosopher John Stuart Mill presented five basic methods of causal investigation (and formulable as patterns of causal inference). Although earlier writers had recognized some of them, he was the first to provide a systematic and comprehensive treatment, though his discussion is flawed in places. The three methods of direct interest here are *the Method of Agreement, the*

Method of Difference, and *the Joint Method of Agreement and Difference.* However, Mill's discussion generally ignores the distinction between necessary and sufficient conditions, and when it is brought to bear explicitly, the three methods become five in number.[11] All of them exemplify eliminative induction: PCPs are eliminated (and those ineliminable confirmed) by experimental testing, careful observation or the analysis of collected data.

Testing for Necessary Conditions: The Direct Method of Agreement When the necessary/sufficient distinction is introduced, the method of agreement splits into two; and the first, the Direct Method, tests for necessary conditions. It has in effect already been described in the previous section; there, the plus/minus tables in which necessary conditions were being sought are straightforward cases of the Direct Method. Still, an example will be useful:

> A medical researcher notices that six patients admitted to her hospital over the past year all suffer from a rare form of cancer. Upon investigation, she finds that they live in different locations in the area and have different medical histories, diet, and personal habits (e.g., smoking, alcohol use). But there is one PCP all share: they are employed at a local agricultural co-op where a newly marketed herbicide is prepared for use on farm crops. The researcher tentatively concludes that exposure to the herbicide caused the disease.

The number of PCPs in this example is quite large (for example, residing in any of several locations, having a particular kind of diet), but in simplified form the researcher's investigation may be summed up as follows (C_5 of course is the property of being exposed to the herbicide, E is that of having the disease and (a)–(f) are the six patients):

	C_1	C_2	C_3	C_4	C_5	E
a.	+	+	+	−	+	+
b.	−	+	−	+	+	+
c.	−	+	+	−	+	+
d.	+	+	+	−	+	+
e.	+	−	−	+	+	+
f.	+	−	+	−	+	+

Here only one PCP was present when the disease was; all of the others, such as living in a certain area, eating a high fat diet, or smoking were eliminated insofar as they were absent in at least one of the patients (of course more than one PCP might prove ineliminable since a given kind of event usually has more than one necessary condition). C_4 is eliminated by patient (a), C_1 and C_3 by (b) and C_2 by (e), leaving C_5 as the probable necessary condition. So in fact only three instances were needed to eliminate C_1 through C_4 as candidates, and hence our already abbreviated table could have been reduced by three lines (and in theory it could have had just one line). As so often happens, the data provide more information than is strictly needed for the elimination process.

The study indicates that C_5 is a "probable" necessary condition; it tells us with regard to the six patients that *if* one of the PCPs is a necessary condition for E, then C_5 is that condition. But it is possible that the "real" necessary condition was not included in the list of PCPs. Perhaps the real cause was not exposure to the herbicide, but emissions from a long forgotten toxic waste dump located near the co-op. Alternatively, it may be that another substance is also a causal agent of the disease, in which case the true necessary condition would be a disjunction of it with C_5. Since the presence of that substance was not on the list of PCPs, discovery of the disjunctive condition is impossible here. And it may also be that the herbicide and this other substance have a common component that would then qualify as the necessary condition. This last point is especially important; it may well be that subsequent investigation reveals victims in other situations who were never exposed to the herbicide but rather to a chemical present in it.

As a result, we should regard our conclusion that C_5 is the probable necessary condition as directly applying only to workers at the co-op and not to the general human population. We would be unwarranted in concluding that all people who contract this form of cancer have been exposed to the herbicide, or equivalently in concluding that anyone *not* so exposed will *not* come down with the disease. Only if we examine more patients and enlarge (and possibly, at a later point, revise) our list of plausible candidates will we be able to draw a more general conclusion. Basically, what the above study tells us is that C_5 is a prime suspect, and that if we wish to pinpoint an exact causal condition, this is the place from which further investigation should begin. This point holds for the other methods discussed later: in many instances of their use the conclusion to be drawn is of limited generality.

It was said earlier that, if one of the PCPs is a necessary condition for E, then C_5 is that condition. But strictly we know from the previous section that disjunctions of simple PCPs are also theoretical candidates and that insofar as C_5 has not been eliminated, neither have any of the disjunctive properties of which it is a component—and in fact a careful study of the previous table will disclose other disjunctions that have not been ruled out; for example C_1 v C_4. Further investigation might eliminate C_1 v C_4, but will never rule out C_1 v C_5 as long as C_5 itself remains. Often in such cases these disjunctive hypotheses are only formalities that are highly unlikely given our background information. Typically they will not be pursued unless there is evidence in advance indicating that they are plausible candidates or unless all of the simple PCPs have been eliminated.

The Direct Method may at first blush seem to be nothing more than simple enumeration inasmuch as it simply records instances in which E and C_5 are jointly present. But in fact it is more: C_5 has been observed to be present whenever E is *under varying conditions* in which plausible alternatives to C_5 have been eliminated. The medical researcher analyzed the given situation into many plausible factors and then detected a unifomity in six disparate instances, ruling out competitors with C_5 in the process. As such, her conclusion has a higher probability than would be warranted by simple enumeration.

Testing for Sufficient Conditions: The Inverse Method of Agreement We saw in the last section that a PCP is eliminated as a sufficient condition by an instance in which it is present but the effect is not, and a PCP that is absent in every such instance is thus a probable sufficient condition. The Inverse Method is the embodiment of this procedure, and for this reason little needs to be said about it here. It is basically nothing more than the Direct Method in reverse: the effect and the probable causal agent are *absent* in all cases instead of present. In the following table, the factors C_1, C_3, and C_4 are present in at least one instance and are thus eliminated as causally sufficient. Of the simple properties, then, only C_2 remains a live candidate:

	C_1	C_2	C_3	C_4	E
a.	+	−	−	−	−
b.	+	−	−	+	−
c.	−	−	+	+	−
d.	+	−	+	−	−

What was said earlier concerning the Direct Method applies here as well. It is possible of course that a relevant condition has been excluded from the list of PCPs and that the causal agent is a conjunction of C_2 with that condition. Moreover, the conclusion in many cases would be of limited generality, indicating that C_2 should be the focus of further investigation that would lead to a more general causal conclusion. Of course *all* conjunctions of C_2 with any of the other listed PCPs remain as at least formal possibilities, and as a quick inspection of the table will show, C_1 & C_4 has not been eliminated either.

Testing for Sufficient Conditions: The Method of Difference. A more common way of testing for a sufficient condition is to resort to experimental manipulation under controlled conditions, and the

modus operandi in such cases is often Mill's Method of Difference
(though it is used in nonexperimental situations too). Here, we begin
with an instance in which the effect E occurs and we wish to determine
which of the PCPs observed to be present *in that instance* is or are
sufficient for E. Our goal in using this method is thus somewhat more
limited than in the Inverse Method; E may have any number of
sufficient conditions but the only ones that can be identified here will
be those from the set of PCPs present in this *particular* instance, in
which E occurred. The task then is to attempt to eliminate the PCPs
present in this instance by finding further instances where they are
present but E is absent; any property that is absent in such attempts
is thus a probable sufficient condition.

There is no method comparable to the Method of Difference in
testing for necessary conditions, and the reason is simple. If E occurs,
then by definition *all* of its necessary conditions occurred too, but only
some or just one of its sufficient conditions had to occur. In a particular
situation where E is present then, we can focus our investigation on
which of the PCPs that occurred with E was operative as a sufficient
condition, and this is what the Method of Difference does. We cannot
similarly narrow our focus for necessary conditions, since in *any*
instance of E all of them had to be present.

The initial instance in which E and the PCPs were observed to be
present together is thus the point from which investigation begins; it
is *not* a test instance but rather the circumstance that initiates the
causal search. To indicate its special status, this instance will be
labeled '*' in our tabular representation of the Method of Difference,
and it will indicate the observed situation in which various PCPs were
present along with E.

The study on tooth decay mentioned in the preceding section was
only partially represented by the presence/absence table used there;
when fully set out, it provides a good example of the Method of
Difference. In the table, C_1 again represents the presence of food
debris; C_2, the presence of microorganisms; and E, the presence of
cavities:

	C_1	C_2	C_1 & C_2	E
*	+	+	+	+
a.	+	−	−	−
b.	−	+	−	−

The initial instance indicated by '*' represents the observed situation prior to testing: both food debris and bacteria are present together
with the occurrecnce of cavities. In test (a) a bacteria-free laboratory

environment was created and the rats developed no cavities; since E is absent in the presence of food debris, C_1 is eliminated as a sufficient condition. In test (b) the rats were fed by tube directly to the stomach; since E again is absent but microorganisms are present C_2 is eliminated, leaving only C_1 & C_2 as a live candidate.

Mill himself claimed that the conclusion to be drawn here is that the PCP that survives the elimination test is either a cause or else an "indispensable part" of the cause of the phenomenon being investigated. In other words, the PCP might not be a sufficient condition by itself, and we have already seen this to be the case in the dental study. Some people do not develop cavities even though they have food particles and bacteria in their mouths, so C_1 & C_2 is not sufficient for E. For reasons not yet clear to us, these subjects have some kind of immunity to cavity formation, and hence the full sufficient condition would consist of C_1 & C_2 conjoined with whatever further properties are responsible for such immunity. C_1 & C_2 then is an indispensable part of a sufficient condition, but it is not the whole story.

As before, the conclusion drawn is also of limited generality but is easily extended from laboratory rats to the entire species because of their genetic similarity. To extend the conclusion to humans requires a further inference (specifically an argument by analogy) based on the known resemblance between the two species concerning dental structure.

Often, the Method of Difference compares just two instances:

	C_1	C_2	C_3	C_4	E
*	+	+	+	+	+
a.	+	+	+	−	−

Therefore the two instances are supposed to differ in only one relevant respect: in this case C_4 is present in (*) and absent in (a), thus paralleling the behavior of the effect E. However, in ordinary non-experimental situations it is often very difficult to find two instances that differ in just one respect, and for this reason the Method of Difference is rarely used in such contexts. It is more commonly employed in scientific experiment where the investigators can exercise considerable influence over the relevant factors. In fact, *controlled experiments,* where data concerning a "control group" and an "experimental group" are compared, are similar in structure to the Method of Difference, the control group functioning much like the initial instance (*).

Sometimes the *absence* of a factor must be taken into account in formulating the initial condition for an application of the Method of Difference. For example, suppose some laboratory animals are fed a diet normal in all respects except for a lack of foods rich in vitamin C, and they consequently develop the disease known as "scurvy." When we add vitamin C to their diet, however, the disease disappears. Let C_5 be the property of having the usual amount of vitamin C present; then we can represent the absence of C_5 in our table as the presence of $\sim C_5$. Where E is the presence of scurvy, and C_1 to C_5 the presence of standard amounts of other vitamins and minerals, we have the following table:

	C_1	C_2	C_3	C_4	C_5	$\sim C_5$	E
*	+	+	+	+	−	+	+
a.	+	+	+	+	+	−	−

Hence the lack of C_5 is a sufficient condition for contracting scurvy. Alternatively, the *presence* of C_5 is a necessary condition for avoiding it.

Testing for Necessary-and-Sufficient Conditions: The Double Method of Agreement. The Direct Method tests for necessary conditions and the Inverse Method for sufficient ones. Combining the two yields the Double Method by which we may identify necessary-and-sufficient conditions. In the table that follows, the first three instances eliminate PCPs C_1 and C_2 as necessary conditions since each is absent in at least one case in which E is present. The last three instances eliminate them as sufficient conditions since each is present in at least one case where E is absent. But C_3 is present when and *only* when E is, making it the probable necessary-and-sufficient condition. Instances (a)–(f) are six patients admitted to a research hospital with a rare and little understood disease:

	C_1	C_2	C_3	E
a.	−	+	+	+
b.	+	−	+	+
c.	+	−	+	+
d.	+	−	−	−
e.	−	+	−	−
f.	−	+	−	−

Each patient had previously been treated with one of two drugs (C_1 and C_2) normally used for related ailments, but so far with no effect. Doctors decided to administer a new experimental drug (C_3), but only three of the patients, (a), (b) and (c), agreed to take it. Shortly afterward, those patients recovered (E is the property of recovering from the disease) but the three who had refused the drug did not. Note that, of the three who recovered, only one of C_1 and C_2 had been prescribed; so each of the two was absent in an instance in which recovery occurred. Note also that of the patients who did not recover, C_1 and C_2 had been given to at least one; thus each was present in an instance in which recovery did not occur. The doctors concluded that C_3 cured the disease.

Testing for Necessary-and-Sufficient Conditions: The Joint Method of Agreement and Difference. Since the Method of Difference tests for sufficient condition, it may also be combined with the Direct Method to yield a test for necessary-and-sufficient conditions. Here again, we begin with an initial occurrence (*) and apply the Method of Difference to see which PCPs remain when the effect is absent. The Direct Method is then used to see which PCPs are absent when the effect is present.

> Smith developed a severe and unusual rash (E). Because of its similarity to certain other skin disorders, doctors told her to eliminate fowl (C_1), red meat (C_2), and dairy products (C_3) from her diet. After doing so the rash cleared up, and she was then told to first resume eating fowl and later red meat. In each instance, the rash did not recur. She was then instructed to resume eating dairy products. When this was done, the rash reappeared and it persisted when she again eliminated red meat and fowl from her diet. The doctors concluded that Smith's rash was caused by the consumption of dairy products.

The following table illustrates this application of the Joint Method:

	C_1	C_2	C_3	E
*	+	+	+	+
a.	+	−	−	−
b.	+	+	−	−
c.	−	−	+	+

There is a fairly significant difference between the two combined methods. In the Double Method all properties that qualify as PCPs are tested whereas the Joint Method tests only those present in the initial occurrence (*). This means that in the latter a PCP not observed in occurrence (*) might not be eliminated as a sufficient condition—it could be absent in all cases where E is absent. Removing this possibility by producing a further instance in which such a PCP is present when E is absent in effect turns the experiment into an application of the Double Method.

The upshot is that which method we choose to employ in a given situation depends on our previously acquired evidence concerning the PCPs. If we observe an occurrence of E and the evidence we have makes it probable that one of the PCPs observed to be present in that occurrence is a sufficient condition, then the Joint Method should be used and the occurrence in question becomes the initial instance (*). On the other hand, if the evidence simply indicates that one or another of the PCPs we have compiled is a sufficient condition, then we would have to resort to the Double Method.

Mill's Methods: Some General Comments. Mill claimed great things for his methods. He regarded them as both methods for *discovering* causal connections (hence falling under the "logic of inquiry") and methods for *proving* that such connections exist (thus part of inductive logic proper). But on both counts he overstated his case. As methods of discovery they are incomplete and in need of supplementation. Nor are they methods of "proof" in any strict sense; rather they provide us with inductive inference patterns that yield their conclusions with probability, not with the certainty found in mathematical proofs.[12]

As mechanisms for discovery, Mill's Methods play only a minor role. Most of the hard creative work in actual causal investigations occurs at the beginning in deciding which properties are to be regarded as PCPs. Only after this has been done can the Methods be applied. The number of properties present in a given situation are countless, and it would be impossible to make a complete list of them, let alone test each one. To obtain a list of reasonable length, we need a way of determining which of these properties are *likely* to be causally relevant, and the only way of doing this is to draw inductive inferences from our previously acquired evidence. This inductive knowledge serves as our guide in setting up a list of PCPs—of what might plausibly be the causal agent—and without it Mill's Methods are useless.

Compiling such a list is not an easy matter, and if it is done poorly then all PCPs might be eliminated, making a reexamination of the previously acquired evidence necessary (of course complete elimination sometimes occurs even with a better analysis). What is worse, a PCP yielding a false conclusion might *not* be eliminated in such a case. An elementary case in point would be our sophomores in search of the cause of intoxication, for their "investigation" may be construed not just as an example of enumerative inference but also as a very simplistic use of the Direct Method (in each instance, water was present whenever the effect was). Their mistake lay not in the use of the Method, but in faulty analysis of the situation. If the various liquors consumed had not been treated as so many single PCPs but instead analyzed into their constituents, the Direct Method would have shown that alcohol as well as water invariably accompanied the effect. Adding a new PCP such as ginger ale would then, after a further test, have eliminated water as causally necessary. The Method of Difference could then have eliminated it as sufficient.

Even though this is a silly example, it should give some idea of the revisions and additions brought about by new evidence and re-analysis that are typical of serious real-life causal investigations. In many investigative contexts, a continual stream of new developments will require scientists to add further simple or complex PCPs to the original list (while at the same time removing others that have been eliminated), leading to further testing and reevaluation of the results. Compiling a list of PCPs is the most important (yet the most obscure) part so far of the discovery process; when done properly we may reasonably expect a good deal of success in using Mill's Methods. When done poorly, those same Methods will be of no help and might even lead us astray.

Although they are not methods of "proof," Mill's Methods may be expressed as forms of inductive inference wherein false causal hypotheses are eliminated and those that resist elimination are confirmed or rendered more probable. But formulating a particular application of one of the methods as a full-fledged inductive argument is a complex task involving far more than just a description of the method employed. The evidence used in determining which properties shall serve as PCPs must be included. As we have seen this is an inductively based judgment that could prove erroneous, thus undermining the conclusion inferred. Moreover, in the typical case a large amount of background information is used—often in the form of previously established laws and principles—and this would also have to be included in the formulation of the argument. Without the background information and a rationale for using the selected PCPs, Mill's Methods will not yield causal conclusions with high probability, and both of these components are themselves the product of inductive inference.

A fully general formulation of such patterns of inference has yet to be given, and inductive rules governing them have never been formulated with any precision or exactitude. Even so, it is as forms of inference in which causal hypotheses are rejected or confirmed that Mill's Methods find their place in causal inquiry. As tools of discovery, they are but a small part of the story.

Exercises

1. Let C_1, C_2, and C_3 be PCPs for E. Using the Method of Difference, construct a plus-minus table in which all simple PCPs but one have been eliminated in two trials beyond the initial case (*). Then list the complex PCPs that have not been eliminated in your table.

2. At Irma's Luncheonette one day, six customers developed stomach cramps after dining. They had drunk different beverages, eaten different salads and soups. However, all had consumed tuna salad sandwiches prepared with different breads. The health department concluded that the tuna salad caused the stomach disorders. Which of Mill's Methods is being used here?

3. At Melman University Hospital, two patients were admitted suffering from a rare disease. Blood tests of the patients revealed that one of them had the virus *Bertolettus* in her blood, while in the other the virus *Ulrichtus* was present. Curious about this, a medical researcher examined the available records and found that of fifty known cases of the disease in which blood tests were given, twenty-six sufferers had *Ulrichtus* in their blood, nineteen had *Bertolettus,* and both viruses were present in five cases. Blood tests on twenty-five other patients at Melman who were not afflicted with the disease showed that *Ulrichtus* was present in five of them, *Bertolettus* in three, and both were present in one case.

Does this evidence indicate a causally necessary condition for the disease? Which of Mill's Methods is used here? Does the evidence indicate a causally sufficient condition? Again, which of Mill's Methods is used?

4.

	C_1	C_2	C_3	C_3	C_4	E
Instance (a).	+	+	−	+	+	+
Instance (b).	+	−	−	+	+	−
Instance (c).	−	+	+	−	−	+

a. Suppose prior investigation makes it very likely that one of the simple PCPs present in Instance (a) is a necessary-and-sufficient condition for E. Which one is it and which of Mill's Methods is being used?

b. Suppose again the evidence strongly indicates that one of the simple PCPs is necessary-and-sufficient for E but you do not know whether it is one present in Instance (a). Moreover an additional test reveals:

Instance (d): −   −   +   −   −   −

Which of the PCPs is the necessary-and-sufficient condition and which of Mill's Methods has been employed?

5. Which of Mill's Methods is used here? Identify the PCPs and construct a plus/minus table.

To determine whether yellow fever is caused by mosquito bites or by contact with excreta of yellow fever patients, investigators constructed a mosquito-proof dwelling in which ten nonimmune volunteers lived for twenty days.

There, they were in constant contact with the unwashed clothing, bedding, and eating utensils of patients who had recently died of the disease—these items being soiled with blood, feces, and vomit from those patients. At the end of this period none of the volunteers had developed yellow fever. It was concluded that yellow fever is transmitted by the mosquito.

Section 6. Causal Laws and Quantitative Laws _____

In some cases it is impossible to find or produce a situation in which a PCP is wholly present or wholly absent, and hence the methods just discussed are inapplicable. Mill himself notes that if we wish to determine whether the moon's gravitational attraction causes the tidal movements here on earth, the Method of Difference will be of no help. We cannot somehow pluck the moon from the heavens for a week or so and then observe what happens to the tides. However, we can do something just as good: through careful observation we may observe that variations in the moon's position are followed by corresponding variations in the time and place of high water, the place always being that part of the earth nearest to—or most remote from—the moon. We thus have a correlation between the distance of the moon from the earth (hence the degree of gravitational influence) and the intensity of tidal movements, thus warranting the conclusion that a causal relation exists.

Thus where we cannot easily vary the occurrence of a PCP, we can often infer a causal connection by observing that variations in magnitude of a PCP are always accompanied by corresponding variations in the phenomena under investigation. Mill calls this the **Method of Concomitant Variation,** and the observed variation can be either *direct* or *inverse.* An increase in water depth is matched by an increase in water pressure (hence the one is directly proportional to the other), but an increase in gravitational force accompanies a decrease in distance (they are thus inversely proportional). We may roughly schematize the method as follows ("#" and "/" here indicate increases and decreases, respectively):

Direct:	C_1	C_2	C_3	E	Inverse:	C_1	C_2	C_3	E
	+	+	+	+		+	+	+	+
	+#	+	+	+#		+#	+	+	+/
	+##	+	+	+##		+##	+	+	+//

In such cases we may infer that a causal connection probably exists between C_1 and E, the degree of probability depending on the number of variations observed, the initial plausibility of C_1, the strength of the background information, and so forth. But, in many applications of the method, we can infer no more than that some sort of causal relation exists: it may be that C_1 causes E or that they are effects of a common cause or even that E causes C_1 (though this latter alternative can be eliminated if our observations show that variations in C_1 occur prior to those in E). Further investigation would be needed in such cases to determine the exact causal agent.

Where a conclusion that C_1 is the causal agent is warranted, however, it will take the form that C_1 is causally sufficient for E since it is highly probable in such cases that, if we could decrease E to the point where it is completely eliminated, C_1 would then disappear also. There would be no case where C_1 is present to any degree and yet E would be absent.

As a case in point, as we saw in the first chapter, Louis Pasteur showed that microorganisms found in fermentable liquids came from the surrounding air, specifically by means of airborne dust particles (thus refuting the theory that they arose through "spontaneous generation"). To further strengthen his conclusion, he repeated the experiments in several widely different locations and found that the purer the air (the fewer the dust particles) the fewer the number of microorganisms observed in the liquids. This simple application of the Method of Concomitant Variation confirmed the conclusion that the presence of dust particles in the contacting air is causally sufficient for the production of bacteria in previously sterilized fermentable liquids.

Mill formulated the Method of Concomitant Variation in purely qualitative terms, and Pasteur's experiment is a good example of a qualitative correlation. But of all Mill's Methods only this one readily lends itself to quantitative formulation, and it is here that its real importance lies. The laws of the most advanced sciences such as physics are quantitative in character; the variations they are concerned with are stated in precise mathematical terms using the notion of a *function*. The length of a rod, for example, is a function of its temperature; the volume of a gas is a function of temperature and pressure; the velocity of a freely falling body is a function of the time elapsed since its descent began. At this stage of scientific inquiry, qualitative variations concerning causes give way to functional correlations between precisely measurable quantities. Compare, for example, the qualitative correlation noted by Pasteur with the correlation stated in Galileo's law of falling bodies:

Qualitative: the purer the surrounding air, the fewer are the microorganisms in fermentable liquids

Quantitative: $d = (1/2)gt^2$

where d is the distance fallen, t the time elapsed (g is a constant, specifically the universal gravitation constant; 32 ft/sec^2 on the earth). Hence given a temporal quantity for t (an *argument* of the function, the "independent variable"), the spatial quantity for d (the *value* of the function for that argument, the "dependent variable") is straightforwardly calculated. A function's value is *uniquely* determined by the argument, and hence as before the latter is a sufficient condition for the former.

But Pasteur's correlation cannot be readily expressed in exact quantitative terms. We would have to know, first, the exact quantity of dust per cubic foot of atmosphere at each of the tested locations; and second, there would have to be an exact correlation between quantity of dust introduced and the number of microorganisms found. It is virtually impossible to fulfill these conditions, but it was not necessary anyway. For Pasteur was searching for a "cause," using the Method of Concomitant Variation in the qualitative form described by Mill. In the more precise quantitative application found in the physical sciences, the commonsense notion of "cause" is superseded by that of a function.

Simple qualitative laws like "Heavy bodies fall when unsupported" or "Sodium salts burn with a yellow flame" involve perceptual properties like *being heavy, falling, yellow,* and so forth. Their uniform connection is of practical interest to us, but for physical scientists they are unsatisfactory as they stand, since the connection between these properties is still in need of explanation. We can *observe* such connections, but as long as we remain at the qualitative level we cannot *deduce* them within a comprehensive system of explanation from more fundamental principles. However, if we can discover uniformities not directly observable to our senses that underly the multiplicity of qualitative laws, then we can formulate relatively simple laws to account for the complexity of observed connections.

To elaborate a bit, consider a simple process like a stick of wood being burnt to a cinder—a continuous gradation of perceptual properties. The physical scientist wishes to know how these perceptible changes are related, and to find out, the period of time in which the stick is heated is split up into very short intervals within which qualitative variations are very slight. Moreover, the stick of wood is analyzed into minute constituents: carbon atoms, hydrogen atoms, and beyond them into electrons, protons, and the like. Such constituents are qualitatively alike: any two carbon atoms—or two electrons— are exactly similar.

Here, we have reached units that are homogeneous, and their arrangement into basic patterns can be stated in simple fundamental laws. By subdividing the observable stick of wood into unobserved but homogeneous components, the observed changes can be connected in an intelligible and systematic fashion. An underlying maxim of scientific inquiry would seem to be that any complex thing, process, or event is analyzable into a pattern of homogeneous units whose behavior can be expressed in quantitative laws. Commonsense analysis leading to discovery of qualitative laws about causes is replaced by functional analysis and the discovery of quantitative formulae.

A functional correlation is always measured in precise units: millimeters, degrees Celsius, pounds per cubic foot. Hence quantitative laws stating such correlations enable us to replace rather vague qualitative concepts like *heavy, falling,* and the like with exact units by means of which we can determine *how much* weight and *how fast* a descent. Focusing solely on qualitative and perceptual concepts has in the past led to false beliefs. Ancient physicists claimed that heavy bodies have a natural tendency to fall—to seek their "natural place"—and the greater is the weight of the body, the faster it would fall. This is a functional correlation of course, but it was never stated in exact quantitative terms. If the ancients had attempted to make it exact—to determine the *rate* of fall—they would quickly have realized their error.

Instead, it was Galileo who determined the rate of fall. He discovered a contradiction in the ancient theory, and hence he knew that it was false before his famous experiment of dropping 1-pound and 100-pound balls simultaneously from the Tower of Pisa.[13] But since the balls landed at the same time, the experiment was useful in that it told him that a body's weight did not affect its rate of fall. Galileo did not remain content with this discovery, however, but wanted to determine exactly what the rate of fall is. It was known in Galileo's day that the velocity of a falling body increases as it falls, so he first conjectured that velocity is proportional to the distance fallen (for example, an object's velocity after a fall of two feet would be twice its velocity at one foot). However, he found a contradiction in this hypothesis too and rejected it.

Next, he hypothesized that acceleration was proportional to the time elapsed; that is, a falling body gains equal increments of velocity in equal increments of time. His problem was that a freely falling body falls too fast for accurate measurement by the instruments available in his day. However, by rolling balls down grooves of an inclined plane, he was able to retard their motion to a degree where exact measurement was possible. He had already discovered the independence of motions and that a body accelerates uniformly, so he knew that using an inclined plane would not distort his conclusions concerning freely falling objects (and by varying the degree of inclination, he could exhibit a 90° fall as a limit of his tests). His findings showed that the distance fallen was proportional to the square of the time elapsed, and since velocity is just distance traversed over time, he was able to confirm his original supposition that the velocity of a falling object is proportional to the time it has been falling from rest. This was a milestone: a quantitative law had been discovered that corrected ancient misconceptions.

What is equally important here are the consequences of discovering such laws. In Galileo's case, he could then deduce, first, that if a falling body is stopped at some point in its fall and projected upward with its velocity at that point, it will rise to the level from which it fell; and second, whatever the angle of descent, velocity will be the same at any given level parallel to the earth's surface. These conclusions paved the way for Newton's laws of motion. When hypotheses are expressed in precise functional terms, we can often deductively infer further conclusions concerning related phenomena, and by such means the facts are fitted into an explanatory system of precise, mathematically based principles. Rarely if ever will the discovery of a qualitative uniformity provide such deductive consequences.

Even so, the process by which Galileo discovered his law resembles that by which we discover causes using Mill's Methods; insofar as he was in pursuit of a functional relationship, he was after a sufficient condition. The "effect" E in this case are the (infinitely many) particular quantities of velocity a falling object can assume, and the search is for a function that takes these quantities as its values. Obtaining a list of PCPs to be tested requires two steps. First, we develop a list of physical properties that on the basis of prior research are likely to be relevant in determining the velocity of a falling body; that is, the particular quantities of these properties will be the arguments of the function. In Galileo's case, he entertained two such properties: distance traversed and time elapsed. The first of these, as we saw, was rejected because it yielded a contradiction (more often they are rejected by empirical tests). The second step is to formulate a plausible list of specific functions involving these properties (in most instances this is easier said than done) and then test them. In a case like Galileo's, using time elapsed, we might test candidates such as $(1/2)gt^2$ or $(1/4)gt^3$. Empirical tests using the inclined plane will eliminate $(1/4)gt^3$ and the like since some of the velocities they specify (for various quantities t) conflict with the data obtained. The testing procedure involved here resembles the Inverse Method of Agreement but differing from typical qualitative applications since the tested PCPs are all incompatible with one another.

While the elimination process itself is thus straightforward and easily understood, the prior task of constructing a list of plausible PCPs is just as obscure here as in qualitative uses of Mill's Methods. We cannot explore this further except to note that the obscurity should not be surprising: compiling such a list is after all an inductively based procedure.

Notes _____

1. Simple Enumeration arguments may appear to be straightforward and unproblematic, and the ensuing discussion might well give that impression. However, they run afoul of a serious philosophical obstacle whose discussion would be inappropriate at this point. For a look at the problem, see the last section of Chapter Six.

2. One such text is William Mendenhall's *Introduction to Probability and Statistics,* 5th ed. (North Scituate, MA: Duxbury Press, 1979). See Chapters 3 and 7.

3. Thomas Reid, *Essays on the Intellectual Powers of Man,* Essay I, Chapter 4.

4. It might be thought that, if persons not in Jones's family were included, this would strengthen the argument by giving us a more diverse sample. But since heart disease has been linked with hereditary factors, perhaps the better course would be to include in the positive analogy the property of family affiliation.

5. Hence although oxygen alone is necessary but not sufficient for combustion, butane by itself is neither necessary nor sufficient.

6. See R. F. Sognnaes, "Tooth Decay," *Scientific American* (December 1957).

7. For a thorough and comprehensive study of eliminative (or "demonstrative") induction, the classic source is G. H. von Wright's *A Treatise on Induction and Probability* (New York: Harcourt, Brace and World, 1951), especially Chapter 4. However, this book demands more background in deductive logic than is assumed in our discussion.

8. Strictly speaking, of course, a conjunction joins two *sentences,* not two properties. But to avoid excessive and contorted verbiage, we will speak of a "conjunction" of sufficient conditions and use expressions like 'C_1 & C_2'. If precision is required, we can always resort to an expression like 'x is an instance of C_1 & x is an instance of C_2' and to the complex condition or property expressed by such a locution.

9. A *conjunction* of two necessary conditions is *not* a further and distinct necessary condition but simply a joint listing of the two original ones. The sentence 'all E are C and D' is *equivalent* to the sentence 'all E are C and all E are D'. The same holds for disjunctions of sufficient conditions: the sentence 'all (instances that are) C or D are E' is equivalent to 'all C are E and all D are E'.

10. For the skeptical, there are, in addition to the 7 possible sufficient conditions, 21 disjunctions with 2 disjuncts and another 21 with 5. Those with 3 or 4 disjuncts number 35 each. There are 7 more with 6 disjuncts and of course 1 more with all 7 as disjuncts.

11. J. S. Mill, *A System of Logic,* Book III (1843). This classification and the terminology used are from von Wright, *Treatise on Induction.*

12. There is a deductive component however. From the premise, 'Either C_1 or ... or C_n is a cause of E' and the premise 'all PCPs except C_1 were eliminated by using such-and-such method', we may *validly* infer that C_1 (or some conjunction/disjunction of it) is a cause of E. But as we have seen the first premise is an inductively based judgment, and even the second premise (because of the possibility of observational or experimental error)

is inferred only with probability. So the entire process of inference is basically inductive in nature.

13. In rough terms, Galileo argued as follows: According to the ancient theory a three-pound ball should fall faster than a two-pound one. But suppose the three-pounder consists of a two-pounder and a one-pounder. Then it would fall more slowly than the solitary two-pound ball, since the one-pound ball will *retard* the motion of the attached two-pounder. For a more complete account of the Galileo saga, see L. Susan Stebbing, *A Modern Introduction to Logic* (New York: Harper and Row, 1961).

CHAPTER 3

Probability and Expected Value

Back in the first chapter the link between probability and inductive inference was established. The concept of *inductive* probability was introduced for the relation of evidential support between the premise and conclusion of an inductive inference. In a statement of the form, 'The inductive probability of p given q is x' (more briefly, '$\Pr(p/q) = x$'), the value x measures the degree to which the premise, q, confirms (supports, provides evidence for) the conclusion p. These were called *inductive probability statements,* and our study of induction can be framed in terms of them to a large extent. We now focus on a set of principles governing the inference of such statements from one another. Collectively known as **the calculus of probability,** they provide us with the mathematical conditions that any probability concept must satisfy, whether it be the inductive one or another species.

The inference (and other) relations specified by the calculus are deductive in nature and are intended not just as a description of a good deal of our actual reasoning about probabilities but also as a model of how we *should* reason about them. In fact, we will examine cases where certain inferences we often draw concerning probability are confused or mistaken, and the calculus will correct our misconceptions. The probability calculus as presented here is thus a deductive apparatus whose subject matter is inductive probability, and it supplies the mathematical underpinnings that govern in part the correct use of that concept. But before developing the calculus, we need to discuss some preliminary matters.

Section 1. The Calculus of Probability: Axioms and Basic Concepts _____

The contrast between logical and factual truth was also developed in Chapter One. Roughly, we said that a statement is logically true just in case it is both a priori true and logically necessary, where this latter requirement means that it is true under all conditions (as in a truth table tautology or statements like 'All bachelors are unmarried' and '2 + 2 = 4'). Thus there is no possible circumstance under which they would be counted as false. A logically false statement, then, is one that is false under all specifiable conditions and would include truth table contradictions and statements like 'Some bachelors are unmarried'.

Factual truths and falsehoods, however, are empirical statements for which there are specifiable conditions under which they would take a different truth value. As we saw, the study of logical truth belongs to deductive logic, whereas factual statements are typically the premises and conclusions of inductive arguments (though of course they often occur in deductive inference too). Even so, we shall here develop the concept of logical truth a bit more since, first, it will assist our exposition of the calculus and, second, it provides us with a sort of limiting case of the probability concept.

Let's use the sign '□' as an operator on sentences; its role will be to ascribe logical truth to a statement. That is,

$\Box p$ if and only if it is logically true that p

So each of the following statements is true:

□ (either it is raining or it is not raining)
□ (2 + 2 = 4)
□ (all bachelors are unmarried)

But all of these are false:

□ (Bush defeated Dukakis in the 1988 election)
□ (sugar is soluble in water)
□ (Mondale defeated Reagan in the 1984 election)
□ (the heavier a body is, the faster it falls)
□ (8 × 5 = 51)

The first two are false because while the statements enclosed in parentheses are true, they are only factually true. The next pair are false because the enclosed statements are factually false, and of course '8 × 5 = 51' is logically false. Since the negation of a logically false statement is a logical truth, we may express logical falsehood as follows:

It is logically false that p if and only if $\Box \sim p$

Care should be taken to distinguish '$\Box \sim p$' from the nonequivalent form '$\sim \Box p$'. The first says that it is logically true that not-p, whereas the second claims that it is not logically true that p. If we replace 'p' by 'Reagan was elected president in 1940', the first is false and the second is true.

We know from the first chapter that the validity of a deductive inference consists in the impossibility of its having all true premises together with a false conclusion, and we saw that the strong sense of 'impossible' operative here can be expressed in terms of the concept of logical truth. That is, a valid argument is one whose corresponding conditional (the conditional whose antecedent is the conjunction of the premises and whose consequent is the conclusion) is a logically true statement. Hence the notion of validity can now be given a more exact expression as follows:

An argument with premises $P_1, \ldots, P_n$ and conclusion C is *valid* if and only if $\Box\,[(P_1 \,\&\, \ldots \,\&\, P_n) \supset C]$.

It will be useful for us to have a special symbol to express the relation between premise(s) and conclusion in a valid inference. Consequently, we shall introduce the new connective '$\rightarrow$' as follows:

$$p \rightarrow q \text{ if and only if } \Box\,(p \supset q)$$

We will read '$p \rightarrow q$' as 'p *logically implies* q,' and it holds just in case the inference from p to q is valid (i.e., logically true that if p then q).

It is vitally important not to confuse '$\rightarrow$' with '$\supset$'. The conditional

If Kennedy won the 1960 election, then the thirty-fifth president was a Democrat

has both a true antecedent and consequent and hence is itself true. But it is not logically true inasmuch as it can intelligibly be supposed to have been false (he won the election but was not a Democrat, or a Republican was the 35th president). Representing antecedent and consequent by 'A' and 'B' respectively, then while 'A $\supset$ B' is true, 'A $\rightarrow$ B' is not. But the statement

If Bert is a bachelor, then he's unmarried

is such that the consequent cannot be false when the antecedent is true. Using 'C' and 'D' for the component sentences, then, both 'C $\supset$ D' and 'C $\rightarrow$ D' are true since the former is a logical truth. Similarly, since the argument from premise '$\sim$A' to conclusion '$\sim$A v $\sim$B' is valid, '$\sim$A $\rightarrow$ ($\sim$A v $\sim$B)' is also true.

It will also be convenient to have a connective expressing the notion of equivalence. We said earlier that a pair of statements are equivalent just in case they are true under the very same conditions; for example, '$\sim$(A & B)' and '$\sim$A v $\sim$B' are equivalent since their truth table columns are identical. We also saw that the equivalence of these statements can be characterized in terms of the logical truth of their corresponding biconditional; that is, they are equivalent if and only if '~(A & B) ≡ (~A v ~B)' is logically true—which it is since the truth table column for this entire statement contains nothing but **T**s.

We now introduce the connective '↔' to convey the idea of two statements being equivalent:

$$p \leftrightarrow q \text{ if and only if } \Box (p \equiv q)$$

Hence '$p \leftrightarrow q$' will mean that p is equivalent to q, and as before, the contrast between '≡' and '↔' should be kept in mind. Both '~(A & B) ≡ (~A v ~B)' and '~(A & B)↔(~A v ~B)' are true, and the latter is true because the former is logically true. But the statement

Bob passed the exam if and only if he studied hard

or in symbols, '$P \equiv S$', is not a logical truth. Of course it is true if both components are, but it is nonetheless possible for them to differ in truth value (he passed but was just lucky or cheated). Consequently P and S are not equivalent and '$P \leftrightarrow S$' is false.

The signs ' $\Box$ ', '→', and '↔' are called *modal connectives,* in contrast to 'v' or '&', which we shall continue to characterize simply as logical connectives. The difference in terminology reflects the fact that there is an important disparity between the two groups. A compound statement containing only logical connectives is one whose truth value is determined *solely* by the truth values of its component statements. If we are given the truth values for a pair of statements, p and q, the truth values for statements of the forms '~p', 'p & q', 'p v q', '$p \supset q$', and '$p \equiv q$' are *thereby* determined, as the truth tables for these connectives show. But '$p \rightarrow q$', '$p \leftrightarrow q$', and ' $\Box p$' are not at all like this; we have just seen examples where p and q are both true but in one case '$p \rightarrow q$' is true and in another case false (and similarly for '$p \leftrightarrow q$'). Hence for a modal compound statement, the truth values of its component statements are not sufficient for determining the truth value of the whole.

So if p and q have the same truth value and the former is replaced by the latter in the negation '~p', the result '~q' *must* have the same truth value as '~p'. But if we replace a true statement p in ' $\Box p$' with another true statement q, we cannot expect ' $\Box q$' always to have the same truth value as ' $\Box p$' (and likewise for contexts involving '→' and '↔'). Where p is 'It is either raining now or it isn't', and q is 'The Redskins won the Superbowl in 1992', then ' $\Box p$' is true but ' $\Box q$' is false, even though p and q themselves are both true. To ensure that ' $\Box p$' and ' $\Box q$' have the same truth value, p and q must be *equivalent,* not merely share the same truth value. To preserve the truth value of the whole, only equivalent statements may replace one another in a sentence governed by a modal connective.

Let's briefly itemize the main elements of the formal language we will use in studying the probability calculus. In addition to the modal and logical connectives, we will use capital letters with or without subscripts as **statement letters**—abbreviations of particular statements of English. We will also employ small letters in the middle of the alphabet, '*p*', '*q*', and so on, with or without subscripts, as **statement variables.** Small letters at the end of the alphabet, '*x*', '*y*', '*z*', will serve as **numerical variables** ranging over real numbers. We will also require the identity sign (=), the customary arithmetic operators (e.g., '+'), and most important the sign 'Pr', meaning of course 'the inductive probability of ...'. We will abbreviate expressions like '$\sim x = y$' in the usual way as '$x \neq y$'.

The calculus will be developed here as an axiomatic system;[1] that is, some of its most fundamental principles will be selected as **axioms**—statements from which the remaining principles are deduced but that themselves do not admit of proof within the system. The derived principles are the **theorems** of our system. Doing this is far preferable to simply listing the principles one by one without providing any sort of rationale. In laying out the calculus axiomatically, the theorems will have an explicit justification, and their informal proofs will enable us to discern many of the logical relations that hold amongst them.

Before stating the axioms, a definition is needed. Consider the following pair:

> The Chicago White Sox will win the American League pennant this year.
> The Kansas City Royals will win the American League pennant this year.

Given the American League rules (and that the Sox and Royals are member teams), cochampions are not allowed. Hence this pair of statements cannot both be true, or in other words *at most one* of them is true. We will say that relative to those rules, these statements are *mutually exclusive.* This example shows that whether or not two statements are mutually exclusive is often conditional upon other information, and it should be clear that such information logically implies that at most one of the statements will be true. We shall thus employ the following definition:

> The statements $p_1, \ldots, p_n$ are **mutually exclusive** on condition q if and only if $q \rightarrow$ (at most one of $p_1, \ldots, p_n$ is true).

In many cases, the information in q concerning mutual exclusivity is minimal. Where the content of q excludes (as we shall hereafter suppose) such outlandish events as a coin splitting lengthwise while in the air, the pair of statements

This coin will come up heads on the next toss
This coin will come up tails on the next toss

are mutually exclusive. Moreover, some pairs of statements are mutually exclusive unconditionally; a truth table will show that statements of the form '*p* & *r*' and '*p* & ~*r*' are mutually exclusive simply because there is no row in which both are assigned a **T**. Here of course the condition *q* is but a formality.

Now the axioms of our system:

Axiom 1: If $p_1, \ldots, p_n$ are mutually exclusive on condition *q*, then

$$\Pr(p_1 \text{ v} \ldots \text{v} p_n / q) = \sum_{i=1}^{n} \Pr(p_i / q).$$

Axiom 2: $\Pr(p_1 \And \ldots \And p_n / q) = \Pr(p_1/q) \times \ldots \times \Pr(p_n / p_1 \And \ldots \And p_{n-1} \And q)$

Axiom 3: If $p \to q$, then $\Pr(q/p) = 1$

Axiom 4: If $p \leftrightarrow q$, then $\Pr(r/p) = \Pr(r/q)$

Axiom 5: $\Pr(p/q) \geq 0$

The expression on the righthand side of '=' in Axiom 1 is just an abbreviation for the sum of the probabilities of the disjuncts.[2] That is, it simply means $\Pr(p_1/q + \ldots + \Pr(p_n/q)$.

To illustrate the first axiom, let 'C' include the information that a card is to be drawn from a standard, well-shuffled bridge deck. Relative to *C* then, the following are mutually exclusive statements:

A: The card drawn is a ten.
B: The card drawn is a face card (king, queen, or jack).

There are twelve face cards and four tens, so $\Pr(B/C) = 12/52$ and $\Pr(A/B) = 4/52$. Axiom 1 thus gives us the chance of drawing either an eight or a face card; that is, $\Pr(A \text{ v } B/C) = 12/52 + 4/52 = 4/13$. Axiom 1 is not an inductive probability statement nor does it contain one; rather it sanctions the inference of one such statement from two others. Through its use, the probability of a mutually exclusive disjunction is found by summing the probabilities of its disjuncts.

Using Axiom 2, we may determine the probability of a conjunction from those of its conjuncts. Let 'B' now contain the information that cards are to be drawn from a shuffled bridge deck with the stipulation that a card drawn is *not* replaced before the next draw. Where 'K$_1$' represents the statement that the first card drawn is a king and 'K$_2$' that the second card is a king, $\Pr(K_1 / B) = 4/52$ and $\Pr(K_2 / K_1 \& B) = 3/51$, since if K$_1$ is true, only fifty-one cards remain, three of which are kings. So Axiom 2 enables us to infer that the probability of two kings in succession is 1/221; that is, $\Pr(K_1 \& K_2 / B) = 4/52 \times 3/51 = 1/221$.

Axiom 3 tells us in effect that valid deductive inference is a limiting case of probability. Where p logically implies q, the probability of q given p is unity and hence, as we shall see shortly, the greatest probability value. This of course is just what we should expect if it is impossible for q to be false when p is true. However, Axiom 3 brings to the fore a requirement governing our use of inductive probability statements: no probability value is assigned to $\Pr(q/p)$ when p is replaced by a logically false statement. Inductive probability is left undefined when p is, for example, a truth table contradiction. Why? An argument with a contradictory premise constitutes a limiting (or perhaps degenerate) case of validity. Since one statement logically implies another when it is impossible for the first to be true and the second false, a contradiction logically implies *anything* inasmuch as it is impossible for it to be true at all. So if we were to allow contradictions to replace p in $\Pr(q/p)$, Axiom 3 would give every statement q a probability of 1 relative to a contradiction. But this would be intolerable since $\Pr(A/B \& \sim B) = \Pr(\sim A/B \& \sim B) = 1$, and by Axiom 1, $\Pr(A \vee \sim A/B \& \sim B) = 1 + 1 = 2$, which conflicts with the claim that 1 is the greatest probability value. On the other hand, logically false statements can legitimately replace q in $\Pr(q/p)$, and we shall shortly establish that in such a case the value is 0.

While Axioms 4 and 5 are of less practical importance, they should be quite evident. Axiom 4 permits interchanging equivalent statements in the evidence position of an inductive probability statement, and Axiom 5 merely states that no negative numbers may serve as probability values.

Exercises

1. You draw a card from a standard bridge deck. What is the probability that it is an ace? A heart? A red six? A card that is not a face card?

2. Cards are to be drawn from a standard bridge deck. Let

    A: the first card drawn is a king
    B: the second card drawn is a black deuce
    C: the first card drawn is a black deuce
    D: the second card drawn is a face card

Let 'E' include the information that once drawn, a card is not replaced. Determine the following probabilities:

a. $Pr(A \& B/E)$

c. $Pr(A \& D/E)$

b. $Pr(A \vee C/E)$

d. $Pr(B \vee D/A \& E)$

3. Is each statement true or false? Briefly explain.

a. $Pr(A \vee B/A) = 1$

b. $Pr(A/B) = Pr[A/B \vee (C \& {\sim}C)]$

c. If A and B are mutually exclusive on C, then $Pr(A \& B/C) = 0$

d. Let 'B', 'C', and 'E' be as in exercise 2. If the nonreplacement condition is dropped, then where 'F' is the new background statement: $Pr(B \& C/E) \neq Pr(B \& C/F)$ and $Pr(B/C \& F) = Pr(B/F)$.

Section 2. The Calculus of Probability: Theorems and Application _____

The theorems to be established now are useful in answering many questions involving probabilities, but a word needs to be said about their proofs. For our purposes it would be both tedious and unnecessary to construct proofs in a fully rigorous manner; so we shall proceed informally using some simple but wide-ranging rules.

We shall often need to replace an expression with its defining expression and vice versa. So we will employ a *rule of definition* (for short, 'DF'); for example, DF permits us to move back and forth between '$p{\rightarrow}q$' and '$\square\,(p \supset q)$'. A rule governing mathematical manipulation is also required—one that allows such moves as substituting "equals for equals" and also for moving from a formula like '$xy = z$' to '$x = z/y$' or vice versa. This *arithmetic rule* will be abbreviated 'AR'. We will also need a rule for truth-functional manipulation. The *rule of truth functions* (for short, 'TF') will be employed to affirm that one statement logically implies another or that a pair of statements are equivalent—in each case where a truth table would justify such a claim. Thus we can write '$p{\rightarrow}(p \vee q)$' or '${\sim}(p \& q){\leftrightarrow}({\sim}p \vee {\sim}q)$,' citing TF as justification.

Finally we shall use two rules that pertain to the modal connectives. The *rule of logical truths* (more briefly, 'RLT') rests on an obvious principle: If p is logically true and it is impossible for q to be false when p is true (i.e., $p{\rightarrow}q$), then q must be a logical truth too. Hence,

RLT: Given $\square\,p$ and also $p{\rightarrow}q$, we may validly infer $\square\,q$.

Our second rule is even more obvious: If one statement implies another and the latter implies a third, then the first statement also implies the third. We shall call this the *rule of implication,* or 'RI' for short:

RI: Given $p{\rightarrow}q$ and also $q{\rightarrow}r$, we may validly infer $p{\rightarrow}r$.

Certain obvious steps will be combined with others for brevity, and we will cite earlier justifying steps only when confusion might otherwise ensue. Steps will be numbered only when complex justifications occur.

Now for our first theorem. Like many others, it is a conditional and our procedure will be to assume its antecedent and then establish its consequent using the preceding rules. Theorem 1 is an easily obtained consequence of Axiom 3 and states that a logical truth has a probability of 1.

Theorem 1: If $\square p$, then $\Pr(p/q) = 1$.

PROOF: Assume $\square p$
      TF: $p{\rightarrow}(q \supset p)$
      RLT: $\square (q \supset p)$
      DF: $q{\rightarrow}p$
      Ax.3: $\Pr(p/q) = 1$ $p\backslash q$ $q\backslash p$

(The expression '$p\backslash q$' means that p has been substituted for q in the statement of Axiom 3.) The derivation of the second step by TF stems of course from the fact that a truth table will easily show that no row in which p is assigned a **T** is one in which $q \supset p$ is assigned an **F;** and this together with the first line justifies our obtaining the third step from the previous two by RLT. Note that q in Theorem 1 may be any statement whatever; since no statement is relevant as evidence for a logical truth (they are true under any and all conditions), the probability of the latter will be 1 regardless of what is specified as the condition q. Logical truth is hence a limiting case of probability, and even though inductive probability is a concept primarily applicable to factual statements, Theorem 1 will turn out to be useful in several ways.

The next theorem is often called the *Subtraction Principle:*

Theorem 2: $\Pr(\sim p/q) = 1 - \Pr(p/q)$.

PROOF: **1.** TF: $\square (p \text{ v} \sim p)$
      2. Thm.1: $\Pr(p \text{ v} \sim p/q) = 1$ $p \text{ v} \sim p\backslash p$
      3. TF: $q{\rightarrow}\sim(p \text{ \& } \sim p)$
      4. DF: p and $\sim p$ are mutually exclusive on q
      5. Ax.1: $\Pr(p \text{ v} \sim p/q) = \Pr(p/q) + \Pr(\sim p/q)$ $\sim p\backslash q$ $q\backslash r$
      6. AR (2), (5): $\Pr(\sim p/q) = 1 - \Pr(p/q)$

Since the probability of drawing a spade from a bridge deck is 1/4, Theorem 2 tells us that the probability of not drawing one is 3/4. Hereafter, for convenience, we shall omit the tiresome background statement common to the probability expressions under consideration. So instead of writing $\Pr(\sim A/B) = 1 - \Pr(A/B)$, where B expresses the usual information about the deck, we shall simply write '$\Pr(\sim A) = 1 - \Pr(A)$'. But it should be kept in mind that '$\Pr(A)$' is just a shorthand device; when our concern is focused on topics unrelated to problem solving (as in stating and proving theorems), the complete expression will be used.

The Subtraction Principle allows us to readily establish our next theorem, which ascribes to logically false statements a probability of 0:

Theorem 3: If $\Box \sim p$, then $\Pr(p/q) = 0$.

PROOF: Assume $\Box \sim p$
    Thm.1: $\Pr(\sim p/q) = 1$ $\sim p \backslash p$
    Thm.2, AR: $\Pr(p/q) = 1 - 1 = 0$.

Theorem 2 also permits the derivation of another very basic principle: that all probability values fall within 0 and 1 inclusive:

Theorem 4: $0 \le \Pr(p/q) \le 1$.

PROOF: The theorem easily follows by Axiom 5 and Theorem 2.

Axiom 4 allows us to substitute equivalent statements in the "evidence" position of a probability expression. Our next theorem permits such replacement in the left position, and it is one of the most useful theorems we will prove. We shall call it the *Substitution Principle;* its proof is lengthy, but fortunately it is the only such proof we will have to tolerate.

Theorem 5: If $p \leftrightarrow q$, then $\Pr(p/r) = \Pr(q/r)$.

PROOF: **1.** Assume $p \leftrightarrow q$
           2. DF: $\Box (p \equiv q)$
           3. TF: $(p \equiv q) \rightarrow [r \supset (p \lor \sim q)]$
           4. RLT: $\Box [r \supset (p \lor \sim q)]$
           5. DF: $r \rightarrow (p \lor \sim q)$
           6. Ax.3: $\Pr(p \lor \sim q/r) = 1$ $p \lor \sim q \backslash q$ $r \backslash p$
           7. TF: $(p \equiv q) \rightarrow [r \supset \sim(p \& \sim q)]$
           8. RLT (2),(7): $\Box [r \supset \sim(p \& \sim q)]$
           9. DF: $r \rightarrow \sim(p \& \sim q)$
        10. DF: p and $\sim q$ are mutually exclusive on r
        11. Ax.1: $\Pr(p \lor \sim q/r) = \Pr(p/r) + \Pr(\sim q/r)$ $\sim q \backslash q$
        12. AR (6),(11): $\Pr(p/r) = 1 - \Pr(\sim q/r)$
        13. Thm.2, AR: $\Pr(q/r) = 1 - \Pr(\sim q/r)$ $\sim q \backslash p$ $r \backslash q$
        14. AR (12),(13): $\Pr(p/r) = \Pr(q/r)$

The TF moves at (3) and (7) are justified by an eight-row truth table; that is, no row in which $p \equiv q$ is assigned a **T** is one where either $r \supset (p \text{ v } \sim q)$ or $r \supset \sim (p \text{ \& } \sim q)$ is assigned an **F**. The Substitution Theorem tells us for example that given $p \leftrightarrow \sim \sim p$, we may infer $\Pr(p/q) = \Pr(\sim \sim p/q)$; also if in a proof we have $p \leftrightarrow \sim \sim p$ and a statement of the form $\Pr(p/q) = x$ on separate lines, Theorem 5 with an obvious AR move will yield $\mathrm{PR}(\sim \sim p/q) = x$ in one step.[3]

The Substitution Theorem points up a similarity between probability expressions like '$\Pr(p/q)$' and compound statements governed by modal connectives. The latter as we saw require that equivalent statements replace one another to ensure that the resulting compound has the same truth value as the original. The same holds for probability contexts; p and q must be equivalent for one to replace the other in such contexts, merely having the same truth value is not enough. To see this let

H$_1$: The coin comes up heads on the first toss
H$_2$: The coin comes up heads on the second toss

and now suppose that in fact both statements are true; then H$_1$ and the conjunction H$_1$ & H$_2$ are both true (but of course not equivalent). Replacing an occurrence of H$_1$ in the obviously true statement, $\Pr(\mathrm{H}_1) = \Pr(\mathrm{H}_1)$, with H$_1$ & H$_2$ yields the obviously false $\Pr(\mathrm{H}_1) = \Pr(\mathrm{H}_1 \text{ \& } \mathrm{H}_2)$.

What is the probability of heads coming up *at least once* in two tosses of a coin? In other words, $\Pr(\mathrm{H}_1 \text{ v } \mathrm{H}_2) = ?$ Our inclination to apply Axiom 1 here quickly disappears when we realize that it yields the disconcerting result

$$\Pr(\mathrm{H}_1 \text{ v } \mathrm{H}_2) = 1/2 + 1/2 = 1$$

Obviously this has got to be wrong since there would be no chance of getting tails. It is not hard to see where the mistake lies: H$_1$ and H$_2$ are *not* mutually exclusive—the coin could show heads on both tosses. So Axiom 1 is inapplicable here, and we must find a new addition principle to handle disjunctions in which more than one disjunct can be true. This is our next theorem:

> ***Theorem 6:*** $\Pr(p_1 \text{ v } \ldots \text{ v } p_n/q) = 1 - \Pr(\sim p_1 \text{ \& } \ldots \text{ \& } \sim p_n/q)$

> PROOF: Th.2, AR: $\Pr(p_1 \text{ v } \ldots \text{ v } p_n/q) = 1 - \Pr[\sim(p_1 \text{ v } \ldots \text{ v } p_n)/q]$
> TF: $\sim(p_1 \text{ v } \ldots \text{ v } p_n) \leftrightarrow (\sim p_1 \text{ \& } \ldots \text{ \& } \sim p_n)$
> Th.5, AR: $\Pr(p_1 \text{ v } \ldots \text{ v } p_n/q) = 1 - \Pr(\sim p_1 \text{ \& } \ldots \text{ \& } \sim p_n/q)$

Where only two disjuncts are involved, we can simplify calculations by using

Theorem 6A: $\Pr(p_1 \vee p_2/q) = \Pr(p_1/q) + \Pr(p_2/q) - \Pr(p_1 \& p_2/q)$

Its proof is left as an exercise. Returning to our problem about the coin,

$$\begin{aligned}
\Pr(H_1 \vee H_2) &= 1 - \Pr(\sim H_1 \& \sim H_2) = 1 - [\Pr(\sim H_1) \times \Pr(\sim H_2/\sim H_1)] \\
&= 1 - (1/2 \times 1/2) = 3/4 \\
&= \Pr(H_1) + \Pr(H_2) - \Pr(H_1 \& H_2) \\
&= \Pr(H_1) + \Pr(H_2) - (\Pr[H_1] \times \Pr(H_2/H_1)] \\
&= 1/2 + 1/2 - 1/4 = 3/4
\end{aligned}$$

The value assigned to $\Pr(H_2/H_1)$ is of course the same that we would assign to $\Pr(H_2)$, and the reason is that the probability of the coin's coming up heads on the second toss is not affected by whether it showed heads on the first. In contrast, when drawing cards *without* replacement, the chance of getting a king on the second draw does indeed depend on what card was drawn first. Hence,

$$\Pr(K_1 \& K_2) = \Pr(K_1) \; \Pr(K_2/K_1) = (4/52)(3/51) = 1/221.$$

In the coin example, the statements H_1 and H_2 are said to be *independent* on the usual condition about the coin, whereas K_1 and K_2 are not independent given the no-replacement stipulation. As a rough characterization of this crucial concept,[4]

> $p_1, \ldots, p_n$ constitute a set of *independent* statements on condition q if and only if relative to q the probability of any one of the ps is not affected by the truth values of the others nor by a truth-functional compound statement containing two or more of the others. For example, $\Pr(p_1/q) = \Pr(p_1/p_2 \& q) = \Pr(p_1/\sim p_2 \& q) = \Pr(p_1/p_2 \& \sim p_3 \& q)$.

It will be convenient to speak not only of statements as independent, but also of the *events* they describe (and similarly for other concepts such as mutual exclusivity). So tosses of a coin, drawings of cards, and so forth will be described as "independent events." Our next theorem concerns independent conjuncts:

Theorem 7: If $p_1, \ldots, p_n$ are independent on condition q, then

$$\Pr(p_1 \& \ldots \& p_n/q) = \prod_{i=1}^{n} \Pr(p_i/q).$$

PROOF: Assume $p_1, \ldots, p_n$ are independent on q
DF: For each i such that $2 \leq i \leq n$,
$\Pr(p_i/q) = \Pr(p_i/p_1 \& \ldots \& p_{i-1} \& q)$

Ax.2, Ar: $\Pr(p_1 \& \ldots \& p_n/q) = \prod_{i=1}^{n} \Pr(p_i/q)$

[The expression on the righthand side of '=' merely abbreviates: $\Pr(p_1/q) \times \ldots \times \Pr(p_n/q)$.] Where K_1 and K_2 are specified as independent, then we have $\Pr(K_1 \& K_2) = \Pr(K_1) \times \Pr(K_2) = (1/13)^2$.

It should be pretty clear by this point that, in calculating the probability of a compound statement, there are two handy rules to keep in mind:

If the statement is a disjunction, determine whether the disjuncts are mutually exclusive. If so, use Axiom 1. If not, use Theorem 6.

If the statement is a conjunction, determine whether the conjuncts are independent. If so, apply Theorem 7. If not, apply Axiom 2.

To illustrate, let's tackle an example. In gambler's parlance, when a pair of dice are tossed and they show a total of 7 or of 11, a "natural" has been thrown. What then is the probability that in two tosses of a pair of dice, a natural is obtained on the first toss and a total of nine on the second? As a first step, we should write out the problem in truth-functional form. Let:

S_1 – a 7 is thrown on the first toss
E_1 – an 11 is thrown on the first toss
N_2 – a 9 is thrown on the second toss

We wish to know the probability of getting either 7 or 11 on the first toss *and* getting a 9 on the second. So our question is: $\Pr[(S_1 \vee E_1) \& N_2] = ?$

The next step is to apply the relevant principles of the calculus. Since S_1 and E_1 are mutually exclusive, Axiom 1 applies to their disjunction, and since tosses of a die are independent, Theorem 7 applies to the entire conjunction. So we have:

$$\Pr[(S_1 \vee E_1) \& N_2] = \Pr(S_1 \vee E_1) \times \Pr(N_2)$$
$$= [\Pr(S_1) + \Pr(E_1)] \times \Pr(N_2)$$

Our final step is to determine the component probability values and calculate. Each die has 6 sides, and there are thus 6×6 or 36 possible combinations of numbers that could turn up on a given toss, ranging from 2 (known as "aces" or "snake eyes") to 12 ("boxcars"). There are 6 possible ways of obtaining a 7 (4–3, 3–4, 5–2, 2–5, 6–1, 1–6), two ways of obtaining 11 and four ways of getting a 9. Hence $\Pr(S_1) = 6/36$, $\Pr(E_1) = 2/36$ and $\Pr(N_2) = 4/36$. With these values, we now calculate:

$$\Pr[(S_1 \vee E_1) \& N_2] = (6/36 + 2/36)(4/36) = 32/1296 = 2/81$$

Now for another question; what is the probability of obtaining either a spade on the first draw from a bridge deck or else kings on the first two draws given no replacement after the first draw? Our problem is $\Pr[S_1 \text{ v } (K_1 \And K_2)] = ?$ Since the king of spades could be drawn, the disjuncts are not mutually exclusive. So Theorem 6 (or its corollary) should be used:

$$\Pr[S_1 \text{ v } (K_1 \And K_2)] = \Pr(S_1) + \Pr(K_1 \And K_2) - \Pr(S_1 \And K_1 \And K_2)$$

$\Pr(S_1 \And K_1 \And K_2)$ is in effect the chance of getting the king of spades on the first draw and another king on the second, and since there is no replacement Axiom 2 must be used here. So the righthand side of the equation becomes

$$\Pr(S_1) + [\Pr(K_1) \times \Pr(K_2/K_1)] - [\Pr(S_1 \And K_1) \times \Pr(K_2/S_1 \And K_1)]$$

The probability of drawing the king of spades first is 1/52, and the chance of getting a king on the second draw given the king of spades on the first is 3/51. Plugging in these and the remaining obvious values, we have

$$\Pr[S_1 \text{ v } (K_1 \And K_2)] = 1/4 + (1/13)(3/51) - (1/52)(3/51) = 0.253$$

Exercises

1. Let $\Pr(A) = 1/2$ and $\Pr(B) = 5/8$. A and B are independent. Determine

a. $\Pr(\sim A)$	**d.** $\Pr(A \text{ v } A)$
b. $\Pr(A \text{ v } \sim A)$	**e.** $\Pr[B \And (A \text{ v } \sim A)]$
c. $\Pr(B \And \sim B)$	**f.** $\Pr(A \text{ v } B)$

2. A card is drawn from a bridge deck. What is the probability that it is

a. Either an ace or a jack?	**c.** Either a face card or a ten?
b. Either a diamond or a spade?	**d.** Either a heart or a face card?

Show your work.

3. Two cards are drawn in succession from a bridge deck. Calculate the following:

a. The probability that both are spades, assuming replacement. Without replacement.

b. The probability that the first card is a king and the second a queen, with replacement.

c. The probability that the first card is a queen and the second a king, with replacement.

d. The probability of getting a king and a queen in two draws, with replacement.

e. The probability that neither card is a spade, without replacement.

f. The probability that not both cards are spades, with replacement.

g. The probability that exactly one card is a spade, without replacement.

4. In draw poker, each player is initially dealt five cards face down. If all five are of the same suit (e.g., all clubs), the hand is a *flush*. If all five are in consecutive order (e.g., 4, 5, 6, 7, 8,), the hand is a *straight*. A *full house* is a hand consisting of three of a kind and a pair (e.g., three kings and two fives).

a. You're playing draw poker and are dealt two aces, two eights, and a deuce. You discard the deuce and draw another card. What is the probability that you now hold a full house? *Note:* since you have not seen the other players' cards, the situation is no different—as far as your present knowledge is concerned—from that of being dealt five cards with no other players present; so you may assume in effect that there are forty-seven remaining cards from which you are making the draw.

b. You are dealt a four, a five, a seven, an eight and finally a king, which you discard. What is the probability that the card you draw will give you a straight?

c. You are dealt four diamonds and then a heart, which you discard. What is the probability of ending up with a flush?

d. You are dealt a five, a six, a seven, an eight, and then a deuce, which you discard. What is the probability that you will obtain a straight?

e. You are dealt a pair of tens, an ace, a three, and a five. You discard the three and the five and draw two more cards. What is the probability of getting either four tens or a full house? Of getting just three tens?

5. Prove that the following is a theorem of the probability calculus: if p and q are mutually exclusive on r and $r \rightarrow (p \lor q)$, then $\Pr(p/r) = 1 - \Pr(q/r)$.

6. Prove Theorem 6A. Hint: $(p_1 \lor p_2) \leftrightarrow [(p_1 \& p_2) \lor (p_1 \& \sim p_2) \lor (\sim p_1 \& p_2)]$. Also keep in mind: $x + y + z = (z + x) + (z + y) - z$.

More Theorems: So far, we've dealt mainly with probabilities for conjunctions and disjunctions having just two components. But of course our axioms and theorems are applicable to compounds of three or more conjuncts or disjuncts too. Axiom 1 tells us that the probability of getting an even number in one toss of a single die is

$Pr(T \lor F \lor S) = 3(1/6) = 1/2$. The probability of drawing four face cards in succession from a bridge deck without replacement is easily determined using Axiom 2: $Pr(F_1 \& F_2 \& F_3 \& F_4) = (12/52)(11/51)(10/50)(9/49) = 0.0018$.

Theorem 7 may be applied if replacement and reshuffling is stipulated after each draw, since here of course the draws are independent of one another:

$$Pr(F_1 \& F_2 \& F_3 \& F_4) = (12/52)^4 = 81/28561 = 0.0028$$

What is the probability that in a toss of ten dice *at least one* of them will show a three? Theorem 6 enables us to handle this problem, and since the conjuncts involved are independent, Theorem 7 applies as well:

$$\begin{aligned} Pr(T_1 \lor T_2 \lor \ldots \lor T_{10}) &= 1 - Pr(\sim T_1 \& \sim T_2 \& \ldots \& \sim T_{10}) \\ &= 1 - [Pr(\sim T_1) \times Pr(\sim T_2) \times \ldots \times Pr(\sim T_{10})] \\ &= 1 - (5/6)^{10} = 1 - 0.16 = 0.84 \end{aligned}$$

Suppose we draw cards from a bridge deck until only eight remain. After looking at the forty-four already dealt, we discover that each of the remaining cards is either a heart or a king (or both). Relative to this information, the statements

The next card dealt will be a heart
The next card dealt will be a king

are such that *at least one* of them is true. In such a case, we shall say that the two statements are *jointly exhaustive* on the background condition. That is,

$p_1, \ldots, p_n$ are **jointly exhaustive** on q if and only if
$q \rightarrow (p_1 \lor \ldots \lor p_n)$

In our example, the statements were not mutually exclusive since the king of hearts remained in the deck. But we will be concerned with sets of statements that are *both* mutually exclusive and jointly exhaustive. Suppose the Blackhawks and the Canadiens are playing; since ties are allowed in hockey, the statements

The Blackhawks win   The Canadiens win   The game ends in
                                             a tie

are mutually exclusive *and* jointly exhaustive given the rules of hockey. At most one of the three is true and at least one of them is true;

therefore one and only one of them is true. That is, if $p_1, \ldots, p_n$ are mutually exclusive and jointly exhaustive on q, then exactly one of them is true.

Our next theorem states a useful and fairly obvious property of mutually exclusive and jointly exhaustive sets of statements:

> **Theorem 8:** If $p_1, \ldots, p_n$ are mutually exclusive and jointly exhaustive on condition q, then $= \sum\limits_{i=1}^{n} \Pr(p_i/q) = 1$.

PROOF: 1. Assume $p_1, \ldots, p_n$ are mutually exclusive and jointly exhaustive on q
2. DF: $q \to (p_1 \vee \ldots \vee p_n)$
3. Ax.3: $\Pr(p_1 \vee \ldots \vee p_n/q) = 1$
4. DF, Ax.1 (1): $\Pr(p_1 \vee \ldots \vee p_n/q) = \sum\limits_{i=1}^{n} \Pr(p_i/q)$
5. AR(3), (4): $= \sum\limits_{i=1}^{n} \Pr(p_i/q) = 1$

So the probabilities of the individual statements in the mutually exclusive and jointly exhaustive set must sum to 1. Suppose your local bookmaker quotes you 3 to 2 odds in favor of the Canadiens, 2 to 1 odds against the Blackhawks, and 14 to 1 odds against a tie. Has your bookie obeyed the dictates of the calculus? The notion of *odds* is of course closely related to probability, and we may translate "odds talk" into probability talk as follows:

If given q, the odds *in favor of* p are x to y, then $\Pr(p/q) = x/(x + y)$.
If given q, the odds *against* p are x to y, then $\Pr(p/q) = y/(x + y)$.

Using some obvious notation, the quoted odds correspond to the values:

$\Pr(C) = 3/5, \qquad \Pr(B) = 1/3, \qquad \Pr(T) = 1/15$

which sum to 1. So your bookie's quotes accord with the calculus (an unusual occurrence in actual practice).

Now suppose that on condition q, the mutually exclusive and jointly exhaustive statements $p_1, \ldots, p_n$ also have the same probability, that is, are equiprobable. Hence for each p_i, $\Pr(p_i/q) = 1/n$. A very basic principle governing such cases may now be derived as a corollary to Theorem 8:

> **Theorem 9:** If $p_1, \ldots, p_n$ are mutually exclusive, jointly exhaustive, and equiprobable on condition q, then for $k = 1, 2, \ldots, n$,
> $\Pr(p_1 \vee \ldots \vee p_k/q) = k/n$.

PROOF: **1.** Assume $p_1, \ldots, p_n$ are mutually exclusive, jointly exhaustive, and equiprobable on q.

2. DF,Th.8: $\Pr(p_1 \text{ v} \ldots \text{v} p_n/q) = \sum\limits_{i=1}^{n} \Pr(p_i/q) = 1$

3. DF (1),(2): each $\Pr(p_i/q) = 1/n$

4. Ax.1, AR: for $k = 1, 2, \ldots, n$,
$\Pr(p_1 \text{ v} \ldots \text{v} p_k/q) = k(1/n) = $ k/n.

Step (3) was obtained using the definition of 'equiprobable'. Where n is the total number of cases, k is described as the number of "favorable" cases. The probability of drawing an ace from a bridge deck is thus the number of favorable cases, 4, divided by the total number of mutually exclusive, jointly exhaustive, and equiprobable cases, 52; hence 4/52. The principle here established as Theorem 9 has sometimes been construed as defining the concept of probability.[5] This approach is no longer prevalent, and it should be remembered that our concept of inductive probability is framed in terms of the relation of evidential support that characterizes inductive inference. Thus, the principle— called the *Principle of Counting Equiprobable Cases*—is a consequence of the axioms for us, not a definition of the concept. But it is important to have shown it to be a consequence; the inductive probability concept would not be worth much if it did not conform to Theorem 9.

A coin is tossed three times. What is the probability that tails will appear on the first two tosses and heads on the third? The tosses being independent, this problem is easily handled by Theorem 7:

$$\Pr(T_1 \text{ \& } T_2 \text{ \& } H_3) = (1/2)^3 = 1/8$$

But now, what is the probability of getting two tails and one head in three tosses? This is a different question since it is not specified in which order the tails and head will appear. Hence, we must determine how many ways there are in which one head and two tails may occur. In a simple case like this, a little reflection is all that is needed to see that there are three such ways: $T_1 \text{ \& } T_2 \text{ \& } H_3$, $T_1 \text{ \& } H_2 \text{ \& } T_3$, and $H_1 \text{ \& } T_2 \text{ \& } T_3$. Our original question may now be rephrased: What is the probability that one of these three combinations will occur? Since the three are mutually exclusive, we may apply Axiom 1:

$$\Pr[(T_1 \text{ \& } T_2 \text{ \& } H_3) \text{ v} (T_1 \text{ \& } H_2 \text{ \& } T_3) \text{ v} (H_1 \text{ \& } T_2 \text{ \& } T_3)] = 3(1/8) = 3/8$$

What is not so obvious, though, is how many combinations are involved in a question like this: what is the probability that in five draws from a bridge deck with replacement, three will be diamonds and two will not be diamonds? The draws being independent, Theorems 7 and

2 are all that is needed to determine the chance of a particular three-diamond–two-nondiamond combination; for example,

$$\Pr(D_1 \text{ \& } \sim D_2 \text{ \& } D_3 \text{ \& } \sim D_4 \text{ \& } D_5) = (1/4)^3(3/4)^2 = 9/1024 = 0.009$$

But of course to solve the problem we need to know the total number of such combinations, and any standard algebra text will supply us with the appropriate formula. A *combination* of a set of objects is a selection of one or more of those objects without regard to the order of selection. In the present case, there are five cards in the set and we are considering a selection in which exactly three of them are diamonds. So we want to know how many combinations there are of five things taken three at a time. Following standard practice, we will abbreviate the expression, 'the number of combinations of x things taken y at a time', by the symbol '$\binom{x}{y}$'; the formula we require is

$$\binom{x}{y} = \frac{x!}{y!(x-y)!}$$

where '$x!$' (read "x factorial") abbreviates '$x \cdot (x-1) \cdot (x-2) \cdot \ldots \cdot 1$'. Thus in our example we have

$$\binom{5}{3} = \frac{5 \cdot 4 \cdot 3 \cdot 2 \cdot 1}{3 \cdot 2 \cdot 1 \cdot 2 \cdot 1} = 20/2 = 10$$

There are therefore ten distinct ways of obtaining exactly three diamonds in five draws, and since the probability of any one of these combinations is 9/1024 and they together form a mutually exclusive set of statements, the solution to our problem is now at hand ('C_i' states that the ith combination occurs); using Axiom 1 we have

$$
\begin{aligned}
\Pr(\text{any } 3\text{-diamond–}2\text{-nondiamond}) &= \Pr(C_1 \text{ v} \ldots \text{v } C_{10}) \\
&= \Pr(C_1) + \Pr(C_2) + \ldots + \Pr(C_{10}) \\
&= 10(9/1024) = 45/512 = 0.088
\end{aligned}
$$

The notion of a combination has many applications in probability contexts. An excellent illustration of this is a version of a well-known puzzle often called "the paradox of the second ace."[6] Suppose we have a twelve card deck consisting of just the aces, kings, and queens; suppose further we are to be dealt a hand of just two cards. Let

A: The hand contains two aces
B: The hand contains at least one ace
C: The hand contains the ace of spades

Our task is to calculate Pr(A/B) and Pr(A/C). Common sense or intuition would appear to tell us that these values should be the same, since the fact that the identity of the ace is made explicit in C but not in B does not seem to be a relevant consideration. If we are dealt two cards face down and told that one of them is the ace of spades, then we are being given more specific information than if we are told simply that one of the cards is an ace. But this difference just does not seem germane to the task of calculating the chance that the other card is also an ace.

To find the desired probability values, we must employ the notion of a combination. And since the draw of any one of the twelve cards is equiprobable with that of the other eleven, *and* since the statements delineating all of the possible hands that may be drawn (statements of the form "cards so-and-so and such-and-such were drawn") are mutually exclusive and jointly exhaustive, Theorem 9 applies here. It tells us that

$$\Pr(A/B) = \frac{\text{number of hands with two aces}}{\text{number of hands with at least one ace}}$$

To calculate the number of hands with two aces, we need to know how many combinations there are of the four aces taken two at a time. Thus,

$$\binom{4}{2} = \frac{4 \cdot 3 \cdot \cancel{2} \cdot \cancel{1}}{2 \cdot 1 \cdot \cancel{2} \cdot \cancel{1}} = 12/2 = 6$$

Finding the denominator is a bit more involved: how many two-card hands are there containing at least one ace? The total number of hands is

$$\binom{12}{2} = \frac{12 \cdot 11}{2} = 66$$

Of these, six as we know are two-ace hands. Of the sixty left, we must determine how many contain exactly one ace. One way of doing this is to determine how many hands contain no aces, and then subtract that figure from 60. Since there are eight nonaces in the deck, we have

$$\binom{8}{2} = \frac{8 \cdot 7}{2} = 28$$

Thus there are 60 – 28 or 32 hands with just one ace, and hence 38 hands with at least one ace. Consequently, by Theorem 9,

$$\Pr(A/B) = 6/(32 + 6) = 6/38 = 3/19$$

Turning now to Pr(A/C), Theorem 9 tells us:

$$\text{Pr(A/C)} = \frac{\text{number of two-ace hands one of which is the ace of spades}}{\text{number of hands with the ace of spades}}$$

Plainly the numerator is three, since the ace of spades can be paired with each of the other three aces. To determine the denominator, we need note only that, in addition to these three hands, there are four in which the ace of spades is paired with a king and four more in which it is paired with a queen. Hence

$$\text{Pr(A/C)} = \frac{3}{3 + 4 + 4} = 3/11$$

which, contrary to common sense, is *different* from Pr(A/B).

Perhaps one way of resolving this "paradox" is to reconsider Pr(A/B) in light of the preceding ratio obtained for Pr(A/C). There are only three two-ace hands with the ace of spades, but six two-ace hands in all. So we know that the numerator as well as the lefthand quantity in the denominator of the ratio for Pr(A/C), that is, of 3/(3 + 4 + 4), must be changed to 6 in calculating Pr(A/B). If we doubled the other quantities in the denominator as well, we would obtain the same value as for Pr(A/C); 6/(6 + 8 + 8) = 3/11. But it is here that the mistake lies; although there are only four hands in which the ace of spades is paired with a king and four more in which it is paired with a queen, there are *sixteen* hands in which an ace is paired with a king and sixteen more with one ace and one queen. Hence, the correct ratio for Pr(A/B) is 6/(6 + 16 + 16) = 3/19. Perhaps this serves to emphasize a point made earlier: the calculus is not only a descriptive model of our probabilistic reasoning but a normative one too.

It remains to state two theorems about combinations; their formulation is complex, but their content is simple and both have already been illustrated.

Let $p_1, \ldots, p_n$ be independent and equiprobable statements on condition r, and similarly for $q_1, \ldots, q_n$. Let each of the pairs $<p_i, q_i>$ be mutually exclusive and jointly exhaustive on r, and let C_k be one of the $\binom{n}{m}$ combinations such that m = the number of cases in which a p_i is true. Then, where $\text{Pr}(p_i/r) = z$:

Theorem 10A: $\text{Pr}(C_k/r) = \text{Pr}(p_i/r)^m \times \text{Pr}(q_i/r)^{n-m} = z^m(1-z)^{n-m}$

Theorem 10B: $\text{Pr}(C_1 \lor \ldots \lor C_{\binom{n}{m}})/r = \binom{n}{m} \times \text{Pr}(p_i/r)^m$

$$\times \text{Pr}(q_i/r)^{n-m}$$

$$= \binom{n}{m} z^m(1-z)^{n-m}$$

Exercises

1. A single die is tossed four times. What is the probability of getting

    a. A three on all four tosses?
    b. A three on none of the four?
    c. Either a three on all four or a five on all four?
    d. A three on the first and third and a five on the other two?
    e. A three on two of the tosses and a five on the other two?

2. What is the probability that in three draws from a bridge deck without replacement at least one card will be a diamond?

3. A gambler is said to have asked Galileo, "Why does a toss of three dice turn up a sum of ten more often than a sum of nine?" Answer the gambler.

4. A box contains eight white and four red cubes. Without looking inside, six cubes are drawn with replacement each time. What is the probability that four were white and two were red? That at least five were red?

5. A single die is tossed four times. What is the probability

    a. That not all of the tosses result in a three?
    b. Of getting a three at least once?
    c. Of getting a three exactly three times?
    d. Of getting a three at least three times?

6. a. At draw poker, you are dealt two kings, a three, a four, and a six. You discard the three small cards and draw three more. What is the probability that you will end up with four kings?
    b. You are dealt the seven, eight, and ten of clubs and the two and three of hearts. You discard both hearts and draw two more cards. What is the probability that you will get a straight flush (i.e., a straight in which all five cards are of the same suit)? A flush *or* a straight?

7. You estimate that the probability that the Bears' star running back has recovered from injury to be 3/4. The odds in favor of their winning the next game given that he's recovered are 5 to 3, but the odds against their winning if he has not are 4 to 1. What is the probability that the Bears will win their next game?

8. Prove that the following are theorems of the calculus:

    a. If p and q are independent on r and $\Pr(p/r) = \Pr(q/r) = x$, then
    $\Pr(\sim p \ \& \ \sim q/r) = 1 - (2x - x^2)$.
    b. If $p_1, \ldots, p_n$ are independent and equiprobable on condition q, and $\Pr(p_i/q) = x$, then
    $\Pr(p_1 \ v \ldots v \ p_n/q) = 1 - (1 - x)^n$.

9. Sketch a proof of Theorem 10A.

10. Here is another solution to the paradox of the second ace. In calculating $Pr(A/B)$ and $Pr(A/C)$, the *order* in which the two cards were dealt was not taken into account. Yet in supposing that the values should be the same we were perhaps tacitly assuming that in statement B an ace—or in C the ace of spades—was dealt first. At any rate, once order of appearance is made explicit, the paradox disappears and the probability values are the same. Let A again be the statement that the hand contains two aces, let B_1 represent the statement 'The first card dealt is an ace', and C_1 the statement 'The first card dealt is the ace of spades'. Using Theorem 9, calculate $Pr(A/B_1)$ and $Pr(A/C_1)$. Then explain why $Pr(A/B_1) \neq Pr(A/B)$.

11. (Hard) Consider the paradox of the second ace for a full bridge deck: Find the probability that a five-card poker hand contains two aces given that it contains the ace of spades; then find the probability that it contains a pair of aces given that it contains at least one ace. If your calculator is not up to the job, just display the appropriate formulae.

12. (Hard) What is the probability that at least two people in a party of ten have the same birthday? An estimate will do if your calculator is anemic.

Section 3. Bayes' Theorem _____

A great deal of scientific investigation is concerned with the testing and retesting of hypotheses, often with the goal of determining which of a number of competing hypotheses should be accepted. Several theorems of the probability calculus are especially relevant to such inquiry, and two of them—the Prediction Theorem and Bayes' Theorem—will be discussed now. First, however, it is necessary to cite a preliminary result (a "lemma"):

Lemma: If $r \rightarrow (p \equiv q)$, then $Pr(p/r) = Pr(q/r)$.

PROOF: Very similar to that for Theorem 5. Hence it will be omitted here.

Now let $p_1, \ldots, p_n$ be mutually exclusive and jointly exhaustive on q; they might, for example, be a complete set of competing hypotheses concerning some phenomenon under investigation. And now consider a statement r that summarizes the results of an experiment concerning these hypotheses. Since the hypotheses are mutually exclusive, the same must hold for the conjunctions $p_1 \& r, \ldots, p_n \& r$, and these express the possible alternatives under which r is true. With this in mind, we now state and prove the Prediction Theorem:

Theorem 11: If $p_1, \ldots, p_n$ are mutually exclusive and jointly exhaustive on condition q, then

$$\Pr(r/q) = \sum_{i=1}^{n} [\Pr(p_i/q) \times \Pr(r/p_i \ \& \ q)]$$

PROOF: **1.** Assume $p_1, \ldots, p_n$ are mutually exclusive and jointly exhaustive on q

2. DF: $q \rightarrow (p_1 \ v \ldots v \ p_n)$

3. TF: $(p_1 \ v \ldots v \ p_n) \rightarrow \{r \equiv [(p_1 \ \& \ r) \ v \ldots v \ (p_n \ \& \ r)\}$

4. RI: $q \rightarrow \{r \equiv [(p_1 \ \& \ r) \ v \ldots v \ (p_n \ \& \ r)]\}$

5. Lemma: $\Pr(r/q) = \Pr[(p_1 \ \& \ r) \ v \ldots v \ (p_n \ \& \ r)/q]$

6. TF, (1): $p_1 \ \& \ r, \ldots, p_n \ \& \ r$ are mutually exclusive on q

7. Ax.1, (1): $\Pr(r/q) = \sum_{i=1}^{n} \Pr(p_i \ \& \ r/q).$

8. Ax.2: $\Pr(r/q) = \sum_{i=1}^{n} [\Pr(p_i/q) \times \Pr(r/p_i \ \& \ q)]$

(If $n = 2$, an eight-row truth table justifies 3; if $n = 3$, a sixteen-row table is needed, and so on. To illustrate the theorem, suppose three bags are identical in appearance, one of which contains eight red and two white cubes, another five red and five white cubes, and a third with four red and six white. A bag is selected at random and three cubes are to be drawn from it with replacement each time. The Prediction Theorem enables us to determine, for example, the probability that all three of the cubes to be drawn will be red. There are thus three hypotheses as to the bag selected:

A: The chosen bag has eight red and two white cubes
B: The chosen bag has five red and five white cubes
C: The chosen bag has four red and six white cubes

Obviously these hypotheses are mutually exclusive and jointly exhaustive in the given context, and since the selection was random we assign the same probability to each such that—as dictated by Theorem 8—they sum to 1.

$$\Pr(A) = \Pr(B) = \Pr(C) = 1/3$$

Now let D represent the statement that in three draws with replacement all the cubes were red. The draws are independent, so we have

$$\Pr(D/A) = (8/10)^3 \qquad \Pr(D/B) = (5/10)^3 \qquad \Pr(D/C) = (4/10)^3$$

Applying Theorem 11, we now calculate $Pr(D)$:

$$Pr(D) = Pr(A)Pr(D/A) + Pr(B)Pr(D/B) + Pr(C)Pr(D/C)$$
$$= (1/3)(8/10)^3 + (1/3)(5/10)^3 + (1/3)(4/10)^3$$
$$= \frac{512 + 125 + 64}{3000} = 701/3000 = 0.234$$

Suppose further that in three independent draws all the cubes were in fact red. Such a result would confirm (raise the probability of) hypothesis A and disconfirm (lower the probability of) hypothesis C. That is, given the evidence in D, we would expect $Pr(A/D) > Pr(A)$ and $Pr(C/D) < Pr(C)$. Determining conditional values like $Pr(A/D)$ and $Pr(C/D)$ is accomplished by our next theorem. It enables us to calculate the probability of a hypothesis given some new evidence from the initial probabilities of the hypotheses together with the "inverse" probabilities like $Pr(D/A)$ and $Pr(D/C)$. Known as "Bayes' Theorem," it provides us with a basic method of determining the extent to which hypotheses are confirmed or disconfirmed on the basis of new evidence.

Theorem 12 (Bayes' Theorem): If $p_1, \ldots, p_n$ are mutually exclusive and jointly exhaustive on condition q, then for $i = 1, \ldots, n$:

$$Pr(p_i/r \ \& \ q) = \frac{Pr(p_i/q) \times Pr(r/p_i \ \& \ q)}{\sum\limits_{i=1}^{n} [Pr(p_i/q) \times Pr(r/p_i \ \& \ q)]}$$

PROOF: Assume that $p_1, \ldots, p_n$ are mutually exclusive and jointly exhaustive on q

TF: $(r \ \& \ p_i)(p_i \ \& \ r)$ for each $i = 1, \ldots, n$

Thm.5: $Pr(r \ \& \ p_i/q) = Pr(p_i \ \& \ r/q)$

Ax.2: $Pr(r/q) \times Pr(p_i/r \ \& \ q) = Pr(p_i/q) \times Pr(r/p_i \ \& \ q)$

AR: $Pr(p_i/r \ \& \ q) = \dfrac{Pr(p_i/q) \times Pr(r/p_i \ \& \ q)}{Pr(r/q)}$

Thm.11 and assumption:

$$Pr(p_i/r \ \& \ q) = \frac{Pr(p_i/q) \times Pr(r/p_i \ \& \ q)}{\sum\limits_{i=1}^{n} [Pr(p_i/q) \times Pr(r/p_i \ \& \ q)]}$$

(It is assumed in all this that $Pr(r/q) > 0$.

Returning to our example, let us now calculate the probabilities of our three hypotheses given the evidence in D. Note that these values must—in conformity with Theorem 8—sum to 1, and hence $Pr(C/D)$ is obtained merely by subtracting the sum of the other values from 1.

$$Pr(A/D) = \frac{Pr(A)Pr(D/A)}{Pr(A)Pr(D/A) + Pr(B)Pr(D/B) + Pr(C)Pr(D/C)}$$

$$= \frac{(1/3)(8/10)^3}{(1/3)(8/10)^3 + (1/3)(5/10)^3 + (1/3)(4/10)^3} = 512/701 = 0.73$$

$$Pr(B/D) = \frac{(1/3)(5/10)^3}{701/3000} = 0.178$$

$$Pr(C/D) = 1 - (0.73 + 0.178) = 0.092$$

As expected, D provides a substantial degree of confirmation for hypothesis A since the new value of 0.73 is much higher than the original value of 1/3. Similarly, the new value of C is considerably lower than 1/3 and therefore has been disconfirmed to a significant degree.

Some terminology will be helpful here. The initial value of a hypothesis, $Pr(p_i/q)$, is said to be the hypothesis's **prior probability**— it is the value prior to factoring in the new evidence. The value $Pr(p_i/r \, \& \, q)$ is hence termed the **posterior probability** of the hypothesis, wherein the influence of result r is taken into account. The values assigned to r for each of the hypotheses under consideration (i.e., the inverse probabilities $Pr(r/p_i \, \& \, q)$) are often called **likelihoods.** Bayes' Theorem is thus a means of calculating the posterior probabilities of a set of mutually exclusive and jointly exhaustive hypotheses from their prior probabilities and their likelihoods. It should also be noted that repeated experimentation among a set of competing hypotheses involves iterated application of Bayes' Theorem; what is a posterior probability at one point in time becomes a prior probability later, when new test results are being sought. Such iteration ideally is to culminate in one of the hypotheses being decisively confirmed.

When only two mutually exclusive and jointly exhaustive hypotheses are at issue, p and q, the latter will be true under exactly the same conditions as the negation of p, hence $q \leftrightarrow \sim p$. This being so, calculating the posterior probabilities in such a case can be streamlined somewhat. By Theorem 5, $Pr(q/r) = Pr(\sim p/r)$, and by Theorem 2 and Bayes' Theorem we have

$$Pr(p/s \, \& \, r) = x/(x + y) \qquad Pr(\sim p/s \, \& \, r) = y/(x + y)$$

where $x = \Pr(p/r)\Pr(s/p \ \& \ r)$, $y = \Pr(\sim p/r)\Pr(s/\sim p \ \& \ r)$, and s contains the new evidence. By AR then, we obtain a corollary to Bayes' Theorem:

$$\frac{\Pr(p/s \ \& \ r)}{\Pr(\sim p/s \ \& \ r)} = \frac{\Pr(p/r)\Pr(s/p \ \& \ r)}{\Pr(\sim p/r)\Pr(s/\sim p \ \& \ r)} = \frac{x}{y}$$

Suppose your friend Al claims that the Celtics are 3 to 2 favorites to win their next game; that is, $\Pr(C) = 3/5$. You later discover that their star forward might not play up to par owing to a recurrent injury. Because of his importance to the team, you estimate the probability that he fails to play up to par (P) *given* that the Celtics do in fact win to be low, say 1/10. Moreover you suppose that the chance he played below par given a victory by the opposition to be much higher, say 7/10.[7] You can now determine the probability that the Celtics will win given a subpar performance by the star:

$$\frac{\Pr(C/P)}{\Pr(\sim C/P)} = \frac{\Pr(C)\Pr(P/C)}{\Pr(\sim C)\Pr(P/\sim C)} = \frac{(3/5)(1/10)}{(2/5)(7/10)} = \frac{3/50}{14/50} = \frac{3}{14}$$

In other words, the odds in favor of the Celts winning are now 3 to 14 and the posterior *probability* is 3/17. Correspondingly, the "posterior odds" favoring the opposition are 14 to 3 and the posterior probability is 14/17.

So if Al is still willing to bet \$3 on the Celtics at 3 to 2, it will be to your advantage—if your estimates are anywhere near correct—to bet against him. On your calculations you stand a 14/17 chance of winning \$3 and only a 3/17 chance of losing \$2 (since Al's odds are 3 to 2 in favor, he is presumably willing to bet \$3 to win \$2).

Bayes' Theorem is of particular relevance to those scientific hypotheses in which exact probability values can be realistically assigned. Such is the case in disciplines like quantum mechanics and genetics, where many laws are statistical in character. The following example drawn from the latter field provides a good illustration.[8]

Biologists have distinguished two genetic varieties of black mice: "homozygotes" that, when mated with a brown mouse, yield nothing but black offspring, and "heterozygotes" that are expected to yield one-half black offspring and one-half brown offspring when mated with a brown mouse. Suppose then a black mouse is to be mated with a brown; we do not know to which genetic type the black mouse belongs, but we do know that each of its parents has already given birth to some brown offspring. The parents thus are both heterozygotes, and a mating of such a pair typically produces a proportion of one homozygote to two heterozygote to one brown.

So prior to the test mating there is a probability of 1/3 that our black is a homozygote and 2/3 that it is a heterozygote. Where H_1 says that it is a homozygote and H_2 a heterozygote, and where T includes the information that both parents are heterozygotes, we have as our prior probabilities:

$$\Pr(H_1/T) = 1/3 \qquad \Pr(H_2/T) = 2/3$$

Now suppose the test mating with a brown mouse produces the result (B) that seven offspring were born, all of which are black. Our likelihoods are

$$\Pr(B/H_1 \text{ \& } T) = 1 \qquad \Pr(B/H_2 \text{ \& } T) = (1/2)^7 = 1/128$$

The Prediction Theorem enables us to find the chance of this result occurring:

$$\Pr(B/T) = (1/3)(1) + (2/3)(1/128) = 1/3 + 1/192 = 65/192$$

We may now determine the posterior probabilities either by using Bayes' Theorem

$$\Pr(H_1/B \text{ \& } T) = \frac{1/3}{65/192} = 64/65$$
$$\Pr(H_2/B \text{ \& } T) = 1 - 64/65 = 1/65$$

or by using our corollary

$$\frac{\Pr(H_1/B \text{ \& } T)}{\Pr(H_2/B \text{ \& } T)} = \frac{64/192}{1/192} = \frac{64}{1}$$

In any case, B obviously provides strong confirmation for H_1.

Several points about this example deserve mention. Note first that a probability of 1 is assigned to $\Pr(B/H_1 \text{ \& } T)$. Now if 'homozygote' is *defined* in terms of producing exclusively black offspring, then of course $(H_1 \text{ \& } T) \rightarrow B$ and by Axiom 3 a value of 1 is correct. If on the other hand—as is in fact the case—H_1 & T do not logically imply B but instead only supply it with an extraordinary degree of confirmation, an assignment of 1 might be questioned. But if in fact through the many years of observation and testing no homozygous mouse has under the stated conditions yielded nonblack offspring, and if there are established laws causally linking the genetic constitution of homozygous mice with exclusively black offspring, then although we may not be certain of the truth of B given H_1 & T in the sense of its being a deductively valid consequence, we nonetheless can accord it a "practical certainty" of being true. And the assignment of unity to $Pr(B/H_1 \& T)$ would be taken to reflect such certainty; the truth of B on condition $H_1 \& T$ is regarded as a bona fide item in our stock of knowledge rather than a hypothesis possibly warranting further investigation. Even so, some philosophers have balked at the idea of assigning a value of 1 to any pair $<p, q>$ where it is false that $q{\rightarrow}p$, so it might be noted in passing that if that value is replaced by, say, 0.99, the resulting posterior probabilities would differ only negligibly from the present ones.

It is also perhaps worthwhile to note some underlying assumptions operative in the example. Theorem 7 was implicitly employed in determining the probability of $Pr(B/H_2 \& T)$, so it is assumed that the seven births constitute an independent set of events. More important, in assigning the value 1/3 to $Pr(H_1/T)$, we have assumed that this value is unaffected by the fact that exactly seven offspring were produced when the mating with a brown mouse occurred. Mendelian genetics is mute on this point, but it might be more—or less—difficult to obtain seven offspring from a homozygous-brown mating than from a heterozygous-brown one.

Often of course we cannot assign specific numerical values to the hypotheses prior to testing, either because we do not know what they are or because such an assignment would be arbitrary or unrealistic. Yet Bayes' Theorem is still very useful. To take the first kind of case, suppose we do not know the specific values for $Pr(H_1/T)$ and $Pr(H_2/T)$; if we simply designate them as x and $1 - x$, respectively, then with some arithmetic maneuvering we have

$$Pr(H_1/B \& T) = \frac{x}{x + [(1 - x)/128]} = \frac{128x}{128x + (1 - x)} = \frac{128x}{127x + 1}$$

$$Pr(H_2/B \& T) = \frac{(1 - x)/128}{x + [(1 - x)/128]} = \frac{1 - x}{128x + (1 - x)} = \frac{1 - x}{127x + 1}$$

Now, $128x > 1 - x$ if and only if $x > 1/129$. Hence $Pr(H_1/B \& T) > Pr(H_2/B \& T)$ if $x > 1/129$. In other words, if the prior probability of our black mouse being homozygous exceeds 1/129, then the posterior probability of his being homozygous given all black offspring in a brown mating will be greater than the posterior probability of it being heterozygous given the same conditions. Moreover, we could determine the degree to which it is greater (or smaller) once we specify a minimum value for x; that is, if for some real number y, $Pr(H_1/T) > y$, then there is a z such that $Pr(H_1/B \& T) > z$. Bayes' Theorem thus does not lose its applicability simply because exact probability values are not known.

A classic illustration of Bayes' Theorem is the clash between the wave (W) and corpuscular (C) theories of light in the mid-nineteenth century. Relative to the evidence then available the two theories were not only mutually exclusive but to an approximation jointly exhaustive; that is, Pr(W & C/E) was virtually 0 (the wave-particle theory of the present day was not to be developed for many years to come). There were advocates on both sides, and the general feeling was that, although some recent findings favored the wave theory, it did not enjoy a decisive advantage over its competitor. Thus in terms of prior probabilities, Pr(W/E) > Pr(C/E) but the difference was not large.

> One of the supporters of the corpuscular theory was the mathematician Poisson, who deduced from the mathematical formulation of the wave theory that, if that theory were true, there should be a bright spot in the center of the shadow of a disk. Poisson declared that this absurd result showed that the wave theory was untenable, but when the experiment was actually performed the bright spot was there. Such a result was unthinkable on the corpuscular theory, so this turned into a triumph for the wave theory . . .[9]

Let S express the result of the experiment. On Poisson's calculations, we should expect Pr(S/W & E) to be very close to 1 (because of factors like the exact formulation of the theory, the design of the experiment, and the accuracy of the observations, it is perhaps best not to assign a value of 1 even though W→S) and conversely the likelihood for the corpuscular theory should be near 0. When we plug these into the Bayesian formula,

$$\frac{xy}{xy + zw}$$

where $y = $ Pr(S/W & E) and $w = $ Pr(S/C & E), it becomes immediately apparent that the posterior probability of the wave hypothesis not only exceeds its prior probability, but is *considerably* greater than the posterior probability of the corpuscular theory—indeed since the quantity in the denominator, *zw,* is so small, the posterior probability of the wave hypothesis is itself very close to unity. The corpuscular theory, in the formulation it had been given prior to the experiment, had to be rejected (however, it often happens in such cases that the refuted hypothesis is subsequently revised to accommodate the new findings).

Note that this application of Bayes' Theorem did not require exact probability values; the fact that the difference between the two likelihoods is so very large means that the difference between the posterior probabilities of the two hypotheses is large enough to be decisive. Of course as later developments dictated, the wave theory eventually underwent revision, evolving over the years into the current theory. Theories often undergo revision and reformulation as new evidence comes to light and as "old" evidence (the information in 'E') is found wanting. In the present case, both theories presupposed the existence of an "ether" as a medium that sustains the waves or corpuscles, a presupposition that was eventually discarded in the late nineteenth century after a famous experiment by Michaelson and Morley. So despite the high value assigned to Pr(W/S & E), the wave theory of the mid-nineteenth century never achieved the status of a "final" answer.

Exercises

1. The odds in favor of Purdue beating Indiana are 7 to 5. The odds against Indiana are 2 to 1, and the odds against a tie are 11 to 1. You hear a rumor from an often reliable source that some gamblers will spike the Purdue water bucket with prune juice, and estimate the chance of that having occurred given an Indiana win to be 4/7. However, you figure that the chance that it occurred is only 1/10 given a Purdue win, and 1/8 given a tie. What is the probability that Purdue will win given the truth of the rumor?

2. A box contains eight red pencils and six blue ones; another box, externally indistinguishable from the first, contains four red ones and six blue ones. One of the boxes is chosen at random and a pencil drawn from it. What is the probability that it is red? Suppose it is red; what is the probability that the box with eight red pencils was chosen? Suppose three pencils are drawn with replacement each time, and two are red and one is blue. What is the probability that the box with eight red pencils was chosen?

3. Suppose we divide a bridge deck into two packs. Pack A contains all the diamonds, three clubs, and seven hearts. Pack B thus contains all the spades, ten clubs, and six hearts. The two packs are placed behind you and a die is tossed. You cannot see the die but are told that if it shows a two or a four, you will be dealt (and shown) a card from pack A. If it shows another number, you will be dealt one from pack B. What is the chance that

    a. You are dealt a heart?
    b. The card was dealt from pack A given that it is a heart?
    c. The card was dealt from pack B given that it is a heart?
    d. The card was dealt from pack A given that it is a heart or a club?

Suppose now you are dealt a second card on the condition that if the first was red, the second will be dealt from pack A, and if it was black, the second will be drawn from pack B (in both cases the first card is replaced). What is the probability that

   e. The second card was drawn from pack A given that it is red?
   f. The second card was drawn from pack A given that it is black?
   g. Both cards are red?

4. The notorious gambler Fingers Schrag offers to toss coins with you. You suspect that the coin he is using may be loaded and consider three hypotheses: a 1/4 chance that it is fair, a 3/8 chance it is loaded so that the probability of heads is 3/4, and a 3/8 chance it is loaded so that the probability of tails is 3/4. Eight tosses give five heads and three tails. What is the probability that it is loaded?

Section 4. Expected Value _____

   "Probability is the very guide of life," according to Bishop Butler, an eighteenth-century philosopher and theologian. In our daily affairs we are constantly faced with making decisions among alternative courses of action. Before the decision, we usually do not know which of the various possible consequences (or outcomes) of each act will occur—we can determine only how *likely* each is to occur. In an investment decision, such as a real estate venture or a stock purchase, we need to determine how likely it is that we will obtain a reasonable return on our investment and what would be the chance of a financially damaging loss. Since we cannot be certain of such consequences in advance, rational decision involves—at least implicitly—probability estimates. But another factor is involved: we must also consider the *values* of the act's consequences—the potential gains and losses on each investment.

   So we will examine here the rudiments of "decision theory"; that is, rational choice among alternative actions in conditions of uncertainty where the consequences of each act are both mutually exclusive and jointly exhaustive. Our main topic is the concept of the *expected value* (sometimes "expected utility" or "expectation") of an action that meets these conditions. Roughly, it is a measure of how advantageous or disadvantageous or how beneficial or harmful an action is, and as we have already seen, this is a function of both the probabilities and values of the act's possible consequences.

   Before going further, we will make some minor additions to our notation. Boldface small letters **'a'** and **'c'** (with or without subscripts) will be employed, respectively, as *act variables* (ranging over courses of action) and *consequence variables*. Boldface capital letters **'A'** and **'C'** with subscripts will express particular acts (e.g., 'bet $1 on red in roulette') and the consequences of those acts (e.g., 'lose $1'), respectively.

In evaluating a course of action, **a,** on condition q, we must examine the likelihood of its consequences, $\Pr(p_1/\mathbf{a}\ \&\ q)$, $\Pr(p_2/\mathbf{a}\ \&\ q)$, and so forth (where '$p_i$' in effect states that consequence $\mathbf{c}_i$ occurs) and the values (gains or losses) that will accrue if they occur. We will express the latter quantities by the expressions 'Val($\mathbf{c}_1$)', 'Val($\mathbf{c}_2$)', and so on. The expected value of the act itself will be expressed by 'EVal($\mathbf{a}/q$)', where q is the information available to the person considering the action. We define the expected value of **a** on q by the following **Principle of Expected Value** ('EVP' for short):

> **EVP:** If $p_1, \ldots, p_n$ are mutually exclusive and jointly exhaustive on condition q, and $\mathbf{c}_i$ is a consequence of act **a** that occurs if p_i is true, then
>
> $$\mathrm{EVal}(\mathbf{a}/q) = \sum_{i=1}^{n} [\Pr(p_i/\mathbf{a}\ \&\ q) \times \mathrm{Val}(\mathbf{c}_i)]$$

To illustrate, let us examine a simple bet. Most casinos permit what is called the "field bet" at a craps table. It is a one-roll bet in which you win the amount of the bet if a three, four, nine, ten, or eleven is rolled with a pair of dice; you win *twice* that amount if a two or twelve is rolled; and you lose otherwise. Let '$\mathbf{A}_1$' represent wagering $1 on the field bet. Let '$\mathbf{C}_1$', '$\mathbf{C}_2$' and '$\mathbf{C}_3$' express relatively the three consequences: win $1, win $2, and lose $1. Let '$\mathbf{B}_1$', '$\mathbf{B}_2$' and '$\mathbf{B}_3$' abbreviate respectively: a three, four, nine, ten, or eleven is rolled; a two or twelve is rolled; a five, six, seven, or eight is rolled. Then we have (dropping the background statement as usual):

$$
\begin{aligned}
\mathrm{Eval}(\mathbf{A}_1 &= [\Pr(\mathbf{B}_1) \times \mathrm{Val}(\mathbf{C}_1)] + [\Pr(\mathbf{B}_2) \times \mathrm{Val}(\mathbf{C}_2)] + [\Pr(\mathbf{B}_3) \times \mathrm{Val}(\mathbf{C}_3)] \\
&= (14/36)(\$1) + (2/36)(\$2) + (20/36)(-\$1) \\
&= -\$2/36 = -\$0.055
\end{aligned}
$$

That is, a single play of the field bet has an expected value of minus five and one-half cents. Now consider act $\mathbf{A}_2$—that of not playing the field bet. We have a probability of one that you will neither win nor lose (a zero gain and a zero loss); hence nothing ventured, nothing gained *and* nothing lost. So $\mathrm{EVal}(\mathbf{A}_2) = 0$, and $\mathrm{EVal}(\mathbf{A}_2) > \mathrm{EVal}(\mathbf{A}_1)$.

The negative expected value for $\mathbf{A}_1$ means in effect that the bet is unfavorable to the player (and of course favorable to the house, which must cover its costs and turn in a profit). In gambler's jargon, the casino has a 5½ percent "advantage" over the player; on average, for every dollar won by the player the casino wins about $1.055. More fully, suppose the bet is made many times and the frequency of winning $1, winning $2 and losing $1 occur at approximately the rate of the stated probability values; that is, $1 is won about 14/36 of the time, $2 about 2/36 of the time, and $1 is lost around 20/36 of the time (it is unlikely that the frequency will equal exactly the probability but it is very likely as play continues that it will be close to the probability). Then the expected value will be about the same as the net loss; if you played seventy times, won $1 twenty-seven times, $2 four times, and lost thirty-nine times, then your net loss would be $4. And 4/70 is about 5.5%.

It is important here at the outset to distinguish between the *expected value of an act*—EVal($\mathbf{a}, q$)—and the *value of a consequence* of the act. The latter is simply the worth attached to the consequence; Val($\mathbf{c}_i$) measures the value of degree of gain or loss that accrues to a possible outcome of the action and does not in itself presuppose the concept of probability. Expected value, however, is a function of these values *and* probability; an act's expected value may be regarded as a weighted average of the values of its mutually exclusive and jointly exhaustive consequences, each such value being weighted by the probability with which we "expect" the consequence to occur.

The expected value of an unfavorable bet is negative and that of a favorable one is positive, but if you and I are tossing a coin and you win $1 if it comes up heads and I win $1 otherwise, then the expected value for each of us is $(1/2)(\$1) + (1/2)(-\$1) = 0$. Obviously then, a *fair bet* is one whose expected value is 0. To carry this a step further, the greater the expected value, the more "desirable" the choice. The **Rule of Maximizing Expected Value** rests on this idea; it tells us that, where we are confronted with a range of alternative actions, *we ought to choose one with maximum expected value,* that is, an act such that its expected value is not exceeded by any of the alternatives. This rule has often been proposed as a standard for rational decision making, and according to it we should opt for *not* making the field bet. Yet of course thousands of people make that bet every day. Are all of them being irrational? Or does this show that the rule of maximizing expected value should be rejected? Clearly there are complications associated with the rule, and we shall discuss some of them later on.

The concept of expected value is most readily applied in situations where both the probabilities and values are assigned real numbers: for probabilities, an x such that $0 \leq x \leq 1$, and for values, a positive or negative number expressing the gain or loss. But the concept is still applicable with some loss of exactitude in cases where assigning a probability value is the result of an estimate rather than a calculation. The more serious obstacle to a wide-ranging use of the expected value notion is that of expressing the values of an act's consequences in numerical terms. Philosophers and other writers historically have grappled with the task of defining a quantitative measure of value, but an examination of what little progress has been made would take us too far afield. For now we will suppose that a real number may be assigned a consequence that is indicative of its worth to the person making the decision, and in the simplest cases we will look at, these numbers represent monetary units. More will be said about this assumption later; we employ it now because it enables us to see clearly how the expected value concept works.

It is sometimes said in gambling books (and western movies) that one should never "draw to an inside straight" when playing draw poker. An inside straight is one where only four out of the remaining forty-seven unseen cards can "fill" the straight; for example, if you were dealt a three, four, six, seven, and an unhelpful fifth card, discarding the latter and drawing one more will complete the straight if and only if the drawn card is a five. Now suppose you are playing poker with five others. Each of you has placed in the pot an "ante" of 25 cents before the cards were dealt. After the deal, the first player bet $1 and was called (matched) by the other four. The bet is now to you and you are holding the aforementioned hand. Do you drop out or do you bet a dollar for the opportunity of drawing one more card?

We will suppose that your knowledge of the other players and the fact that a straight is a strong hand in this game makes you confident that you will win if you draw a five. Ignoring any betting that may occur after the draw, let us evaluate the two courses of action. There is now $6.50 in the pot and a 4/47 chance of winning it, but there is a probability of 43/47 that you will lose your dollar (your 25 cent ante occurred at an earlier stage of the game and your decision *now* should be based on a potential prize of $6.50 and a potential loss of $1). We thus have

$$\text{EVal}(\mathbf{A}_1) = (4/47)(\$6.50) + (43/47)(-\$1) = -\$17/47 = -\$0.36$$

On the other hand, the expected value of dropping out $(\mathbf{A}_2)$ is of course 0; since $\text{EVal}(\mathbf{A}_2) > \text{EVal}(\mathbf{A}_1)$, $\mathbf{A}_2$ is the better course, as the maxim states.

Had you held a "bobtail" straight, matters would have been different. Here you hold, for example, a four, five, six, and seven. Now either a three or an eight will fill the straight, and the expected value of this act $(\mathbf{A}_3)$ exceeds 0:

$$\text{EVal}(\mathbf{A}_3) = (8/47)(\$6.50) + (39/47)(-\$1) = \$13/47 = \$0.28$$

Suppose however it is stipulated that at least one player must have a hand containing a pair of jacks or better (a higher pair, two pair, or stronger hand) for play to continue. If no player announces holding a hand of that quality, the cards are returned and the deck reshuffled. A new hand is dealt *and* another 25 cent ante is contributed. Let us imagine that four deals have been made with no player having jacks or better. On the fifth, the first player announces jacks and bets a dollar; the bet is called by the other four. You again hold the three, four, six, and seven and are faced with the question of whether to call the bet and draw one more card. Since the pot now holds $12.50, the calculation is much different this time:

$$\mathrm{EVal}(\mathbf{A}_4) = (4/47)(\$12.50) + (43/47)(-\$1) = \$7/47 = \$0.15$$

Whereas $\mathrm{EVal}(\mathbf{A}_1) < 0$, $\mathrm{EVal}(\mathbf{A}_4) > 0$. Though it lacks the rhetorical appeal, perhaps we should adopt the new maxim: *almost* never draw to an inside straight.

Some gamblers have claimed that on an otherwise fair bet one is sure to win over the long run by making the same bet consistently (always betting heads, for example) and *doubling* the bet after each loss. Thus if you bet a dollar on heads and tails comes up, you should wager $2 on the next toss. According to their reasoning, you are sure to win eventually because extended runs of all tails are extremely unlikely. Even the longest run will end sometime, and when that occurs you will be money ahead since you "pyramided" your bets all along the way (i.e., doubling after each loss including the one just before you won).

If this is sound reasoning, every casino would now be in bankruptcy. Of course since you have only a finite amount of wealth, an extended run of tails could, if it lasted long enough, exhaust it. But such a run is indeed very unlikely, so let us suppose that you have decided in advance how long to play (say, until you lose all your funds or until you win some particular amount—though in such a case the game conceivably might go on forever). To keep things to a manageable size, suppose you are betting on heads and will begin with a $7 stake, intending to play exactly three times (the most you can play if you lose each time). You bet $1 on the first toss. After each win, you bet $1, and after each loss you double your previous bet. There are eight possible outcomes with the payoffs listed in the table that follows. Note that the figures on the far right sum to 0. Hence the expected value of the doubling strategy is exactly the same as that of betting $1 on each toss regardless of what occurred on previous tosses, or for that matter, betting all $7 on a *single* toss of the coin.

First toss	Second toss	Third toss	Pr	Gain/loss	Pr × gain/loss
H	H	H	1/8	$3	3/8
H	H	T	1/8	$1	1/8
H	T	H	1/8	$2	2/8
H	T	T	1/8	−$2	−2/8
T	H	H	1/8	$2	2/8
T	H	T	1/8	$0	0
T	T	H	1/8	$1	1/8
T	T	T	1/8	−$7	−7/8

Moreover, it should be clear (though the reader is invited to verify these matters) that, if we extend the number of tosses or enlarge the stakes or set a maximum on winnings, the expected value will remain 0. The doubling strategy does not provide an advantage over the house.

But gambling is not the only activity where EVP is readily applied. Determining whether to insure a person's home, car, or life is basically similar to assessing the attractiveness of a wager. Of course it is a much more complex calculation, but both probabilities and gains or losses can be given quantitative expression and the latter specified in units of currency. As an example, suppose Smith's only major asset is a collection of precious gems valued at $30,000. Suppose further his insurance company determines from their records and data that the chance of loss (owing to theft or accident, say) for a person in Smith's circumstances is 0.004 in a given year (to keep things simple, we shall ignore any appreciation or depreciation in value over the year). Where P_1 says that the gems are lost, we set the expected value to 0 and solve for x:

$$\Pr(P_1)[-(\$30{,}000 - x)] + \Pr(\sim P_1)x = 0$$
$$(0.004)[-(\$30{,}000 - x)] + (0.996)x = 0$$

The amount, x, the company must charge to break even works out to $120. But of course insurance companies are not charities and must charge more than this amount to cover operating costs and profits. The actual yearly premium, then, will be larger; if on a probability of 0.004 the company charges at the rate 0.0045, then the premium will be 0.0045 × $30,000 or $135 and the expected value for the insurance company will be $15.

But now let us look at the matter from the insured's viewpoint. Smith is faced with two alternatives:

A_1: Not to insure with either loss of his asset at probability 0.004 or an asset at the end of the year worth $30,000 at probability 0.996.

A_2: Purchase insurance, in which case he is worth $30,000 less the premium at the end of the year.

Not surprisingly, if we calculate the expected value in dollars, it would appear that insurance is not worth it:

$$\text{EVal}(A_1) = (0.004)(0) + (0.996)(\$30,000) = \$29,880$$
$$\text{EVal}(A_2) = \$30,000 - \$135 = \$29,865$$

By the Rule of Maximizing Expected Value, Smith should not insure, but this surely seems incorrect not only for Smith but for most people. Once we move beyond acts like wagering and attempt to apply the rule in practical everyday choice contexts, values are not in general to be measured in monetary units.

The reason is simple and basic: For most rational agents in most situations, the value of money does not increase at the same rate as its quantity. To see this, let us first examine a not-so-everyday choice. Suppose you are asked to make two draws with replacement from a bridge deck. Let

P_1: At least one of the cards is a diamond
P_2: Both cards are diamonds

Now suppose one of the Rockefellers offers you the following choice:

A_3: $1 million tax free if P_1, nothing otherwise
A_4: $10 million tax free if P_2, nothing otherwise

Note what happens when we calculate the expected value in dollars:

$$\text{EVal}(A_3) = (7/16)(\$1,000,000) + (9/16)(0) = \$437,500.00$$
$$\text{EVal}(A_4) = (1/16)(\$10,000,000) + (15/16)(0) = \$652,343.75$$

In this calculation, $\text{EVal}(A_4) > \text{EVal}(A_3)$ and by the Rule of Maximizing Expected Value (hereafter, 'RMV' for short) A_4 should be chosen. But this would be a ludicrous choice for most people—certainly for those of us who have not *already* acquired a million dollars and may never have another opportunity. Unless you are a millionaire or in some other way a special case, you would surely choose A_3 since it gives you nearly a one-half chance at $1 million dollars while A_4 gives you a 15/16 chance at gaining nothing at all. Moreover, a 7/16 shot at $1 million dollars is worth more than a 1/16 shot at an amount ten times larger since $10 million dollars is simply not worth ten times $1 million for the vast majority of people. $10 million would not make ten times as much difference to us in terms of our well-being, security, happiness, and so on. This example illustrates what is called the **Diminishing Value of Money Principle:** *The value of money increases at a slower rate than its quantity.*

To spell this out a bit, suppose for the moment that the value of money is proportional to *the cube root* of the number of dollars; that is, $\text{Val}(\$x) = x^{1/3}$ units of value. We shall call these nonmonetary value units *utiles;* hence $\text{Val}(\$8) = 2$ utiles but $\text{Val}(\$27) = 3$ utiles, only a 50% increase in value but over a threefold increase in money. We now recalculate acts $\mathbf{A}_3$ and $\mathbf{A}_4$ using utiles as specified by this function. Since $(1{,}000{,}000)^{1/3} = 100$ and $(10{,}000{,}000)^{1/3} \approx 216$, we have

$$\text{EVal}(\mathbf{A}_3) = (7/16)(100) = 43.75 \text{ utiles}$$
$$\text{EVal}(\mathbf{A}_4) = (1/16)(216) = 13.5 \text{ utiles}$$

Now by the RMV we should choose $\mathbf{A}_3$, which is what we should expect. The cube root function is used here because it is relatively simple and provides a clear illustration of the diminishing value principle. It is not being claimed that this particular function is an especially appropriate one, either as a description of or a prescription for our value estimates. The point could have been made using a variety of such "utility functions."

Thus many of the decisions to be made using EVP ought to employ the notion of a utile—a unit of value related to money by a utility function. Otherwise it would be difficult indeed to take RMV seriously, and there is no better example of this than the insurance decision cited earlier. But if we calculate in utiles—using the cube root function—insurance is worth it for Smith:

$$\text{EVal}(\mathbf{A}_1) = (0.004)(0) + (0.996)(31.07) = 30.94 \text{ utiles}$$
$$\text{EVal}(\mathbf{A}_2) = (\$30{,}000 - \$135)^{1/3} = 31.03 \text{ utiles}$$

The diminishing value principle thus provides a justification for insuring, at least where the company's add-on for costs and profit is "reasonable." By insuring we obtain security in that we avoid risk and at a small cost are assured of a specific amount of wealth. Insurance enables us to eliminate some of the uncertain and unpredictable elements of our lives, and most people find that desirable since they wish to know their fates to whatever extent possible. Gamblers on the other hand enjoy uncertainty, deliberately incurring risk in order to maximize their wealth. Most of them, however, are willing to wager only on small quantities of their total wealth—hence an insured homeowner may nonetheless participate in small stakes poker games.

It should not be thought, therefore, that a person who engages in the diametrically opposed activities of gambling and insuring is *thereby* irrational. Perhaps the enjoyment derived from wagering small amounts balances the risk undertaken, or it might be that for some people a principle of *increasing* value is operative for smaller sums of money, that is, the value of money increases faster than its quantity up to a point (a crude example would be $\text{Val}(\$x) = x^2$ utiles, for relatively small x). The diminishing value principle would then come into play for more substantial portions of the total wealth. An increasing value principle would thus justify gambling for smaller sums, while insuring for much larger sums would be justified as well. At any rate, it seems clear that most of us enjoy *some* uncertainty in a controlled situation, but not too much.

A constraint on our use of the expected value concept must be mentioned: first, the values placed on the consequences of the acts a person is to choose from must be finite, and second, one of the following should be stipulated:

a. Each act has only finitely many consequences, *or*
b. Values must be "bounded," i.e. there are numbers n and m such that no value to be assigned a consequence exceeds n or is less than m.[10]

The reason for these restrictions is best brought out by considering a very simple act known as the *St. Petersburg Game:* A coin is tossed until heads first appears, at which point the game ends. If heads first appears on the nth toss, the player is paid 2^n utiles.

What is the expected value of a single play of this game? The coin may come up heads on the first toss or not until the fourth toss or the tenth or the one-hundredth or the one-millionth. Clearly these latter cases are *very* improbable, but they are not impossible and hence must be considered as possible consequences of the act. The nth such consequence has a probability of $(1/2)^n$ and a value of 2^n, and there are infinitely many of them. So we have

$$(1/2)(2) + (1/2)^2(2^2) + \ldots + (1/2)^n(2^n) + \ldots = 1 + 1 + \ldots + 1 + \ldots = \infty$$

A single play would thus have an infinite expected value! The *St. Petersburg Paradox* is simply the observation that a play of the game obviously is not worth anywhere near that much. If it were, then by RMV it would be preferable to an act like receiving a gift of a billion dollars; conversely, you should be willing to put up your entire fortune if someone should offer you a single play of the game. To generate the paradox, however, it is essential that the payoff for the nth consequence be at least 2^n; if for example the payoff were n itself, the game would have an expected value of only 2 utiles.[11]

The upshot of the paradox is that if there is such a thing as an infinite value, then acts and consequences that involve it are beyond the scope of the expected value concept. In fact, however, this constraint may not be a serious one; historically, philosophers and others who have wrestled with such issues have found the notion of infinite value a rather dubious one (though see Pascal's Wager later). In any case, we may avoid the paradox if we require that values for consequences be finite and require in addition statement (a); it will follow that the expected value of any act is finite. Alternatively, we may use (b) together with the restriction on finite consequence values to accomplish the same end. That is, if there is a greatest value that is finite, then the paradox disappears.

To drive this home, suppose a benevolent multimillionaire worth exactly \$16,777,216 offers you a single play of the St. Petersburg game with a payoff of $\$8^n$ for the nth consequence. Since \$16,777,216 = $\$8^8$, you will win every cent he owns if you are so fortunate as to have heads not appear until the eighth toss! Now suppose further that the value of money, as before, equals the cube root of the number of dollars. The value of \$16,777,216 is thus 256 utiles. Your calculation then becomes

$$(1/2)(2) + (1/2)^2(2^2) + \ldots + (1/2)^8(2^8)$$
$$(1/2)(2) + (1/4)(4) + \ldots + (1/256)(256)$$

If \$16,777,216 is the greatest monetary value at stake, then the act has only eight possible consequences and its expected value is finite (8 utiles).

Addendum: Pascal's Wager: One of the founders of probability theory was the seventeenth-century philosopher-mathematician-theologian Blaise Pascal, who put forward a very provocative argument for believing in God and joining the Church.[12] If you adopt Christianity, he argued, salvation becomes a possibility for you, and if you are saved you will gain infinite value in the form of eternal life in heaven. Now at the very least there is some probability that Christianity is true, and moreover some probability that you will obtain salvation if you become a believing Christian. Since the chance of success is finite and the value to be gained is infinite, the expected value of adopting Christianity is infinite. So to maximize your expected value, join the Church and believe in God; the expected value of not becoming a Christian is after all only finite. As the difference in expected value shows, if you do not join the Church but Christianity is true, you will have lost out on enormous value; and if you do join but Christianity turns out not to be true, you have lost nothing.

When a decision to adopt a religious faith is made in the calculating manner of a poker player deciding whether to draw to a four-flush, one wonders how sincere such belief can be and whether it could bring about salvation. Moreover as noted earlier it is not at all clear that there is such a thing as an infinite quantity of value, and in any case we have just examined a good reason for supposing that expected values must be finite. But Pascal at least thought that life in heaven was of infinite (positive) value, so perhaps we can grant him that for the sake of argument. For in fact neither of these objections has much to do with the logic of Pascal's argument, and that as we shall see is where the most basic problem lies.

Let us suppose that in southern California there is a weird religious cult, Mephisto we shall call it, whose major tenets are that, first, God does not exist; second, a devil of great power and evil intent does exist; third, the devil rewards believers in Mephisto and punishes all those (including Christians) who do not believe; and last, believers in Mephisto will experience eternal happiness in the afterlife while nonbelievers will be condemned to endless pain and suffering. From the standpoint of Mephisto the expected value of becoming a Christian is not only not infinite but not even positive. Less facetiously, the same could be argued for any of Christianity's genuine competitors (e.g., Islam) as long as, first, they hold that salvation is possible only within their faith and damnation will be the result for nonbelievers, and second, there is a nonzero chance that their doctrines are true.

What the Mephisto case points up is that Pascal's argument assumes one of the major points at issue; viz., whether adopting Christianity will enhance your prospects for salvation. To ascribe such an enormously greater expected value to Christianity over its competitors it must be tacitly assumed that the probability of a contrary faith is nil. As we saw at the beginning, expected value is a conditional concept. EVal($\mathbf{a}/q$) expresses $\mathbf{a}$'s expected value relative to q. If in Pascal's argument, q implicitly includes the claim that competitors such as Islam have no chance of being true, then perhaps the expected value is infinite; but the argument is then worthless—of course Christianity is the better pick if it is assumed at the outset that these competing faiths are all false! But if q does not include this claim, Pascal is just wrong in holding that we lose nothing if we adopt Christianity and it turns out to be false; should a competing faith be true we could lose a great deal. His calculation is simply wrong when contrary faiths are assigned nonzero probabilities.

Exercises

Unless otherwise noted, make calculations in monetary units.

1. What are the expected values of the following choices?

    a. You will receive $500 if an ace is drawn from a bridge deck, otherwise you pay $40.

    b. You bet $5; if heads comes up once in two tosses you win $2; if it comes up heads both times you win $3; otherwise you lose.

    c. You receive a $5 birthday check from Aunt Mabel.

    d. You estimate there is only one chance in twenty of being detected by the IRS if you cheat on your income tax in such a way as to save yourself $150 in tax; on the other hand, if you are caught you will be fined $3,000.

2. After perusing the Racing Form, you estimate the probability of Freddy Favorite winning the Podunk Stakes to be 0.45 while that of Longshot Lou is only 1/11. If Freddy pays even money and the odds offered against Longshot are 8 to 1, which is the better bet?

3. You decide to use the original doubling strategy to win just $1, meaning you will play until you win just once (then quitting) or until you go broke. If you begin play with a stake of $3, what is your expected value? Suppose we extend the doubling strategy to four tosses and triple the stakes after each loss. Will this alter the expected value? Explain.

4. Figure 2 shows a (partial) illustration of a typical Nevada crap table.

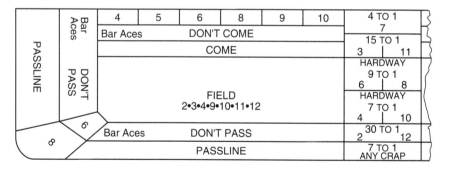

Figure 2.

Terminology: A *natural* is a seven or eleven. A *crap* is a two, three, or twelve. A *hardway* four is a two-two combination. A *soft* four is a one-three or three-one combination. *Aces* is a two. *Center bets* are those in the center of the table (here on the right) except those labeled "hardway." *Corner bets* are those in the lower left corner.

    a. Center bets are one-roll bets. You win if the number bet is rolled and lose otherwise. You are paid according to the stated odds. Calculate the expected values of any three of the six center bets (use $1 bets).

    b. In a hardway bet, the dice are rolled until *either* the hardway number you bet is rolled—in which case you win—or a seven or soft combination of the same number is rolled—in which case you lose. You are paid according to the stated odds. What are the expected values of $1 hardway bets on six and on ten?

    c. Like the hardway bet, in a corner bet you bet that the shooter will toss the number bet *before* tossing a seven. You win the amount you bet. What is the expected value of the eight bet?

    d. The pass line bet (the basic bet): if the shooter rolls a natural, you win; if a crap is rolled, you lose. If another number is rolled, the shooter keeps rolling until *either* that number is rolled again—in which case you win—*or* a seven is rolled—in which case you lose—whichever comes first. You win the amount bet.

        1. Calculate the expected value of the first roll of the pass line bet.

        2. (Hard) Calculate the expected value of the complete pass line bet.

    e. The don't pass bet wins when the pass line bet loses and loses when it wins *except* when an ace is rolled (hence "bar aces") in which case you neither win nor lose. You win the amount bet. What is the expected value of the don't pass bet? (Use your answer to part 2 of (d).)

5. The Monumental Insurance Company has agreed to insure your copy of the first issue of *Mad* magazine for $1,000. Given the precautions you have taken, they figure there is a 2/100 chance in the coming year that it will be lost, stolen, or destroyed. If they wish their venture to have an expected value of $12, what will your yearly premium be?

6. In Section 2, you were asked to calculate the probability of drawing either a flush or a straight when you held the seven, eight, and ten of clubs and discarded the two and three of hearts. Suppose you are in a game and are dealt this hand. Snake-Eyes Schrag bets $5 and is called by Bad News Bertolet; all of the other players fold. The bet is now to you. You are sure that neither Snake-Eyes nor Bad News will be able to beat a flush or a straight, and you also feel sure that both will check and merely call a $5 bet after the draw. How much money must now be in the pot for your call to be worth $5?

7. A ticket to the big game—which you want very badly to see—costs $10, but at the moment (just before game time) you only have $9. Someone offers to toss a coin with you for $1. Would you accept? What is the expected value of the wager? Do you think the bet is worth more than its expected value under the circumstances? Why or why not?

8. Suppose an infinitely powerful deity offers you the following choice:

a. A guaranteed seventy more years of life, enjoying on average 1 utile/hour, then death.
b. A single play of the St. Petersburg Game, enjoying the utiles won at the rate of 1 utile/hour, then death.

What is the expected value of act (a)? Which act would you choose? Why?

Notes

1. The system presented here was first developed by J. Hosiasson-Lindenbaum in "On Confirmation," *Journal of Symbolic Logic* 5 (1940): pp. 133–48. However, it more closely resembles the version given by Arthur Burks in *Cause, Chance and Reason* (Chicago: University of Chicago, 1977).
2. Axiom 1 makes clear that condition r typically contains more information than just that relating to mutual exclusivity; namely, material that would be considered evidence for p, and so forth. But this information in no way precludes r logically implying that p and q are not both true, since for any statements s and t, if $s \to t$, then $(s \& u) \to t$.
3. Because of space limitations—and because the idea should now be familiar—substitutions for the variables in the axioms and theorems cited in our proofs will be dropped hereafter. Also, to increase readability the use of single quotes to indicate when an expression is being mentioned, rather than used, will be relaxed.
4. More precisely (if less lucidly), where $s_1, \ldots, s_2 2^{n-1}$ express all truth functions of $n - 1$ of the ps (i.e., each s_k expresses a distinct column of **T**s and **F**s for $n - 1$ of the ps), we may say that $p_1, \ldots, p_n$ are an independent set of statements on r just in case where $1 \leq i \leq n$, $\Pr(p_i/r) = \Pr(p_i/s_k \& r)$ for each s_k that is a truth function of the ps less p_i. For an infinite set of statements, we may say: $p_1, \ldots, p_n$, are independent on q if every finite subset of the ps is independent on q.

5. See for example Pierre Simon de Laplace, *A Philosophical Essay on Probabilities* (New York: Dover Press, 1951); original French ed., 1814.

6. For more on this and similar problems, see W. Ball, *Mathematical Recreations and Essays* (London: Macmillan, 1940). See also Burks, *Cause, Chance and Reason.*

7. Note that the likelihoods for the hypotheses need not sum to 1.

8. This example is discussed in detail in R. A. Fisher, *Statistical Methods and Scientific Inference,* 2nd ed. (New York: Hafner Press, 1959), pp. 18–20. See also J. L. Mackie, *Truth, Probability and Paradox* (Oxford: Oxford University Press, 1973), pp. 214–215.

9. From W. Salmon, "Inquiries into the Foundations of Science," in *Probabilities, Problems and Paradoxes,* ed. S. Luckenbach (Encino, Calif.: Dickenson, 1972).

10. In technical jargon, values and expected values on this condition are said to be bounded both "from above" and "from below." In the example to be discussed here, however, only the "above" requirement is relevant.

11. It is perhaps best to state the payoffs in terms of utiles rather than currency, for otherwise it might be thought that the Diminishing Value of Money Principle could be invoked to solve the paradox (for example, 2^{100} would be worth much less than 2^{10} times 2^{10}). In fact, however, the paradox arises whenever the payoff is 2^n or more for the nth consequence.

12. B. Pascal, *Pensées,* no. 233. Actually, Pascal was a Roman Catholic and his argument was directed at becoming a Catholic. But it is perhaps of more interest to extend the argument to Christianity in general.

CHAPTER 4

More on Probability and Expected Value

Section 1. Why Accept the Calculus? The Dutch Book

Your friends Art and Bob are eager to bet on the Sox's next game. Art is pessimistic about the Sox's chances and quotes you odds of 2 to 1 against their winning. Bob, however, is optimistic and quotes you odds of 3 to 2 in favor of the Sox winning. Where A represents the statement that the Sox win, the situation may be described as follows: if you bet *on* A with Art, he will pay you $2 if A is true while you will pay him $1 if it is false, and if you bet against A (on ~A) with Bob, he will pay you $3 if A is false and you will pay him $2 if A is true. In other words, Art is willing to bet $2 on the Sox losing in order to win $1 from you, and Bob is willing to bet $3 on the Sox winning in order to win $2 from you.

Now if you take these bets *and* choose the right amount to wager on each, you will be in an enviable position. Your bets are

B_1: Bet on A with Art at 2 to 1 odds against A
B_2: Bet on ~A with Bob at 3 to 2 odds against ~A

And if you bet $2 on A (winning $4 if true) and $2 on ~A (winning $3 if true), the "sum" of your two bets is a net gain for you regardless of how the game turns out:

A	B_1	B_2	sum(B_1, B_2)
T	$4	-$2	$2
F	-$2	$3	$1

(The italic capital '*B*' will be used throughout to represent bets.) By determining which way to bet (on or against) and how much to bet, you have assured yourself a profit no matter what happens. A gambler who manages to do this is said to have made a *book* against his opposition.

This—on a larger scale—is what a professional bookmaker tries to do. He will offer bets on a number of statements and then attempt to set the odds in such a way as to both attract customers and also guarantee himself some amount of gain no matter what the outcome. Since a bookmaker has many clients, he, like you in our example, can make a book against his collective opposition without making one against any single client. However it is also possible for a single bettor to be so foolish or careless as to make a bet or series of bets such that a loss is suffered no matter how things turn out; in such a case we will say that the gambler's opponent has made a **Dutch Book** against him or her. To take a very simple case, if someone were so irrational as to bet $1 on each number of a single die and agree to collect $5 if a number bet appears on a given toss, then on each toss the bet would be $6 and the payoff only $5 for a net loss of $1. The wagerer is thus in a Dutch Book situation; it is not merely that the expected value is negative, rather *a loss is incurred no matter what the outcome.*

The notion of a Dutch Book is crucial for our next topic: Why should we accept the principles of the calculus of probability? These principles are often presented as if their truth was beyond question and in no need of justification. But a request for justification is not unreasonable; where A and B are mutually exclusive on condition E and we have determined that $\Pr(A/E) = x$ and $\Pr(B/E) = y$, why should we accept the claim that the inductive probability of A v B given E is $x + y$ rather than some other figure? It would be far better to have some rational grounds for believing Axiom 1 than merely to accept it as an article of faith. More generally, we would like to find a justification for supposing that assignments of inductive probability values to pairs of statements, $<p, q,>$ should conform to the principles of the calculus— that the inductive probabilities we assign should behave according to the mathematical characterization of probability specified by the axioms of the calculus.

Since the calculus was developed axiomatically in previous sections, the justification of its theorems of course resides in their being provable from the five axioms. What is required now is that we step outside the system and find rational grounds for accepting those axioms as a basis for making inductive probability assignments to statement pairs under various conditions. The results obtained will be developed informally with a minimum of technical apparatus (more complete and rigorous discussions may be found elsewhere), and they will be framed initially in terms of rational betting behavior.[1] We will then move beyond the gambling arena and briefly discuss our results in more general terms.

Let us first be a little more precise about bets. A bet *on* a statement at odds x to y against its being true will be abbreviated as, "a bet on p

at odds x to y." But inductive probability is a conditional concept, and in fact we generally make bets only when evidence is at hand. Consequently we will be concerned mainly with bets on pairs of statements, $<p, q>$ (read, "p given q"), where q expresses the available evidence for p. Bets B_1 and B_2 therefore are better represented as bets made with respect to the pair $<A, E>$, where E includes relevant information about the game available to the wagerer. Should it turn out that the Sox pull a surprise and start a different pitcher from the one earlier announced, you might exercise your option to cancel the bet. A bet on $<p, q>$ is thus a conditional bet, and we shall stipulate

> **A bet on $<p, q>$ at odds x to y** is one in which the bettor wins $x if $<p, q>$ and loses $y if $<\sim p, q>$ (if $\sim q$, then the bet is off).

A bet against $<p, q>$, then, is a bet on $<\sim p, q>$ and wins $y while losing $x. In bet B_1 with Art, you bet on $<A, E>$ at 4 to 2 (or 2 to 1) odds. Art's bet was thus on $<\sim A, E>$ at 2 to 4 odds, winning $2 if $<\sim A, E>$ and losing $4 if $<A, E>$.

The sum $x + y$ is the **stakes** of the bet, and the **betting quotient** of $<p, q>$—which we abbreviate as '$BQ<p, q>$'—is $y/(x + y)$. In B_1 the stakes are $6 and $BQ<A, E> = \frac{1}{3}$ (for Al of course $BQ<A, E> = \frac{2}{3}$); in B_2 the stakes are $5 and $BQ<A, E> = \frac{2}{5}$. The betting quotient is the ratio: loss/stakes.

Keep in mind that in bets B_1 and B_2 your success in making a book depended on three factors:

the odds (and hence betting quotients) in each case,
the stakes chosen for each bet, and
whether you bet on or against the statement pair.

Had the odds been 1 to 1 ("even money") in both cases, no book could have been made; similarly if the stakes of B_1 had been $12 instead of $6; and had you bet in the opposite direction in each case a book would have been made against you. When two wagerers have come to an agreement on these three matters, they have determined what we will call a **betting system.** Whether a clever gambler can arrange a betting system that amounts to a Dutch Book against his or her unwary opponent depends on each of the three, and our task now is to examine more closely the first of them.

Suppose Smith and Jones agree to make bets with each other on a set of statement pairs, and further agree on the odds for each pair. Then they have agreed on a *set of betting quotients,* and such a set gives rise to a set of bets on or against the pairs involved. If they agree to wager with respect to the pairs $<p, r>$ and $<q, r>$ and assign a betting quotient of $y/(x + y)$ to the former and $w/(z + w)$ to the latter, then four bets result. These are shown in Table 4–1.

Table 4–1

B_1: bet on $<p, r>$ at odds x to y
B_2: bet on $<q, r>$ at odds z to w
B_3: bet on $<\sim p, r>$ at odds y to x
B_4: bet on $<\sim q, r>$ at odds w to z

Smith will take two of these bets and Jones of course the other two. We may now consider the "sum" of the two bets each wagerer has agreed to; that is, the set of net gains or losses that result from the possible outcomes. In the present case, there are four outcomes. Supposing that Smith makes bets B_1 and B_2 at stakes $x + y$ and $z + w$ respectively, they and their sum are as shown in Table 4–2.

Table 4–2

	Outcome	B_1	B_2	sum(B_1, B_2)
Case 1	$<p, r>$ $<q, r>$	x	z	$x + z$
Case 2	$<p, r>$ $<\sim q, r>$	x	$-w$	$x - w$
Case 3	$<\sim p, r>$ $<q, r>$	$-y$	z	$z - y$
Case 4	$<\sim p, r>$ $<\sim q, r>$	$-y$	$-w$	$-(y + w)$

Again, this is Smith's betting table; the one for Jones will display bets B_3 and B_4 together with their sum, and of course the payoff values will be just the reverse of Smith's (positive where Smith's are negative and vice versa).

In our discussion of expected value, we noted that a *fair* bet is one whose expected value is 0. So far, we have spoken only of odds and betting quotients, but the concept of fairness enables us to connect these topics with that of inductive probability:

B is a **fair bet** on $<p, q>$ at odds x to y if and only if $\text{EVal}(B/q) = \Pr(p/q)x + \Pr(\sim p /q) - y = 0$.

From this definition it is easy to show that a fair bet is one in which the probability and the betting quotient of the relevant statement pair are identical. By the same token the betting quotient itself may be described as fair just in case it is identical to the probability. The derivation of these principles requires only Theorem 2 and a little arithmetic:

B is a fair bet on $<p, q>$ at x to y if and only if:

$$\mathrm{EVal}(B/q) = \mathrm{Pr}(p/q)x - \mathrm{Pr}(\sim p/q)y = 0$$
$$= \mathrm{Pr}(p/q)x - [1 - \mathrm{Pr}(p/q)]y = 0$$
$$= [\mathrm{Pr}(p/q)x + \mathrm{Pr}(p/q)y] - y = 0$$
$$= \mathrm{Pr}(p/q)(x + y) - y = 0$$
$$\text{Hence } \mathrm{Pr}(p/q) = y/(x + y)$$

Since $y/(x + y)$ was defined as the betting quotient of $<p, q>$ when the odds are x to y, it follows from the foregoing that

> A bet on $<p, q>$ (hence $\mathrm{BQ}<p, q>$) is fair if and only if $\mathrm{BQ}<p, q> = \mathrm{Pr}(p/q)$.

This result should come as no surprise, though it is worthwhile to have a demonstration for it. If Smith bets \$1 on heads and Jones \$1 on tails, then the odds on heads are 1 to 1 and the betting quotient is $1/(1 + 1)$ or $\frac{1}{2}$. If the chance of heads is also $\frac{1}{2}$, the expected value is obviously 0. If unbeknownst to Jones, the coin is weighted so that the probability of heads is $\frac{3}{4}$, then Smith has a favorable bet: $(\frac{3}{4})(\$1) + (\frac{1}{4})(-\$1) = \$0.50$.

Let us say that a betting system has been *obtained* from a set of betting quotients when the stakes of each bet have been determined and the bettors have decided on who will make which bet. A Dutch Book, then, is simply a betting system in which all payoffs are positive for one of the bettors and hence negative for the other: in such a case we will say that the former has *made a Dutch Book against* the latter. We can now state our main thesis:

I. Where S is a set of fair betting quotients (that is, $\mathrm{BQ}<p, q> = \mathrm{Pr}(p/q)$ for each pair $<p, q>$), no Dutch Book can be obtained from S if and only if each inductive probability value, $\mathrm{Pr}(p/q)$, conforms to the axioms of the calculus of probability.

Now (I) is a biconditional, and so it consists of two claims:

II. If no Dutch Book can be obtained from S, then the inductive probability values from which S was derived conform to the axioms of the calculus.

III. If the inductive probability values from which S was derived conform to the axioms of the calculus, then no Dutch Book can be obtained from S.

We will discuss (II) and (III) separately. Claim (II) will receive the most attention for it in effect claims that a *necessary* condition for avoiding the possibility of a Dutch Book is the assignment of probability values as dictated by the five axioms—a clever antagonist will be unable to make a Dutch Book against you *only if* the probabilities determining the set of betting quotients do not violate those axioms. Claim (III), which will be covered in less detail, states that such an assignment of probability values is in addition *sufficient* for avoiding the Dutch Book spectre.

We now turn to the task of establishing (II), and it will help if we first reword it. Since 'if *p* then *q*' is equivalent to 'if not-*q* then not-*p*,' (II) will be established if we can show

II a.   If one or more of the probability values from which S was derived violate the axioms, then a Dutch Book *can* be obtained from S.

It will be useful—and perhaps add a bit of drama—if we look at the matter as follows. Smith allows Jones to determine the set of fair betting quotients; they are fair inasmuch as they are equal to the inductive probability values Jones assigned to the statement pairs involved. *Then* Jones allows Smith to determine the rest of the betting system—to specify the stakes and who will bet on what pair (since Jones regards each bet as fair, it presumably would not matter to her whether she bets on or against a pair as long as the odds reflect the betting quotient she has assigned). The idea is that if Jones's probability values—which are also her betting quotients—violate the calculus, then she lays herself open to a Dutch Book. It would be possible for Jones to enter into a series of bets each of which she considers fair, and yet for Smith to make a Dutch Book against Jones. That, according to (IIa), is what happens if you fail to adhere to the calculus of probability.

To establish (IIa), then, we will consider each of the five axioms in turn and show how a Dutch Book can be obtained if they are flouted. To simplify things, the first two axioms will be stated with respect to just two disjuncts or conjuncts, but our reasoning can be extended to longer compounds.

Axiom 1: If *p* and *q* are mutually exclusive on *r*, then $\Pr(p \lor q/r) = \Pr(p/r) + \Pr(q/r)$.

It will be helpful to begin by establishing the following claim:

If *p* and *q* are mutually exclusive on *r*, then the sum of bets on $<p, r>$ and $<q, r>$ at equal stakes is a bet on $<p \lor q, r>$ at the same stakes.

Consider any pair of statements p and q that are mutually exclusive on r, and let B_1 be a bet on $<p, r>$ at odds x to y and B_2 be a bet on $<q, r>$ at odds z to w. Suppose further that $x + y = z + w$. Since the statements are mutually exclusive, we need only consider three cases:

	B_1	B_2	sum(B_1, B_2)
Case 1: $<p, r> <\sim q, r>$	x	$-w$	$x - w$
Case 2: $<\sim p, r> <q, r>$	$-y$	z	$z - y$
Case 3: $<\sim p, r> <\sim q, r>$	$-y$	$-w$	$-(y + w)$

If the values in the top two rows of the column for sum(B_1, B_2) are identical, then the sum is itself a *bet* that wins if either p or q occurs and loses when neither does. In such cases, the sum column specifies a bet, B_3, on the pair $<p \lor q, r>$, which wins $x - w$ (i.e., $z - y$) in cases 1 and 2 and loses $y + w$ in case 3. Since $x + y = z + w$, plain arithmetic tells us that $x - w = z - y$, so that in the present case the sum is indeed such a "disjunctive" bet. And since B_1 is a bet on $<p, r>$ at x to y and B_2 is a bet on $<q, r>$ at z to w, sum(B_1, B_2) is a bet B_3 on $<p \lor q, r>$ at odds $x - w$ to $y + w$. So the stakes of B_3 are $(x - w) + (y + w)$, and this is easily shown to be the same quantity as $x + y$ and $z + w$.

Suppose Smith and Jones wish to bet on the Blackhawks' next game. Where A is the statement that the Hawks win, B that the game ends in a tie, A and B are mutually exclusive on evidence C. Suppose also Jones specifies that $\Pr(A/C) = \frac{3}{8}$ and $\Pr(B/C) = \frac{1}{4}$. Jones would thus regard the following bets as fair:

B_1: Bet on $<A, C>$ at 5 to 3
B_2: Bet on $<B, C>$ at 3 to 1

The principle just proved tells us that sum(B_1, B_2) is a bet on $<A \lor B, C>$ at the same stakes as those for B_1 and B_2, and by Axiom 1, $\Pr(A \lor B/C) = \frac{5}{8}$. So this bet should be considered fair at 3 to 5 odds. But suppose Jones violates the axiom by specifying that $\Pr(A \lor B/C) = \frac{1}{2}$, and hence considers the bet fair at 1 to 1 odds. Clearly Jones would also regard as fair a certain bet against either a Hawk win or a tie:

B_3: Bet on $<\sim(A \lor B), C>$ at 1 to 1

To obtain a Dutch Book, all Smith need do is have Jones accept all three of these bets at the same stakes. If the stakes are $8, then the sum of all three constitutes a Dutch Book against Jones:

		B_1	B_2	B_3	sum (B_1, B_2, B_3)
Case 1: <A, C> <B, C>	<A v B, C>	5	−2	−4	−1
Case 2: <~A, C> <B, C>	<A v B, C>	−3	6	−4	−1
Case 3: <~A, C> <~B, C>	<~(A v B), C>	−3	−2	4	−1

No matter what happens Jones suffers a net loss of $1. Had Jones obeyed the calculus and assigned <A v B, C> the value ⅝ and hence <~(A v B), C> the value ⅜, the payoff column for B_3 would have been −$3 for the first two cases and $5 for the third. For all three cases sum(B_1, B_2, B_3) would then be 0 and no Dutch Book would have been possible.

On the other hand, if Jones had violated Axiom 1 by assigning <A v B, C> a value *greater* than ⅝, Smith could not have made a Dutch Book in this same fashion. Had Jones specified that Pr(A v B/C) = ¾, she would regard as fair a bet against <A v B, C> at odds 3 to 1; such a bet—at $8 stakes—loses $2 in the first two cases and wins $6 in the third. The sum of this bet with B_1 and B_2 would thus be a $1 *gain* for Jones in all three cases. Obviously, then, for Smith to obtain the Dutch Book he must reverse gears and have Jones bet against <A, C> and <B, C> but on <A v B, C>. Jones would thus consider fair

B_4: Bet on <~A, C> at 3 to 5
B_5: Bet on <~B, C> at 1 to 3

and given the new value for <A v B, C> the following would also be considered fair

B_6: Bet on <A v B, C> at 1 to 3

Once again Smith has a Dutch Book against Jones:

	B_4	B_5	B_6	sum(B_4, B_5, B_6)
Case 1:	−5	2	2	−1
Case 2:	3	−6	2	−1
Case 3:	3	2	−6	−1

Since only rudimentary arithmetic considerations were used in these examples, we may generalize as follows:

If p and q are mutually exclusive on r and a bettor specifies that Pr(p/r) = x, Pr(q/r) = y and Pr(p v q/r) = $z \neq x + y$, and agrees to fair bets with respect to these pairs at equal stakes, then a Dutch Book can be made against him by having him accept bets

1. On $<p, r>$, on $<q, r>$ and against $<p \vee q, r>$ if $z < x + y$
2. Against $<p, r>$, against $<q, r>$ and on $<p \vee q, r>$ if $z > x + y$.

Violation of Axiom 1 thus lays one open to a Dutch Book; one can enter into a series of the bets each of which one considers fair and yet not only is the sum of the bets unfair (a negative expected value) but a net loss will occur no matter what the outcome.

Axiom 2: $\Pr(p \ \& \ q/r) = \Pr(p/r) \times \Pr(q/p \ \& \ r)$.

Let A represent the statement that the Bears' quarterback remains healthy all season; B is the statement that they make the playoffs; and C is a statement including the relevant evidence available to Smith and Jones. We may thus consider bets with respect to the pairs $<A, C>$, $<B, A \ \& \ C>$ and $<A \ \& \ B, C>$, where the second of these is a bet that the Bears make the playoffs given that their quarterback stays healthy and the third is a bet that both events occur. In the second pair B is conditional on A as well as C, and so if the Bears' quarterback is seriously injured, the bet made with respect to $<B, A \ \& \ C>$ is cancelled.

Now suppose that Jones specifies that $\Pr(A/C) = \frac{3}{5}$ and $\Pr(B/A \ \& \ C) = \frac{5}{8}$. Axiom 2 requires that $\Pr(A \ \& \ B/C) = \frac{3}{8}$, but suppose further that Jones violates the axiom by assigning $\Pr(A \ \& \ B/C)$ the value $\frac{1}{4}$. Smith can now make a Dutch Book by, first, having Jones accept the following bets each of which she regards as fair:

B_1: Bet on $<A, C>$ at 2 to 3
B_2: Bet on $<B, A \ \& \ C>$ at 3 to 5
B_3: Bet on $<\sim(A \ \& \ B), C>$ at 1 to 3

Second, Smith sets the following stakes: \$$x$ for both B_2 and B_3; and for B_1, \$$xy$, where $y = \Pr(B/A \ \& \ C)$. If Jones agrees to \$8 stakes for B_2 and B_3, then the stakes for B_1 will be $(\frac{5}{8})8$ or \$5. Using these stakes, Smith can now make a Dutch Book, for there are three outcomes (though B_2 is cancelled on one of them) and on all Jones suffers a net loss:

	B_1	B_2	B_3	sum (B_1, B_2, B_3)
Case 1: $<\sim A, C> \text{---} <\sim(A \ \& \ B), C>$	−3	—	2	−1
Case 2: $<A, C>$ $<\sim B, A \ \& \ C>$ $<\sim(A \ \& \ B), C>$	2	−5	2	−1
Case 3: $<A, C>$ $<B, A \ \& \ C>$ $<A \ \& \ B, C>$	2	3	−6	−1

Had Jones specified a value for Pr(A & B/C) greater than ⅜, Smith could have obtained the Dutch Book by having Jones bet *against* <A, C> and also <B, A & C> but *on* <A & B, C>. The stakes would be determined as before. Constructing the Dutch Book is left as an exercise.

Violation of Axiom 2 thus can lead one to accept as fair three bets resulting in a net loss without exception. Some elementary arithmetic reasoning (that we will forego here) suffices to show that

> If a bettor specifies that $Pr(p/r) = x$, $Pr(q/p \& r) = y$ and $Pr(p \& q/r) = z \neq xy$, and agrees to fair bets with respect to these pairs at stakes w for <q, p & r> and for <p & q, r> and stakes yw for <p, r>, then a Dutch Book can be made against him or her by having that bettor accept these bets:

> **1.** On <p, r>, on <q, p & r> and against <p & q, r> if $z < xy$
> **2.** Against <p, r>, against <q, p & r> and on <p & q, r> if $z > xy$

Obtaining a Dutch Book for the remaining axioms is easier. Since the truth of each is more evident on first inspection, we must suppose that Jones is *very* foolish.

Axiom 3: If $p \rightarrow q$, then $Pr(q/p) = 1$.

By definition of '$\rightarrow$', q must be true if p is true (i.e., $\square(p \supset q)$), and since $1 = 1/(0 + 1)$, a fair bet on <q, p> in such a case has odds of 0 to 1. That is, you would "bet" any amount for no potential gain; given p, q cannot be false and thus you cannot lose the bet. The bet's fairness, moreover, is reflected in the consideration that you gain nothing in betting on a certainty. Assigning a probability value other than 1 should thus produce a Dutch Book, so let us suppose that Jones, while agreeing that A→B, assigns such a value to Pr(B/A). There are two cases to consider: Pr(B/A) < 1 and Pr(B/A) > 1.

First, Pr(B/A) < 1. If for example Jones claims that Pr(B/A) = ⅞, then she would regard as fair a bet *against* <B, A> at 7 to 1 odds; that is, BQ<~B, A> = 1/(7 + 1). Smith of course has Jones accept this bet—meaning that where the stakes are $8 Jones cannot but lose $1 since B cannot possibly be false when A is true. Since Jones cannot possibly win the $7 prize, Smith has a Dutch Book. The same result holds regardless of what value Jones chooses for Pr(B/A) as long as it is less than 1. Since y is a positive quantity and $y/(x + y) < 1$, plain arithmetic tells us that $x > 0$. Hence there will always be *some* gain if—as Smith did—one bets on <B, A> in these circumstances.

Second, Pr(B/A) > 1. Suppose Jones claims that Pr(B/A) = 1.2. Now of course Theorem 4 guarantees that no probability value exceeds 1, but its proof obviously requires an axiom of the calculus, so we would beg the question were we to dismiss this case on such grounds. Indeed, a closer examination should help make clear why probability values should not exceed 1. Since Jones's value is 1.2, the fair betting quotient needed is $12/(-2 + 12)$; hence Jones must consider a bet on $<B, A>$ fair at the very unusual odds of -2 to 12 or -1 to 6. In having Jones take this bet, Smith obtains a simple Dutch Book since there are "negative winnings," that is, losses, if—as it must—$<B, A>$ occurs. Jones "can't win for losing" because for every \$6 wagered, the "winnings" are $-\$1$ (a one dollar loss) $<B, A>$ being the only possible outcome. And *any* value greater than unity could have been chosen; if y is positive and the ratio $y/(x + y) > 1$, it is clear that x must be a negative quantity, and hence only "negative gains" can occur.

Axiom 4: If $p \leftrightarrow q$, then $\Pr(r/p) = \Pr(r/q)$.

If two statements are equivalent, they naturally should confirm a third statement to the same degree. Suppose however that Jones agrees that $A \leftrightarrow B$ but claims that $\Pr(C/A) = \frac{1}{4}$ and $\Pr(C/B) = \frac{5}{8}$. Simple arithmetic considerations make it apparent that Smith can obtain his Dutch Book by having Jones bet *on* the pair with the greater value and *against* the pair with the smaller at the same stakes—in this instance on $<C, B>$ and against $<C, A>$ at, say, \$8 stakes. A bet B_1 on $<C, B>$ is fair at 3 to 5 odds and a bet B_2 on $<\sim C, A>$ is fair at 1 to 3. There are only two cases to consider, so we have

	B_1	B_2	$\text{sum}(B_1, B_2)$
Case 1: $<C, A>$ $<C, B>$	3	-6	-3
Case 2: $<\sim C, A>$ $<\sim C, B>$	-5	2	-3

Axiom 5: $\Pr(p/q) \geq 0$.

If for whatever reason Jones assigns $\Pr(A/B)$ the value $-\frac{1}{4}$, then since the betting quotient is $1/(-5 + 1)$, a bet on $<A, B>$ would have to be considered fair by him at odds -5 to 1. Thus again we have a bet with negative winnings, making it an easy matter for Smith to obtain a Dutch Book:

	Bet on $<A, B>$
Case 1: $<A, B>$	-5
Case 2: $<\sim A, B>$	-1

Negative winnings and positive losses will always result when a betting quotient is negative, for if $y/(x + y) < 0$ and y is positive, then x must be negative and a loss is in order no matter what the outcome.

So far, we have outlined a proof that one can avoid the Dutch Book possibility *only if* the probability values determining fair betting quotients obey the axioms of the calculus. That is, we have shown (IIa)—and hence (II)—by showing that unless the assigned values comply with the calculus we cannot avoid the threat of a Dutch Book being made against us by a shrewd opponent. But will compliance with the calculus *suffice* to protect us from a Dutch Book? This is what (III) claims, and we must now examine it a little further.

It is natural to suppose that if one makes a series of fair bets, their sum will be fair too. Let A and B be independent on C and let $Pr(A/C) = \frac{1}{2}$ and $Pr(B/C) = \frac{1}{4}$. A bet B_1 on <A, C> is thus fair at 1 to 1 odds, and a bet B_2 on <B, C> is fair at 3 to 1 odds. To obtain a betting system from the set of quotients, let us suppose one bettor agrees to bet B_1 and B_2 and that he and his opponent agree to stakes of \$2 for the first and \$4 for the second. His betting table is

	B_1	B_2	$sum(B_1, B_2)$
Case 1: <A, C> <B, C>	1	3	4
Case 2: <A, C> <~B, C>	1	-1	0
Case 3: <~A, C> <B, C>	-1	3	2
Case 4: <~A, C> <~B, C>	-1	-1	-2

What is the expected value of the sum of these bets? Since B_1 and B_2 are both fair, their expected values are 0, and we would expect the same to hold for their sum. This is in fact the case:

$$EVal[sum(B_1, B_2)/C] = Pr(A \& B/C)(\$4) + Pr(A \& {\sim}B/C)(0) + Pr({\sim}A \& B/C)(\$2) + Pr({\sim}A \& {\sim}B/C)(-\$2)$$
$$= (\tfrac{1}{8})(4) + (\tfrac{1}{8})(2) + (\tfrac{3}{8})(-2)$$
$$= \tfrac{1}{2} + \tfrac{1}{4} - \tfrac{3}{4} = 0$$

A little reflection will show that *any* betting system obtained from the quotients in question will have a 0 expected value no matter how the stakes are varied and no matter who makes which bet. If, say, we change the stakes to \$10 for B_1 and \$8 for B_2 and our bettor bets against <B, C>(let this be bet B_3), the expected value is $(\frac{1}{8})(-\$1) + (\frac{3}{8})(\$7) + (\frac{1}{8})(-\$11) + (\frac{3}{8})(-\$3) = -\frac{1}{8} + \frac{21}{8} - \frac{11}{8} - \frac{9}{8} = 0$. In general then, *if each bet of a set of bets is fair, their sum is fair too* (moreover it can be shown that any sum of fair sums will likewise be fair). But the converse of this principle does not hold—if the sum is fair, the individual bets need not be fair (if the expected values of two bets are \$3 and -\$3, the sum is fair even though they are not).

These calculations of expected value of course presuppose the principles of the calculus, and this leads to the following supposition: If the probability values determining a set of *fair* betting quotients conform to the axioms of the calculus, then the sum of any set of fair bets arising from those quotients will itself be fair. Since a betting system is basically just a sum of bets, this is to say that any betting system obtainable from the set of fair betting quotients will have an expected value of 0. A complete proof of this principle is beyond our scope but it might aid our understanding of the matter if we consider a more specific version of it for the case of two bets.[2] We will show that if we adhere to the calculus, then

If $EVal(B_1/r) = 0$ and $EVal(B_2/r) = 0$, then $EVal[sum(B_1,B_2)/r] = 0$.

Now assume $EVal(B_1/r) = 0$ and $EVal(B_2/r) = 0$, where B_1 is a bet on $<p, r>$ at x to y and B_2 is a bet on $<q, r>$ at z to w. By EVP we have

$$Pr(p/r)x + Pr(\sim p / r)-y + Pr(q/r)z + Pr(\sim q / r)-w = 0$$
$$Pr(p/r)x - Pr(\sim p / r)y + Pr(q/r)z - Pr(\sim q / r)w = 0$$

Since $p \leftrightarrow [(p \& q) \text{ v } (p \& \sim q)]$ and $\sim p \leftrightarrow [(\sim p \& q) \text{ v } (\sim p \& \sim q)]$—and similarly for q and for $\sim q$—and since the disjuncts are mutually exclusive in each case, we obtain by Axiom 1 and Theorem 5

$$[Pr(p \& q/r) + Pr(p \& \sim q /r)]x - [Pr(\sim p \& q/r)$$
$$+ Pr(\sim p \& \sim q/r)]y + [Pr(\sim p \& q/r) + Pr(p \& q/r)]z$$
$$- [Pr(p \& \sim q/r) + Pr(\sim p \& \sim q/r)]w = 0$$

Factoring and regrouping these results gives

$$Pr(p \& q/r)x + Pr(p \& q/r)z + Pr(p \& \sim q/r)x - Pr(p \& \sim q/r)w +$$
$$Pr(\sim p \& q/r)z - Pr(\sim p \& q/r)y - Pr(\sim p \& \sim q/r)y - Pr(\sim p \& \sim q/r)w = 0$$

And with a little more maneuvering we obtain

$$Pr(p \& q/r)(x + z) + Pr(p \& \sim q/r)(x - w) + Pr(\sim p \& q/r)(z - y)$$
$$+ Pr(\sim p \& \sim q/r) - (y - w) = 0$$

Now compare this formula with Table 4–2—displayed earlier in this section—where the gains and losses for $sum(B_1, B_2)$ were schematically laid out. The sum $x + z$ is the payoff for outcome $<p, r>$ and $<q, r>$, that is, for $<p \& q, r>$; $x - w$ is the payoff for $<p \& \sim q, r>$; $z - y$ is the payoff for $<\sim p \& q, r>$; and $-(y + w)$ (i.e., $-y - w$) is the payoff for the last outcome. Therefore the lefthand side of this equation is identical to the expected value of $sum(B_1, B_2)$, hence

$$EVal[sum(B_1, B_2)/r] = 0$$

which is what we had to show. These considerations should provide a reasonably clear indication that

IV. If the inductive probability values that determine a set of fair betting quotients conform to the axioms of the calculus, then each betting system obtainable from that set is fair.

To establish (III) we need only combine (IV) with the straightforward claim:

V. A Dutch Book is an unfair betting system.

That is, if we adhere to the calculus in determining expected value (thus eschewing ludicrous "probability" values like $-\frac{1}{4}$ and 1.2), any Dutch Book has a negative expected value for one of the players. For example, the first Dutch Book made against Jones in the discussion of Axiom 1 has a value of $-\$1$:

$$\begin{aligned} \text{EVal}[\text{sum}(B_1, B_2, B_3)] &= \text{Pr(case 1)Val(case 1)} + \text{Pr(case 2)Val(case 2)} \\ &\quad + \text{Pr(case 3)Val(case 3)} \\ &= (\tfrac{3}{8})(-\$1) + (\tfrac{1}{4})(-\$1) + (\tfrac{3}{8})(-\$1) = -\$1 \end{aligned}$$

An inspection of the betting tables displayed earlier for Axioms 1, 2, and 4 will show that each of the outcomes is negative and at least some of the probability values are positive; consequently the expected value must be a negative quantity. Our sketch of a proof for (III) is now complete, for plainly (III) validly follows from (IV) and (V)—hence if the probability values from which a set of fair betting quotients are derived conform to the calculus, no Dutch Book can be obtained from that set. Having now established (II) and (III), we have thereby established (I)—the "Dutch Book theorem."

The ramifications of (I) extend well beyond wagering contexts and affect all people whether they gamble or not and even if they find gambling morally objectionable. It is worth recalling Bishop Butler's remark, "Probability is the very guide of life." Inductive probability values are measures of the beliefs we acquire through reasoning from evidence and observation and hence are determinants of many actions undertaken in various circumstances where uncertainty is present— and uncertainty is always present in our lives to some extent. In a statement of the form, '$\text{Pr}(p/q) = x$', the value x provides us, implicitly at least, with a betting quotient for accepting and acting on p given the evidence contained in q, and hence in a much broader sense most of our deliberate actions are expressions of "betting" behavior. We "gamble" in this sense whenever we travel, buy a house, or even cross a busy street, for in all such cases we willingly undertake some risk to obtain a desired end.

Now a Dutch Book will arise when someone accords a degree of belief to a statement (or statement pair) that conflicts with the degrees assigned to certain others. In our discussion of Axiom 1 we saw that the probabilities, and hence betting quotients, assigned to <A, C> and <B, C> meant that Jones was willing to make a fair bet on the former at 5 to 3 odds and another on the latter at 3 to 1 odds. The *sum* of the bets on these pairs would be a fair bet on <A v B, C> at 3 to 5 odds and hence a bet against this pair would be fair at odds 5 to 3. This of course agrees with the probability value specified by Axiom 1: Pr(A v B / C) = ⅝. Instead however Jones claimed that Pr(A v B / C) = ½ and consequently was willing to bet against <A v B, C> at the quite different odds of 1 to 1. These odds mathematically conflict with the numerical sum of the odds assigned to <A, C> and to <B, C>. Violation of Axiom 1 thus exposes Jones's inconsistency by yielding a Dutch Book. Adherence to the calculus of probability is a condition for our degrees of belief being internally consistent with one another. Therein lies the justification of the calculus and the true significance of the Dutch Book theorem.

As a final point, a **partial book** is a betting system in which one of the bettors never wins but does not always lose; that is, each outcome is either 0 or else negative.[3] We have seen that no Dutch Book can be made if and only if our probability values conform to the calculus; however it is still possible for a partial book to be made. As we noted in the discussion of Axiom 3, if one holds that Pr(A/B) = 1, then a fair "bet" on <A, B> will be at 0 to 1 odds. If in fact B→A, then it is impossible to lose the bet but nothing is gained in winning it. Suppose however that it is *false* that B→A; perhaps B highly confirms A but does not logically imply it. Then it is possible at least for A to be false when B is true, and a fair bet on <A, B> results in a partial book:

	bet on <A, B>
Case 1: <A, B>	0
Case 2: <~A, B>	−1

If we hold Pr(A/B) = 1 when it is false that B→A, then we lay ourselves open to a partial book. So to avoid the specter of such a book, our probability values must conform not only to the axioms of the calculus *but also to the converse of Axiom 3:*

If Pr(q/p) = 1, then p→q.

This principle is not a theorem of the calculus—it cannot be proven from the five axioms. In our discussion of Bayes' Theorem we briefly considered some reasons for thinking it false; the partial book possibility constitutes a reason for thinking it true. At any rate, the foregoing remarks provide us with an informal demonstration of

> **VI.** If no partial book can be obtained from a set of fair betting quotients, then the inductive probability values from which those quotients were derived conform to the axioms of the calculus *and* the converse of Axiom 3.

Exercises

1. Famed commentator Will George estimates the chance that his beloved Cubs will win the pennant given the evidence obtained during spring training to be ⅝ while that of the Dodgers winning is only ⅛. He insists, however, that the chance of either the Cubs or the Dodgers winning is 2/3. Moreover, he is willing to make fair bets with you. Make a Dutch Book against Will.

2. You are beginning to feel a little sorry for Will and decide that a partial book is good enough. Make a partial book against him.

3. A not-so-great philosopher, Philo of Kokomo, once claimed that Theorem 7 of the calculus is false—that in fact $\Pr(p \,\&\, q/r) > \Pr(p/r) \times \Pr(q/r)$. Make a Dutch Book against Philo.

4. Suppose Jones violates Axiom 2 by claiming that $\Pr(A \,\&\, B/C) = \frac{1}{2}$ even though she also holds that $\Pr(A/C) = \frac{3}{5}$ and $\Pr(B/A \,\&\, C) = \frac{5}{8}$. Make a Dutch Book against Jones.

Section 2. Probability, Frequency, and the Gambler's Fallacy _____

Frequency and probability are of course closely related, so close in fact that they are often confused with one another. Perhaps the best way to begin a study of their connection is to start with the concept of a sequence of events (possibly infinite) in which each event is *independent* of the others and all are *equiprobable*. Repeated tosses of a coin or a die are examples. Such a sequence will be called a **basic sequence.** We will designate one of the possible outcomes of the events a **success;** for example, heads in the coin tossing sequence. The expression 's_n' will mean "the number of successes in n events." We will use the small Greek letter 'α' to represent the probability of each event of the sequence, and the **relative frequency** of success in n trials will be designated by 'fr_n'. If a standard coin is tossed ten times and shows heads on six tosses, then $\alpha = \frac{1}{2}$, $s_{10} = 6$, and $fr_{10} = \frac{6}{10}$. By definition, then

$$fr_n = s_n/n.$$

If the coin is tossed six times, it could show heads on none of the tosses or, say, just one, two, etc. But some of these outcomes are more likely than others. What is the *most probable* number of successes? Common sense would say that, since the probability of success in each event or trial is $\frac{1}{2}$, the most likely number of successes in six trials is three. By the same token, if we designate an occurrence of a two or a four on a toss of a die as a success, then the probability of success on a given toss is $\frac{1}{3}$ and the most likely number of successes in six tosses is two. On this score, common sense is right as the calculations in Table 4–3 show. The expression '$\Pr(s_n = k/q)$' means "the probability that the number of successes in n trials is k, given q" (hereafter, the background condition 'q' will be dropped).

Table 4–3

Outcomes	Coin $\alpha = \frac{1}{2}$	Die $\alpha = \frac{1}{3}$
$\Pr(s_6 = 0) = \Pr(fr_6 = 0)$	$(\frac{1}{2})^6 = \frac{1}{64}$	$(\frac{2}{3})^6 = \frac{64}{729}$
$\Pr(s_6 = 1) = \Pr(fr_6 = \frac{1}{6})$	$6(\frac{1}{2})^6 = \frac{6}{64}$	$6(\frac{1}{3})(\frac{2}{3})^5 = \frac{192}{729}$
$\Pr(s_6 = 2) = \Pr(fr_6 = \frac{2}{6})$	$15(\frac{1}{2})^6 = \frac{15}{64}$	$15(\frac{1}{3})^2(\frac{2}{3})^4 = \frac{240}{729}$
$\Pr(s_6 = 3) = \Pr(fr_6 = \frac{3}{6})$	$20(\frac{1}{2})^6 = \frac{20}{64}$	$20(\frac{1}{3})^3(\frac{2}{3})^3 = \frac{160}{729}$
$\Pr(s_6 = 4) = \Pr(fr_6 = \frac{4}{6})$	$15(\frac{1}{2})^6 = \frac{15}{64}$	$15(\frac{1}{3})^4(\frac{2}{3})^2 = \frac{60}{729}$
$\Pr(s_6 = 5) = \Pr(fr_6 = \frac{5}{6})$	$6(\frac{1}{2})^6 = \frac{6}{64}$	$6(\frac{1}{3})^5(\frac{2}{3}) = \frac{12}{729}$
$\Pr(s_6 = 6) = \Pr(fr_6 = 1)$	$(\frac{1}{2})^6 = \frac{1}{64}$	$(\frac{1}{3})^6 = \frac{1}{729}$

These calculations involve simply an application of Theorem 10B, and the maximum values are $\Pr(s_6 = 3)$ in the coin example and $\Pr(s_6 = 2)$ in the die case. A little inspection of these examples—taking note of the required combinations and exponents in each outcome—should be all that is needed by way of justification to show that common sense is correct. The most probable number of successes is that positive integer obtained by multiplying the number of trials and the probability of each trial, or if this figure is not an integer, the positive integer(s) closest to it. Accordingly, the most probable relative frequency of success is α itself. More fully,

Where the number of trials of a basic sequence is n and the probability of each trial is α:

1. The most probable number of successes = $n\alpha$ (or the integer(s) nearest $n\alpha$)
2. The most probable relative frequency of success = $n\alpha/n = \alpha$

However, even though $n\alpha$ and α are more probable than any of their respective alternatives, both are quite improbable where the number of events is large. Table 4–4 shows the probability values for the most likely number of successes (and frequencies) for 6, 10, 100, 1,000, and 10,000 trials, where $\alpha = \frac{1}{2}$.

Table 4–4

    Probability that $s_n = n(\frac{1}{2})$ and $fr_n = \frac{1}{2}$

$\Pr(s_6 = 3)$	$= \Pr(fr_6 = \frac{1}{2})$	$= 0.313$
$\Pr(s_{10} = 5)$	$= \Pr(fr_{10} = \frac{1}{2})$	$= 0.246$
$\Pr(s_{100} = 50)$	$= \Pr(fr_{100} = \frac{1}{2})$	$= 0.080$
$\Pr(s_{1000} = 500)$	$= \Pr(fr_{1000} = \frac{1}{2})$	$= 0.025$
$\Pr(s_{10,000} = 5000)$	$= \Pr(fr_{10,000} = \frac{1}{2})$	$= 0.008$

So the longer the basic sequence, the *less* likely is the most probable number of successes, and hence the less likely the *observed* number of successes will equal exactly the most probable number (similarly, the less likely will the observed relative frequency equal the probability of each event).[4]

On the other hand, the longer the basic sequence, the *more* likely that the observed number of successes (observed frequency) will fall within a certain percentage range of the most probable figure. For a divergence from the most probable value of 10 percent on either side, the chance that the observed values will be within these bounds rises dramatically as the number of trials increases (see Table 4–5).[5]

Table 4–5

    Probability that s_n (fr_n) falls within 10 percent of $n\alpha$ (of α)

$\Pr(4 \leq s_{10} \leq 6)$	$= \Pr(0.4 \leq fr_{10} \leq 0.6)$	$= 0.656$
$\Pr(40 \leq s_{100} \leq 60)$	$= \Pr(0.4 \leq fr_{100} \leq 0.6)$	$= 0.965$
$\Pr(400 \leq s_{1000} \leq 600)$	$= \Pr(0.4 \leq fr_{1000} \leq 0.6)$	$= 1 - 2.1 \times 10^{-10}$
$\Pr(4000 \leq s_{10,000} \leq 6000)$	$= \Pr(0.4 \leq fr_{10,000} \leq 0.6)$	$= 1 - 4.5 \times 10^{-90}$

We have seen that the most probable relative frequency of success is the probability α of each event, and moreover that, although it is in general unlikely that the actual relative frequency, fr_n, will be *exactly* α (and indeed the longer the sequence the less likely it is), it is *very* likely that fr_n will be close to α (and the longer the sequence the more likely it is). In fact, as an inspection of the decimal figures in Table 4–5 shows, the probability that the observed relative frequency is within a certain percentage deviation of the most probable frequency (of α) increases toward 1 as the number of trials increases. This point may be formulated as the **Law of Large Numbers,** which for now will be stated informally as follows:

Over the long run, the observed relative frequency for a basic
sequence tends to approach the probability of each event (fr_n
tends to get closer and closer to α as n increases), and the
longer the sequence the greater is the tendency; that is to say,
the longer the sequence, the higher is the probability that the
observed frequency will be very close to the most probable
frequency.[6]

The expected value calculations made by casinos and insurance
companies clearly presuppose this law. A bet on red at roulette has as
we saw an $^{18}/_{38}$ chance of winning; therefore, according to the law if
the bet is made many times, the frequency of winning should be very
close to $^{18}/_{38}$. If it could not reasonably "expect" the frequency to be in
this area, a casino would not be able to count on having an advantage
over its customers of about 5% a play at 1 to 1 odds. Casinos,
insurance firms, and indeed rational agents generally can reduce
their exposure to risk and uncertainty by focusing attention not on a
single event but on a large number of similar cases and formulating
strategies for coping with them. A casino cannot be certain that you
will lose on your next play of roulette, but it can be confident that you
will lose if you play a great many times. Your insurance company has
no idea of when you will file a claim, but it knows that the chance of
all of its policyholders filing claims within a few days of one
another—and very likely causing bankruptcy—is extremely low. The
Law of Large Numbers plainly underlies our calculations of expected
value, and our next task will be to formulate the law more precisely.
Our formulation requires the familiar mathematical notion of a limit.
Since its formal definition often produces mystification rather than
enlightenment, we shall remain content for now with the intuitive
idea: to say that a sequence of real numbers has a limit is to say that
it gets closer and closer to a particular real number as we move
through the sequence.[7] Thus the sequences that follow have limits of
0 and 1, respectively:

$$\tfrac{1}{2}, \tfrac{1}{4}, \tfrac{1}{8}, \ldots, \tfrac{1}{2^n}, \ldots$$
$$\tfrac{1}{2}, \tfrac{3}{4}, \tfrac{7}{8}, \ldots, (2^n - 1)/2^n, \ldots$$

We are now in a position to state the Law of Large Numbers more
precisely:

LN: Where n is the number of trials of a basic sequence, fr_n the
relative frequency of success and α the probability of each trial,
then for any positive real number ϵ between 0 and 1:

$$\underset{n \to \infty}{\text{Limit}} \, \Pr(\alpha - \epsilon \leq fr_n \leq \alpha + \epsilon) = 1$$

(The expression '$n \to \infty$' conveys the idea of n increasing indefinitely.)

The real number ϵ in effect specifies a deviation from the most probable relative frequency α, and (LN) thus tells us that for any deviation from α *no matter how small,* the probability that the observed frequency will be *within* that figure increases toward 1 as the number of trials gets larger and larger. Hence as n increases, the ratio fr_n tends to approach α, that is, to be within ϵ of α for any value of ϵ regardless of how close it is to α. In Table 4–5, $\epsilon = \frac{1}{10}$, and we can now reexpress the table in conformity with (LN) in Table 4–5A. (The sign '$|\alpha - \epsilon|$' expresses the *absolute value* of the difference between α and ϵ; for example, $|4 - 3| = |3 - 4| = 1$.)

Table 4–5A
Probability that fr_n is within $|\alpha - \epsilon|$ of α

$$\Pr(\tfrac{1}{2} - \tfrac{1}{10} \le fr_{10} \le \tfrac{1}{2} + \tfrac{1}{10}) \quad = 0.656$$
$$\Pr(\tfrac{1}{2} - \tfrac{1}{10} \le fr_{100} \le \tfrac{1}{2} + \tfrac{1}{10}) \quad = 0.965$$
$$\Pr(\tfrac{1}{2} - \tfrac{1}{10} \le fr_{1000} \le \tfrac{1}{2} + \tfrac{1}{10}) \quad = 1 - 2.1 \times 10^{-10}$$
$$\Pr(\tfrac{1}{2} - \tfrac{1}{10} \le fr_{10,000} \le \tfrac{1}{2} + \tfrac{1}{10}) = 1 - 4.5 \times 10^{-90}$$

The column of values on the right obviously approaches 1, as (LN) requires.

The probability values of the original Table 4–5 were expressed both in terms of relative frequency and number of successes. The Law of Large Numbers, however, has been formulated only with respect to the former concept. It might be thought that the law can be equivalently expressed in terms of the latter simply by replacing 'fr_n' with 's_n' and by replacing 'α' with '$n\alpha$'. However, the matter is more subtle, and if we make these replacements we run into trouble. Let m be an integer expressing a deviation from $n\alpha$ (thus if $m = 10$ and $n = 100$, then we are considering the probability that the observed number of successes falls between 40 and 60 inclusive; i.e., $50 - 10 \le s_{100} \le 50 + 10$), and consider what we obtain when such replacement takes place:

1. Over the long run, the observed number of successes for a basic sequence tends to approach the most probable number of successes (i.e., s_n tends to get closer and closer to $n\alpha$ as n increases), and the longer the sequence the stronger the tendency.
2. For any positive integer m, $\displaystyle \lim_{n \to \infty} \Pr(n\alpha - m \le s_n \le n\alpha + m) = 1$

The trouble with (1) and (2), quite simply, is that they are false; and in fact the very opposite of what they claim holds true. The actual number of successes not only does not approach the most probable figure, the difference between them tends to *grow without limit* as the length of the sequence increases. To appreciate this point, let us imagine that a fair coin has been tossed 10,000 times (heads again counting as a success) with the observed *frequency* of success through the course of the sequence conforming in a straightforward way to the probabilistic assertion made by the Law of Large Numbers (it is not being claimed of course that the results always fall into place as neatly as they do here). We shall suppose that we have kept a careful record of s_n and fr_n with the results shown in Table 4–6.

Table 4–6

Tosses	s_n	fr_n	$n\alpha$	$\lvert n\alpha - s_n \rvert$	$\lvert \alpha - fr_n \rvert$
10	6	$60/100$	5	1	$10/100$
100	57	$57/100$	50	7	$7/100$
1000	440	$44/100$	500	60	$6/100$
10,000	5500	$55/100$	5000	500	$5/100$

Note first that, as predicted by the Law of Large Numbers, fr_n is getting closer and closer to α or $\frac{1}{2}$ as the number of trials increases, and hence the figures in the column on the far right are getting smaller, expressing as they do the difference between the most probable and the observed relative frequency. On the other hand, the observed number of successes is *not* approaching $n\alpha$; rather the difference between the most probable and the observed number of successes (second column from the right) is steadily growing larger as the number of trials increases. There should no longer, therefore, be anything surprising in the claim that the more the coin is tossed, the *frequency* of heads tends to approach the most probable frequency while the *number* of heads tends to diverge more and more from the most probable number. It is worth noting that, in comparing (LN) with (2), the numbers α, ϵ, and m are fixed while $n\alpha$ increases as n does. So the quantity $\lvert \alpha - \epsilon \rvert$ remains fixed while $\lvert n\alpha - m \rvert$ grows without limit.

Now if $m = 10$ and the number of trials n increases from 10 to 10,000 as in Table 4–6, the value $\Pr(n\alpha - m \leq s_n \leq n\alpha + m)$ in fact becomes smaller as n gets larger. In our example, $\Pr(0 \leq s_{10} \leq 15) > \Pr(40 \leq s_{100} \leq 60)$ since the first is obviously unity and the second, as we saw in Table 4–5, is 0.965. And the latter in turn is considerably greater than either of the quantities $\Pr(490 \leq s_{1000} \leq 510)$ or $\Pr(4990 \leq s_{10,000} \leq 5010)$, which are approximately 0.31 and 0.16, respectively. So $\Pr(n\alpha - m \leq s_n \leq n\alpha + m)$, far from approaching 1, as (2) claims, is instead approaching 0. Statements (1) and (2) must therefore be rejected, and in their place we have the **Law of Huge Integers:**

> **HI:** Where n is the number of trials of a basic sequence, and s_n and α are as usual, then for any positive integer m:

> 1. Over the long run, the observed number of successes tends to diverge from the most probable number (i.e., the difference between s_n and $n\alpha$ grows larger as n increases), and the longer the sequence the stronger the tendency.
> 2. Limit $\Pr(n\alpha - m \leq s_n \leq n\alpha + m) = 0$
> $n\rightarrow\infty$

Suppose a coin is tossed one hundred times and heads (a success) has come up only forty times. Some gamblers are inclined to reason that on the next toss or several tosses, heads is more likely to occur than tails since presumably "not enough" of them have occurred thus far. But obviously the coin is either fair or it is not. If it is not, then the results to this point are evidence that *tails* is more likely. And if the coin is fair and the tosses independent, then the probability on any given toss is ½ regardless of previous results. In no case, therefore, can one reasonably maintain that heads is more likely on upcoming tosses. To maintain it is to commit "the gambler's fallacy."

Yet there is a strong tendency to reason in just this way. This slot machine has not paid off in 500 attempts, so I've got a better than usual chance at a jackpot in my upcoming plays. The roulette wheel has not stopped at sixteen for the last 120 plays, hence it is a favorable number to bet on now (and if it has stopped at seventeen several times, I should *not* bet on it). We seem to reason: there's been a run of bad luck, but by "the law of averages" things must eventually even out. So events will change for the better soon.

There is much loose talk among gamblers about the law of averages, and it is doubtful that any of them have anything clear in mind. But if there is something precise *and* true to be discerned in such talk, it is simply the Law of Large Numbers: the greater is the number of trials, the more likely the frequency of success will approach the probability of each event. The gambler's fallacy, however, appears to arise as a result of confusing the law with the false statements (1) and (2)—or better, an illicit inference from the law to such statements. After observing forty heads in one hundred tosses we note that the sequence exhibits ten fewer successes than the most probable number, and since the sequence should move in the direction of a frequency of ½ it should likewise move toward the most probable number of heads—thus rendering it more likely that heads will occur on subsequent tosses. But it is here that the mistake lies: all that we are entitled to infer is that the frequency will likely approach ½, not that the number of heads will approach $n(½)$. The following argument has a true premise and a false conclusion and is therefore invalid:

The more the coin is tossed, the greater is the chance that the frequency of heads will be very close to the most probable frequency of ½. Hence, the more it is tossed, the greater is the chance that the number of heads will be very close to the most probable number of ½ the tosses.

Consequently, heads is more likely on the next toss, so the reasoning goes, since the sequence will tend to "make up" for the "below normal" number of heads on the first one hundred tosses. But as (HI) makes clear, the likelihood is that the number of heads will diverge even more from $n(½)$.

Principle (HI), or the Law of Huge Integers, leads to a very startling consequence. Suppose Smith and Jones agree to toss a fair coin repeatedly with Smith winning $1 if it shows heads and losing $1 if it does not. The probability of winning—and losing—on each toss is of course ½ for both players and their expected values are 0. What can we conclude about winnings and losses in a fair, purely chance game like this if the game continues indefinitely? Since each player has a ½ chance of winning on a given toss and the frequency of success tends to approach ½, it might be thought that the more the coin is tossed the greater is the likelihood that the two players will end up even— neither of them showing a gain nor a loss. In fact, however, just the opposite is true. If each player begins with a finite amount of money, the more the game is played the greater the chance that one of them will wind up with *all* the money. To see this, let us reconsider the sequence of tosses in Table 4–6. Where heads is a success, note that Smith's net gain or loss at any point in the game is twice $|n\alpha - s_n|$, and this latter figure, we know, increases without limit as the number of tosses increases (see Table 4–7).

Table 4–7

Tosses	s_n	$|n\alpha - s_n|$	Net gain/loss
10	6	1	+ $2
100	57	7	+$14
1000	440	60	–$120
10,000	5500	500	+$1000

If each player had begun the game with $1000, then by the 10,000th toss Jones would be completely broke. Since the difference between the actual and most probable number of successes tends to grow indefinitely, so does the net gain or loss as the game progresses. We may not be able to say which player will be the victor (note Smith's loss after 1000 tosses), but we can be confident that the players' gains and losses tend to increase in proportion to the number of tosses. Let t be the time at which one player possesses all the wealth, then as t increases, the probability *that* one of them will be in this position at t approaches a limit of 1. This is often called the **Law of Gambler's Ruin;** and to put it more lucidly, even though the chance of winning on each toss is ½ and the expected value is 0, it is inevitable that if they play long enough with finite stakes, one of the players will win everything!

Exercise

Baseball announcers are wont to say things like: "Slugger Grogan (or some other dangerous long ball hitter) is coming up to the plate, and he hasn't hit a home run in his last twenty games. Boy, he's due for one!" Has the announcer committed the Gambler's Fallacy? Discuss.

Section 3. Frequency Probability _____

The only species of probability employed so far is that of inductive probability, and many if not most of our everyday probability claims are of this kind. Sometimes, however, we attribute a probability value to a statement by itself, rather than—as in our general form, 'Pr(p/q) = x'—to one statement conditional upon another. But even here the probability claim is often just an abbreviated statement of inductive probability. A weather forecaster who says that the chance of rain is 80% generally means that the (inductive) probability of rain given the available meteorlogical data and so forth is approximately 0.80. Not all unconditional probabilities can be handled in this way, but there can be little doubt that the operative concept in remarks like the weather forecaster's is that of evidence and thus inductive probability.

However, suppose a quality control analyst for International Widget says that there is a 3% chance of a widget coming off the assembly line being defective. Such a probability claim would normally be understood in a quite different manner from the weather forecaster's. For the probability value of ³⁄₁₀₀ is arrived at not on the basis of measuring the degree to which some evidence confirms a hypothesis, but rather by observing over a fairly long run the relative frequency with which widgets that are defective occur on the assembly line—on average, of every one hundred produced three are no good. This is a very common way in which we think of and employ the notion of probability, and it is thus another sense in which words like 'probable', 'chance', and the like are used in everyday and scientific discourse. We shall call it the *descriptive* sense, and instead of stating the degree to which a statement is confirmed by some evidence, it simply makes a factual claim that can in principle be verified (or falsified) by empirical investigation. To take a more illustrative case, consider:

1. The probability of an American man over 50 years of age dying of heart disease is 0.35.

This is obviously a claim that would interest an insurance company, and to determine whether or not it is true, no doubt they would simply examine the available statistical data. If approximately 35 percent of the male Americans over 50 have in fact died of heart disease, (1) would be considered true. Here, then, (1) is understood not as meaning that one statement confirms another to the degree 0.35, but rather that a certain relative frequency is in fact 0.35. Whereas the question of whether or not inductive probability statements are empirical in character is controversial (to be explored later), these descriptive probability claims beyond question are empirical.

To drive home the empirical nature of descriptive probability claims, we will consider another example. A coin that falls heads half the time is a quite different physical specimen from one that does so 70 percent of the time. To determine whether a given coin is of one of these kinds, we might subject it to a long sequence of tosses. The sequence would thus be a simple empirical investigation testing each of the descriptive statements:

2. The probability that this coin will fall heads is ½.
3. The probability that this coin will fall heads is 7/10.

So understood, (2) and (3) are clearly empirical statements making no reference to concepts like evidence or confirmation. Rather, the *results* obtained after many tosses will constitute confirming or disconfirming evidence concerning the two. That is, inductive probability comes into play in the evaluation of claims like (2) and (3). Suppose we obtain the following result:

E: In 1000 tosses of the coin 710 were heads.

Obviously (E) strongly confirms (3) and disconfirms (2), and we may express this conclusion by the *inductive* probability statements:

Pr[statement(3)/E] is high
Pr[statement(2)/E] is low

Hence the inference from (E) to (3) is inductively strong, whereas the inference to (2) is weak. Because inductive inference is crucial to empirical inquiry and because descriptive probability statements are empirical, it would appear that inductive probability is the more fundamental concept in that it is presupposed in determining a descriptive probability value.

Consequently, a descriptive probability statement like (2) must be sharply distinguished from the following inductive statement:

4. $\Pr(H/A) = \frac{1}{2}$

where 'H' represents the statement, "This coin will fall heads on the next toss"; and 'A', the statement, "This coin appears symmetrical and such coins fall heads about half the time."[8] For one thing, (2) is defined for a sequence of tosses, whereas (4) pertains to a single event—a feature characteristic of many inductive probability statements. More important, although the result (E) offers evidence against (2), it neither confirms nor disconfirms (4) since the latter merely expresses an assessment of the bearing of certain evidence on statement (H). Instead of being disconfirmed by (E), (4) is now a dead issue for us, since the relevant inductive probability value at this point is $\Pr(H/A \ \& \ E)$.

Descriptive probabilities may be found in disciplines ranging from genetics to demography, and thus it is important that we clarify them and give a precise account of the intuitive idea. Although the correct analysis of inductive probabilities remains a controversial matter, this is fortunately not the case with descriptive ones. Because of their indisputably empirical character and because the mathematical machinery of the probability calculus may be applied to them, there is widespread agreement among probability theorists that a satisfactory analysis of our descriptive use of 'probable' is provided by the precisely defined concept of **frequency probability** and by the **frequency interpretation** of the calculus. We will now spell out these notions.

As before, we use the italicized capital letters, '*F*' and '*G*' as predicate letters representing properties of objects. Where '*F*' represents the property of dying of heart disease and '*G*' the property of being an American man over age 50, the descriptive probability value of statement (1) would appear to be nothing more than a "conditional" relative frequency. We shall designate this frequency by the term '$fr_n(F/G)$', and it is to be understood as follows:

$$fr_n(F/G) = \frac{\text{number of individuals having both } F \text{ and } G}{\text{number of individuals having } G}$$

The subscript attached to '*fr*' again expresses the number of instances or trials in the sequence under investigation. If we have health and mortality records for n U.S. citizens, then '$fr_n(G)$' expresses the percentage of those that are American men over age 50 and '$fr_n(F \& G)$' is the percentage of such persons who also died of heart disease. Using these unconditional frequencies, we can give a more general account of the conditional version:[9]

$$fr_n(F/G) = \frac{fr_n(F \& G)}{fr_n(G)}$$

G is called the **reference property,** and the set of objects that have it is known as the **reference class.** Suppose we have observed one hundred birds, sixty of which are swans, and thirty-five of the swans are white. Where G is the reference property of being a swan, and F is the property of being white, the relative frequency of a bird's being white given that it is a swan may be expressed:

$$fr_{100}(F/G) = \frac{35/100}{60/100} = 7/12$$

Where the reference property holds of every item in the sequence (if for example all of the birds observed had been swans), then of course we may reduce $fr_n(F/G)$ to the unconditional form $fr_n(F)$, for here each item in the sequence is a member of the reference class and vice versa. This form would apply to statements (2) and (3), for there the reference class is simply the tosses of the coin and 'F' represents the property of showing heads on any such toss.

But is it enough to just equate a descriptive probability with a relative frequency? Suppose n is very small; for example, we have records for only forty American men over age 50 and thirty of them have died of heart disease. How confident would we feel about taking ¾ to be a *probability* value in any reasonable sense? Suppose on the other hand we consider very long sequences. The relative frequency value of our coin falling heads was $71/100$ in 1000 tosses. Let us imagine that on the next 1000 the frequency is $41/100$, a mere $22/100$ on the next, and on tosses 3000 to 4000 the frequency is $81/100$. If such a strange result had occurred, we might be very reluctant to take the frequency value for all 4000 tosses as a probability value: the coin's behavior was too erratic or indeed "unpredictable." At the least, we might feel that continued testing would be needed to see if the sequence eventually shows signs of approaching a single value instead of oscillating back and forth forever. And *if,* despite fluctuations it approaches a certain frequency over the long run, no doubt we would regard that frequency as the best candidate for a probability value.

What we have here of course is the notion of a limit again, or more fully a *limiting relative frequency,* and the concept of frequency probability rests on this idea. The limit notion was introduced in the previous section in an intuitive way, but the time has now come for the full definition:

> A sequence of real numbers, $x_1, x_2, x_3, \ldots$ has a **limit** σ if and only if for any positive real number, ϵ, there is a positive integer, y, such that for all positive integers, z, if $z > y$, then $\mid \sigma - x_z \mid < \epsilon$.

The value ϵ is a deviation or error tolerance, and the claim is that no matter how small a value for we choose, there is a member y of the sequence, beyond which each subsequent member z is within ϵ of α. An artificial example will be useful here (artificial because the sequence is simply stipulated rather than inferred from observations of some portion of it). Suppose a coin shows heads on its first four tosses and then alternates between tails and heads indefinitely. Where 'F' represents the property of showing heads and where 'Ft_1' means "Toss t_1 was heads," we have

sequence: Ft_1, Ft_2, Ft_3, Ft_4, $\sim Ft_5$, Ft_6, $\sim Ft_7$, Ft_8, $\sim Ft_9$, Ft_{10}, . . .

fr_n sequence: 1   1   1   1 $\frac{4}{5}$ $\frac{5}{6}$ $\frac{5}{7}$ $\frac{6}{8}$ $\frac{6}{9}$ $\frac{7}{10}$ . . .

The lower sequence clearly approaches $\frac{1}{2}$ as a limit. So if we pick a deviation from $\frac{1}{2}$, say $\frac{1}{4}$, then we can find a member of the sequence—in this case, trial 8—such that all trials beyond it are within $\frac{1}{4}$ of $\frac{1}{2}$; for example, $\mid \frac{1}{2} - \frac{6}{9} \mid < \frac{1}{4}$. The same must hold for any ϵ we pick *no matter how small;* if we travel far enough through the sequence, we will always find the appropriate trial y. This is the full meaning of the claim that as we move through the sequence, we get closer and closer to the limit of $\frac{1}{2}$.

We can now define frequency probability. Consider an infinite sequence of events with each event, n, being characterized as F or $\sim F$ and, where G is the reference property, as G or $\sim G$. To distinguish frequency from inductive probability, we shall express the former as 'Pr_f':

I. $Pr_f(F/G) = \underset{n \to \infty}{\text{Limit}} \, fr_n(F \, /G)$

if this limit exists, otherwise '$Pr_f(F/G)$' is left undefined (and of course if all events lack the reference property, it is not defined either). If our coin had—as in the first 4000 tosses—continued to fluctuate instead of approaching a particular frequency, we would simply refrain from ascribing a probability value. If G holds in each event of the sequence, then (I) may be simplified to

$$\mathrm{Pr}_f(F) = \underset{n \to \infty}{\mathrm{Limit}}\ fr_n(F)$$

Accordingly, in our coin example we can say that the frequency probability of heads in that sequence is ½. The account of frequency probability given here should be compared with the Law of Large Numbers of the last section, according to which the relative frequency tends over the long run to approach the probability of each individual event (though this latter probability was there construed as inductive).

Although frequency probability has been defined for infinite sequences, many probability theorists maintain that it may still be applied without violating the basic idea to finite but very long sequences. Hans Reichenbach, a noted frequency theorist, puts it as follows:

> If a sequence of roulette results or mortality statistics were to show a noticeable convergence only after billions of elements, we could not use it for the application of probability concepts, since its domain of convergence would be inaccessible to human experience. However, should one of the sequences converge "reasonably" within the domain accessible to human observation and diverge for all its infinite rest, such divergence would not disturb us; we should find that such a *semiconvergent* sequence satisfies all the rules of probability.[10]

Such a sequence has what Reichenbach calls a "practical limit," and it is this sort of limit with which we are concerned in most concrete situations. As in the insurance example earlier, we often do not wish to consider the limit of an infinite series of events; instead we are concerned with a frequency, *x/y,* for a finite but very long series. Thus we might consider the frequency probability of *F*'s being *G* as a convergence to *x/y* for a *y* that is large enough for our purposes. Although such a modification is easy and obvious, keep in mind that it is made at the price of undermining the simplicity and mathematical precision of definition (I). It is perhaps best to regard (I) as an "idealization" of our use of 'probable' in a descriptive sense.

As Reichenbach's reference to "the rules of probability" suggests, the calculus of probability may be regarded as an apparatus for calculating frequency probabilities as well as inductive ones. This "frequency interpretation" of the calculus is applicable to a set of frequency statements concerning a given sequence. The axioms and theorems of this version of the calculus are about limits of sequences and as such are logically true statements of mathematics. To clearly distinguish the frequency and inductive interpretations, some notational changes are desirable. Replacing 'Pr' with 'Pr$_f$' and statement variables such as 'p', 'q', and so forth with predicate letters 'F', 'G', and the like, Axiom 2 on the frequency interpretation may be expressed

$$\text{Pr}_f(F \ \& \ G/H) = \text{Pr}_f(F \ /G) \times \text{Pr}_f(G/F \ \& \ H).$$

While the principles of the frequency calculus are logical truths, it should not be thought that the same holds of particular frequency probability statements like '$\text{Pr}_f(F/G) = \frac{1}{2}$'. Rather, such a statement is definitely *empirical* in character, since it asserts that $\frac{1}{2}$ is the limit of a certain sequence; to determine whether that figure is correct, observation of an accessible finite portion of the sequence is required. Frequency probability statements about empirically observable sequences are thus factually true-or-false.

The concept of frequency probability therefore provides us with a good analysis of our descriptive use of the word 'probable' and its relatives, for it preserves the empirical character of our descriptive probability claims and clarifies and makes more precise the status of their probability values. Moreover, the frequency interpretation of the calculus may be brought to bear in reasoning pertaining to a set of such statements and in calculating a correct value. Hence descriptive statements will hereafter be construed as frequency probability claims. Although more could be said about developing and justifying a frequency interpretation of the calculus, the problems encountered in such a task are manageable and in any case beyond our scope.[11]

Two quite different probability concepts have now been distinguished: probability in the sense of the evidential bearing of premise to conclusion, or *inductive probability;* and probability in the sense of limiting relative frequency, or *frequency probability*. They are not to be thought of as competitors, but simply as different meanings of 'probable', 'chance', and so on; hence as different interpretations of the calculus of probability. The contrast between them perhaps can best be brought out by considering their associated statements. In an *inductive* probability statement like '$\text{Pr}(A/B) = \frac{1}{2}$', the letters '$A$' and '$B$' represent *statements* (the conclusion and premise, respectively, of an argument) and '$\frac{1}{2}$' measures the degree to which the latter statement provides evidence for the former. In a *frequency* probability statement such as '$\text{Pr}_f(F/G) = \frac{1}{2}$', the italicized predicate letters 'F' and 'G' express *properties* applicable to individual events of a sequence and '$\frac{1}{2}$' designates the real number that is stated to be the limiting relative frequency with which events that are F accompany those that are G.

A frequency statement is essentially about a particular infinite sequence of events, whereas in an inductive statement the conclusion 'A' may be a singular statement about one event ('It will rain tomorrow'), a generalization ('All ravens are black'), or even a statement form applying to an arbitrary event of a finite sequence ('Toss x_i will be heads' for i = 1,2,3). And by using the limit concept, we saw in our discussion of the Law of Large Numbers that we can extend the application of inductive probability to infinite sequences as well.

We saw earlier that inductive probability is presupposed in the empirical confirmation of statements like (2) and (3), and nothing would appear to change now that they are analyzed as statements of limiting relative frequency. We can directly observe only a finite segment of an infinite sequence, and to determine whether the sequence has a limit and if so what it is, we must draw inferences from our observations. Consider again the inferences from (E) to both (2) and (3). As frequency statements the latter make conflicting claims about an infinite sequence of tosses while (E) describes only a finite portion of it. Now *any* actual results observed in a finite segment are logically compatible with whatever limit the entire sequence might have. Since it is therefore possible for (E) to be true and for (2)—and for (3)—to be false, both inferences are simply invalid from a deductive standpoint with nothing more to be said. The same holds even if we construe the values in (2) and (3) as "practical limits"—convergent frequencies in a finite but very long sequence only part of which has been observed. Here, (2) would assert that in the total sequence of, say, 1 million tosses, about half of those tosses will be heads while (3) claims that approximately 70 percent will be heads. Observation statement (E) is compatible with both the figures 500,000 and 700,000, since it merely restricts the number of heads to a range of 710 to 999,710.

On the other hand, from an *inductive* standpoint, (E) is strong evidence for (3) and against (2)—the former is more *likely* to be true given (E) than the latter. The empirical verification of a frequency probability statement would thus appear to presuppose inductive inference and hence the concept of inductive probability, though as we shall see later some probability theorists have denied this claim.

Exercises

1. Does the following sequence have a limit? Explain.

   Fx_1, followed by five occurrences of $\sim F$, 25 occurrences of F, 125 of $\sim F$, 625 of F, and so on.

2. An illustration of one of the problematic aspects of a frequentist analysis: each of the following infinite sequences contain the same members (though they are of course *distinct* sequences). For each, determine the frequency probability with which a member is an even integer.

   1, 2, 3, 4, 5, 6, 7, 8, 9, 10, . . .
   1, 3, 2, 5, 7, 4, 9, 11, 6, 13, 15, 8, . . .

3. In the Dutch Book discussion, we saw that the converse of Axiom 3 of the calculus (interpreted, as it was there, in terms of inductive probability) is controversial, though the partial book idea offers a reason for believing it. There is, however, no controversy about the *frequency* interpretation; it is most definitely false. Describe a sequence that shows this false:

If $\Pr_f(F/G) = 1$, then for each event x, $Gx \supset Fx$.

Notes

1. See for example A. Shimony, "Coherence and the Axioms of Confirmation," pp. 1–28, and J. Kemeny, "Fair Bets and Inductive Probabilities," pp. 264–273, both in *Journal of Symbolic Logic* 20 (1955). The present discussion is indebted to the latter essay especially, though it should be noted that Kemeny's use of 'fair' is different from the one used here.
2. For proof of a related principle, see Kemeny, ibid.
3. The concept of a partial book and the related principle (VI) are due to Shimony, "Coherence and the Axioms of Confirmation."
4. Obviously these values are not readily calculated by hand, but they may be determined with the aid of such exciting works as *Tables of the Cumulative Binomial Probability Distribution.*
5. The number on the third line of Table 4–5 is approximately $1 - (\frac{1}{210}$ billion) and that on the fourth line is even closer to unity.
6. The Law of Large Numbers is a theorem of the calculus, but its proof is complex and beyond our scope. Strictly, this is what is sometimes called the "weak" version of the law; there is a "strong" version that is not of interest to us here. The word 'tends' as used in the statement of the law and the ensuing discussion is being used here in a probabilistic sense.
7. The formal definition of a limit will be given in the next section.
8. Of course a relative frequency value is here included as part of the *evidence,* but '½' in (4) does not express a relative frequency as such; rather, it provides a measure of the degree to which A confirms H.
9. As in Chapter Two, the use of logical connectives with predicate letters is an abbreviatory device to save space and verbiage.
10. H. Reichenbach, *Theory of Probability* (Berkeley: University of California Press, 1949).
11. See for example R. von Mises' *Probability, Statistics and Truth* (New York: Macmillan, 1957), in particular his discussion of "random sequences" in the first two lectures. See also G. von Wright, *A Treatise on Induction and Probability* (Paterson, N.J.: Littlefield, Adams and Co., 1960), p. 80.

CHAPTER 5

The Justification of Induction

Section 1. Inductive Rules and the Calculus _____

The calculus of probability is an instrument by which we can infer certain inductive probability statements from others, but except for some special cases those statements are not deducible from the axioms *alone*—they are not themselves theorems of the system. Without some prior input, the calculus will not enable us to determine whether, for example, the statement 'Pr(C v D/E) = ¼' is true. Rather, it provides us only with a means of determining the truth value of an inductive probability statement *if* we are given the truth values of certain others. If we know that ⅛ is the correct value for Pr(C/E) and for Pr(D/E)—and we have determined that C and D are mutually exclusive—the calculus tells us that 'Pr(C v D/E) = ¼' is a true statement and that 'Pr(C v D/E) = ⅜' and so forth are false ones. But without such prior knowledge the calculus cannot tell us whether ¼ is the correct value. Moreover, if C and D are not truth-functional compounds, then the truth values of the input statements 'Pr(C/E) = ⅛' and 'Pr(D/E) = ⅛' typically are not determined by the calculus. Knowing those truth values is knowledge that goes beyond anything the axioms and theorems can tell us.

There are some exceptions to this. Since A→(A v B), then of course by Axiom 3 alone we know that Pr(A v B/A) = 1; so the calculus can determine *some* inductive probability values. But this is a special case because A and A v B are not "logically independent." To spell this out a bit, *p* and *q* are *logically independent* statements only when each of the four rows of their truth table presents a genuine, logical possibility; in other words, none of the following four cases is logically impossible:

p and *q* are both true   *p* and *q* are both false
p is true but *q* is false   *p* is false but *q* is true

So the truth value of one of the statements does not logically *require* the other to have a particular truth value.[1] Statements A and A v B are not logically independent since it is impossible for A v B to be false when A is true. By the same token, a pair of mutually exclusive statements are not logically independent since it is impossible for both to be true.

But in the standard case the component statements of an inductive probability statement—representing as they do the premise and conclusion of an inductive inference—are in fact logically independent, and in such a case neither the probability statement nor its negation is a theorem of the calculus. We will express this point as a "metatheorem"; it is not a theorem because it is not a statement *of* the calculus but one *about* it.[2]

> **Metatheorem I:** For any statements p and q and real number x between 0 and 1 inclusive, if p and q are logically independent, then the inductive probability statement '$\Pr(p/q) = x$' is *not* a theorem of the calculus of probability nor is its negation.

How then do we determine the truth value of a statement of the form '$\Pr(p/q) = x$' (determine that x is—or is not—the correct value for '$\Pr(p/q)$')? The question takes us directly back to the discussion in the first chapter concerning the relation between inductive inference and inductive probability: The latter measures the degree to which the premise of the inference supports or confirms the conclusion. Now consider again Pasteur's experiment with the goosenecked flasks also discussed in that chapter. Let A abbreviate his conclusion that microorganisms enter fermentable liquids from the air, and let us compress a description of the structure of the experiment, the results observed and other relevant data into the premise B. We now have the statement:

Pr(A / B) is high

How do we know this statement is true? A complete answer is a complex and controversial matter, but we can say this much for now: we know it in part because the premise and the conclusion are related by inductive rules governing evidence. There are rules of inductive logic that determine the truth values of inductive probability statements—rules for assessing empirical evidence that are not part of the calculus but that are the most important component of inductive logic. We have already looked at simple examples of such rules; for example, rules governing arguments by analogy or rules for causal investigation (such as Mill's Methods). It is rules like these that determine (with varying precision) the degree to which we should accept the conclusion of a species of inductive reasoning given the evidence in its premise and hence determine also the truth values of the related inductive probability statements.

We should recall the notion of a *system of inductive logic* introduced in Chapter One; when the calculus of probability is supplemented by a precise account of the inductive probability concept, together with rules for constructing inductively strong inferences and for arriving at inductive probability values, the result is such a system. Perhaps the single most important goal of inductive logic (and one that is far from attainment at the present time) is the construction of a complete inductive system that clarifies and makes explicit the patterns of reasoning found in scientific investigation and everyday affairs, and in which the inductive rules underlying such inferences are formulated precisely and demonstrated rigorously. The study of inductive rules goes hand in hand with the task of developing such a system, and while there is still much progress to be made, it is possible for us to examine some relatively simple systems in which many of the most basic and elementary inductive rules may be developed. We will take a brief glimpse of such systems in the last section of this chapter; for now we have other matters to consider.

Let us call the inductive system actually used (and occasionally misused) by scientists, attorneys, detectives, and the rest of us in our everyday affairs **Scientific Inductive Logic**, or for short SIL. We have just seen that we know only in outline what a formal construction of this system would look like, but insofar as we employ inductive reasoning, we implicitly draw upon—often in a vague and inexact fashion—a body of inductive rules that govern such reasoning and assign probability values to statements (even if the values are sometimes only qualitative ones like "high" and "low"). Some of the simplest and most widely applicable of these rules were examined earlier in connection with analogical arguments and Mill's Methods, but SIL contains a vast number of more complex rules that would be difficult, to say the least, for us to formulate precisely and that in many instances are of interest only to a small minority of us who employ inductive inference (certain rules might be of use mainly to geneticists, for example, others to statisticians or medical researchers).

Rather than examine such rules, then, we need to step back and look at SIL as a whole, for it raises an acute philosophical problem that will be discussed in this chapter. However, it will be useful for us to have an example of an inductive rule on which to focus our inquiry, and to that end we will use what is perhaps the simplest and most basic inductive rule of all, the **Rule of Induction by Simple Enumeration**, or RSE.

RSE: Where *F* and *G* are any properties, the inductive probability that the next object observed to be *F* will be *G* *increases* as the number of already observed instances of *F* that are *G* increases, assuming there are no counterinstances (an *F* that is not *G*) and that statements of the forms '*x* is *F*' and '*x* is *G*' are logically independent.

Section 2. Hume on Justifying Induction _____

We draw inferences according to RSE and other elementary rules of SIL every day; indeed, they are so ingrained in us that we would never consider giving them up. Yet it would be desirable if we could produce an argument that would rationally justify our use of them, and it is to philosophers that such tasks fall. This might initially seem like an easy job, but as we will see the job is at best difficult and at worst impossible. The problem centers around a line of argument first put forth by the eighteenth-century Scottish philosopher David Hume to the effect that an attempt to provide a rational justification of our use of SIL must inevitably be circular—it must end up assuming the very thesis to be proved.[3] Hume's argument is a powerful one, and it has served as a springboard for all subsequent discussions of the issue both pro and con. We shall now sketch that argument, explaining his basic premises as we proceed.

1. *Our past observations of two kinds of events that have constantly occurred together are construed by SIL as evidence of a causal connection between those events, and on that basis we make predictions about future conjunctions of them.* Having established from a vast amount of evidence that fire and smoke are causally related, we immediately and without hesitation infer inductively the presence of fire when we see smoke off in the distance. Through observation and experiment we have noted many such uniformities in our world: litmus paper always turns red when immersed in acid, gases always expand when heated, unsupported objects near the surface of the earth always fall to the ground. And in all such cases, these uniformities form the basis for predicting what will happen to the *next* piece of litmus paper dipped in acid, the *next* quantity of heated gas, and so forth.

2. *In licensing such predictions, SIL presupposes that the uniformities observed in the past will continue into the future; that is, that the future will be like the past.* In short SIL assumes a "uniformity of nature" principle: heated gases will continue to expand, the law of gravity will not cease to operate, and in general "instances, of which we have had no experience, must resemble those of which we have had experience, and . . . the course of nature continues always uniformly the same."[4] To be sure, there are some observed uniformities that are not a reliable basis for prediction: every bird we have ever observed was hatched before or during the twentieth century, but we can hardly project such a uniformity indefinitely into the future. Therefore, ideally, a complete and exact formulation of the uniformity of nature principle would exclude such cases while allowing for those about heated gases and freely falling bodies. Finding such a formulation, as we shall see later, is a far more difficult task than one might first suppose. It is at least as difficult—and indeed part of the same enterprise—as constructing a comprehensive system of Scientific Induction. But let us suppose for the sake of continuing the argument, that some such version of the uniformity principle is available to us.

3. *The uniformity of nature principle is not a logical truth and therefore cannot be established by deductive reasoning alone, that is, by the kind of proof found in mathematics and logic.* Though we are all no doubt firmly convinced of its truth, the uniformity principle is not logically true since we can, in Hume's felicitous phrase, "conceive of a change in the course of nature." There is no *logical* absurdity or contradiction in supposing that the law of gravity ceases to operate at some point in the future or that heated gases fail to expand; and in this respect the principle is unlike a tautology or algebraic equation. It clearly makes a factual and empirical claim about the universe, and thus its truth does not arise solely from its logical form or the meanings of its component expressions. As such, we cannot hope to establish its truth merely by reflection, intuition, or deductive inference from logically true principles. On the latter point, since we can suppose a change in nature's course, there are specifiable conditions under which the uniformity principle *would* be false, but logical truths hold regardless of how the universe is constituted. Hence an argument for the uniformity principle from such truths as premises is simply invalid.

4. *The uniformity of nature principle is therefore a factual truth and as such requires for its verification inductive inference from our observational data.* Any empirical law, even highly abstract ones like Newton's Law of Gravity, must ultimately trace back to our observational experience of the world. It is from such experiences that our laws and generalizations ultimately find their verification, and this is of course accomplished by *inference* from the statements describing those experiences. These inferences, deductively considered, are not valid, for competing statements are at least compatible with the same body of experiential observation. We can say only that the laws and generalizations arrived at by such inference are more *probable* than their competitors. As such, these inferences are inductive. The uniformity principle is empirical, and thus induction is required for its verification too.

5. Therefore, *since our use of inductive inference presupposes the truth of the uniformity of nature principle and its truth can be determined only through inductive inference from our experience, any attempt to rationally justify our use of SIL must be circular.* To attempt to establish the uniformity principle on empirical grounds requires inductive reasoning, and hence we are arguing in a circle if we attempt to use that principle to justify SIL. Moreover, we have just seen that the principle cannot be established on purely deductive grounds either. It follows, according to Hume, that there are no rationally acceptable grounds for our use of inductive inference.

This compelling argument has been accepted by many philosophers past and present. Others have attacked Hume's reasoning and some have proposed justifications of SIL that they claim are not circular. We shall look at two such approaches later in this chapter.

In any case, few philosophers—at least nowadays—would go along with some rather drastic consequences Hume drew from his result. First, Hume claimed that we no longer have any right or justification for making inductive judgments like, "We have strong evidence for the sun's rising tomorrow" or to *predict* the sun's rising tomorrow. But to many writers on induction this is a case of carrying things too far. The meanings of the terms in our inductive vocabulary (like "strong evidence," "probable," "unlikely," or "confirm") are governed in part by SIL. Thus it is quite correct for us *as users of SIL* to assert that we have strong evidence for the sun's rising, since the rules of Scientific Logic ascribe a very high probability to that claim given the vast amount of evidence available. It is only when we step outside the system and raise the question of justifying it as a whole that Hume's argument becomes relevant.

Second, Hume argued that, failing a rational justification, inductive inference is not to be thought of as "reasoning" at all. As a mental process, it falls outside the scope of human reason and in fact is simply a matter of psychic conditioning or "habit." Having experienced many times smoke occurring concurrently with fire, we develop the expectation of the one upon perceiving the other, and inductive "inference" amounts to no more than this. Yet it is not at all clear why we must regard "reasoning," at least construed as the passage from premises to conclusion according to a logical rule, and "habit" as mutually exclusive alternatives; and for many later philosophers Hume is guilty here of an illicit mixing of logical and psychological issues.

But regardless of such matters, Hume's basic point remains: to attempt to justify our use of SIL by an appeal to a uniformity-of-nature principle is to argue in a circle.

Section 3. Another Approach to the Problem _____

Scientific Inductive Logic consists of a body of inductive rules together with the principles of the calculus. But now an important point emerges: we can formulate *alternative* sets of inductive rules— competitors with those we actually employ—that produce different assessments of our inferences and hence justify different inductive probability statements. In other words, we can in principle develop other inductive logics whose rules conflict with our own. For example, we could introduce an alternative enumeration rule, call it RSE-C:

> **RSE-C:** The inductive probability that the next *F* observed will be *G decreases* as the number of observed instances in which *F* has been *G* increases, assuming no counterinstances and that '*x* is *F*' and '*x* is *G*' are logically independent.

Let us call the system of inductive logic that contains, in addition to the calculus, RSE-C and other such alternatives to our own rules **Counterinductive Logic** (for short, CIL). Consider a simple argument whose premise states that hundreds and hundreds of swans have been observed and all have been white and whose conclusion states that the next swan observed will also be white. Whereas our own rule RSE assigns a high probability to the conclusion, RSE-C adjudges the inference to be a weak one—and the more white swans observed, the weaker it becomes. Plainly there is something very strange about this system of inference, and we will return to it later on. All that is important for the present is that it is a *possible alternative* to our own; someone could for whatever reason draw inferences according to RSE-C rather than RSE (no doubt such a person would regard it as extremely improbable that the sun will rise tomorrow).

Other alternatives are available too. For example, one might introduce the rule RSE-R:

> **RSE-R:** The inductive probability that the next *F* observed will be *G does not depend on* the number of observed instances in which *F* has been *G*, assuming no counterinstances and so forth.

Thus the probability that the next swan observed will be white is the same regardless of whether just 3 or 3 million white swans have been observed so far. When the calculus is supplemented by RSE-R and similar alternatives to our own inductive rules, the result is a system we will call **Random Inductive Logic.** It should be noted that, unlike SIL and CIL, the past has no bearing on the future in Random Logic; inductive probabilities are assigned without regard to what our experience of the past has been like.

There are thus alternative inductive logics that may in principle be applied to the real world; in fact of course we all employ SIL and would not consider for a moment using the others, which after all make very bizarre predictions. And though someone who drew inferences according to one of the other logics and acted upon the conclusions drawn would no doubt be regarded as behaving irrationally (if indeed that person managed to survive at all), the important point to be gained here is that it can be supposed without contradiction (i.e., it is logically possible) that someone employs one of these logics. The claim that no one uses them is only a factual, not a logical, truth.

There are cases where it might superficially seem that we ourselves sometimes use CIL or RIL, but in fact we do not. The following inference, taken at face value, is an instance of RSE-C, but in the sense in which *we* would consider it an inductively strong argument, it belongs to SIL:

> This auto has been driven many times for nearly 400 miles without running out of fuel. Therefore, it will run out of fuel the next time.

Taken as it stands, this inference is a poor one in SIL and a good one in CIL. Why then do we as users of SIL consider the conclusion to be probable? Because we are tacitly adding an unstated premise, something like

> Very few automobile fuel tanks hold enough fuel for more than 400 miles of driving.

With the addition of this premise—itself confirmed through SIL inference patterns from extensive data—the argument becomes an inductively strong one in SIL, but is no longer an instance of RSE-C. That is, without the additional premise the argument is an instance of RSE-C and a weak one by SIL standards; *with* that premise it is no longer a case of RSE-C but a more complex argument that SIL sanctions as inductively strong. It is this latter argument that we as users of SIL are actually employing.

We can now pose Hume's question in a slightly different form: Can we rationally justify our use of SIL over alternatives like CIL and RIL? We might imagine ourselves attempting to convince a hypothetical advocate of CIL—"Countero" we will call him—that he should give up his logic and adopt our own. Countero's inductive standards are topsy-turvy relative to ours in that a vast number of arguments that are considered inductively strong on SIL are inductively weak on CIL and vice versa.

But while Countero and the rest of us are at odds inductively, no disagreement exists concerning deductive logic. That is, from a purely deductive standpoint Countero is as rational as anyone else in that, for example, if he knows that either p or q and observes that not-p is true, he will infer that q is true as well. Moreover, being a deductive instrument, Countero accepts the calculus as well: If the probability of p is $\frac{1}{3}$ and that of q is $\frac{1}{6}$ and p and q are mutually exclusive, he will infer that the probability of p or q is $\frac{1}{2}$. It is in the *initial* probability values that our dispute lies, for if these were not also determined using the calculus, then they were arrived at through inductive inference. If Countero assigns values like $\frac{1}{3}$ and $\frac{1}{6}$, our own assignments will typically be much higher.

Before going further, we might observe that the common acceptance of deductive logic by advocates of SIL, CIL, and for that matter RIL shows that inductive logic is not a part of deductive logic and that we cannot hope to justify our use of SIL by an appeal to the rules, principles, and apparatus of deductive logic. The latter is compatible with, and underlies, the use of any particular inductive system, and as such no one of them can be validly derived from deductive rules and principles.

Returning to our main point, how might we convince someone like Countero that Scientific Induction is the best choice? Surely the most natural, commonsense approach would be to point to the success our logic has enjoyed in the past; in other words, our logic has worked well and Countero's has not. Predictions made using SIL have in general been successful whereas those made by CIL (or by RIL) have by and large been wrong—and often disastrously wrong. If 87 percent of 100 hypotheses had turned out to be true and SIL had predicted each with a probability of 0.9 and CIL had assigned each a value of 0.15, this is clearly a victory for our side and a failure for Countero; and it is just this sort of thing that has happened in the past. Arguments that SIL has sanctioned as inductively strong have in fact had true conclusions accompanying true premises most of the time while those CIL considered strong did not—indeed CIL's success rate was extremely low. Conversely, arguments whose conclusions were assigned a low probability by SIL rarely had true conclusions accompanying true premises, whereas the frequency was much higher with arguments that CIL adjudged inductively weak. So the success rate of true conclusion to true premise was roughly matched by the probability assigned by SIL but was nowhere close to the value CIL assigned. In fact, CIL has been *so* wrong that Countero should consider himself lucky to be alive; after all it is he, not us, who upon encountering a raging forest fire reasons: "Many times in the past people have come in contact with fire and in each case they have been badly burned, so it is very unlikely that I will be burned this time."

However, the appeal to past success will leave Countero unmoved. There are many things he can say in response, among them:

1. Most of our knowledge of the past has been obtained not through direct observation but by *inference* from historical records and data (none of us of course ever witnessed the age of the dinosaurs or the fall of Rome). These inferences however are inductive, and hence our reconstruction of the past involved the use of SIL. That is, in justifying the contention that the use of SIL has been highly successful in the past, we have employed a picture of the past constructed with the aid of SIL. Countero will point out that he used CIL in developing *his* account of the past, and in that account SIL was not nearly as successful.

2. Countero generously gives us our account of the past for the sake of argument. We have argued that, because SIL has been successful, he should now adopt it to make predictions about the future. But this is to presuppose the very logic we are arguing for. It surely is not a logical truth that SIL will enjoy continued success; the most we can say is that it is very probable that it will. But guess which logic assigns this probability value? Countero, using a rule like RSE-C, can equally well argue that because his logic has been *un*successful in the past, it is highly probable that it will be successful in the future!

3. An inductive logic provides us with criteria for evaluating our inductive reasoning, and to the extent that we are rational creatures, our beliefs and hence our actions are determined by such inference. Our three alternative inductive logics thus yield three competing behavior patterns for coping with the real world. As the forest fire case showed, Countero will behave very differently from the rest of us. Now the expected value concept is supposed to provide us with a rational means of deciding among alternative courses of action, but when the alternatives are inductive logics any attempt to show that one of them has a higher expected value than the others can lead only to circularity. Probability values must be fed into the expected value calculation, and these values are supplied only through the use of an inductive logic. If the question is which inductive logic to accept, then what is accepted and the basis for accepting it are the same.

To follow up on this last point a bit, the consequences of the courses of action being evaluated are the successes and failures that result from using that inductive logic. But we cannot know before they occur what the consequences will be. All we can do at that point is make predictions about what will occur based on information obtained about the past. But making predictions and, as we saw earlier, learning what the past was like both involve inductive inference. So evaluating the actions and behavior prescribed by an inductive logic require the use of just such a logic.

Of course after the consequences are known, we can indeed look back and determine which logic worked best, but even here an inductive logic is required to answer the question of whether what occurred was mere coincidence or part of a broad pattern that will likely continue into the future. The procedure of rational choice among alternative actions presupposes use of an inductive logic, and hence cannot be applied to choosing among inductive logics themselves.

The line of argument just sketched—or something like it—has been offered by several twentieth-century philosophers,[5] and differs from Hume's in that it appeals to the concept of alternative inductive systems and makes no reference to the Uniformity of Nature principle (though we shall see later that a concept of uniformity is at work under the surface). But both Hume's argument and the present one lead to the following skeptical conclusions: first, a system of inductive logic cannot be rationally justified by an appeal to a logical truth or by purely deductive reasoning; second,

> Any attempt to justify rationally a system of inductive logic by an appeal to a factual statement (such as the uniformity of nature principle or a statement asserting the past success of the logic) is circular.

Section 4. An Attempt to Answer Hume: The Inductivist View _____

Not surprisingly, there are philosophers who have refused to take Hume's argument lying down. In this section and the next we will look briefly at two responses to Hume that have gained some support among writers on induction. There are other replies as well, but two of the most widely discussed are embedded in theories of inductive probability and hence will be explored in the last chapter. First, however, it will perhaps clarify matters if we consider some natural—if misguided—rebuttals to Hume.

Upon first encountering Hume's argument, there is often an inclination to react somewhat as follows. Our thought processes, our acquisition and use of language, and indeed our ability to cope successfully with nature and survive through the unfolding course of evolution all presuppose a highly uniform universe in which learning from experience serves as a generally reliable guide for future action. And it is through the use of SIL inference patterns that such learning occurs. The human race would never have evolved—or if it had it would never have survived—in a universe in which SIL was not a reliable and successful instrument. Moreover, since we are evolutionary products of such a universe, SIL is embedded so deeply in our psychic (and perhaps even physiological) makeup that we could not give it up even if we wanted to. Fundamental concepts like causality, in terms of which we interpret and categorize the data provided by our senses, presuppose SIL. Its justification consists simply in the fact that it is so ingrained in us and so crucial to our survival and well-being.

But consider, for example, the claim that we would never have learned the use of language had we not used SIL or that we would never have survived in a world in which SIL was not the correct logic. Are these statements *logically* true? Presumably not, for we can at least conceive of circumstances in which such things occurred without employing SIL. They are, then, factual and empirical claims, and the most we can say is that they are very *probably* true. Any current state of affairs—such as our linguistic behavior—is a possibility in *any* logic, even Counterinductive Logic. They differ only on how probable such events are and hence on whether their occurrence is fortuitous or else part of a regular pattern. But these probability values are supplied by SIL itself, and so once again we are arguing in a circle: The statements used to justify SIL are themselves justified through the assignment of high probability values by SIL.

Moreover, it might well be true that we are psychologically incapable of using a different inductive logic, but of course it is also beside the point since no one—not even Hume—ever advocated that we jettison SIL. And aside from hardliners like Hume, more moderate skeptics could grant that from a purely practical standpoint SIL does not stand in any need of justification. Rather, the point is a theoretical one: were we to attempt a justification of SIL as a whole, we would by the nature of the case argue in a circle.

The Inductivist Justification: A more serious proposal for justifying inductive inference has been made by some twentieth-century philosophers who maintain, surprisingly, that the basic inference rules of SIL can be supported by inductive reasoning without producing circularity. One of the more prominent advocates of this approach is Max Black,[6] who maintains that inductive rules of inference can be justified (or "supported" as he prefers to call it) by "second-order" inductive arguments. As an example, he uses a very simple and basic inductive rule, R, which is a statistical version of simple enumeration:

Rule R: Most instances of A observed in a wide variety of
conditions have been B.
$\therefore$ The next A observed will be B.

Thus the rule governs arguments like

> Most species of fish observed have been edible, hence the next
> species we discover will be edible.
> Most tickets purchased in the state lottery have been losers,
> hence the next ticket purchased will be a loser.

since they exhibit the form of argument specified in R. It must be kept
in mind of course that the inductive strength of particular arguments
of this form will vary according to the quantity and variety of favorable
instances mentioned in the premise: if the proportion of favorable instances is high and a very large sample has been observed, the argument will have a high inductive probability, whereas small samples and
low ratios will yield an inductively weak one. Black claims that rule R
can be supported by the following inductive argument:

> **(a)** In most instances of the use of rule R in arguments with
> true premises under a wide variety of conditions, R has
> been successful (the conclusion has also been true). Hence
> in the next instance encountered of the use of R in an
> argument with a true premise, R will be successful.

Note first that this argument is of the very form specified in R, and
thus it uses R in showing that R will be successful in the future, citing
its success in the past as evidence. Note also that instead of being an
argument about, say, fish species or lottery tickets it is an argument
about arguments and hence what Black calls a "second-order" argument.

Are we arguing in a circle if we use argument (a) to support R?
Black maintains that we are not, since a circular argument is always
a deductively *valid* one (though of course worthless nonetheless). In a
circular argument the conclusion is presupposed as a premise, and
hence it is impossible for the conclusion to be false when all premises
are true. But argument (a) is certainly *not* valid. The most that can (or
for that matter, should) be claimed for it is that it is inductively
strong—the premise confers a high probability on the conclusion being
true. Indeed, that is the whole point of claiming that rule R is being
supported on inductive grounds.

Moreover, says Black, argument (a) can be inductively strong even
though it is governed by the very rule it is intended to support.
Imagine a computer that has been programmed to produce conclusions
according to rule R from the evidence fed into it. When the computer is
given the data: "In most of the examined workings of this machine
under a wide variety of conditions a true conclusion was derived when
a true premise was furnished," it duly reports the conclusion: "The

next instance of the application of this machine to a true premise will result in a true conclusion." There is no reason why this conclusion should not be true, at least in the majority of cases, which is all that is needed. Nothing in the nature of the data supplied in *this* particular instance prevents the computer from drawing the correct conclusion, just as it had before. Thus there is nothing paradoxical in the contention that it can make true predictions about its own reliability.

Further, inductive rules like R are "self-supporting" in that they can, under favorable circumstances, be inductively supported by the second-order arguments governed by them. That is, an argument like (a) can actually raise the degree of reliability of the rule it is concerned with (raise the probability of the conclusions of arguments covered by the rule), and in a later essay Black spells out more fully how this can happen.[7] Suppose we have evidence for the premise of the following "first-order" argument and intend to infer its conclusion according to rule R:

> 4/5 of the As so far observed under varying conditions have been *B*.
> Hence, the next *A* encountered will be *B*.

Now we know from before that the observed frequency is not always to be identified with the probability with which the conclusion is true, but for simplicity let us suppose that SIL in this instance does just that: The chance of the conclusion being true given the premise is also 4/5. Suppose also that we examine past uses of rule R and have determined that the premise of the following second-order argument is true:

> In 9/10 of the instances in which R has been used with respect to arguments with true premises observed under a variety of conditions, R has been successful.
> Hence, in the next instance encountered of the use of R in an argument with a true premise, R will be successful.

Again, let us suppose SIL assigns the conclusion a probability of 9/10 relative to the premise. Now note that the "next instance" in this context is the first-order argument, and for R to be successful here is for the conclusion of that argument to be true. The inductive strength of the second-order argument, says Black, is thus immediately transferred to the first-order argument, raising the probability of the latter's conclusion from 4/5 to 9/10. The evidence cited in the second-order argument amplifies the relevant evidence for the first-order one in the following way:

> It is, however, permissible to view the situation . . . as concerned with the extrapolation of an already observed statistical association between

true premises of a certain sort and a corresponding conclusion. The evidence takes the form: In nine cases out of ten, the truth of a statement of the form *m/n Xs have been found to be Ys* has been found associated in a wide variety of cases with the truth of the statement *The next X to be encountered was Y.* This is better evidence than that cited in the premise of the original first-order argument: it is therefore to be expected that the strength of the conclusion shall be raised.[8]

Such second-order arguments thus can in favorable cases increase the inductive strength of the conclusions of arguments covered by rule R, and in that way provide inductive support for R itself. And nowhere in any of this can any circularity or question begging be detected. Black also claims that it does not follow from the preceding that a first-order argument must actually be checked against a corresponding second-order argument before the former can properly be used; if there is no basis for thinking R is unsuccessful most of the time or is objectionable on some logical grounds, that is sufficient to render our use of it reasonable. Rather, "the function of higher-order arguments in the tangled web of inductive method is to permit us to progress from relatively imprecise and uncritical methods to methods whose degrees of reliability and limits of applicability have themselves been checked by inductive investigations. It is in this way that inductive method becomes self-regulating and, if all goes well, self-supporting."[9]

But what has any of this to do with meeting Hume's objection to justifying SIL? The approach just outlined simply bypasses the skeptics' arguments and in fact presupposes the uniformity of nature principle rather than attempting to give a noncircular justification of it. In general, inductivists place no stock in sweeping arguments concerning SIL as a whole; it is sufficient, they contend, to give a piecemeal, rule-by-rule justification of inductive inference so long as no circularity enters in. Black in particular claims that it is senseless to attempt to justify induction in general, "for there is no relevant and authoritative standard of justification to which appeal could be made."[10] That is, skeptics have a misguided or confused notion of what would constitute an acceptable justification.

To briefly spell out this charge, Black contends that Hume and other skeptics have upheld a deductive standard of justification—that the premises of inductive inference, usually with supplementary "assumptions" like the uniformity principle, should *validly* yield the conclusion or else a probabilistic assertion of what the conclusion says (e.g., "Very probably, the next *A* encountered will be *B*"). In other words, the skeptics demand that, for induction to be considered an acceptable mode of inference, it must be reconstructed as a species of deduction; since the truth of the conclusion is *guaranteed* in valid inference, they at least implicitly regard deductive validity as the only standard against which the strength of an argument can be measured. But for Black and other inductivists, induction is not "reducible" to deduction; to suppose that it is—or that doing so would be a desirable goal—is to misunderstand the nature of inductive inference.

No doubt this would be a misunderstanding, but whether all skeptics are guilty of misconstruing induction in this way is debatable. The arguments presented in the previous sections do not, at least on the surface, appear to presuppose such a standard for justification. It is not at all clear why the skeptics who accept those arguments are thereby required to reconstrue inductively strong arguments as yielding their conclusions with certainty rather than high probability. For like Black, they can grant that such arguments by the nature of the case occasionally lead us from true premises to a false conclusion—the improbable sometimes happens. What the skeptic wants is a rational justification for believing that this failure rate will not drastically change in the future. The problem is not that it is possible for inductively strong inferences to go wrong occasionally—the problem is rather that it is possible in theory for arguments assessed as inductively strong by SIL to lead us to false conclusions most of the time and for an alternative logic to be more successful.

In any case, it would be fatal to Black's view if it could be shown that the second-order, "self-supporting" arguments he invokes do in some way beg the question, and several philosophers have attempted to show just that.[11] It is clear, they argue, that in using an inductive inference to show that its conclusion is highly probable, the user must assume that the inference is inductively strong. Now to suppose that argument (a) is inductively strong logically requires us to assume that the rule of inference governing (a), specifically R, will probably be successful in the next instance of its use. But that is to say that the assumption that (a) is inductively strong requires the assumption that (a)'s conclusion (viz., that R will be successful in the next instance of its use) is probable. Consequently, it is claimed, in using (a) to show that the statement 'R will be successful in the next instance of its use' is probable, it must already be *assumed* probable that R will be successful in the next instance of its use. Black's second-order argument is circular in this sense: although—as he rightly notes—the conclusion is not being assumed as a *premise* of the argument, the rule that governs the argument must, in some reasonable sense of the term, be "assumed" reliable by one who uses the argument and yet the point of the argument is to provide support for using that very rule (in effect, to argue for its reliability). While this may not be circular in the strict sense, it is enough, according to Black's critics, to warrant rejection of his attempt to justify induction inductively.[12]

Black's program has also been attacked on another front.[13] Exactly the same reasoning as Black uses to provide inductive support for rules of Scientific Logic can be used to support rules of Counterinductive Logic as well. But any proposal that justifies equally the rules of two opposed systems of inductive logic is in effect a justification for neither of them. To whatever extent Black's argument (a) supports rule R of SIL, to that same extent, say his critics, may the counterinductive rule.

> **Rule R′:** Most instances of *A* observed in a wide variety of
> conditions have not been *B*.
> ∴ The next *A* to be encountered will be *B*.

be supported by the following argument:

> **(a′)** In most instances the use of R′ in arguments with true
> premises in a wide variety of conditions, R′ has been
> *un*successful. Hence, in the next instance to be
> encountered of the use of R′ in an argument with a true
> premise, R′ will be successful.

To justify the use of the rules of SIL is at the least to give grounds for using them *rather than* the rules of another logic, but the inductivist program does not appear to meet this condition.

Section 5. Another Response:
The "No-Problem" Approach _____

Here is a familiar puzzle: "If a tree falls in the forest and there's no one around, does it make a sound?" This question is readily answered, but notice that it is not an "answer" in the usual sense but a reply that claims to show that the question was an improper one to begin with. For the puzzle trades on a confusion between two different meanings of the word 'sound'. If we mean by it what a physicist means, that is, certain waves of various frequencies being propagated through the atmosphere, then of course a sound is made. Those waves will be produced regardless of whether any human beings are present. On the other hand, if by 'sound' we mean an auditory *experience* of hearing something, then it is obvious that no sound is produced inasmuch as no human being is there to have such an experience or sensation. Once a clear sense has been attached to 'sound', our initial puzzlement disappears, and a "yes" or "no" answer becomes obvious. We might say that the original "problem" has not so much been solved but *dissolved;*

it was not a legitimate problem but a "pseudo-problem" that arose because of some sloppy and confused thinking.

Some philosophers of the twentieth century have taken a similar attitude toward the "problem" of justifying inductive inference; it is, they contend, a philosophical pseudo-problem and nothing more. We will here briefly examine the views of perhaps the most prominent advocate of this approach, the British philosopher P. F. Strawson.[14]

One component of the No-Problem view is shared with Black: The demand for a rational justification for Scientific Logic as a whole arises out of a tacit but mistaken conviction that the deductive concept of validity is the only legitimate criterion for evaluating the strength of arguments. The skeptics, hence, are demanding a justification that would make induction a species of deduction, which it is not and cannot be. Since this view has already been discussed in connection with Black's approach (together with an objection to it), it will not be pursued any further here.

More important, Strawson and his allies argue that the skeptics' demand for a "rational" justification for SIL rests on a conceptual error that is reflected in the misuse of expressions such as 'reasonable procedure', 'good evidence for', 'rational grounds for', and so forth. For they hold that the acceptance and use of Scientific Logic as the instrument for shaping our expectations of the future is part of what is meant by "being rational"; a person who based all or most daily decisions concerning future action on, say, voices he or she claimed to hear would for that very reason be considered irrational. The demand for an argument showing that acceptance of SIL is rational—that it is a "reasonable procedure"—makes about as much sense as demanding to know why all bachelors are unmarried.

> ... to ask whether it is reasonable to place reliance on inductive procedures is like asking whether it is reasonable to proportion the degree of one's convictions to the strength of the evidence. Doing this is what "being reasonable" *means* in such a context. ...
>
> In applying or withholding the epithets 'justified', 'well founded', etc. in the case of specific beliefs, we are appealing to and applying inductive standards. But to what standards are we appealing when we ask whether the application of inductive standards is justified or well-grounded? If we cannot answer, then no sense has been given to the question. Compare it with the question: Is the law legal? It makes perfectly good sense to inquire of a particular action ... whether or not it is legal. The question is answered by an appeal to a legal system, by the application of a set of legal (or constitutional) rules or standards. But it makes no sense to inquire in general whether the law of the land, the legal system as a whole, is or is not legal. For to what legal standards are we appealing?[15]

Since SIL is a *standard* of rational behavior and hence determines at least in part the meanings we give to expressions like 'rational grounds for' and 'good evidence for', asking for a rational justification is like asking whether the standard meter bar in Paris is 1 meter in length. Those who question the rationality of using Scientific Logic have simply failed to grasp the meanings of their own words.

But can't there be alternative methods of making decisions and predicting the future, and isn't there then a legitimate question of rationally justifying our use of SIL over these others? Strawson replies that it is a mistake to think that there are alternatives in this sense. He allows that we might stumble across a person whose only means of making decisions about future action is to close his eyes and accept the first answer that pops into his head, and he further allows that this person just might—to our amazement—be correct a large percentage of the time. But it is wrong, according to Strawson, to suppose that this strange but successful method is a noninductive one. By the very fact of its success, the method is inductively supported by Scientific Logic; each use of it falls under the statement "The first answer that comes into my head is usually the correct one," and there is inductive evidence in support of this generalization in the form of a sustained high proportion of successes to total number of cases. To say that the method is successful is to say that it has been applied repeatedly with success, and successful repetition like this is just what we *mean* when we say that it has inductive evidence in its favor. The method thus is not an alternative to SIL, but an auxiliary to it whose legitimacy is sanctioned by the rules of Scientific Logic. However,

> Pointing out this fact must not be confused with saying that 'the inductive method is justified by its success.' ... I am not seeking to 'justify the inductive method', for no meaning has been given to this phrase. ... I am saying rather that any successful method of finding out about the unobserved is necessarily justified by induction. ... The phrase 'successful method of finding things out which has no inductive support' is self-contradictory.[16]

Not only do the skeptics misunderstand the word 'rational' when they demand a "rational justification," they also have committed foul play on 'justification'. For to speak sensibly of justifying a particular doctrine, theory, or principle, we must presuppose a rational framework in terms of which the purported justification can be stated and argued. And since the justifying argumentation often must employ inductive inference, SIL is an essential component of such a framework. To ask for a justification of *it,* therefore, is to ask for something that by the nature of the case cannot be supplied.

This is not to say that SIL is *un*justifiable in the sense in which, say, the theory of spontaneous generation is. It is rather that adherence to the standards of SIL is a condition necessary for formulating and discussing a legitimate justification of *any* subject matter that falls beyond the bounds of mathematics and deductive logic. To ask for justification at this stage is at least implicitly to question the legitimacy of the apparatus by means of which any justification could be given. We reach the point at which it no longer makes sense to speak of justification; the word has been drained of all meaning.

Nearly all philosophers nowadays—even many who remain skeptics in one form or another—would grant that Strawson and his allies have given us a convincing argument for holding that acceptance of SIL is part of what we mean by being rational and that SIL constitutes a standard or norm that governs our use of such inductively loaded expressions as 'probable', 'strong evidence for', 'chance', 'confirm', 'support', 'reliable', 'safe bet', and 'rational'. Words like these would not mean what they do without our tacit commitment to Scientific Logic as an instrument for forming expectations about the future. Consequently, hardline skeptics like Hume are simply wrong when they maintain that we no longer have any rational grounds for believing that the sun will rise tomorrow or that the next gas that is heated will expand. Nor does it make sense to clam that the scientific method is no more reliable than witchcraft or voodoo, yet that is the suggestion in these remarks by Hume: "The *intense* view of these manifold contradictions and imperfections in human reason has so wrought upon me, and heated my brain, that I am ready to reject all belief and reasoning, and can look upon no opinion even as more probable or likely than another."[17] But this frenzied handwringing is uncalled for and only illustrates Hume's own misunderstanding of the words he is using. Because of our commitment to SIL as a standard for forming and expressing rational opinion, it is quite correct for us (Hume included) to assert that the sun's rising tomorrow is "more probable" than its not rising and that we have (to say the least) "strong evidence for" the belief that heated gases will continue to expand.

Yet despite this contribution Strawson has made to the debate, doubt remains as to whether he has succeeded in establishing his main point: that the justification of induction is only a pseudo-problem. Hume's histrionics aside, the question is whether the basic problem he posed and the updated version of it discussed in Section 3 have been "dissolved." Strawson has argued that there are no real "alternatives" to SIL, and he has made a plausible case for saying that a method like that of using the first idea that pops into one's head is not a genuine competitor. But we have already seen that there are in principle methods of forecasting and deciding that are alternatives in a stronger sense, for unlike Strawson's example, Counterinductive Logic and Random Inductive Logic provide alternative *standards* of rationality. Our hypothetical friend Countero behaves irrationally by our standards, and no doubt many of us would consider him insane. An insane person, such as a paranoic, is one who among his many problems persistently violates the canons of inference set down by SIL; the insane person will for example infer conclusions from very scanty evidence with a much higher probability than is warranted by the rules of Scientific Logic.

But when Countero does such things, it is not because he is suffering from a mental affliction that prevents him from abiding by SIL rules, it is because he has adopted a completely different set of rules according to which his behavior is eminently rational. Far-fetched though it may be, we might still imagine a community of such people (a "counterculture") who use CIL and regard it as a standard of rational prediction and decision just as we so regard SIL. Hence if we ask them to justify their commitment to CIL, they could reply, in true Strawsonian spirit, that the question is absurd; relying on CIL is part of what is meant (in their society) by being rational and to raise such a question is to misunderstand the words used in it. And in a way they are right; when *we* use the word 'rational' we mean something quite different from what they mean. So let us use a different word, 'contrational,' for their conception. Using CIL, then, is part of what is meant by being contrational; and Countero can readily agree that he acts irrationally but what is of far more significance to him is that he behaves contrationally.

Notice that the statement, 'It is contrational to accept CIL' is logically true just as is 'It is rational to accept SIL'; both are true solely in virtue of the meanings of their component expressions, and hence if the latter is on the same footing with 'Bachelors are all unmarried', so is the former. On the other hand, although it is rational to believe that the sun will rise tomorrow, it is contrational to *dis*believe that statement, since the two logics assign quite different probability values based on the same body of evidence. Suppose, then, we point out to members of the counterculture that CIL has been very unsuccessful in the past. They might well admit that CIL has had an extended run of bad luck, but that it is highly likely that things will change for the better soon—after all, they use rule RSE-C. And if we further ask how in light of its past track record they can justify their reliance on CIL, they might reply that the question is like asking why bachelors are all unmarried; using CIL is part and parcel of what they regard as "contrational" behavior.

How might we get members of the counterculture to change their ways? Notice that this is not to ask how we can convince them that SIL is the rational choice, for they already know that. It is a logical truth that it is rational to accept SIL, and since they accept the principles of deductive logic just as the rest of us do, they will in the abstract agree with that claim. Rather, the question is, how can we convince them to reject contrationality (and hence CIL) and adopt rationality (and SIL)? Note first that this is not a pseudo-question: it is an intelligible and substantive question that does not trade on any confusion over what the component expressions involved mean, nor in asking it do we betray any misunderstanding of the terms contained in it. It is true that it is of only theoretical import since there never has been nor is it likely (an SIL likelihood of course) that there ever will be such a counterculture. Hence there is no compelling need to justify the use of SIL over its hypothetical competitors, but we can still raise the question in theory. Note, second, that there seems to be no way of answering the question except by arguing in a circle. For the only sorts of reasons that appear to be available at this point are that SIL has been much more successful in the past and that reliance on a logic embodying a commitment to a uniformity principle would stand its users in better stead. And we have already seen that these reasons beg the question.

We have also seen that No-Problem advocates contend that to ask for a rational justification of SIL is to call into question the apparatus of justification giving, and hence that we have reached the point where justification no longer makes sense. But even this seems doubtful. There is of course the common ground of deductive logic (including the probability calculus), accepted and used by both the counterculture and ourselves. However this is not of much help since Hume has argued convincingly that a purely deductive justification is impossible, a conclusion shared (though in a somewhat different form) by the No-Problem approach. Even so, there is a further point of departure that the counterculture and the rest of us can agree on: that it is better to be successful in one's prediction and decision making than not. All of us, as users of an inductive logic, have a vested interest in predictive success, at least as far as the rest of our lives here on earth are concerned. Thus we can raise the legitimate if somewhat abstract question of whether the inductive logic (and the conception of rationality it embodies) that has worked best so far will continue to be a successful prediction- and decision-making instrument in the future or whether an alternative logic might be a better choice.

In asking for a rational justification of this kind, we do not appear to have reached a point where justification no longer makes sense, though we may have reached the point where none is needed in any practical sense. None of us has ever seriously considered using a different logic, and it is fanciful at best to suppose there will ever be a counterculture whose predictive success will cause us to reconsider our very deep commitment to SIL. It is true that as 'justify' is typically used, it presupposes an apparatus that includes the rules of Scientific Logic; in saying, for example, that we are justified in rejecting the theory of spontaneous generation we are at least tacitly saying that the rules of SIL assign a negligible probability to that theory given the evidence available. It is also true that there are alternative theories (such as biogenesis) that we are justified in believing, again by the rules of SIL. But when it is said that SIL has no justification, it does not follow that we are warranted in rejecting it, much less that an alternative to it is justifiable. Clearly CIL and RIL cannot be given noncircular justification either.

What sense, then, can the skeptics give to 'justify' in this context? They might argue as follows: to justify a system of rules is to appeal to a more fundamental system that requires justification less than the one in question, deriving the basic principles of the latter from those of the former. In the case of SIL, the only such system would seem to be the rules and principles of deductive logic, which we have already seen to be inadequate to the task. There exists no system more fundamental than SIL, CIL, and RIL that can provide a rational basis for making a theoretical choice between the three logics and the conceptions of rationality they exemplify.

Although much more could be said about this dispute, enough has been done here to indicate where the main sources of disagreement lay.

Section 6. Alternative Systems of Induction _____

We will now outline how systems of inductive logic may be constructed using the calculus of probability as a common base. The material presented here is a simplified version of the pioneering work done by Rudolf Carnap in his classic work *The Logical Foundations of Probability* and elsewhere.[18] Later, we will reconsider Hume's conclusion in light of the apparatus laid out here. However it should not be thought that all of the material in this section is uncontroversial; some writers on induction and probability would disagree with the approach taken here.

We begin with a set of objects (or individuals) and a finite number of basic properties that the objects may—or may not—possess. The collection of objects and properties will be termed a **domain.** In addition, our formal language for the domain will contain **proper names**—one name for each object—and also **predicate letters**, each of which expresses one of the basic properties. For the names we will use small letters at the beginning of the alphabet (with or without subscripts), and as before we will use italicized capital letters for the predicate letters. The statement '*a* is *F*' (or '*a* has the property *F*') will be abbreviated '*Fa*'; it is an example of an *atomic* statement, a noncompound statement wherein a property is ascribed to an object. The language will also contain, of course, the five logical connectives. The properties are to be logically independent in a sense derivative from that defined at the opening of this chapter: *F* and *G* are logically independent properties if and only if statements of the forms '*Fx*' and '*Gx*' are logically independent. The objects may be ordinary individuals (people, places, and things) or something more esoteric (such as processes or space-time regions). The only requirement is that they be logically disconnected objects, that is, where *x* and *y* represent any pair of names, statements of the forms '*Fx*' and '*Fy*' are logically independent.

It will help to have an example as we proceed, so we will use a domain D containing just two objects and two basic properties. The corresponding language L contains just two names, '*a*' and '*b*', one for each object, and two predicate letters, '*F*' and '*G*', one for each property. This is a very simplistic domain used only for illustration; it is worth noting that the results to be developed here have been extended by Carnap and others to more sophisticated domains that more closely approximate those underlying "the real world," for example, domains with relations (such as "larger than") as well as properties, domains in which the logical independence requirement has been dropped (thus permitting "families" of mutually exclusive predicates, such as color predicates), and so forth. Domains with infinitely many objects may be characterized as well.

A **Q-property** of a domain is a complex property expressed by a conjunction that contains exactly one occurrence—negated or unnegated—of each predicate letter of the language. Each object of the domain will have exactly one Q-property. If the domain has n basic properties, then it has 2^n Q-properties. For example, our domain D has 2^2 or four Q-properties; they are

$$Fx \ \& \ Gx \qquad Fx \ \& \ \sim Gx \qquad \sim Fx \ \& \ Gx \qquad \sim Fx \ \& \ \sim Gx$$

Each object of the domain will exhibit exactly one Q-property, and we must now consider statements in which Q-properties are ascribed to them.

> A **state description** of a language is a conjunction that specifies a Q-property for each object of the corresponding domain. If the domain contains n basic properties and m objects, then there are 2^{mn} state descriptions of the language.

In language L, there are 2^4 or 16 state descriptions. In any given state description, each of the two objects in D is asserted to have one or another of the four Q-properties. Two examples of such state descriptions are

$$Fa \ \& \ {\sim}Ga \ \& \ Fb \ \& \ Gb \qquad Fa \ \& \ Ga \ \& \ Fb \ \& \ {\sim}Gb$$

Since a state description tells us for each object and property whether or not the object has the property, it describes what we will call a **possible world** with respect to the domain. In our domain D each conjunct of a state description is logically independent of the others, and no state description of L is logically false (specifies a logically impossible situation). Hence each succeeds in specifying a possible world. Of the sixteen possible worlds of D, one will be the *actual* world—the other fifteen being alternatives that might have occurred but in fact did not. So the sixteen state descriptions form a set of mutually exclusive and jointly exhaustive statements, and each is factually true-or-false. Exactly one of them is true, and of course it is the one describing the actual world. For convenience, equivalent state descriptions are treated as one; for example, the conjunctions '*Fa & Ga & Fb & Gb*' and '*Fb & Gb & Fa & Ga*' will be regarded as one and the same state description.

Now, for a very important definition

> An **inductive logic** for a domain and language is a set of rules that determines a unique probability value for each pair of statements, $<p, q>$, of the language; that is, a real number x such that $\Pr(p/q) = x$.

Hence, the rules of an inductive logic determine the truth value of every inductive probability statement that can be formulated in the language for a given domain. We will shortly establish a crucial metatheorem for inductive logics, but first we must prove one more theorem of the calculus and then two lemmas, which taken together constitute a proof of the metatheorem.

Theorem 13 relates conditional probability statements (of which inductive probability statements are a species) with unconditional ones. The latter are statements wherein a probability value is ascribed to a statement without being relativized to an evidence condition or other statement. Unconditional probabilities may be defined in terms of conditional ones as follows:

$$\Pr(p) = \text{def. } \Pr(p/q) \text{ where } \Box\,q.$$

So p's unconditional probability is specified as its conditional probability given a logical truth (a statement having no evidential bearing on p). Theorem 13 provides us with a formula for retrieving conditional from unconditional probabilities:

Theorem 13: $\Pr(p/q) = \dfrac{Pr(p \ \& \ q)}{\Pr(q)}$

PROOF: Axiom 2, the preceding definition and AR.

Now for the lemmas.

Lemma A: Any assignment of values between zero and 1 inclusive to the state descriptions of a language that sums to 1 constitutes an assignment of unconditional probability values to those state descriptions.

Proving Lemma A is a very straightforward matter. By Theorem 8, if the numbers assigned to a set of mutually exclusive and jointly exhaustive statements are to be probability values, they must sum to 1. And since the set of state descriptions are mutually exclusive and jointly exhaustive on purely logical grounds (that is, not relative to any further statement), these probability values are unconditional ones.

Lemma B: For any statement p of a language, its unconditional probability, $\Pr(p)$, is calculable from an assignment of unconditional probabilities to the state descriptions of the language, and the conditional probability of a pair of statements, $\Pr(p/q)$, is calculable from the unconditional probabilities of each.

PROOF: Axiom 1, Theorem 5 and Theorem 13 (as illustrated later).

Putting together lemmas A and B, we obtain

Metatheorem II: Any assignment of values to the state descriptions of a language that sums to one determines (in the presence of various theorems of the calculus) an inductive logic for the domain of the language.

To understand the metatheorem more clearly (as well as the proof of Lemma B), let us return to domain D and language L. How might we calculate, for example, the value of the conditional probability, $\Pr(Gb/Fa \ \& \ Ga \ \& \ Fb)$? First note that $Fa \ \& \ Ga \ \& \ Fb$ is equivalent to the disjunction of all state descriptions in which it occurs: by TF $p \leftrightarrow [(p \ \& \ q) \ \mathrm{v} \ (p \ \& \ {\sim}q)]$, so we have

$(Fa \ \& \ Ga \ \& \ Fb) \leftrightarrow [(Fa \ \& \ Ga \ \& \ Fb \ \& \ Gb) \ \mathrm{v} \ (Fa \ \& \ Ga \ \& \ Fb \ \& \ {\sim}Gb)]$

Applying Theorem 5 followed by Axiom 1 gives

$Pr(Fa$ & Ga & $Fb) = Pr[(Fa$ & Ga & Fb & $Gb)$ v $(Fa$ & Ga & Fb & $\sim Gb)]$
$= Pr(Fa$ & Ga & Fb & $Gb) + Pr(Fa$ & Ga & Fb & $\sim Gb)$

Now suppose the probability of the state description on the left is $\frac{1}{10}$ and that of the other is $\frac{1}{20}$, then $Pr(Fa$ & Ga & $Fb) = \frac{1}{10} + \frac{1}{20} = \frac{3}{20}$. Using Theorem 13, then, we have

$$Pr(Gb/Fa \text{ \& } Ga \text{ \& } Fb) = \frac{Pr(Fa \text{ \& } Ga \text{ \& } Fb \text{ \& } Gb)}{Pr(Fa \text{ \& } Ga \text{ \& } Fb)} = \frac{\frac{1}{10}}{\frac{3}{20}} = \frac{2}{3}$$

We have said in general what an inductive logic is and how to determine probability values with it. We now specify in more exact terms particular systems of inductive logic and show how they apply to our simple domain D. First, however, a few more definitions.

Two state descriptions are *isomorphic* if and only if one can be transformed into the other by a succession of interchanges of their proper names, all occurrences of one proper name replacing all occurrences of another.

For example, $\sim Fa$ & Ga & Fb & $\sim Gb$ and Fa & $\sim Ga$ & $\sim Fb$ & Gb are isomorphic to one another (interchange the as and bs and then put the components containing the former on the left). They are *not* isomorphic to Fa & Ga & $\sim Fb$ & $Gb,$ which is instead isomorphic to $\sim Fa$ & Ga & Fb & Gb. While this may seem complicated, the intuitive idea behind isomorphism is very simple: isomorphic state descriptions describe "qualitatively similar" possible worlds. For example, the first pair of state descriptions describe worlds in which one object has G but lacks F and the other has F but lacks G. In the second pair, however, both worlds have one object with both F and G and one that has G but not F.

The *isomorphism measure* of a state description d—written '$I(d)$'—is the number of state descriptions isomorphic to d, including d itself.

Thus $I(\sim Fa$ & Ga & Fb & $\sim Gb) = 2$. It is isomorphic to Fa & $\sim Ga$ & $\sim Fb$ & Gb and also to itself. Note that isomorphism is a "symmetric" relation: If one state description is isomorphic to another, the latter is isomorphic to the former as well. Two isomorphic state descriptions have the same isomorphism measure. We need just one more definition:

A **structure description** is a disjunction of all state descriptions isomorphic to one another (if a state description is isomorphic to itself only, it alone serves as the structure description).

Table 5–1 lists all sixteen state descriptions for our domain D, along with their isomorphism measures. The braces on the left group to- gether those that are isomorphic to one another. Therefore, each of the state descriptions braced together are disjuncts of the same structure description. The probability assignments on the right side of the table will be explained momentarily.

Table 5–1

State description (d)	Isomorphism Measure I(d)	Pr(d) in SIL	Pr(d) in CIL	Pr(d) in RIL
{ 1. *Fa & Ga & Fb & Gb*	1	$\frac{2}{20}$	$\frac{1}{28}$	$\frac{1}{16}$
{ 2. *Fa & ~Ga & Fb & ~Gb*	1	$\frac{2}{20}$	$\frac{1}{28}$	$\frac{1}{16}$
{ 3. *~Fa & Ga & ~Fb & Gb*	1	$\frac{2}{20}$	$\frac{1}{28}$	$\frac{1}{16}$
{ 4. *~Fa & ~Ga & ~Fb & ~Gb*	1	$\frac{2}{20}$	$\frac{1}{28}$	$\frac{1}{16}$
5. *Fa & Ga & Fb & ~Gb*	2	$\frac{1}{20}$	$\frac{2}{28}$	$\frac{1}{16}$
6. *Fa & ~Ga & Fb & Gb*	2	$\frac{1}{20}$	$\frac{2}{28}$	$\frac{1}{16}$
7. *Fa & Ga & ~Fb & Gb*	2	$\frac{1}{20}$	$\frac{2}{28}$	$\frac{1}{16}$
8. *~Fa & Ga & Fb & Gb*	2	$\frac{1}{20}$	$\frac{2}{28}$	$\frac{1}{16}$
9. *Fa & Ga & ~Fb & ~Gb*	2	$\frac{1}{20}$	$\frac{2}{28}$	$\frac{1}{16}$
10. *~Fa & ~Ga & Fb & Gb*	2	$\frac{1}{20}$	$\frac{2}{28}$	$\frac{1}{16}$
11. *Fa & ~Ga & ~Fb & Gb*	2	$\frac{1}{20}$	$\frac{2}{28}$	$\frac{1}{16}$
12. *~Fa & Ga & Gb & ~Gb*	2	$\frac{1}{20}$	$\frac{2}{28}$	$\frac{1}{16}$
13. *Fa & ~Ga & ~Fb & ~Gb*	2	$\frac{1}{20}$	$\frac{2}{28}$	$\frac{1}{16}$
14. *~Fa & ~Ga & Fb & ~Gb*	2	$\frac{1}{20}$	$\frac{2}{28}$	$\frac{1}{16}$
15. *~Fa & Ga & ~Fb & ~Gb*	2	$\frac{1}{20}$	$\frac{2}{28}$	$\frac{1}{16}$
16. *~Fa & ~Ga & ~Fb & Gb*	2	$\frac{1}{20}$	$\frac{2}{28}$	$\frac{1}{16}$
Sum over all d		1	1	1

We are now in a position to specify Scientific Inductive Logic. SIL is the inductive system containing the five axioms of the calculus *plus* a very important sixth principle that enables us to determine the truth values of inductive probability statements from the standpoint of rules such as RSE. We shall call it "The Principle of Scientific Logic," or for short, "PSL":

PSL: For each state description d, $Pr^s(d) = 1/(I(d) \times g)$, where g is the number of structure descriptions.

The 's' superscript merely indicates probability in the SIL sense. For D, $g = 10$ (again, just count the number of braces in Table 5–1). PSL together with Theorem 8 determines an assignment of unconditional probabilities to all state descriptions. Each receives a value, $Pr^s(d)$, inversely proportional to $I(d)$, and the values sum to 1. The values assigned are listed in the table. As we have seen, any such assignment of unconditional probabilities determines an inductive logic.

The result of adding PSL to the calculus is to give us probability values for expressions of the form '$Pr(p/q)$' that conform to the inductive rules of SIL as we intuitively understand them. To illustrate, we will use the rule RSE as it applies to domain D. The statement Fb & Gb is equivalent to the disjunction of state descriptions (1), (6), (8) and (10) as displayed in Table 5–1, since it occurs in each of them and in no others. Likewise, Fb is equivalent to the disjunction of those state descriptions along with (2), (5), (12) and (14). Thus,

$$Pr^s(Gb/Fb) = \frac{Pr^s(Fb\ \&\ Gb)}{Pr^s(Fb)} = \frac{1/10 + 3(1/20)}{2(1/10 + 6(1/20))} = 1/2$$

For example, the probability that b is white given that it is a swan is ½. According to RSE, the probability should increase as the number of confirming instances increases, so we should expect that

$$Pr^s(Gb\ /\ Fa\ \&\ Ga\ \&\ Fb) > Pr^s(Gb/Fb)$$

And this is exactly what happens. In our example earlier illustrating how Theorem 13 is used to calculate conditional probabilities, we used what in fact were SIL assignments to the relevant state descriptions in calculating the value for $Pr^s(Gb/Fa\ \&\ Ga\ \&\ Fb)$. That value, it will be recalled, was ⅔, and hence our two calculations conform to RSE.

The increase from ½ to ⅔ is of course too dramatic for a single confirming instance, but this is because D is such a simplistic domain. In one with a great many more properties, the values would be much more realistic. Though it will not be shown here, PSL assigns values in conformity with RSE for any domain of the kind specified earlier. Moreover, more sophisticated inductive rules of SIL can be proven as theorems of the system, and hence PSL gives us a good though very simplified model of SIL.

To obtain Counterinductive Logic, we add a different principle:

PCL: For each state description d, $Pr^c(d) = I(d)/g_c$, where g_c is the sum of the isomorphism measures of all state descriptions.

In D, $g_c = 28$, and the values assigned for CIL are listed in Table 5–1. PCL assigns each state description a probability value in proportion to the number of state descriptions isomorphic to it. Thus in the presence of the principles of the calculus, PCL specifies an inductive logic and so determines the truth value of each inductive probability statement formulable in language L, though of course those truth value assignments differ greatly from those we as users of SIL would assign.

We will show that the inductive logic specified by PCL is a species of CIL by showing with respect to domain D again that the probability values assigned accord with the rule RSE-C.

$$\text{Pr}^c(Gb/Fb) = \frac{\text{Pr}^c(Fb\ \&\ Gb)}{\text{Pr}^c(Fb)} = \frac{1/28 + 3(2/28)}{2(1/28) + 6(2/28)} = 1/2$$

$$Pr^c(Gb/Fa\ \&\ Ga\ \&\ Fb) = \frac{\text{Pr}^c(Fa\ \&\ Ga\ \&\ Fb\ \&\ Gb)}{\text{Pr}^c(Fa\ \&\ Ga\ \&\ Fb)} = \frac{1/28}{1/28 + 2/28} = 1/3$$

So the values conform to CIL; the probability that the next F will be G *decreases* as the number of instances in which G has accompanied F increases. Similarly, other rules of CIL correspond to certain theorems provable in this system.

To obtain Random Inductive Logic, we add the principle

PRL: For each state description d, $\text{Pr}^r(d) = 1/g_r$, where g_r is the number of state descriptions.

Unlike other systems, in RIL the possible worlds are equally likely; hence in D each state description is assigned the value $1/16$. PRL hence determines an inductive logic and thereby determines the truth value for each inductive probability statement of language L. Here, calculating inductive probabilities is an easy matter.

$$Pr^r(Gb/Fb) = \frac{4(1/16)}{8(1/16)} = 1/2$$

$$Pr^r(Gb/Fa\ \&\ Ga\ \&\ Fb) = \frac{1/16}{2/16} = 1/2$$

The calculations obviously conform to the rule RSE-R; the probability that the next F will be G does not depend on the number of instances in which G has accompanied F. Note that in the other inductive systems the probability of a prediction about a future event is made relevant to events observed in the past, but not with RIL. In SIL and CIL, $\text{Pr}(Fa) \neq \text{Pr}(Fa/Fb) \neq \text{Pr}(Fa/{\sim}Fb)$; but RIL assigns the same value to each of them. For all three logics of course a statement about one object is *logically* independent of a statement about any other, but in RIL a pair of statements like Fa and Fb are *inductively* independent as well.

A possible world in which objects tend to be similar (or share the same properties) is a more "uniform" or "regular" world than one where they tend to differ in the properties they possess. We have already seen that isomorphic state descriptions are those that describe qualitatively similar worlds, or what comes to the same thing: they are state descriptions that agree on the number of objects said to have each Q-property. An inspection of the state description table for domain D shows that the *greater* the number of state descriptions isomorphic to a given one (i.e., the higher the isomorphism measure), the *less* uniform the possible world it describes. State description (1) has a low $I(d)$ and describes a uniform world, but (11) has a higher $I(d)$ and describes a less uniform world. This point holds generally for domains of any number of objects; in a three-object–two-property domain the state description *Fa & Ga & Fb & Gb & Fc & Gc* has an isomorphism measure of 1, but the description *Fa & ~Ga & ~Fb & Gb & Fc & Gc* has an isomorphic measure of 6 (there are five distinct state descriptions isomorphic to it). So, *a state description's isomorphism measure is inversely proportional to the degree of uniformity exhibited by the possible world it describes;* the higher the $I(d)$, the less uniform the world.

Therefore, as Table 5–1 illustrates, SIL assigns higher unconditional probabilities to the more uniform worlds—it exhibits so to speak a "bias" toward uniformity. The bias is reflected in the fact that, unlike RIL where all state descriptions are equiprobable, all *structure* descriptions are equally likely in SIL (for D they all take the value $\frac{1}{10}$). On the other hand, CIL behaves in diametrically opposed fashion: higher unconditional probabilities are assigned to the less uniform worlds—it exhibits a bias toward irregularity. RIL of course is bias free.

Thus a primitive concept of uniformity is embedded in our characterization of SIL for simple domains. Hume's original question now becomes, "Is there any rational, noncircular justification for assigning higher unconditional probabilities to state descriptions describing uniform worlds?" To argue that such an assignment yields a logic that has been successful in the past is simply to raise once again all of the difficulties that were discussed earlier concerning this approach.

But there is another consideration as well. Keeping in mind the risk involved in generalizing from simple domains like *D* to that underlying our real world, we might imagine a (no doubt gigantic) state description giving a complete past history of our universe, as well as a description of its present state. SIL would presumably assign this statement a very low probability (because of the vast number of possible alternatives to the actual universe), and since our world is a uniform one CIL would assign an even lower value. Our friend Countero can now argue that for a statement with an extremely low unconditional probability to come true (and with it, the fact that he would not have survived in the world it describes) shows only that we as users of SIL were the beneficiaries of good fortune, not that his choice of CIL was unjustified or irrational. It shows, that is, only what we all knew from the outset: that improbable events sometimes happen. To argue that SIL is the correct logic to use on the basis of what has actually happened in the past and the present is simply a bald-faced attempt to maximize the probability of our current information about the world, and as such is circular. The criterion for judging how successful a logic has been is not what did in fact happen (for that, after all, has at least some nonzero probability in *any* logic) but what would probably happen and to determine that we must use an inductive logic. Once again, the attempt to justify our use of SIL on the basis of its alleged success in the past leads to circularity.

Final Comment: The foregoing argument belongs to the same family as those found in Section 3 of this chapter; they are intended to show that any attempt to justify SIL on the basis of its success in the past will inevitably be circular. We saw in Section 2 that Hume argued the same point with respect to the uniformity of nature principle, and we have seen in the present section a connecting strand between the two lines of argument: SIL probability assignments to state descriptions exhibit a bias toward "uniform" worlds. The general thesis that emerges here is that circularity must be the result if we attempt to provide a rational justification for a system of inductive logic by appealing to a factually true principle.

However, we have also considered two responses to skeptics like Hume. Black attempted to show that noncircular justifications can be given for SIL rules on a piecemeal basis, and Strawson has argued that there is no legitimate question of justification with regard to inductive inference. Both writers agree on one basic point: the question of justifying SIL *as a whole* is a pseudo-question resting on confusion and misunderstanding of the standards by which inductive inferences should be appraised. The skeptic raises the question of justifying a system of induction and then argues that there is no solution. For Black and Strawson, it is wrong to suppose that the question can be legitimately raised at all. We have, of course, examined an objection to their view.

Not all responses to the skeptic are like this. In Chapter Seven we will look at two more proposals; unlike Black and Strawson, both take the question of rationally justifying SIL as a system to be legitimate and claim that noncircular grounds can be provided in support of our use of SIL.

There are still further responses to the skeptic. We left open in Chapter One the question of whether there are statements that are neither logically nor factually true or false, and some philosophers have proposed that the uniformity of nature principle is not an empirical truth as the skeptic assumes, nor of course is it a purely logical one either. Rather, they claim that it is a priori (and "necessary" in some sense), but nonetheless has factual content in that it conveys substantive information about the underlying structure of the universe. It is thus a *metaphysical* principle on this view, not a scientific one. Some proponents attempt to deduce the principle from (what they take to be) more fundamental metaphysical claims, while others despair of proof and maintain that it must be assumed or "presupposed" if scientific inquiry is to be regarded as a legitimate enterprise. On the first approach, one must be prepared to "buy" the entire metaphysical system to obtain a justification; on the second, it is hard to see how such a presupposition amounts to anything more than a pious hope that it be true. And in any case, skeptics would argue that the uniformity principle simply is not a metaphysical one. Further discussion of this approach would take us beyond inductive logic.[19]

The uniformity principle was never stated in a precise form in our discussion, and it was said in Section 1 that to do so we must first have a means of distinguishing genuine uniformities, such as 'All observed emeralds are green' from accidental ones that do not provide us with a sound basis for prediction, such as 'All past Democratic presidents of the United States have been righthanded'. As with the problem of justification, this might initially seem like an easy task, but as we will see in the next chapter it is in fact quite difficult, and no generally satisfactory theory has yet been proposed.

Exercises

1. Using the sample language and domain of this section, calculate the following unconditional probabilities for SIL. Then do the same for CIL.

    a. $\Pr(\sim Fa)$ **b.** $\Pr(Fa \ \& \ Gb)$ **c.** $\Pr(Fa \ v \ Ga)$

What are the following conditional probabilities for SIL? For CIL?

    e. $\Pr(Ga/\sim Fa)$ **f.** $\Pr(\sim Ga/Fa \ \& \ Fb \ \& \ Gb)$

2. Consider a domain with three properties, represented by 'F', 'G', and 'H', and one object designated by 'a'. How many state descriptions are there? List them. Specify their isomorphism measures. So how many *structure* descriptions are there? List them. Determine the unconditional probability assignments to the state descriptions for SIL, and then do the same for CIL. Now calculate the following probabilities for SIL and then for CIL.

a. $\Pr(Fa)$ c. $\Pr(Fa/\sim Fb)$
b. $\Pr(Fa/Fb)$ d. $\Pr(Fa/Fb \ \& \ Fc)$

Notes

1. Logical independence, of course, must be distinguished from the probabilistic sense of 'independent' defined in connection with Theorem 7. See Section 2 of Chapter Three.
2. The theorem may be proven by first showing that, for any arbitrarily chosen inductive probability statement, there is an interpretation of its component statement letters on which it is false but the five axioms of the calculus are true, and then showing that there is an interpretation that does the same for its negation. This is easily done and will be omitted here. For a proof along similar lines, see Arthur Burks, *Cause, Chance and Reason* (Chicago: University of Chicago Press, 1977), Chapter 3.
3. David Hume, *A Treatise of Human Nature,* ed. L. A. Selby-Bigge (London: Oxford University Press, 1888); originally published 1739. See also Hume's *Enquiry Concerning Human Understanding* (Chicago: Gateway Editions, 1956).
4. Hume, *Treatise,* p. 89.
5. A particularly good example is provided by Arthur Burks in "The Presuppositions of Induction," *Philosophy of Science* (1953).
6. Max Black, "The Inductive Support of Inductive Rules," in *Problems of Analysis* (Ithaca, N.Y.: Cornell University Press, 1954), Chapter 11.
7. Max Black, "Self-Supporting Inductive Arguments," *Journal of Philosophy* 55 (1958): 718–725.
8. *Ibid.,* p. 722.
9. *Ibid.,* p. 723.
10. Max Black, *Language and Philosophy* (Ithaca, N.Y.: Cornell University Press, 1949), Chapter 3, p. 86.
11. See Wesley Salmon's "Should We Attempt to Justify Induction?" *Philosophical Studies* 8 (1957): 45–47; and Peter Achinstein's "The Circularity of a Self-Supporting Inductive Argument," *Analysis* 22 (1960–1961): 138–141.
12. For more on this, see Black's reply to Achinstein in *Analysis* 23 (1962–1963): 43–44, and Achinstein's rejoinder, *Analysis* 23 (1962–1963): 123–127.
13. See Salmon, "Should We Attempt?"
14. P. F. Strawson, *Introduction to Logical Theory* (New York: John Wiley and Sons, 1952); see Chapter 9.
15. Ibid., p. 257, his italics.
16. Ibid., p. 258.

17. Hume, *Treatise,* pp. 268–69.
18. *The Logical Foundations of Probability,* 2nd ed. (Chicago: University of Chicago Press, 1962). We will depart a bit from Carnap's procedure, but the results will be essentially the same.
19. Immanuel Kant, in his *Critique of Pure Reason,* trans. N. K. Smith, (London: Macmillan, 1933), exemplifies the first of these approaches. John Maynard Keynes illustrates the second; see his *A Treatise on Probability,* London: Macmillan (1952).

CHAPTER 6

Confirmation and Its Problems

Back in the second chapter we looked at some simple forms of inductive inference used in scientific investigation, and in the third chapter Bayes' Theorem was discussed in connection with evaluating rival hypotheses. Now we will undertake a more general examination of the role induction plays in the confirmation of scientific hypotheses. Initially, the logical form of these inferences seems simple enough, but a deeper inspection reveals complexities and problems that have generated a good deal of controversy. Since inductive probability is probability in the sense of degree of confirmation, the issues and problems raised here fall not just within the realm of the philosophy of science but inductive logic as well.

Section 1. The Confirmation/Disconfirmation Process _____

Unfortunately, even nowadays we sometimes find scientific practice described as a gathering of facts and data followed by generalizing from such evidence to universal laws. In fact, very little investigation proceeds in this way; while simple enumeration is a basic and elementary form of inductive inference, its role in actual scientific work is minimal.

A few writers have gone much further, claiming that induction plays *no* fundamental role in science and denying that there is any form of inference from experimental data to general hypotheses. The philosopher Karl Popper[1] maintains that the only legitimate form of scientific argument is the purely deductive reasoning used in rejecting hypotheses. What is crucial to scientific method for these writers is the free and open process by which hypotheses are constructed, followed by the subjection of these hypotheses to the most severe and rigorous tests that can be devised. But the question of how the hypothesis was arrived at is of no importance; it might have been suggested by careful observation, consulting work in related fields, or it might simply be a seat-of-the-pants hunch. None of this is of any relevance in providing an account of the underlying logic of scientific investigation. What is important is whether the hypothesis can survive the experiments constructed to test it.

While most philosophers of science agree with Popper on the importance of hypotheses and the unimportance of their origins, few share his more extreme view that scientific method does not employ inductive inference. So we will examine now the much more widespread view that, while simple enumeration has little role to play, induction nonetheless has its place in scientific method.[2] To do this, we first need to explore the notion of a hypothesis a bit more.

The terms 'hypothesis', 'theory' and 'law' are used in various ways: A law is often regarded as a well-confirmed statement (Kepler's "laws" for example), and 'theory' is sometimes reserved for very general or comprehensive theses (as in the "theory" of special relativity). However, for simplicity we shall just use 'hypothesis' to cover all such cases. Hypotheses come in a variety of forms. We might determine that a particular coin is not "loaded" by confirming the *statistical* hypothesis that in one hundred tosses it will show heads between 40 and 60 percent of the time (a probability of 0.965). Such hypotheses and their confirmation, however, are best left to the statisticians, who have sophisticated mathematical tools for dealing with them.

Instead, we will focus on two other kinds. *Universal* hypotheses are general claims such as Galileo's famous law, $d = (1/2)gt^2$ or Pasteur's thesis that microorganisms in fermentable liquids enter those liquids by way of dust particles in the surrounding air. However some hypotheses are not generalizations, but are instead *particular* in form. For example, when perturbations in the orbit of the planet Uranus were detected in the nineteenth century, it was hypothesized that there was another planet beyond Uranus's orbit whose gravitational influence was responsible for the disparity between Uranus's predicted and observed motions (subsequently discovered, of course, and named "Neptune"). Universal hypotheses are very often theoretical in nature, making reference to entities that cannot be directly observed (photons, force fields) and can be tested only indirectly. Many of them, like Pasteur's, state a causal connection, while others, as in Galileo's case, state a functional correlation.

Moreover, 'hypothesis' will be used to cover complex and highly general theories such as Newtonian Mechanics. Hypotheses like these are of great importance in the advancement of scientific knowledge because of their comprehensiveness. For one thing, they enable us to explain an enormous range of diverse phenomena, and for another, they often serve as unifying mechanisms, bringing a large number of more specific hypotheses into a systematic arrangement. For many years, Kepler's laws (concerning "celestial" motion) and Galileo's law (about "terrestial" motion) were thought to have little connection with one another, but with Newton's work (his law of gravitation and three laws of motion) they both became subsumable under a more general theory that explained many other kinds of phenomena as well. Newton provided a comprehensive system that far exceeded anything before it in its ability to both explain and predict. It also led to the development of new hypotheses whose confirmation can be achieved through a much greater range and quantity of evidence than was possible before.

Rather than simply generalizing from collected data, scientists employ hypotheses to guide their investigations. Faced with some problematic or puzzling data, a hypothesis is formulated that provides a possible explanation. One or more statements describing testable consequences are then inferred from the hypothesis—we shall call these **observation statements**. Through observation or experiment we then determine whether these statements are true. If they are, they provide supporting evidence and hence confirm the hypothesis. The inference from observation statement back to hypothesis is thus an inductive one. The whole procedure is usually termed the **hypothetico-deductive method**.

Where H represents a hypothesis and O an observation statement, then as we saw in the first chapter the schema:

I. If H then O

O

∴ H

is an invalid argument form from a deductive standpoint. Its importance emerges when it is considered as an *inductive* inference, for if tests show that O is true, then O provides *confirmation* for H—the probability of H given O exceeds the probability of *H* without it.

Why, then, call the method "deductive" instead of "inductive?" We must again consider the initial inference *from* the hypothesis *to* the observation statement, which finds its expression in the first premise of schema (I). In a great many cases the inference of O from H is one of valid deductive reasoning—the hypothesis (usually in conjunction with other statements to be described later) *implies* the observation statement. The first premise is thus what we earlier called the "corresponding conditional" of the inference from H to O, and it is logically true. The first four examples of experimental confirmation to be presented are all of this character, and if all instances of reasoning from H to O were like this, the first premise of the preceding schema could be written 'H→O'.[3] However, sometimes the derivation of observation statement from hypothesis is a matter of probability and hence of inductive reasoning. In such cases, the hypothetico-deductive method, as we will see later in connection with our fifth example, is basically just an application of Bayes' Theorem. We turn to our first two examples.

Example 1: Where g is the gravitational constant (32 feet/second), t is the time elapsed, and d the distance fallen, then from Galileo's hypothesis, $d = (\frac{1}{2})gt^2$, and the fact that this object has been falling for exactly 2 seconds, we may validly infer the observation statement that it has fallen 64 feet. If our measurements of a particular freely falling body bear this out, the hypothesis has gained additional confirmation.

Example 2: Galileo and other scientists were puzzled by the fact that a liquid sucked up a tube will not run out of the tube when its top is sealed, and that suction pumps used to drain water would not work if placed more than 33 feet above the water level. A student of Galileo's, Evangelista Torricelli, offered a hypothesis to explain these facts: first, the earth is surrounded by an "ocean of air" that has weight and exerts pressure just as water does; second, a vacuum is created in the tube or pump so that there is no atmospheric pressure in the top to counteract the air pressing against the bottom, and lastly, the water is thus supported at a certain height in the tube when the weight of the water is equalled by the weight of the air. Since mercury is 13.6 times denser than water and the atmosphere supports a column of water 33 feet, Torricelli deduced the following observation statement: atmospheric pressure would also support a column of mercury a little over 29 inches high in a tube sealed at the top ($\frac{33}{13.6} \times 12$ in. $= 29$ in.). Another observation statement was deduced: The column of mercury would descend if transported to a higher altitude where because of the thinner air the pressure is lower. Experiments were devised to test these statements (giving us the world's first barometer) and both were shown to be true, thus confirming Torricelli's hypothesis.

However, examples (1) and (2) show that schema (I) is inadequate as a general account of the hypothetico-deductive method (hereafter, HDM). For one thing, statements concerning proper testing conditions must be incorporated into it. As a generalization, Galileo's hypothesis tells us nothing about the behavior of any particular object, and hence by itself it does not validly yield the conclusion that the falling object has descended 64 feet. We need in addition a statement of **initial conditions,** in this case that the object in question has been in free fall for 2 seconds. One of the conditions in Torricelli's case is that no air can enter the tube of mercury from the top. In more advanced cases, as in the discovery of Neptune or Pasteur's experiments, the formulation of initial conditions can be quite complex. So 'If H then O' must be replaced with 'If H & I_1 & ... & I_m then O' where I_1, ..., I_m describe such conditions.

But more is needed, for nearly all scientific investigation proceeds against a background of previously tested and accepted hypotheses that are being assumed in the current experiment. These are **auxiliary hypotheses** that typically (though not always) have gained high confirmation in the past and whose truth is relevant to the hypothesis under study. In Torricelli's case, an obvious example would be that mercury is 13.6 times denser than water. Similarly, if we attempt to establish the curvature of the earth's surface by observing that a ship sailing away from us disappears gradually from sight—its decks falling from view before its masts—we must assume the auxiliary hypothesis that light travels in straight lines. Auxiliary hypotheses are used not only to establish the truth or falsehood of observation statements, but sometimes to support certain statements of initial conditions. In any case, it now appears that a better formulation of the HDM would be

II. If H & I_1 & ... & I_m & A_1 & ... & A_n then O
     O
     ∴ H

where the A_1 ..., A_n express the relevant auxiliary hypotheses.

Disconfirming a Hypothesis: Suppose now that the observation statement inferred from a given hypothesis together with the auxiliary hypotheses and statements of initial conditions has been shown experimentally to be false. Suppose also that the auxiliary hypotheses and initial condition statements are all true. What can be inferred about the hypothesis H itself? By purely deductive reasoning it follows that H is also false. The result ~O means that the antecedent of the first premise in schema (II) is false, and since H is the only conjunct whose truth is still in question, it is H that must be rejected. The argument that follows (where the third premise expresses the working assumption that all initial condition statements and auxiliary hypotheses are true) is valid and can be shown so on truth table grounds:

(H & I_1 & ... & I_m & A_1 & ... & A_n) ⊃ O
~O
I_1 & ... & I_m & A_1 & ... & A_n
∴ ~H

Clearly the only way an investigator might still maintain H in the face of the result ~O would be by rejecting one or more statements conjoined in the third premise (or by holding that O is really true despite the observed results, which is also in effect a rejection of some of the initial conditions). It is of course possible but usually very improbable that at least one of the initial condition statements or auxiliary hypotheses is at fault. Occasionally, though, such cases do occur.

> *Example 3*: From Newton's hypotheses about motion and gravity together with the initial conditions concerning known bodies of our solar system, the orbital motions of Uranus were deduced. However it was observed that the planet's motions were quite different from what was predicted. Rather than reject Newton's theory, several astronomers hypothesized that another planet existed whose gravitational influence would account for the observed disparities. Neptune was later discovered telescopically, and the information acquired about its own movements led to a revised set of initial conditions that made possible the deduction of Uranus's true orbit.

When, as here, an otherwise well-established hypothesis suffers an ostensible disconfirmation, it is not rejected unless and until we acquire adequate data that renders likely a correct prediction. If a hypothesis like Newton's is to be rejected, there must exist a competing hypothesis to supplant it with strong and independently acquired evidence backing it up; and if initial conditions or auxiliary hypotheses are to be altered, again there must be independent evidence that the new conditions or hypotheses are true (as when Neptune was actually located telescopically). No rival hypothesis was available of course at the time when Uranus's peculiarities were observed.

Later, however, Einstein developed his general theory of relativity, which received a great deal of confirmation from experiments performed in the early twentieth century, and just prior to this, perturbations in Mercury's orbit had also been detected. To account for them on Newton's theory, it was hypothesized that a planet ("Vulcan" it was called) existed whose orbit was between Mercury's and the Sun. Unfortunately, all attempts to find this planet ended in failure. But from Einstein's hypotheses one could deduce an orbital path very similar to the observed orbit of Mercury without resorting to the Vulcan conjecture, and hence the observed data concerning Mercury's orbit turned out to be a major blow to the Newtonian theory. In this case, then, instead of continuing to uphold Newton and seeking revised initial conditions, the emergence of an independently confirmed rival hypothesis led astrophysicists to regard the Vulcan episode as a case of authentic disconfirmation of Newton's laws.

Of course Newton's work was never completely rejected as, say, the theory of spontaneous generation was following Pasteur's experiments. Although no longer considered to be literally correct, Newton's laws still have a useful if limited application to relatively "short" distances on earth, to bodies moving at speeds much slower than that of light, and to gravitational fields not as strong as those often found in outer space. Within this realm of application, his laws may still be regarded as highly confirmed.

Confirming a Hypothesis: Returning to schema (II), we have seen that from the standpoint of deductive logic, the argument is simply invalid; even though all initial condition statements and auxiliary hypotheses are true and O has been shown true experimentally, we cannot *validly* infer the truth of H. However, for an H and an O like those, say, in example (2), it would appear that we have an *inductively strong* inference. H is very probably true; that is, highly confirmed by O in the presence of the initial conditions and auxiliary hypotheses. Yet such an appearance can be misleading in many cases, for schema (II), although less of an oversimplification than schema (I), still ignores some of the complexities involved in scientific confirmation.

One complexity is this: While O may confirm H, it may also confirm (and to a roughly similar degree) a *competing* hypothesis H'. In such a case, the probability of H is not significantly raised. When Copernicus developed his heliocentric theory, according to which the earth and other planets revolve about the sun, his mathematical machinery enabled him to predict with high accuracy the paths of the known planets through the sky. However, it was noted in the first chapter that the Ptolemaic theory prevalent at the time, in which the earth is stationary and the Sun and planets revolve about it, could predict those paths with similar accuracy. Consequently, the truth of observation statements describing those paths did little by themselves to win adherents to the heliocentric view.

Thus, consideration of rival hypotheses from which the same true observation can be deduced must be worked into a complete formulation of the HDM. And to see how serious the problem is, let us consider example (1) again. Galileo's formula, '$d = (\frac{1}{2})gt^2$', is of course very highly confirmed, and measurements have been made for many values of the variable t. But what about the *other* values of t, those for which there has been no actual empirical test? If for example no one has ever tested the formula for $t = 17.2$ seconds, we would still infer that were we to do so, an object would have fallen 4733.4 feet. But there are other formulae of the general form '$d = f(t)$' that agree with Galileo on the observed values but that depart from it in many of those that in fact have never been tested; for our case of 17.2 seconds, one hypothesis might predict 4800 feet, another 4571.3, and so forth.

These other hypotheses, then, are competitors with Galileo's *and* are confirmed by all the available empirical evidence that confirms his. Where H is Galileo's hypothesis, then, imagine replacing H in the first premise of schema (II) by the theoretical rivals H', H", and so forth. In each case, that premise might well remain true, for in conjunction with the initial conditions and auxiliary hypotheses (or appropriately altered versions of them), its antecedent could still logically imply the truth of O. Of course we could presumably falsify some of the competitors by further testing, but no amount of finite testing would eliminate all possible rivals to the Galilean formula. The question then is this: Given that further tests cannot disconfirm all possible competitors to Galileo, what rational justification can be supplied for accepting Galileo's formula and thereby rejecting those confirmed by the same body of evidence?

This problem leads us directly into another complexity involved in giving a precise and general account of the HDM: that of the *prior probabilities* (as in Bayes' Theorem) of the hypotheses. A necessary condition for determining the degree to which an experimental finding O confirms H is that we have a reasonably good idea of the probability H has before the testing that showed O to be true; that is, of the value for $Pr(H/E)$, as opposed to $Pr(H/E \& O)$, where E includes the previously acquired evidence for H.[4] A prior probability is not to be thought of as simply a scientist's personal estimate, but rather as the degree to which the existing evidence E in conjunction with certain other factors to be mentioned later makes H a "plausible candidate" for testing. If the prior probability is very low, scientists will be reluctant to spend time and money testing the hypothesis; and if it is very high, as in the case of Newton's laws in example (3), they will try to save it from apparent disconfirmation by questioning the initial conditions or auxiliary hypotheses.

A full-scale examination of prior probabilities is a topic for the philosophy of science and will not be undertaken here; their theoretical status and their role in scientific method are matters of considerable dispute at the present time. But regardless of such concerns, the theoretical competitors to Galileo's formula presumably are much less plausible prior to any new testing, and so we should now take a brief look at the kinds of considerations involved in determining a hypothesis's prior probability.

First, of course, some hypotheses are assigned low prior probabilities simply because of the known data concerning their subject matter. It is doubtful that a serious investigation will ever be undertaken over the question of whether eating chicken soup will cure a cold. We know enough about the ingredients of chicken soup to know that it is unlikely that they have any real curative properties whether singly or in combination.

Second, we have already noted a rule from the logic of inquiry concerning simplicity: If two or more competing hypotheses are supported by roughly the same body of evidence, we should choose the simplest of them. And historically, the simplest hypotheses in the natural sciences have tended to be the best ones. The as-yet-unrefuted alternatives to Galileo are vastly more complicated than his equation and do not yield as simple and uniform an increase in velocity. Simplicity is surely the major factor in the assignment of high prior probability here.

Third, another rule of inquiry concerns compatibility with known laws. If a hypothesis is incompatible with well-confirmed hypotheses and has little going for it by way of hard evidence, a low prior probability is warranted. Hypotheses concerning the powers of witches or mediums often conflict with accepted laws of physics and hence are not taken seriously.

This list is far from exhaustive, but should give the general idea. The determination of a prior probability is typically anything but easy, though a careful estimate is often enough for many purposes. In fact, usually it is sufficient to know that the value is not close to 0—that the hypothesis is not fanciful, capricious, or downright ludicrous. For if it is near 0, a confirming observation statement will not in general increase its probability to a significant level.

On the other hand, a hypothesis with a high prior probability can be highly confirmed by an observation statement that testing has shown to be true. The problem, however, lies in *finding* such hypotheses. Thinking them up requires imagination, insight, ingenuity; scientific creativity is no less difficult than that of the painter or composer (although this problem will be lessened if progress is made in the logic of inquiry). Consequently, in a typical testing situation there are but a few competing hypotheses to be taken seriously. In those rare cases in which there are many competitors, each with a respectable prior probability, the emphasis is on disconfirmation and hence elimination.

The foregoing shows that, to obtain a more accurate and general version of the HDM, schema (II) needs to be supplemented. Where 'Pr(H/E)' expresses the prior probability of the hypothesis, we have

III. If $H \& I_1 \& \ldots \& I_m \& A_1 \& \ldots \& A_n$ then O
   O
   Pr(H/E) is not negligible
   Pr(H/E) exceeds that of every competing hypothesis that
       would also be confirmed by O
   $\therefore$ H

Crucial Tests: Suppose H and H′ are the only competing hypotheses with a nonnegligible prior probability and are unquestionably mutually exclusive (not, as sometimes happens, just alternative characterizations of the same explanation). Ordinarily, both, in conjunction with their initial conditions and auxiliary hypotheses, will validly yield a number of observation statements in common, as the example about the heliocentric and Ptolemaic hypotheses shows. However, there will also be cases where H will yield an observation statement O that is *incompatible* with an O' yielded by H'. Hence at least one of O and O' must be false, and ideally a crucial test can be devised to determine which if either is true. If O' is shown to be false, H' is strongly disconfirmed; and if O is true, we have good grounds for accepting H inasmuch as it has been substantially confirmed by the evidence obtained in the test. Perhaps the most famous example of crucial testing is the nineteenth-century dispute between the wave and corpuscular theories of light mentioned briefly in Chapter 3 in connection with Bayes' Theorem. It well illustrates why such tests rarely yield results that are as decisive as the word "crucial" would suggest.

> *Example 4*: By 1830 the wave theory, as a result of some experiments by the physicists Young and Fresnel, had acquired a higher probability than the corpuscular theory, but the dispute was by no means settled. The wave theory (H) validly yields the observation statement (O_1) that a phenomenon known as Newton's rings should not appear if there is no reflection from the first surface of a thin plate, while the corpusular theory (H') implies that they should still be seen under these conditions. An experiment by G. B. Airy in 1831 showed that O_1 was true. Moreover, the wave theory holds that light travels more rapidly in air than in water (O_2) while the corpuscular theory maintained the opposite. In 1850 the physicists Foucault and Fizeau were able to measure experimentally the two speeds with the result that it travels more rapidly in air. These experiments decisively confirmed the wave theory at the time.

Where E summarizes the evidence available by 1830, then, $Pr(H/E) > Pr(H'/E)$, but the latter value was still reasonably high. As a result of the Airy and Foucault-Fizeau experiments, however, $Pr(H/E \& O_1 \& O_2)$ was *much* greater than $Pr(H'/E \& O_1 \& O_2)$, so much so that the former value is close to 1 while the latter is near 0.

Why "close to 1" and "near 0" instead of an unqualified 1 and 0? After all the observation statements were validly *deduced* from the hypotheses, and hence their probabilities *given* the wave hypothesis should be 1, and they should be 0 for the corpuscular thesis. These probabilities are essentially what were termed "likelihoods" in our coverage of Bayes' Theorem back in Chapter Three. Where x and y are the prior probabilities respectively of the wave and corpuscular theories, Bayes' Theorem may be used to represent the situation as follows:

$$\text{Posterior probability of } W = \frac{1x}{1x + 0_y} = 1$$

$$\text{Posterior probability of } C = \frac{0y}{1x + 0_y} = 0$$

Of course these calculations are unrealistic. As the first premise of schema (III) shows, the hypotheses validly yield the observation statements only in conjunction with initial-condition statements and auxiliary hypotheses, and these point up various sources of difficulty in the confirmation process that make assignments of 1 or 0 to the likelihoods unwarranted. Despite the fact that O_1 and O_2 are deductively implied by the wave hypothesis together with initial condition statements, auxiliary hypotheses, and previously acquired evidence (and their negations are similarly implied by the corpuscular hypothesis), there is always the probability however small that one or more of those further statements is false. Concerning initial conditions, it is possible though improbable that Airy and Foucault-Fizeau did not really succeed in establishing the truth of O_1 and O_2. For example, the latter researchers did not directly observe light traveling faster in air; their observations were made using a complicated apparatus composed of a rapidly revolving mirror and lens along with stationary mirrors and other devices. Error is always possible in such cases.

In addition, many auxiliary hypotheses were assumed, the most important of which was that there existed an "ether" through which the waves were propagated. This hypothesis was later rejected by Einstein and other twentieth-century physicists following a well-known experiment by Michaelson and Morley that turned up no evidence of such an ether. Hence this auxiliary hypothesis was eventually rejected, leading to a reexamination of the wave theory despite the confirmation it had received from Airy and Foucault-Fizeau.

Moreover, the corpuscular theory itself was a complex thesis, and consequently the outcome of the Foucault-Fizeau experiment (even granting the truth of all auxiliary hypotheses) warrants only the inference that not all of the theory is true or, in other words, that at least one of its components is false. But the experiment could not tell us which elements are to be rejected and thus leaves open the possibility that some sort of particle-like conception of the propagation of light is correct. This fact, together with further developments like the Michaelson-Morley results, led to the particle/wave hypothesis of the present day.[5]

Thus a value of 1 or 0 is as unrealistic in the case of posterior probabilities as it is with likelihoods, no matter how "decisive" the experimental outcome may appear. Because of its complexity and its reliance on inductive reasoning, the confirmation process never makes a hypothesis 100% certain regardless of how carefully the tests are conducted or how compelling the truth of the auxiliary hypotheses may be. And there are yet further factors that may adversely affect the determination of a posterior probability. For example, the investigator could be wrong in the assessment of a hypothesis's prior probability or there might be a competing hypothesis with a higher prior probability that no one has yet thought of. Moreover, hypotheses are not always given precise expression and are constantly subject to change and reformulation. In fact, one reason why the wave theory had a higher probability prior to the experiments outlined in example (4) was because of some alterations proposed by Young and Fresnel.

Rarely if at all, then, does a "crucial" experiment definitively reject one of the two competing hypotheses. A hypothesis can be saved in the face of a negative test result by rejecting an auxiliary hypothesis or else by reformulating the hypothesis, rejecting certain components of it thought to be at fault. Nor does such an experiment establish beyond question the truth of the hypothesis confirmed; as we saw in the Galileo example, there will always in theory be alternatives left that are confirmed by the same evidence. In a strict sense, then, perhaps there are no crucial experiments, but in a more pragmatic construal of the term, tests such as those of Airy and Foucault-Fizeau are "crucial" in that they, first, point up that one of the two rival theories is seriously flawed and, second, provide considerable evidential support for the other. Consequently, such experiments always have a definitive impact on the future course of hypothesis construction and testing.[6]

The second experiment described in the Torricelli example (i.e., showing that the column of mercury descends with an increase in altitude) can also be considered a crucial experiment in this sense. Torricelli's atmospheric pressure hypothesis was proposed in opposition to the prevailing theory of the time; viz., that "nature abhors a vacuum." On this latter theory, water rises in the pump cylinder to fill the vacuum created by the upward movement of the piston. Moreover, the theory offered plausible accounts of other kinds of phenomena as well, such as why it is necessary to punch a hole in the top of a wine cask as well as the bottom in order to drain its contents. But the theory ran into trouble with other data, including why the pumped water would rise no further than 33 feet. The results of the altitude test were widely regarded at the time as a decisive refutation of the abhorrence hypothesis and likewise a dramatic confirmation of Torricelli's.

Of course we could try to save the older theory by adding a new auxiliary hypothesis; viz., that nature's abhorrence of vacuums decreases with increasing altitude. But although this thesis is not absurdly false, there was not the slightest evidence for thinking it to be true. The most objectionable feature of it, however, is that it would be introduced in a purely ad hoc manner; that is, its only rationale would be that of salvaging a hypothesis that has been dealt a severe experimental blow. Not all ad hoc hypotheses are objectionable in this way, but if—as in the present example—they fail to account for other relevant phenomena requiring explanation and yield no further significant test implications, then they are unacceptable as a component of a scientific explanation. However, the atmospheric pressure hypothesis explains a wide range of phenomena and readily yields further testing consequences; for example, that a partly inflated balloon at sea level will be more fully inflated on a mountaintop and also (in conjunction with other accepted hypotheses) that water will boil at a lower temperature atop a mountain than it will at lesser elevations.[7]

In the examples considered so far, the hypothesis (in conjunction with the initial condition statements and auxiliary hypotheses) validly yields its observation statements, and thus the first premise of schema (III) expresses a deductively correct inference (in effect, it is a logical truth). However, there are many cases where the inference from the hypothesis to the observation statement is only one of probability. Here, then, the inference embodied in the first premise is inductive and may be expressed by a type of inductive probability statement found in the formula for Bayes' Theorem. To take a very simple (and fictional) example

Example 5: Let us suppose that there are two genetic varieties of terriers, Type 1 and Type 2, we will call them. Your terrier Spot is one of the two but you do not know which (hence hypotheses H_1 and H_2), but he was recently bred with a Type 1 female. When two Type 1 dogs are mated, the resultant litter typically produces a ratio of five black puppies to one brown; and when a Type 1 and Type 2 are mated the result is a ratio of two blacks to three brown. In a few months we observe the new litter (giving us observation statement O): when Spot was mated with a Type 1, the result was two brown puppies and one black. Statement O thus provides significant confirmation of H_2 and correspondingly disconfirms H_1.

Given the minimal information about Spot available to us, then where E compresses the relevant auxiliary hypotheses, and so forth, the prior probabilities of our two hypotheses are presumably

$$\Pr(H_1/E) = 0.5 \qquad \Pr(H_2/E) = 0.5$$

Of course neither H_1 nor H_2 even in conjunction with the initial condition data and auxiliary hypotheses *implies* statement O—the inference is not valid since it is quite possible in both instances for the litter to have been different. On the other hand, O is much more *probable* if H_2 were true than if H_1 were, and in the present case numerical probabilities are assignable:

$$\text{Pr}(O/H_1 \text{ \& } E) = \binom{3}{2} (1/6)^2(5/6) = 0.069$$

$$\text{Pr}(O/H_2 \text{ \& } E) = \binom{3}{2} (3/5)^2(2/5) = 0.432$$

Note that these conditional probabilities are precisely what were called "likelihoods" in our discussion of Bayes' Theorem back in the third chapter, and they in effect express the probability of the first premise of schema (III)—the likelihood of O being true given H. The HDM, construed as the pattern of inference spelled out in that schema (and referring as it does to the prior probabilities of rival hypotheses) thus can be more precisely expressed as an application of Bayes' Theorem. The degree to which our observation statement confirms or disconfirms the two hypotheses is now just a simple and by now quite familiar calculation:

$$\text{Pr}(H_1/O \text{ \& } E) = \frac{(0.5)(0.069)}{(0.5)(0.069) + (0.5)(0.432)} = 0.138$$
$$\text{Pr}(H_2/O \text{ \& } E) = 1 - 0.138 = 0.862$$

Finally, the characterization of the HDM in terms of schema (III) and the examples used here to illustrate it can perhaps be misleading in one respect: that in confirming a hypothesis we deal with just one or two potentially confirming observation statements. On the contrary, to avoid accepting hypotheses based on inadequate evidence or biased data, a hypothesis should be tested many times under the most diverse conditions achievable. An accurate picture of scientific investigation requires emphasis on repeated application of the HDM toward the end of acquiring a large and diversified body of confirming evidence.

Section 2. Some Confirmation Principles and a Paradox _____

Philosophers of science have expended much effort over the years exploring the logic of the confirmation concept, and while much progress has been made, a full examination of their efforts is beyond the scope of a book on inductive logic.[8] Instead, we will focus on some principles that most writers on the subject regard as conditions that must be satisfied by any satisfactory analysis of scientific confirmation. We shall also look at a problem that has arisen in the quest for such an analysis. Both the principles and the problems fall within the province of inductive probability and hence inductive logic.

The principles we will look at may, with some minimal assumptions, be deduced as theorems of the probability calculus. In what follows, we shall use the variable h (with or without subscripts) to range over hypotheses, o (again with or without subscripts) for observation statements, and e to express previously acquired evidence for h. To conserve space, we will write the denominator in the formula for Bayes' Theorem simply as '$\Pr(o/e)$' instead of the long summation used in Chapter Three, a move justified by a previous theorem (i.e., the Prediction Theorem, Theorem 11) that simply identifies $\Pr(o/e)$ with that summation. We will need to make the following obvious assumption:

o confirms h if and only if $\Pr(h/o \ \& \ e) > \Pr(h/e)$

Our first principle basically states that logical implication—the relation between premise and conclusion of a deductively valid argument—is a limiting case of confirmation. Since, for example, A v B validly follows from A, the latter is also confirmation of A v B (and of course confirms it to the degree 1 according to Axiom 3 of the calculus). In the typical case, as we have seen, while h often validly yields o (at least in conjunction with initial condition statements and auxiliary hypotheses), the reverse does not hold. The first principle, however, states that where it *does* hold, o is also to be considered as confirming h as well. Its proof depends on the very plausible assumption that $\Pr(h/e) < 1$.

> ***The Entailment Condition:*** If o implies h, then o confirms h; that is, if $o \rightarrow h$, then $\Pr(h/o \ \& \ e) > \Pr(h/e)$.

PROOF: Assume $o \rightarrow h$
TF: $(o \ \& \ e) \rightarrow o$
RI: $(o \ \& \ e) \rightarrow h$
Ax.3: $\Pr(h/o \ \& \ e) = 1$
Since $\Pr(h/e) < 1$: $\Pr(h/o \ \& \ e) > \Pr(h/e)$; that is, o confirms h.

We have seen that on the HDM a hypothesis receives confirmation whenever one of the observation sentences that validly follow from it is established.[9] In other words, if h implies o, then o would provide confirmation of h. Making the very natural assumptions that $\Pr(h/e) = 0$ and that $0 < \Pr(o/e) < 1$, this principle is readily proved.

Converse Entailment Condition: If h implies o, then o confirms h; that is, if $h{\rightarrow}o$, then $\text{Pr}(h/o \ \& \ e) > \text{Pr}(h/e)$.

PROOF: **1.** Assume $h{\rightarrow}o$ (and $\text{Pr}(h/e) = 0$ and $0 < \text{Pr}(o/e) < 1$)
　　　2. TF: $(h \ \& \ e){\rightarrow}h$
　　　3. RI: $(h \ \& \ e){\rightarrow}o$
　　　4. Ax. 3: $\text{Pr}(o/h \ \& \ e) = 1$
　　　5. AR (1): $\text{Pr}(o/e) < 1$
　　　6. AR (1), (5): $1/\text{Pr}(o/e) > 1$
　　　7. AR (4), (6): $\dfrac{\text{Pr}(h/e)\text{Pr}(o/h \ \& \ e)}{\text{Pr}(o/e)} > \text{Pr}(h/e)$
　　　8. Thm.12 (Bayes' Theorem): $\text{Pr}(h/o \ \& \ e) > \text{Pr}(h/e)$; that is, o confirms h.

Step (7) is obtained from (6) by multiplying through with $\text{Pr}(h/e)$, and by replacing '1' with '$\text{Pr}(o/h \ \& \ e)$' according to step 4.

A seemingly plausible confirmation principle (sometimes called the "Special Consequence Condition") asserts that whatever confirms a hypothesis also confirms any hypothesis that validly follows from it. That is,

If o confirms h and $h{\rightarrow}h'$, then o confirms h'.

For example, the principle requires that an observation confirming Newton's Law of Gravitation would also confirm any of Kepler's laws of planetary motion (since the former in conjunction with the laws of motion implies the latter).

Yet, as the following counterexample shows, acceptance of this principle would seem to commit us to the intolerable result that o confirms *every* statement whatever! Let h be the conjunction of *any* pair of statements, A and B (they might be 'grass is green' and 'Lincoln was a Republican', respectively), and let o be A and h' be B. Now A confirms A & B and it is obvious that (A & B)${\rightarrow}$B, so the Special Consequence Condition requires us to hold that A also confirms B, that is, that 'grass is green' confirms 'Lincoln was a Republican' or any other statement substituted for h'. It thus appears that we must reject the principle.

However, the matter is not that simple. The American philosopher Nelson Goodman has argued that while A "supports" A & B in the sense of "reducing the net undetermined claim," it does not confirm it since "establishment of one component endows the whole statement with no credibility that is transmitted to [the other component]." Confirmation, he says, "occurs only when an instance imparts to the hypothesis some credibility that is conveyed to other instances," as in the instance '$Fa \ \& \ Ga$' confirming 'All F are G'.[10] Here, the former genuinely confirms the latter since it also increases the credibility of further instances like '*Fb* & *Gb*' and '*Fc* & *Gc*', while A does not do the same for the right conjunct of A & B. So on Goodman's view, although every case of confirmation is one of support, not every case of support is one of confirmation. Insofar as its inductive probability is raised, A & B is supported by A, and the same holds for 'All *F* are *G*' relative to '*Fa* & *Ga*'; but only the latter case involves confirmation. For writers like Goodman, genuine confirmation is essentially linked to the notion of prediction; the predictive power of 'All *F* are *G*' is enhanced relative to future instances given the observation '*Fa* & *Ga*'.

In Goodman's approach, although every valid deductive consequence of a hypothesis supports that hypothesis, not all of them confirm it (in the proposed counterexample, A supports A & B since it validly follows from it, but does not confirm it). As a result, our "obvious" assumption made earlier,

$$o \text{ confirms } h \text{ if and only if } \Pr(h/o \ \& \ e) > \Pr(h/e)$$

would have to be altered by replacing 'confirms' with 'supports'. Moreover, the Converse Entailment Condition as stated previously would have to be dropped; but again, if 'confirms' is replaced by 'supports' it would presumably be legitimate in Goodman's usage. Most important, the Special Consequence Condition would be immune to the counterexample just cited, and it is an accepted principle for writers like Goodman and Carl Hempel.

We cannot pursue this matter any further here, and for the balance of our discussion we will continue to use 'confirm' in the broader sense employed to this point, where in effect it means what Goodman intends by the word 'support'. For our main concern is the concept of inductive probability or *degree* of confirmation, in other words "quantitative" confirmation. However, Goodman and Hempel are chiefly concerned with giving a precise explication of "qualitative" confirmation that forgoes distinctions of degree and construes confirmation simply as a relation between an evidence sentence and a hypothesis. As such, it is the inductive counterpart of the relation of logical implication in deductive logic, and traditionally the starting point for studying it is the notion of confirmation as applied to a generalization and its confirming instances. Indeed, Goodman's usage seems tied to hypotheses that are generalizations, and it is not clear what becomes of the confirmation concept when applied to "particular" and "statistical" hypotheses.

If a hypothesis h validly yields two observation statements, o_1 and o_2, and o_1 describes a more surprising or unexpected phenomenon than o_2 (prior to the consideration of h), then o_1 confirms h to a higher degree than o_2. For example, we saw in the last section that observations of Mercury's orbital motions made around the turn of the century were puzzling to astronomers of that day; let these be described in o_1. However, Einstein's general theory of relativity (hypothesis h) was developed shortly after this and could account for those otherwise problematic movements. We should expect o_1, then, to provide greater confirmation of Einstein's theory than the measurement of an ordinary and well-known phenomenon such as (let this be o_2) the motion of a pendulum. That the theory could accurately predict the pendulum's movements was to be expected; that it could predict Mercury's was a surprising and important development (especially in light of the failure of Newton's theory to do so). We may now formulate the principle involved here as follows:

> ***Principle of Unexpected Evidence:*** If $h{\rightarrow}o_1$ and $h{\rightarrow}o_2$ and $\Pr(o_2/e) > \Pr(o_1/e)$ then $\Pr(h/o_1 \,\&\, e) > \Pr(h/o_2 \,\&\, e)$.

A proof of the principle is easily sketched. Assuming the antecedent, it follows from the first two conjuncts by reasoning exactly similar to the first four lines of the preceding two proofs that

$$\Pr(o_1/h \,\&\, e) = \Pr(o_2/h \,\&\, e) = 1$$

From the righthand conjunct of the antecedent (together with the obvious assumption that $\Pr(o_2/e)$ is less than 1), we obtain by AR

$$1/\Pr(o_1/e) > 1/\Pr(o_2/e)$$

From the previous two steps, multiplying through by $\Pr(h/e)$—which is naturally assumed to be greater than 0—we get

$$\frac{\Pr(h/e)\Pr(o_1/h \,\&\, e)}{\Pr(o_1/e)} > \frac{\Pr(h/e)\Pr(o_2/h \,\&\, e)}{\Pr(o_2/e)}$$

which by Bayes' Theorem yields $\Pr(h/o_1 \,\&\, e) > \Pr(h/o_2 \,\&\, e)$. By AR then we have

$$\Pr(h/o_1 \,\&\, e) - \Pr(h/e) > \Pr(h/o_2 \,\&\, e) - \Pr(h/e);$$
$$\text{that is, } o_1 \text{ confirms } h \text{ more than } o_2 \text{ does.}$$

A very basic and transparent confirmation principle is the **Equivalence Condition:** If an observation statement confirms a hypothesis, then it confirms any equivalent hypothesis and to the same degree. Its proof is easy since it is but a corollary to Theorem 5 of the calculus (The Substitution Theorem).

The Equivalence Condition: If o confirms h_1 and $h_1 \leftrightarrow h_2$, then o confirms h_2 and to the same degree.

PROOF: **1.** Assume o confirms h_1 and $h_1 \leftrightarrow h_2$

2. DF (1): $\Pr(h_1/o \,\&\, e) > \Pr(h_1/e)$

3. Thm. 5 twice, (1): $\Pr(h_1/o \,\&\, e) = \Pr(h_2/o \,\&\, e)$ and $\Pr(h_1/e) = \Pr(h_2/e)$

4. AR (2),(3): $\Pr(h_2/o \,\&\, e) > \Pr(h_2/e)$; that is, o confirms h_2

5. AR (2),(3),(4): $\Pr(h_1/o \,\&\, e) - \Pr(h_1/e) = \Pr(h_2/o \,\&\, e) - \Pr(h_2/e)$; that is, o confirms h_2 to the same degree as h_1

The Equivalence Condition is a widely accepted principle and its truth seems obvious and unquestionable. Yet it runs afoul of a problem often called *the Raven Paradox* (it has nothing per se to do with birds, it is just that the example commonly used involves them). The problem is one to be taken seriously, not only because of the trouble it creates for the notion of confirmation, but because failure to find a solution would require us to reject Theorem 5 of the calculus, and with it the axioms from which it is deduced.

The Raven Paradox. Consider a simple generalization like

1. All F are G

for example, "All ravens are black." Observing an object a that is both a raven and black would obviously be considered confirmation of the statement to some (perhaps small) degree. That is, an observational instance like

2. $Fa \,\&\, Ga$

would be taken as offering some evidence for (1). But now consider the equivalent generalization:

3. All non-G are non-F

or in other words, "All nonblack things are nonravens." Just as (2) would confirm (1), so it would appear that observing an object b such that

4. $\sim Gb \,\&\, \sim Fb$

confirms generalization (3). That is, observation of a nonblack nonraven offers some confirmation of the hypothesis that every nonblack object is not a raven. But, as any elementary deductive logic text will tell us, (3) is equivalent to (1), and since (4) clearly confirms (3) it must also according to the Equivalence Condition confirm (1) as well.

But it seems absurd to say that (4) confirms (1). After all, the object *b* mentioned in (4) could be any number of things that would seem to have nothing at all to do with confirming the hypothesis that all ravens are black. Object *b* could be a white tennis shoe or a blue waterbed or a red Chevy Nova or . . ., and it just seems ludicrous to suppose that observing such things somehow confirms generalization (1). How could the observation of green swimming trunks possibly confirm (hence raise the probability of) all ravens being black?

This, then, is the Raven Paradox. Plain common sense would appear to tell us that (4) does not confirm (1) even though it obviously confirms (3), and yet the Equivalence Condition tells us it *must* confirm it since (1) and (3) are equivalent. The upshot is that unless we are prepared to say what seems grossly wrong—that (4) confirms (1)—we must reject the Equivalence Condition and accept some highly undesirable consequences concerning confirmation and the probability calculus.[11]

Before looking at proposed solutions to the paradox, a clarification about statements (1) and (3) is appropriate. It is sometimes (mistakenly) thought that a generalization like (1) is to be understood as a statement strictly about the members of its subject class, about the class of things that have *F* (ravens in our example), whereas (3), then, would be about the quite different class of things that are non-*G* (i.e., nonblack objects). As such, so it is thought, they make different claims, and an instance like (2) would confirm only (1) but not (3), and by the same token (4) would confirm only (3) and not (1).

Perhaps from a psychological or pragmatic standpoint there is some plausibility in this; in saying 'All ravens are black' we express our interest in (and our wish to "talk about") ravens, but from a *logical* point of view a generalization—*any* generalization—must be taken as an assertion about *all* objects whatever. To say that all ravens are black is to say something about each and every object, viz., that it either is not a raven or else is black; to put it equivalently, *if* it is a raven *then* it is black. And this in fact is how generalizations are treated in formal deductive logic; (1) and (3) become

For every object *x*, if *x* is *F* then *x* is *G*.
For every object *x*, if *x* is not *G* then *x* is not *F*.

Logically considered, then, (1) and (3) are about the same things and are indeed equivalent. Hence by the Equivalence Condition (2) must confirm (3) as well as (1), and (4) must confirm (1) as well as (3). Just as (1) and (3) must be jointly true or jointly false, so (2) and (4) must stand together as mutually confirming or nonconfirming instances of both (1) and (3).

We will now take a brief look at two common approaches to resolving the paradox. It should be emphasized that there are other proposals too, but space does not permit further discussion here.[12]

A Proposed Solution: Perhaps it is *not* so odd to suppose that (4) confirms (1). By the Rule of Total Evidence we should make use of all relevant background information available to us in drawing inferences (information to be included in *e* in 'Pr(*h/e*)'), and among the items in our backlog of knowledge is that there are a great many more nonblack things in the universe than there are ravens and in general vastly more non-*G*s than *F*s. Hence we can argue on quantitative grounds that, since the number of instances of nonblack objects far exceeds those of ravens, then for anyone cognizant of this fact, an observation of an instance of the first kind offers considerably less confirmation of (1)—and of course (3)—than one of the second kind. In other words, if there are any counterexamples to (1) and (3), they have a greater relative frequency with respect to the class of *ravens* than they do with respect to the much more numerous class of *nonblack things*. So we have done more to show that the generalizations are true when we eliminate a member of the first class as a counterexample than when one of the latter class is eliminated. And elimination is tantamount to confirmation inasmuch as the generalizations are equivalent to the statement that *denies* that there is an object which is both a raven and nonblack (all *F* are *G* ↔ there is no *F* that is not *G*). On this approach, then, the Equivalence Condition is preserved at the expense of holding that an observational instance of form (4) offers some (though a miniscule amount of) confirmation for all ravens being black.

But we should not balk at (4) providing some confirming evidence. For advocates of this view, observing a nonblack thing that in addition is not a raven removes what would otherwise be a counterexample to both (1) and (3)—had the nonblack object turned out to be a raven both generalizations would have been falsified. Again, elimination in such a context amounts to confirmation; the statements are confirmed at least to the extent that they have successfully run the risk of falsification. So once we realize that, first, (4) does indeed offer evidence for (1), but second, an amount even less than the small amount provided by (2), the paradox disappears.

Yet many will find this approach unsatisfying. For one thing, there appear to be generalizations where the class of non-*G*s is not larger than the class of *F*s, and yet the paradoxicality of the situation remains. Consider

All atomic particles are inorganic.

The class of noninorganic things has fewer members presumably than the class of atomic particles, and yet to whatever extent it is puzzling that an observation of a pair of green swim trunks confirms (1), it is equally puzzling that observing your pet dog (a noninorganic thing that is a nonatomic particle) confirms the preceding generalization.

For another, to many writers it is just intuitively obvious that observing a pair of green swimming trunks offers *no* evidence whatever for all ravens being black—not a negligibly small amount of evidence but none at all. And if we try to spell out the uneasiness felt in holding that (4) confirms (1), it is perhaps this: The multitude of nonblack things may be sorted out into various "kinds" such as shoes, waterbeds, automobiles, swim trunks, and so forth, and it should be obvious to us *before* making any observations that none of these things is a raven. Since we know in advance they are not ravens, how could such an observation count as empirical evidence? The only way to refute the generalization is to produce an object that *is* a raven (and of course not black), so why bother to examine anything we already know is not a raven?[13]

A More Complete Proposal: For many writers, the preceding proposal is not completely wrong. Although flawed and incomplete, it points the way to a better solution, especially in its emphasis on the importance of background information. However, we will have to consider information beyond that of the ratio of nonblack things to ravens.

Our current proposal builds on the objection to the first one. Let us take as a working example the following generalizations of forms (3) and (1) respectively:[14]

a. Everything that does not burn with a yellow flame is not a sodium salt

b. All sodium salts burn with a yellow flame

Now let us imagine two different situations:

Scenario I: We hold a chunk of ice (or anything else that obviously is not a sodium salt) to a burner and note that it does not burn with a yellow flame.

Scenario II: We are given a substance whose identity is completely unknown to us and when it is held to a burner, we note that it does not burn with a yellow flame. Further investigation shows moreover that it is not a sodium salt either.

In each case we have a non-yellow-burning thing that is not a sodium salt, but there the resemblance ends. In the first scenario, our intuitions tell us that the observation does not confirm (b)—any more than observing the swim trunks confirms the raven generalization—though it might offer a little confirmation of (a). In the second scenario, we are inclined to say that the observation does indeed confirm both (a) and (b) to a small extent.

The only difference between the two cases is that in the first scenario we know beforehand what the test substance is, and it is a matter of common knowledge that ice is not a sodium salt. But the end result of this is that the outcome of the flame test is irrelevant for us as far as confirming (b) is concerned. The flame's not burning yellow would normally indicate of course that the substance is not a sodium salt, but we knew that already inasmuch as we could tell right off that it was a piece of ice. In the first scenario, then, we have more than just an instance of form (4) as relevant information; in addition we are at least tacitly making use of the background evidence:

c. The substance put to the flame is ice
d. Ice contains no sodium salts

Where '*i*' designates the chunk of ice, then, the statement '~*Yi* & ~*Si*' is not a *confirming* instance of either generalization because it is basically old news. We knew in advance, and independent of holding the ice to a flame (i.e., of observing that '~*Yi*'), that the conjunct '~*Si*' was true. Hence the previous conjunction tells us nothing we did not already know—our prior knowledge includes the fact that every specimen of sodium salt ever tested burned yellow and that many things that were not sodium salts (including ice) did not. Thus, if we explicitly include (c) and (d) along with (4) in our body of evidence, then the observed result of not burning yellow adds no new confirmation of (b). Note also that, despite what we might have at first said, it offers no confirmation of (a) either, and for the same reason.

On the other hand, if we *lack* additional information of this sort—as we do in the second scenario—then the nature of the experimental situation changes completely. It now becomes a genuine (if minimal) *test* of hypotheses (a) and (b). Given an object whose chemical makeup is not part of our prior information and when tested does not produce a yellow flame, then our observation of this fact constitutes confirming evidence for (b) as well as (a). For if, as in the second scenario, the other customary tests for sodium salinity are subsequently conducted and all turn out negative, then we may conclude inductively that the substance is not a sodium salt. That it is not is hence a conclusion we arrive at after further investigation; it is not, as in the first scenario, something we already knew on independent grounds. In a context such as this, these tests including the initial flame test show that our hitherto unknown substance will not undermine generalization (b), and to that extent will offer at least some confirmation for it. So an observational instance like (4) without information like (c) and (d) provides some evidence for (b), but with the inclusion of (c) and (d) under ordinary circumstances it does not.

Returning to the raven case, it is worth noting that if the observation of a nonblack nonraven were the *only* bit of evidence available to us (thus lacking information like the mutual exclusivity of ravens and swim trunks), we would regard it as confirmation to whatever small degree of the generalizations:

> All nonravens are nonblack.
> Everything (whatever) is neither a raven nor black.

Of course we hold these statements to be false because of enormous quantities of evidence to the contrary; observations of black coats and black cats clearly undermine them as (in the case of the second statement) does our highly confirmed belief that ravens exist. But without such information at hand, observing a nonblack nonraven is evidence however small for each of them, just as in the unknown substance case. If even these generalizations would be regarded as confirmed in such a circumstance, it should not be surprising that the narrower claim 'All ravens are black' is confirmed as well. After all, it is equivalent to saying of every object whatever either that it is not a raven or else is black, and in lieu of any background information, observations of green swim trunks and other nonblack nonravens are confirming instances of it. To observe the trunks is to observe an object that meets the complex condition of either-not-being-a-raven-or-being-black, and in a context devoid of any other information such an observation provides genuine evidence.

In summary, we have considered three types of cases:

1. Given a situation like scenario II in which no background information is available (or taken into account), observations of form (4) do indeed provide some confirmation of hypothesis (1), and these considerations should suffice to show that there is nothing paradoxical about this fact.
2. Given a situation in which the only relevant background information is that there are vastly more non-Gs than there are Fs (vastly more nonblack things than ravens), our first proposal applies: Observations like (4) also provide some small amount of confirmation of (1), and again there should no longer be anything puzzling about this. Our inclination to think otherwise results from tacitly making use of further information (e.g., that swim

trunks and ravens are distinct and readily distinguishable types of things) and leads us to misconstrue a small amount of confirmation for none at all.

3. Given a situation like scenario I in which the customarily large amount of background information is available and brought to bear (e.g., that swim trunks are not ravens or that ice is not a sodium salt), ordinary and casual observations of form (4)—as opposed to those that may be part of a genuine scientific test—do not confirm (1).

Hence everyday observations of green swim trunks and the like typically would not provide confirmation of the hypothesis that all ravens are black. Moreover, the Equivalence Condition would be preserved: In the first two cases, (4) confirms both (1) and (3) and in the last case it confirms neither. The words "ordinary and casual" here are important, for as J. L. Mackie and others have argued, if in a scenario I context our observations were somehow part of an experimental testing situation, confirmation to some degree would be present.[15] In any case, we have pursued the paradox as far as we can here; for more extensive discussion the reader should consult the essays cited in the notes to this section.[16]

Section 3. The New Riddle of Induction _____

In our discussion of the justification of induction back in the fifth chapter, we noted that Scientific Inductive Logic assumes a uniformity of nature principle: that, for example, heated gases will continue to expand in the future; that the law of gravity will not cease to operate; that metals will continue to conduct electricity; and more generally, as Hume put it, "instances of which we have had no experience must resemble those of which we have had experience, and . . . the course of nature continues always uniformly the same." However, we also noted that there are some observed uniformities that unlike those just cited are not a reliable basis for prediction: If a historian were to inform us that every Democratic U.S. president has had a younger sister, this is not a regularity that we would want to use as a basis for predictions about future Democratic presidents; or again, even though all birds ever observed have been hatched before the year 2020 AD, we would balk at projecting such a regularity indefinitely into the future. While we have no qualms about predicting the behavior of the next heated gas we encounter, it would be foolish to make predictions on the basis of these latter uniformities.

We initially tend to think that an inductive rule of inference of the following form is a sound one (indeed it is a version of Simple Enumeration). To put it very roughly: an argument of the form

> All observed *F*s have been *G*
> ∴ The next *F* to be observed will be *G*

is to be considered inductively strong if its premise is supported by many examined instances (expressed in statements like '*Fa* & *Ga*') under a variety of conditions with no counterexamples having ever been observed. In other words, generalizations (or uniformities or regularities) that are consistently supported by the acquired evidence are reliable instruments for making predictions. Indeed, it is just this sort of inference that Hume seems to have in mind in the passage cited previously.

But we can now see that this rule (let's call it *Rule E*) is no good as it stands and must be somehow modified or amended if it is to be considered an acceptable rule of SIL. For although it works fine with regularities about the expansion of gases and the conductivity of metals, it tells us the wrong thing with respect to "coincidences" or accidental correlations like the one about American presidents. To put this contrast in better focus, argument (A), which follows, is inductively strong, but argument (B) is not even though Rule E tells us otherwise:

A. All observed pieces of copper conduct electricity.
∴ The next piece of copper observed will conduct electricity.

B. All men observed who work in the Sears Tower are over 6 feet tall.
∴ The next man observed who works in the Sears Tower will be over 6 feet tall.

We will pretend for now that the premise of (B) is true; the point then is that even though it happens to be true, it is a poor instrument for forecasting the height of male workers at Sears Tower. In contrast, the premise of (A) is a generalization that provides a sound basis for prediction and thus is said to be a projectible regularity.

Therefore Rule E needs to be amended so that it still sanctions arguments like (A) as inductively strong but no longer does the same for a weak one like (B) containing an unprojectible regularity. And more generally, an adequate construction of Scientific Logic must contain rules for distinguishing projectible regularities from those that are not. An argument like (B) shows us that SIL assumes only that *certain kinds* of observed uniformities will continue into the future, not that all of them will; it assumes that nature is uniform but not with respect to *all* of the recurring patterns that have been observed. To say that sound predictions are those based on observed regularities in the past, without being able to say *which* regularities, is hence pointless; regularity in conductivity justifies prediction of future cases, but regularity in height range of male workers at Sears Tower does not. So Rule E as stated is unacceptable as a component of SIL because it fails to recognize projectibility differences in the statements serving as its premises.

Rule E, then, must be restricted to arguments with projectible premises, but it will do no good simply to insert a clause to this effect in the formulation of the rule. To amend the rule by having it read, "is inductively strong if *its premise is projectible* and is supported by many observed instances and so forth" is to turn it into a worthless platitude. For projectibility has so far been characterized only in terms of being a sound basis for prediction, and the notion of inductive strength of the argument in this context comes to the same thing. So in this emendation we are simply being told that the argument supplies us with a well-based prediction if its premise provides us with a sound basis for prediction. What is needed here is an independent account of projectibility, a criterion that can be cast in the form of a rule of SIL that tells us when a regularity does in fact provide us with a sound basis for supposing that it describes a uniformity that will continue into the future.

Projectibility of course is a matter of degree; we can speak of one regularity being more or less projectible than another. Presumably the premise of argument (A) exhibits a high degree of projectibility (but for short will simply be described as "projectible") whereas the premise of (B) has a very low or negligible one (hence is "unprojectible" and "accidental"). Projectibility is directly related to the degree of inductive strength (and hence predictive soundness) of the arguments themselves. So the problem for SIL is one of formulating rules governing the spectrum of projectibility, and for determining when in a given instance we have a degree of projectibility sufficient to warrant predictions about the future. And it is worth noting in this regard that even if Hume's problem was somehow laid to rest, the problem concerning projectibility would still remain. That is, even if an acceptable, noncircular justification for SIL *as a whole* was provided, we would still need to get down to cases and formulate rules for distinguishing genuine instances of uniformity upon which we may base our predictions from those where, as in the premise of (B), we cannot. If SIL presupposes that nature is uniform, and this thesis could be developed in some noncircular fashion, the problem would still remain of distinguishing cases of genuine uniformity—as in argument (A)—from those of the purely accidental variety. We must be able to say, in effect, in what respects nature is presupposed to be uniform, and that means that we must have a firm basis for determining which regularities SIL should recognize as projectible. As argument (B) shows us, to say that it is uniform in *all* respects lets in too much.

Defining projectibility might initially seem to be an easy task, but as the balance of this section will show it is very difficult and in fact worse than it has been made out to be thus far. But for now let us consider some fairly natural attempts to deal with it. The form of inference governed by Rule E is one of simple enumeration, and we saw back in Chapter Two that these sorts of arguments—as found in practical everyday contexts—often presuppose a large amount of background information. Perhaps, then, if we try to make such information explicit, we will have a means of distinguishing between projectible and unprojectible hypotheses, thus providing us with a basis for amending Rule E so that only arguments like (A) are sanctioned by it. But what sort of background information will help us here?

One natural attempt along these lines is this: projectible regularities like 'All copper items conduct electricity' are confirmed not only by their own instances (e.g., 'this wire is made of copper and conducts electricity') but are also indirectly confirmed by similar evidence for related hypotheses. Our evidence concerning other materials confirms regularities like 'All items made of iron (or silver or gold) conduct electricity' and in addition confirms those like 'No items made of wood (or rubber or paper) conduct electricity'. These hypotheses and the vast amounts of evidence for them impart to 'All observed copper items conduct electricity' its character of projectibility. On the other hand, no such indirect evidence is available for an unprojectible hypothesis like all men observed working in the Sears Tower being within a certain range of height. Indeed, evidence concerning groups of men working at other locations *disconfirms* many generalizations about the height range of men at the same workplace. Information such as this, so the argument goes, precludes all such hypotheses, including the one about the Sears Tower, from being projectible.

However, if this proposal is to work, we must be more precise about the relevant respects in which these various hypotheses are similar. The evidence confirming hypotheses about the conductivity of iron and the lack of conductivity of wood are supposed to warrant the conclusion that 'All observed copper items conduct electricity' is projectible. Presumably this is because all such regularities fall under the more inclusive hypothesis that

1. All things made of the same material are uniform in conductivity. On the other hand, the evidence for these same regularities is *not* supposed to permit an inference to the generalization: All

items in my closet conduct electricity. The reason is that this generalization does not fall under the above hypothesis. Rather, it can only be grouped with the others under a quite different claim like

2. All things either made of the same material or found in my closet conduct electricity.

The thesis thus comes down to this: any regularity falling under (1)—such as 'All observed copper items conduct electricity'—is rendered more probable by the evidence for the *other* regularities that fall under it. But this feature does not hold for regularities such as 'All items in my closet conduct electricity', which fall under (2); in other words, the totality of evidence for (1) gives us an inductively strong inference and hence a sound basis for prediction whereas that for (2) does not.

But notice that this is only to say that (1) is projectible and (2) is not! So the very problem we were trying to solve is simply raised all over again. The attempt to say why the regularity about copper is projectible but the one about items in my closet is not comes down to saying the former falls under a projectible hypothesis like (1) whereas the latter only falls under unprojectible hypotheses like (2). We are faced with the same problem with which we began, since (1) and (2) are of no help to us unless we have independent grounds for saying which of *them* is projectible.

Another proposal would exclude from projectibility those generalizations containing expressions that refer to specific objects or that involve some sort of spatial or temporal restriction. Thus regularities with terms like 'man who works *at Sears Tower*', 'item *in my closet*', and 'hatched *before 2020 AD*' would be rejected, and only those with purely general terms ('man', 'man who works', 'hatched') would remain as candidates. However, many expressions involving reference to specific things, places, or times have abbreviations (e.g., 'Hoosier' for 'person who resides in Indiana'), and they would also have to be excluded somehow. Moreover, for those without abbreviations, we could simply devise some. We could define *'towman'* as 'man who works at Sears Tower', and 'persital' as 'person over six feet tall', and we would thus have a true regularity, 'All observed towmen are persital', which clearly is not projectible even though it is not excluded as such by our proposal. In fact, the proposal as it stands excludes nothing at all.

The natural response here would be to revise the proposal so that we exclude not only regularities that actually contain terms for specific times, places, and objects but also all those *equivalent* to others that do contain such expressions. This would get rid of 'All observed towmen are persital' all right, but the trouble is that it would rid us of everything else as well, even the regularities that *are* projectible. The regularity, 'All observed copper items conduct electricity' is projectible, but it also equivalent to 'All observed copper items in Chicago or elsewhere conduct electricity.' Since the latter contains reference to a specific place, it would be unprojectible on this proposal, but that would mean that the former would have to be counted as unprojectible as well—even though it obviously *is* projectible. On this revision, everything is excluded.

Goodman's Paradox: The task of distinguishing between projectible and unprojectible regularities is thus more daunting than it at first seemed. But as the philosopher Nelson Goodman has shown,[17] the problem is even worse than imagined. For it is not just that we need some way of excluding unwanted regularities like the Sears Tower example from projectibility, it is rather that *we can find pairs of regularities—one projectible and the other not—that are supported by the same body of evidence but lead to incompatible predictions about the future.*

To state it more fully, the problem with the initially plausible Rule E is not merely that it sanctions arguments like (B) as inductively strong, it also sanctions arguments

  i. Whose premises, though unprojectible, are supported by the same evidence that supports projectible ones of certain inductively strong arguments, and
  ii. Whose conclusions make predictions incompatible with those of the inductively strong arguments.

In a word, indiscriminate use of Rule E results not just in countenancing unwanted projectibilities but in outright paradox.

Let us then look at Goodman's argument. All emeralds we have ever examined have been green, none have been blue. The generalization

  3. All observed emeralds are green

is a projectible regularity while 'All observed emeralds are blue' is not, and Rule E in effect tells us to predict that the next emerald we examine will be green rather than blue. So far, so good. But now, let us define two new terms:

  An object x is **grue** at time t if and only if either x is green at t
      and t is before the year 2100 AD or x is blue at t and t is during
      or after 2100 AD

An object x is **bleen** at time t if and only if either x is blue at t and t is before 2100 AD or x is green at t and t is during or after 2100 AD

These are indeed strange definitions, but let us examine them more closely. Any object that is *now* (prior to 2100 AD) green is also by our definitions grue; the grass on my lawn is grue as well as green. But after 2100 AD, if the lawn is still there and is green, it would be incorrect to say that it is grue; it is at that point bleen. Similarly, the sky is now both blue and bleen, but after 2100 if it is still blue it is also grue. Further, we would expect an emerald that is green now to remain so in 2100—it would not change color—but in the grue-bleen language it would in such a case "change" from grue to bleen. On the other hand, if the sky miraculously turned green on New Year's Day of 2100, while this would count as a change in color in our terms, it would be correct in the grue-bleen terminology to say that it had remained bleen all along.

Thus the regularity

4. All observed emeralds are grue

is, like (3), true; each and every emerald examined, insofar it has been green, has also been grue. But unlike (3), we would certainly not want to say that it is projectible.

Let us now consider the following arguments to which Rule E is supposed to apply; (3) is the premise of the first one and (4) of the second one:

C. All observed emeralds are green.
∴ The first emerald observed in 2100 AD will be green

D. All observed emeralds are grue.
∴ The first emerald observed in 2100 AD will be grue

Argument (C), like our original argument (A), has a well-confirmed, projectible premise, and therefore yields its conclusion with high probability just as Rule E dictates—it is inductively strong. But as in argument (B), we have an unprojectible premise in (D) and an inductively weak inference, thus again showing that Rule E requires revision and pointing up the need for a means by which we can determine when a regularity is projectible. Only *now* we can see how much more difficult the problem of characterizing projectibility is. We can state it in two parts.

First, although intuition or common sense tells us that (3) is projectible and (4) is not, they are supported by *exactly the same body of evidence*. Any confirming instance of (3) ever noted is also supporting evidence for (4) and vice versa—all past observations of green emeralds are equally observations of grue emeralds. Since they are supported by the same data, then lacking any rules for projectibility of regularities, we would have to say that either *both* are projectible or else *neither* is. And since (3) would seem to be projectible if anything is, then despite what we are told by common sense the same would have to be said of (4).

Second, the conclusion of argument (D) contradicts that of (C)—they make *incompatible* predictions about the future; to predict that the first emerald observed in 2100 will be grue is, in effect, to predict that it will be blue rather than green. This would, of course, be a ludicrous prediction for anyone to make, but even so it is a projection into the future of an observed regularity by Rule E—a thoroughly unprojectible regularity but nonetheless having the same evidential support as a genuinely projectible one. Thus the accumulated body of evidence that warrants the prediction of a green emerald in 2100 also warrants the prediction of a grue, and thereby a blue, emerald.

The problem is thus more severe than we had at first supposed. The error in making predictions using an unprojectible regularity not only leads us to make grossly implausible forecasts, it can also lead to one that contradicts a quite legitimate prediction, which arises from using a projectible regularity supported by the very same evidence. All the more reason, then, to avoid employing unprojectible regularities (and Rule E), and all the more reason for SIL to contain projectibility rules and for having a clear account of what projectibility is. As Goodman says, "what may at first have seemed a minor technical difficulty has taken on the stature of a major obstacle to the development of a satisfactory theory of confirmation. It is this problem that I call the new riddle of induction."[18]

The grue example shows that the terminology we use to describe phenomena may determine which regularities we discover in our various and sundry observations (the same observations that give rise to example (3) give rise to (4) as well). To carry this a step further, with a little ingenuity and linguistic license, we can find a regularity that by Rule E will authorize *any* prediction we might wish to make, no matter how ridiculous. For example, suppose every book on my shelf is under 600 pages, and suppose also I wish to predict that the automobile in the garage down the street is orange. Define 'boomob' as anything that is either a book on my shelf or an automobile in the garage down the street, and define 'pagoran' as anything that is either a book under 600 pages or else not a book and orange. Then we have the regularity, 'Every observed boomob is pagoran,' and each instance of a boomob observed thus far has in fact been pagoran. Rule E thus licenses the inference that the next boomob to be observed (which might be the auto in question) will be pagoran (hence orange).

Now obviously this regularity is not projectible, and our example points up not only the need to rule out predictions based on un-projectible regularities, but also how easy it is to find regularities that will "support" any off-the-wall prediction we might wish to make. As Goodman puts it, "Regularities are where you find them, and you can find them anywhere."

This example shows in addition that the problem Goodman poses is a wide-ranging one and attempts to resolve it by focusing on purely perceptual properties like colors are bound to miss the mark. We could define 'green' and 'grue' for instance in purely physical terms, and the problem would still remain. 'Green' could be defined in some such terms as 'reflects light waves of frequency n' and 'grue' as 'reflects light waves of frequency n before 2100 and of frequency m during and after 2100,' with the result that 'All observed emeralds are green' is projectible but that 'All observed emeralds are grue' is not. And as before, both are supported by the same evidence and yet lead to incompatible predictions. The contrast between arguments (C) and (D) is thus the very same as we had before without the physicalistic definitions.

But perhaps the most natural objection to Goodman's thesis is that, while 'green' is a legitimate color word, 'grue' is not, since it involves reference to a specific point in time. Generalizations containing the latter term would thus not qualify for projectibility. We have already seen that attempts to characterize projectibility in terms of expressions lacking reference to times, places, and particular things have come up short of the mark, so this objection does not look promising and indeed it is easily answered. As speakers of the green-blue language we must of course include a temporal reference in our definitions of 'grue' and 'bleen.' But a hypothetical speaker of the grue-bleen language would do the same for our own 'green' and 'blue'; definitions of these latter words for such a person will also contain reference to a particular date. That is, 'grue' and 'bleen' would be basic in this language while our color terms 'green' and 'blue' would be derivative as shown by the definitions:

x is green at t if and only if either x is grue at t and t is before 2100 AD or x is bleen at t and t is during or after 2100 AD

x is blue at t if and only if either x is bleen at t and t is before 2100 AD or x is grue at t and t is during or after 2100 AD

So defining our own color words would involve temporal references too, and the symmetry of these definitions with respect to those given earlier for 'grue' and 'bleen' undercuts the claim that only our words qualify as "legitimate."

Still, this is a difficult conclusion for some to accept, and they have countered as follows: let us imagine all of the many objects to which 'grue' correctly applies—past, present, *and* future—ordered or lined up in the chronological sequence in which they are observed. Then we will find a radical shift in reference at 2100 AD, since those things examined prior to that date are green and those examined thereafter are not green. On the other hand, the term 'green' does not radically shift its reference at *any* point in time, so there is still a sense in which 'grue' has an essentially temporal meaning whereas 'green' does not.

The problem here is that the notion of a "shift in reference" is a relative one. Just as regularities may be found anywhere, so can nonregularities like "reference shifts" or "discontinuities." What counts as a reference shift depends on which class of things serves as a standard for judgment; in the present case whether we take the class of green objects as our reference point or whether, as in the grue-bleen language, the class of grue objects. Just as 'grue' shifts at a point in time from green things to certain other things that are not green, so 'green' shifts at that point from grue things to others that are not grue. It depends on whether we take 'green' as the primitive term and 'grue' as derivative or whether we do it the other way around.

Presumably, the core idea in this objection is that green things to be observed in the future will "look like" green things already observed whereas the same cannot be said for grue things. But this principle does not solve the problem, it just seems to raise it all over again in a somewhat different form. Green things observed in the past have all looked alike, but equally so have all observed grue things. On the other hand, while we regard the first fact as something to be projected into the future, we do not so regard the second one. The contrast between these two is the same as that between examples (3) and (4): one is projectible and the other is not, but both are supported by the very same body of evidence. What is needed, then, is just what Goodman has been demanding all along: rules for determining when a regularity is projectible, ones that will provide a rational justification for our intuitions about what is and what is not projectible. Barring that, it is perhaps not too difficult to imagine a tribe of grue-bleen speakers who would be aghast if on the first day of 2100 AD all grue things abruptly became bleen!

Indeed, Goodman and his supporters hold that temporal specifications are not essential to the new riddle. As Israel Scheffler says,

> Time reference is certainly useful in *explaining* the problem, but is *not* an essential feature of it. What *is* essential is the membership of all actual evidence cases in classes that diverge beyond the evidence. All emeralds in the class of evidence cases, for example, *belong both* to the class of green and to the class of grue things, which, unfortunately, *diverge* for emeralds outside the evidence class.[19]

And in this regard we might note the "alternatives" to Galileo's law of falling bodies discussed in the first section. Each of them is supported by the same confirming instances that support his law, but lead to incompatible predictions about future observations.

A few writers have accused Goodman of violating the Rule of Total Evidence in formulating his riddle. In predicting that a future emerald will be grue, they argue, we know *more* about the situation than just the fact that all observed emeralds have been grue. We know in addition that the observed emeralds were examined *before* 2100 AD, and argument (D) does not include this piece of crucial evidence. However, though it cannot be spelled out here, it has been shown that when this information is included, the New Riddle still remains in full force.[20] If the evidence statements for regularities (3) and (4) are amended to read '*a* is an emerald *examined before 2100 AD* and is green' and '*a* is an emerald *examined before 2100 AD* and is grue,' then with the inclusion of a further premise concerning date of examination, we would still be led to make incompatible predictions—based on the very same body of evidence—about the color of an emerald observed in 2100.

The inclination for some at this point, perhaps born of frustration, is to ask why we need worry about bizarre terms like 'grue' or about accidential hypotheses like the one about workers at Sears Tower. After all, we are unlikely to use them for making predictions anyway. Rule E and similar principles appear to work well enough for the hypotheses we normally employ, so isn't that all we need?

> In a sense, yes; but only in the sense that we need no definition, no theory of induction, and no philosophy of knowledge at all. We get along well enough without them in daily life and in scientific research. But if we seek a theory at all, we cannot excuse gross anomalies resulting from a proposed theory by pleading that we can avoid them in practice. The odd cases we have been considering are clinically pure cases that, though seldom encountered in practice, nevertheless display to best advantage the symptoms of a widespread and destructive malady.[21]

Goodman's Proposed Solution: Goodman himself has offered a tentative and somewhat limited answer to the problem. It is a complex theory (with few competitors so far) and only a brief sketch can be given here.[22]

Goodman notes first that even though the concepts of confirmation and sound projection apply strictly to the relation between evidence and hypotheses, a theory of projectibility may have to involve elements that go beyond this relation, in particular it should take into account the historical record of past predictions and their outcomes. This is legitimately available information that will help us learn how human beings come to sort out the predictions they make as sound or unsound. We are not concerned here with the psychological question of how the mind works in such cases, but rather with characterizing the intuitive distinction it makes between projectible and unprojectible hypotheses.

Suppose, then, someone projects the hypothesis that all observed emeralds are grue; on what basis are we to rule out such cases? It will help to take note of the fact that projections of this kind often *conflict* with other projections. For example, if 'All observed emeralds are green' is also projected, then as we have seen the two projections will disagree concerning certain yet-to-be examined emeralds. So how might we devise a rule that will make the proper choice between the conflicting predictions? The question seems especially vexing inasmuch as 'green' and 'grue' are symmetrically related in terms of their definitions.

Goodman's answer is that we should consult the record of actual past predictions using regularities containing these terms. When we do, we will see that 'green' has, as he puts it, "the more impressive biography"—it has been projected in the past both earlier and with much more frequency than has 'grue'. In other words, 'green' is much more *entrenched* than 'grue'. Of course, any occasion on which a regularity containing the former was projected (or could have been projected), the same *might* have happened for the latter, but in fact this was hardly ever the case. Hence, Goodman suggests that a basic principle for ruling out predictions made with regularities containing terms like 'grue' is that they conflict with predictions made with those containing much better entrenched terms like 'green'. Roughly then, a distinguishing mark of those recurrent features of our experience that underlie the genuinely projectible cases is that they are features for which we have adopted terms that have been *habitually projected* in the past; that is, terms that are highly "entrenched."

Goodman's proposal is therefore to make use of historical information concerning past linguistic practice that may reasonably be assumed to be available to us. Our hypotheses are chosen for prediction not merely on the basis of the evidence for them (on the "confirming instances" we know about and the lack of any known counterexample), but also on how the language in which they are formulated conforms with that of past inductive judgments. In determining degree of projectibility, we tacitly appeal to "recurrences in the explicit use of terms as well as to recurrent features of what is observed." For hypotheses containing terms with extensive biographies like 'conducts electricity', our implicit judgment of their projectibility arises from our habitual projection of them, rather than habitually projecting them because of a prior judgment of projectibility.

However, two qualifications are in order. First, the entrenchment of a term results not only from the projection of hypotheses containing it, but also from the projection of hypotheses containing different terms that apply to the same class of objects. The degree of projectibility possessed by 'green', for example, is due as much to the use of terms like the French '*vert*' in projective contexts as it is to its own employment. For Goodman, entrenchment applies as much to the class of things to which a word applies as it does to the word itself, but it must be kept in mind that the class becomes entrenched only through the use of words that correctly apply to its members; after all, entrenchment can result only from actual linguistic usage.

Second, we must not confuse entrenchment with familiarity. An entirely unfamiliar term (as 'conducts electricity' was at one time) may be highly entrenched if terms coextensive with it have frequently been projected. Conversely, a very familiar term may be poorly entrenched since entrenchment depends not just on frequency of use but frequency of use *in projective contexts*. Blanket elimination of unfamiliar or little used terms, according to Goodman, would seriously inhibit the growth of scientific language. New and useful terms like 'positron' are constantly being introduced and they are not ruled out in his theory simply because of their novelty.

Goodman's theory is not offered as the last word on the subject. For one thing it is limited to simple universal hypotheses, and for another it is concerned only with the preliminary notion of projectibility-at-a-given-time. Temporally unqualified projectibility still awaits explication. Many will feel dissatisfied with the theory since it offers no explanation of the phenomenon of entrenchment itself—of what underlies it or what would account for the basic fact that the hypotheses we deem projectible are the ones whose terms are highly entrenched. But further explanation has not been ruled out either, and in any case Goodman's chief aim has been to lay down clearly stated conditions, based on familiar and available data, for determining projectibility. Moreover, his conditions do seem to work for the kinds of cases he considers. "Ultimate" or metaphysical explanations are something else again.

Notes

1. K. Popper, *The Logic of Scientific Discovery* (London: Hutchinson and Co., 1959).

2. For a more complete introduction to induction and scientific method, see Carl Hempel, *Philosophy of Natural Science* (Englewood Cliffs, N. J.: Prentice-Hall, 1966), chapters 2, 3, and 4. A shorter but quite readable introduction may be found in W. Salmon, *Logic*, 3d ed. (Englewood Cliffs, N. J.: Prentice-Hall, 1984), chapter 3, especially section 30. The explicit formulation of the hypothetico-deductive method given later in this chapter is Salmon's.

3. Being a logical truth, the first premise of schema (I) has a probability of 1. But the *entire* argument constituting schema (I) would of course typically have an inductive probability less than 1 (i.e., $Pr[H/O \& (H \supset O)] < 1$), but the closer it is to 1 the greater the confirmation O provides for H.

4. The prior probability of a hypothesis is to be arrived at independent of any new tests devised for it by way of deduced observation statements. In fact, the word 'prior' here need not be understood temporally—a prior probability may be determined after the test results are examined. What matters is that those results not affect the assignment of prior probability.

5. For more on the Foucault-Fizeau experiment and its aftermath, see Hempel, *Philosophy of Natural Science,* chapter 2.

6. For more on crucial experiments, see Hempel, ibid., chapter 2. See also J. Carney and R. Scheer, *Foundations of Logic* (New York: Macmillan, 1974).

7. For more on ad hoc hypotheses, see I. Copi and C. Cohen, *Introduction to Logic,* 8th ed. (New York: Macmillan, 1990), chapter 13.

8. A pioneer effort in this regard is Carl Hempel's "Studies in the Logic of Confirmation," *Mind* 54 (1945); reprinted in S. Luckenbach, ed., *Probabilities, Problems and Paradoxes* (Encino, Calif.: Dickenson, 1972). In fact he discusses several of the principles to be introduced in this section.

9. We have seen that ordinarily the hypothesis validly yields these statements only in conjunction with auxiliary hypotheses and so on. For simplicity, however, we shall hereafter suppress these.

10. See Goodman's *Fact, Fiction and Forecast,* 2nd ed. (New York: Bobbs Merrill Co., 1965), p. 69. See also Mary Hesse, *The Structure of Scientific Inference* (Berkeley: University of California Press, 1974). For a more telling version of the counterexample to the Special Consequence Principle, see Ellery Eells, *Rational Decision and Causality* (Cambridge: Cambridge University Press, 1982), pp. 56–57.

11. Note that since 'all ravens are black' is also equivalent to 'everything is either not a raven or else is black', an observation of a black lump of coal would also confirm the former generalization. Not only nonblack nonravens but also black nonravens will confirm it on such reasoning.

12. The ensuing discussion roughly follows the line of argument offered by Hempel in "Studies in the Logic of Confirmation," and by J. L. Mackie in "The Paradox of Confirmation," *British Journal for the Philosophy of*

Science 13 (1963): 265–277, also reprinted in Luckenbach, *Probabilities, Problems and Paradoxes*. A different response to the problem—one in keeping with Karl Popper's views on confirmation—is offered by J. W. N. Watkins, "Between Analytic and Empirical," *Philosophy* 32 (1957): 112–131. Yet another approach is offered by G. H. von Wright, "The Paradoxes of Confirmation," in Hintikka and Suppes, eds., *Aspects of Inductive Logic* (Amsterdam: North Holland Publishing Co., 1966).

13. For more on this proposal, see J. Hosiasson-Lindenbaum, "On Confirmation," *Journal of Symbolic Logic* 5 (1940): 133–148, and D. Pears, "Hypotheticals," *Analysis* 10 (1950): 49–63. For criticism of it, see Hempel, "Studies in the Logic of Confirmation," 24.

14. This example is borrowed from Hempel, *ibid.* It should be noted, however, that Hempel's general discussion in this and other related essays concerns the quest for a definition of "qualitative" confirmation whereas the focus in our coverage has been on the "quantitative" variety (i.e., involving "degrees" of confirmation corresponding to inductive probability values). This difference though does seem to undermine the applicability of his remarks.

15. See Mackie's penetrating essay in Luckenbach, *Probabilities, Problems and Paradoxes*. He would qualify the conclusion for scenario I contexts to do not confirm 1 to a worthwhile degree. And as he points out, the exact conclusion to be drawn here depends on just how broadly or narrowly we are willing to construe the notion of a *test*.

16. For a thorough and in-depth discussion of the Raven Paradox and Hempel's views on confirmation, see Israel Scheffler, *The Anatomy of Inquiry* (New York: Alfred A. Knopf, 1963). See Part III, especially Sections 5 and 6.

17. Goodman, *Fact, Fiction and Forecast,* Chapter 3. For further discussion, see Scheffler, *Anatomy of Inquiry*, pp. 291–314; and Brian Skyrms, *Choice and Chance,* 3rd ed., (Encino, Calif.: Dickenson, 1983), chapter 3.

18. Goodman, *ibid.,* pp. 80–81. It should be noted that in his discussion Goodman uses *confirm* in the narrower sense discussed in the last section, and hence he would say that only projectible generalizations receive confirmation from their observational instances. Observing a grue emerald or a 6 foot 1 inch male worker at Sears Tower offers *no* confirmation (in his sense) of the corresponding regularities since such instances do not increase the credibility of other instances of those regularities.

19. Scheffler, *Anatomy of Inquiry,* p. 307. For an attack on the claim of symmetry concerning the definitions in our language and the grue-bleen one, see S. Barker and P. Achinstein, "On The New Riddle of Induction," *Philosophical Review* 69 (1960): 511–522. See also Goodman's response in the same volume.

20. This has been clearly and convincingly demonstrated by Hugues Leblanc in "That Positive Instances Are No Help," *Journal of Philosophy* 60 (1963): 453–462. Reprinted in Luckenbach, *Probabilities, Problems and Paradoxes*.

21. Goodman, *Fact, Fiction and Forecast,* p. 80.

22. See *ibid.,* Chapter 4. For further discussion see Scheffler, *Anatomy of Inquiry,* pp. 310–314; and B. Grunstra, "The Plausibility of the Entrenchment Concept," *American Philosophical Quarterly Monograph Series,* no. 3 (1969): 100–127, also reprinted in Luckenbach, *Probabilities, Problems and Paradoxes.* For an alternative to Goodman's view, see Richard Jeffrey, *The Logic of Decision,* 2nd ed. (Chicago: University of Chicago Press, 1983), pp. 187–190.

CHAPTER 7

Theories of Inductive Probability

Inductive probability is the most important concept of inductive logic, and the time has come to examine its foundations. What sort of explanation can be given for it, and what exactly does it mean to interpret the 'Pr' symbol of the calculus as meaning *inductive* probability rather than another species? Can the concept be analyzed, and if so, into what further concepts? We shall look into these questions in this chapter.[1]

Theories about the nature of inductive probability have their origin in a consideration of how we actually determine the truth values of inductive probability statements—that is, of how we determine correct inductive probability values. For instance, in our discussion of the calculus we used examples concerning cards, dice, and other gambling devices. The initial probabilities to which the principles of the calculus were then applied were arrived at usually by considering the ratio of "favorable" possibilities to the total number of possible cases. Thus the probability of obtaining a three in a single toss of a die is ⅙ since there are six possible cases only one of which is favorable. The earliest theory of inductive probability, the Classical View as we shall call it, takes its cue from this method, as does a more recent and sophisticated theory, the Logical Theory.

On the other hand, we might determine that ⅙ is the correct value not by an a priori consideration of possible cases, but by noting that over a long series of tosses the frequency with which a three has occurred is trending toward ⅙. This is the approach taken by the Frequency Theory, which in effect maintains that inductive probabilities, like the "descriptive" probabilities discussed in Chapter Four, are nothing more than long-run relative frequencies of a certain sort—yet, of a certain sort. Still another approach centers around the question of what a person would consider to be a reasonable bet on a three appearing. If the potential winnings must be at least five times the amount of money risked, then the odds for this agent are five to one against a three being tossed and the probability estimate is ⅙.

Considerations concerning our willingness to bet in a given situation have led to a fourth theory, the Subjective Theory, which takes our actual, subjective degrees of belief as its starting point.

Section 1. The Classical View _____

The Classical View arose in the late eighteenth century and provides an approach that at first sight seems quite plausible.[2] The method of considering all possible cases is offered as a general account of inductive probability. That is, probability is defined as the ratio of favorable alternatives to the total number. To say that the chance of the die showing a three is ⅙ is to say that out of the total number of possibilities or alternatives (in this case the faces of the die) only one is designated as "three" (is favorable). The probability of drawing a spade from a full bridge deck is ¼ since of fifty-two total cases thirteen are favorable.

But suppose someone says that the probability of the die showing a three is ½ since there are just two possible cases, three and nonthree. Obviously something is wrong here; we cannot count just *any* set of possible cases, we need the "right" kind of alternatives. The Classical View takes the position that the nonthree case is not a genuine alternative since it subdivides into five further cases that, along with the "three" alternative, are *equally possible.* Hence there are six total cases to be considered. But what does 'equally possible' mean here? Would we consider all six faces to be equally possible if, say, the die was "loaded" in favor of one of the sides? Presumably not, so the Classical View holds that 'equally possible' must here mean 'equiprobable'. The die presents us with six equiprobable alternatives, hence the chance of a three is ⅙.

But now it would appear the Classical View is in trouble. After all, it is an attempt to explain what the concept of probability is, but we have just seen that to make the view hold up we must appeal to the notion of two events having the same probability. Hence the Classical View seems to be caught in a circle, assuming the very concept it is attempting to explain. Of course advocates of the view are aware of this point, and reply that it is harmless *if* we can define the notion of equiprobability without reference to any probabilistic concept. This they attempt to do by invoking the **Principle of Indifference.** We may state it as follows: two alternatives (or possibilities) are *equiprobable* if and only if there are no relevant, rational grounds for choosing among them. The six faces of a well-balanced die are like this, but the faces of a loaded die are not. In the latter instance there is a sound reason (whether we know about it or not) for choosing one face rather than the others. So a more complete statement of the Classical View would run as follows: *Inductive probability is the number of favorable alternatives over the total number of alternatives where the latter are equiprobable according to the Principle of Indifference.*

However appealing the Classical View may seem at first blush, hardly anyone subscribes to it nowadays, and it will be instructive to see why. For one thing, although the theory seems to work well with respect to dice, cards, and the like, what are we to make of, say, a physicist who claims that given our present knowledge, the probability that Einstein's Special Theory of Relativity is correct is about ⁹/₁₀? What are the alternatives of which approximately 90 percent are in some sense "favorable"? Can we specify them? Can we say even in principle what they are? And if we can, what would it mean to mark out a subset of them as "favorable"? Can we ask the same questions about the probability of the Red Sox winning the pennant in the coming year or of a cure for lung cancer being developed? There are many probabilistic contexts to which the favorable-to-total analysis does not seem to apply.

But the more important problem is the Principle of Indifference itself. Ever since it was first proposed, philosophers and other probability writers have been devising counterexamples to it—examples wherein the principle, despite its initial plausibility, is shown to lead us to logically absurd or contradictory consequences. It will suffice for us to consider just two of the examples that have been proposed.[3]

Our first case concerns an automobile that traverses a measured mile. We do not know the exact time it took, but are told by an eyewitness that it covered the distance in no less than 1 minute and no more than 2 minutes, thus averaging somewhere between 30 and 60 miles per hour. We know *nothing more* about the situation than this. Now consider the probability that the car averaged between 45 and 60 miles per hour versus the probability that it averaged between 30 and 45 miles per hour. Because these are equal intervals and because of our very scanty knowledge of the situation, the PI would presumably tell us to assign a probability of ½ in each case—we have no grounds for preferring one of the intervals to the other. On the other hand, consider now the probability that the car traversed the mile in 1.5 to 2 minutes versus the probability that it did so in 1 to 1.5 minutes. Again, these are equal intervals and the Principle of Indifference would as before assign a probability of ½ to each. But now we have a logical inconsistency; to say that the car took between 1.5 and 2 minutes to make the trip is to say that it averaged between 40 (*not* 45) and 60 miles per hour, and a probability of ½ was assigned this alternative.

But we *also* assigned ½ to the statement that it averaged between 45 and 60 miles per hour. The Principle of Indifference thus leads us to make inconsistent probability assignments.

For a second example, consider the sixteen state descriptions for the domain D listed in the last section of Chapter Five. If we survey them a priori, we find that each is a logical possibility and that there are no grounds for singling out one of them as the "actual" state of affairs rather than any of the others. By the Principle of Indifference, then, we assign them equal probabilities. But as we saw in Chapter Five the result is Random Inductive Logic, which is *not* the logic we use for the very good reason that it does not enable us to revise our expectations of the future in light of new evidence. Applying the principle to state descriptions gives us an inductive logic in which the past has no evidential bearing on predictions about the future—a logic quite at odds with the one we in fact employ.

Now if we apply the principle to *structure* descriptions—assigning them equal probabilities—the result is Scientific Induction. Recall that a structure description is a disjunction of isomorphic state descriptions, and a state description isomorphic only to itself qualifies as a structure description too. A glance at the chart in Chapter Five shows that there are ten structure descriptions (indicated by the lefthand braces), six of which are two-component disjunctions, the other four solitary state descriptions. Applying the Principle of Indifference to structure descriptions gives a value of ⅒ for each and hence leads to the state description assignments that characterize Scientific Logic. So the principle gives us just what we want when applied to structure descriptions.

Unfortunately we have no more grounds for applying it to structure description alternatives than we had for applying it to the "alternatives" of three and nonthree. We ruled out the nonthree alternative by showing that it subdivided into five possible cases, and the same considerations rule out applying the PI to structure descriptions of two or more disjuncts. If it is logically unfair to assign equal values to three and nonthree, the same must hold for assigning equal probabilities to both a "one-disjunct" structure description and a two-disjunct one. After all, the latter one covers two distinct possible worlds just as the nonthree alternative breaks down into five distinct possibilities. Just as there are more ways to obtain a nonthree, so there are more ways for the two-disjunct structure description to be true. Thus, although there is an a priori basis for applying the Principle of Indifference to state descriptions—producing the unfortunate result of Random Logic—it cannot be so applied to structure descriptions, though here the result is a desirable one.

The principle, at least in its full blown form, has therefore been rejected by modern-day writers on probability and, with it, the Classical View. Yet many of them continue to think that there must be *something* right about it if only we could draw the limits of its applicability. After all, it or something very like it seems to be what we implicitly have in mind when we determine that the probability of drawing a spade is ¼ or of tossing a three is ⅙. Later on, we will consider a more recent and widely held theory that attempts to pinpoint what it considers to be the element of truth in the Principle of Indifference.

Section 2. The Frequency Theory _____

In an earlier chapter, we looked at the Frequency Theory of Descriptive Probability and saw that most writers on probability agree that it gives a satisfactory account of descriptive probability statements as they are found in science and everyday affairs. But some probability theorists go much further and advocate a frequentist account of virtually all probability worthy of the name, and in particular of inductive probability. The result is the Frequency Theory of Inductive Probability, a much more controversial position which we will now examine, along with some objections to it.[4]

There are several versions of the Frequency Theory, but we will concentrate on what is perhaps the most influential one: that of Hans Reichenbach.[5] An important component of this account, to which many other frequentists subscibe, is Reichenbach's attempt to justify inductive inference, which will be discussed later.

We will here look at two major features of the Frequency Theory. First, an inductive probability statement is to be analyzed as a form of frequency probability statement, and hence *the concept of inductive probability is just a special case of the more general concept of frequency probability*. More fully, an inductive probability statement— whose probability value ostensibly measures the degree of confirmation one statement provides for another—is on analysis a statement of the limiting relative frequency with which one property accompanies another. A degree of confirmation is nothing more than a long-run frequency with respect to a certain sequence of events. Second, *inductive probability statements are factually true-or-false,* since determining a long-run frequency requires that we observe some finite portion of an empirically given sequence to ascertain the limit.

Inductive probability statements are formulated in terms of statements, whereas we have seen that frequency statements talk about properties occurring in a sequence of events. Probability statements about mass phenomena such as 'The probability of an American man over age 50 dying of heart disease is 0.35', are of course tailor made for the Frequency Theory since the value 0.35 is readily construed as a limiting frequency with which a certain property (here, that of dying of heart disease) accompanies the reference property (being a U.S. man over age 50). But what about probability statements concerning single events; for example, the *next* U.S. man over age 50 to be observed? Inductive probability statements about single events are to be analyzed as statements about the "weight" of a prediction. The statement 'Pr(*Fa*/*Ga*) = *x*' is reexpressed as 'Wgt(*Fa*/*Ga*) = *x*', in which *x* is asserted to be the limiting frequency with which the property *F* occurs in the presence of a reference property *G*. In other words, Wgt(*Fa*/*Ga*) is the long-run frequency with which "*F*-type" predictions are true in instances where *G* is present.

So while we cannot speak directly of the probability of a single event in the Frequency Theory, we can make predictions about such events and speak of the weight of such predictions. This, it is claimed, is sufficient for actual purposes. For example, consider again the frequency statement that the probability of an American man over age 50 dying of heart disease is 0.35 (a statement of the form 'Pr$_f$(*F*/*G*) = *x*'). We now consider the singular prediction that Smith, a particular U.S. man over age 50 will die of heart disease; the *weight* of this prediction, or Wgt(*Fa*/*Ga*), where '*a*' designates Smith, is 0.35, meaning that over the long run about 35 percent of such predictions will be true.

The rationale for this definition of weight is that it can be shown from the definition of a limit that if we always wager on the statement having higher weight, we will more often be right over the long run than if we bet on one with lesser weight. Since statements about the limits of frequencies for sequences like that in the preceding example are empirical, 'Wgt(*Fa*/*Ga*) = 0.35', and hence the inductive probability claim it purports to analyze, is empirically true or false.

Back in Chapter Four frequency probability was characterized as

$$\text{Pr}_f(F/G) = \underset{n \to \infty}{\text{Limit fr}_n(F/G)} \ [\text{if no limit exists, Pr}_f \text{ is left undefined}]$$

So inductive probability is defined on the Frequency Theory in terms of the limit of an infinite sequence. Yet we have seen that the sequences with which the theory is directly concerned are empirical and hence in general finite. We cannot have infinitely many men over age 50 living in a particular social and cultural environment. Further, any frequency value of a finite segment of an infinite sequence is logically compatible with the limit of the entire sequence, no matter how divergent the two are. Still further, earthly human interests do not extend over an infinite time span. An insurance company may be interested in long finite sequences, but no human interest in predictive success is of genuinely eternal scope.

But we saw in Chapter Four that frequentists acknowledge these facts and maintain that for practical purposes we may regard probability as relative frequency over long finite runs—a "practical limit" as it was called—even though this complication undercuts the precision and simplicity of the previous definition (so much so that in the mathematical development of his theory, Reichenbach relies entirely on the precise limit notion tied to infinite sequences since some of his theorems do not strictly hold for finite cases). Frequentists admit that there is an element of idealization in their theory, just as in geometry where we speak of "perfect" triangles and points without magnitude. But their account, they claim, gives an abstract mathematical model of our more customary usage of the probability concept. The problem of *applying* the model in concrete situations is best left to statisticians, scientists, and others who employ probability on a day-to-day basis. To critics of the theory, this is a cop out; to defenders, it is merely being realistic.

Since a frequency probability statement makes a theoretical assertion about the limit of an infinite sequence, no set of empirical observations will *conclusively* determine whether it is true or false. We will never be in a position to *know* the value of $\text{Wgt}(Fa/Ga)$ inasmuch as we will not be able to examine all members of the reference class. The best we can do is make estimates of the limit and revise them as more information comes in. Over time we can usually make more reliable estimates, but by the nature of the case we cannot decisively verify the limit assertion. For frequentists, this again is a problem of applying the concept. Determining the truth or falsity of a frequency statement, according to them, is no more nor less problematic than that of other empirical statements involving highly abstract scientific concepts.

For a statement of the form '$\text{Wgt}(Fa/Ga) = x$', there are typically many reference classes (or choices for 'G') to choose from in determining the value of x; that is, sequences into which to place the event expressed by 'Fa'. Let 'Fa' represent 'Smith will die of heart disease', where Smith is a healthy American man over age 50. We could choose as a reference class: (a) all American men, (b) all such men over age 50, (c) all such men over age 50 who are at present healthy. The probability will no doubt be different in all three cases. Frequentists say that we should choose case (c) since it makes use of the most information we have about people like Smith. On the other hand, if Smith has red hair, we cannot use that information since we have no reliable data on red-haired men dying of heart disease. The general rule is this: Use the smallest relevant reference class for which there is reliable information. This rule (and others often used) is not part of the meaning of the probability concept for a frequentist, but rather part of a cluster of practical factors that govern its application (strictly, the meaning is simply that of limiting frequency since this is all that is relevant in giving a frequency interpretation of the probability calculus).

We have seen that complete verification of a frequency probability statement is not possible, but now a more severe problem arises. As we saw in our discussion of descriptive probability, frequency statements are empirically true-or-false and hence would seem to presuppose inductive probability for their verification. But inductive probabilities are supposed to be nothing more than a subspecies of frequency probabilities, so the Frequency Theory, like the Classical View, at first sight appears to be caught in a circle: inductive probability is analyzed as limiting relative frequency, but to ascertain rationally what the frequency value is we must use inductive inference and hence inductive probability.

This is a serious problem, for if frequency probability presupposes inductive inference, then the Frequency Theory cannot possibly succeed. So let us examine the problem more closely. On the theory, inductive probability statements are to be analyzed as "weight" statements asserting a limiting frequency. Since a statement like '$Wgt(Fa/Ga) = x$' is empirical, we must evaluate whether or not x is the correct value on the basis of empirical observations expressed, say, in the statement E. But if we are *inferring* that x is the proper value from the premise E, such an inference surely would be an inductive one. Not only that, to determine the truth value of the weight statement we must *first* determine empirically the truth value of the weight statement '$Wgt[Wgt(Fa/Ga) = x/E] = y$'. And to determine *this* truth value we must first find the truth value of '$Wgt \{Wgt [Wgt(Fa/Ga) = x/E] = y/E'\} = z$' and so forth. We would thus generate a regress in which infinitely many higher level weights would have to be known in order to determine rationally whether x is the correct value, and the concept of weight would be useless as a means of making predictions about the future. At least this would appear to be the consequence for a theory that analyzes inductive probability statements as making empirical claims. Many critics have claimed that in the last analysis the Frequency Theory cannot escape this objection, but since frequentists are well aware of it we must now examine their response.

The Self-Corrective Method: To avoid this problem, the Frequency Theory proposes a self-correcting inductive method and a justification for its use. The purpose of the method is to provide a means of rationally selecting weights in the simplest and most basic cases where the only relevant knowledge is the frequency observed thus far, and it consists in an indefinite repetition of the following procedure: we observe a sequence, $k_1, k_2, \ldots, k_n$; if $\mathrm{fr}_n(F/G) = x/y$, we accept this *tentatively* as the correct value, making predictions *as if* it were true. If x/y is an erroneous value, it will not survive our subsequent observations and will be replaced by a new value, w/t. If this value is in error, it too will eventually be corrected. We thus obtain a succession of values, x/y, w/t, u/v, . . . that approaches a limit, $\mathrm{Wgt}(Fa/Ga)$, which is the correct probability value.

At work in the self-corrective method is what Reichenbach and others call the **Straight Rule of Induction:** If x out of y Gs have been F, predict that the limiting frequency for the entire sequence will be x/y. The self-corrective method just consists in repetitive use of the Straight Rule, and that use, it is claimed, does not involve inductive inference. But a rational justification is needed for its use since there are obviously alternatives to it (to take an extreme case, predict that $1 - x/y$). We now turn to this topic.

The Pragmatic Justification of Induction: Frequency theorists admit that a general justification of our inductive rules is impossible, as Hume showed. Accordingly, the Straight Rule merely permits us to act on the assumption (or "posit" as Reichenbach calls it) that in the rest of the sequence we will approach x/y as a limit; it is not to be regarded as a full-blown inductive rule since it does not sanction drawing a conclusion as such. But though it is weaker than such a rule, it has the virtue according to some frequentists of having a rational justification; more precisely, a pragmatic "vindication" can be provided for it. The basic problem is to show that we can vindicate the principle that what has worked well in the past, will work in the future; and for a frequentist, this means vindicating the Straight Rule as a principle for estimating frequency values. A vindication is sort of a "conditional" justification; that is, we attempt to show that *if* the goal of predicting the future can be achieved, the Straight Rule is a way to achieve it. Perhaps it cannot be achieved, or maybe other principles will achieve it as well. But the basic idea is that, if *anything* will work, the Straight Rule will.

The pragmatic justification divides into two cases. *Case 1:* no limiting frequency exists. If so, then there is nothing to find; no rule will work, and the Straight Rule is no worse off than any alternative to it. Our only chance for success is to assume the limit exists and follow the self-corrective method; without this assumption, scientific investigation—and indeed any endeavor in which probabilistic predictions are employed—would be impossible. *Case 2:* a limit exists. Then it follows deductively from the definition of a limit that the Straight Rule will find it sometime. To say that the sequence, x/y, w/t, u/v, . . .

has a limit is just to say that for any amount of error, ϵ, no matter how small, there is a trial, n, such that for all subsequent trials, the observed fr_{n+m} is within ϵ of the limit value. Less formally, if the relative frequency of Fs with respect to G approaches a limit, our successive estimates based on repeated use of the Straight Rule will—as more and more members of the reference class are observed— approach that limit over the long haul. The self-corrective method thus has the advantage over other rules in that it *guarantees* eventual attainment of probabilistic success *if* success is attainable at all.

It can be shown (and will in the next section) that the predictions made by the Straight Rule will over time approach those made by Scientific Inductive Logic and therefore vindicating the Straight Rule is very similar to giving at least a partial justification of SIL (however, a "counterinductive" rule, if it could be vindicated, would do the same for CIL). It is worth noting that the Rule of Simple Enumeration is just a special case of the Straight Rule, where *all* observed Gs have been F, and simple statistical inferences (cases where some but not all Gs have been F) fall under its umbrella too. Reichenbach regards simple enumeration and these statistical cases to be the most basic forms of inductive reasoning and goes on to show that the more complex inductive rules used in science and everyday affairs can be generated (and hence vindicated) by means of them. The rule that we should avoid predicting on the basis of small samples, for instance, is justified by showing that the frequency of success in making such predictions is very low. The Straight Rule is the foundation upon which the more sophisticated inference forms may be vindicated.

The self-corrective method provides us with knowledge of the most elementary and basic probability statements, those in which no prior probability values are needed for determining their truth values. Using this stock of probabilities (or "primitive knowledge," as Reichenbach calls it), we may then, through the use of the calculus and of general inductive patterns from the known data, arrive at knowledge of higher level probabilities ("advanced knowledge"). It is mostly this advanced knowledge that we employ on a day-to-day basis, and weights assigned at the advanced level will often override the corresponding primitive weights. But of course advanced knowledge would not exist without a prior stock of primitive knowledge, and the vindication of our advanced probabilistic knowledge ultimately rests on that for the primitive form: the pragmatic justification of induction.

Since we must make some judgments as to the strength of inductive arguments if we are to survive in our world, we must, as is argued in Case (1) assume that a limit exists. Case (2) then tells us that on this assumption the Straight Rule will lead us to success. We may formulate the frequentist's reasoning as follows:

P1. If nature is uniform, use of the Straight Rule will be successful (because of the pragmatic vindication).

P2. If it is not, no method will be successful (the Straight Rule is no worse off than any other).

∴ If *any* method will succeed, the Straight Rule will.

By premise (P2) if the future is not like the past, there is presumably no limit and hence nothing to find. But suppose that in a random, disorderly world some method, M, somehow predicts successfully (meaning that arguments it deems inductively strong have been observed to have true conclusions accompanying true premises with a frequency roughly matching the high probability value assigned). Then, says Reichenbach, we do have a uniformity, namely that of M's success, and the self-corrective method will discover *it*. If M is successful in the preceding sense, the self-corrective method will be too since it will discover M's reliability and will in effect sanction M as an auxiliary method. Thus the eventual success of the self-corrective method is a necessary accompaniment of any successful method of prediction—the latter will succeed *only if* the self-corrective method does too (but not vice versa).

> A blind man who has lost his way in the mountains feels a trail with his stick. He does not know where the path will lead him, or whether it may take him so close to the edge of a precipice that he will be plunged into the abyss. Yet he follows the path, groping his way step by step; for if there is any possibility of getting out of the wilderness, it is by feeling his way along the path. As blind men we face the future; but we feel a path. And we know: if we can find a way through the future it is by feeling our way along this path.[6]

Some Objections to the Frequency Theory: The Frequency Theory is less popular now than it was some twenty or thirty years ago, largely because of serious criticism by its major opponents. An in-depth discussion of these objections is out of the question, but the gist of them is sketched here. Those wishing to follow up should consult the notes at the end of this chapter.

1. It is not clear that Reichenbach's reply adequately supports premise (P2) of the preceding argument. It is true that if M is successful, the self-corrective method will score a success too; namely, detecting and projecting into the future M's reliability. But what Reichenbach needs to show is that if M is successful with respect to arguments about swans, coin tosses, heart disease mortality, and the like, then the self-corrective method will *also* be generally successful with those same kinds of arguments, not just with an argument concerning M's reliability. It seems possible at least that the SCM might be successful when applied to M's past history without enjoying the kind of success M has had with respect to these other arguments. Nothing that Reichenbach has said would appear to justify our immediately ruling out such a possibility.

2. In the Frequency Theory there are no a priori probabilities, although intuitively we seem to countenance them in many contexts. To take an extreme case, suppose that from time immemorial no coin has ever been tossed, and now finally someone is about to do so. What is the probability that it will come up heads? Commonsense considerations about symmetry and the like (along with perhaps some version of the Principle of Indifference) would seem to tell us to assign a value of ½, but in a frequentist account of probability we must refrain from making *any* assignment. Since there is no sequence of prior tosses, there is no projectible relative frequency value. On intuitive grounds, there seem to be a priori probabilities, but if inductive probability is just a subspecies of frequency probability, there cannot be such values.

3. Hence there must *be* a past sequence, but now another problem arises. The strict definition of frequency probability given earlier requires an infinite sequence, but the empirical sequences to which it is applied (coin tosses, uses of a particular inductive argument form) would appear to be finite. Some frequentists thus have gone so far as to claim that we must presuppose an unlimited continuation of such sequences—that coins will continue to be tossed, arguments will not cease to be propounded, and in general that scientific inquiry will extend indefinitely into the future. Such a sweeping, empirical presupposition is too much for most probability theorists to swallow, especially as a foundation for an a priori discipline like logic.

Now as we have already seen, other frequentists take a less drastic approach, claiming that when we apply the concept of frequency probability to finite cases we are making an "idealization" of the sort common in many sciences. But this move strikes many critics as merely papering over a difficult problem: We must on this approach draw *inferences* from finite sequences describing the past and present to the limits of infinite ones, and they have argued that these inferences are essentially inductive. The frequency value of the sequence generally is not known to us by direct observation, rather it is inferred from accumulated data, records, and human memory. This inference can only be inductive and sanctioned by a rule of Scientific Inductive Logic—had someone used a very different inductive logic, this account of the past could be wrong in such a fashion that such use of the Straight Rule would never approach the limiting frequency. It thus appears that use of the Self-Corrective Method implicitly presupposes the use of SIL (or a very similar inductive method) and hence inductive probability—the very concept the frequentist is attempting to analyze away in terms of limiting frequency.

4. There are further problems in applying frequency probability to finite sequences. First of all, we need "long" sequences; if in all of the past, present, and future of the universe, there were just two cases of a coin being tossed and both resulted in tails, then the frequency probability of heads would be 0. Second, it would be very strange and counterintuitive simply to *identify* the probability with the relative frequency for the entire finite sequence (e.g., if in 1 million tosses a coin came up tails 530,131 times, we took the probability to be 0.530131). For we know from our discussion of the Law of Large Numbers that an event of probability α very often does not occur exactly $n\alpha$ times in a sequence of n members. Hence frequentists are inclined to say that the probability is "approximately equal" to the relative frequency over the whole sequence. Since the idea here is that "the longer the sequence, the better the approximation," it would be desirable to have a formal, mathematical account of such approximations. Reichenbach has claimed that it is possible to reconstruct the calculus of probability so that it does strictly apply to finite sequences, but because such a calculus would be very complex and unwieldy, he prefers the standard version in which only the nonfinitistic frequency concept holds. Some critics have expressed strong doubt over the possibility of ever developing such a calculus, and Reichenbach has not shown that it can be done.

5. Many inductive probability statements involve singular predictions; that is, the 'p' in '$\Pr(p/q) = x$' is a statement like "The next toss will be heads" or "The next swan observed will be white." Yet the frequentist analyzes inductive probability statements into frequency claims, and as we have seen the latter are statements about mass phenomena in that they concern the occurrence of properties in a hypothetically infinite sequence of events. Some frequentists admit their theory cannot handle single-case statements and consequently either maintain that another theory must be invoked for them or else take the more drastic course of claiming that the concept of probability—appearances to the contrary—has no meaning in such contexts. But Reichenbach and his followers introduced the concept of the "weight" of a statement as their analysis of single-case inductive probabilities.

Many critics, however, argue that to identify single-case probabilities with "weights," so defined, is grossly implausible. If "probability" in its various forms is to be analyzed solely in terms of mass phenomena, then it simply becomes meaningless when applied to single events, much as the term 'numerous', though it makes sense when applied to species (as in 'Horses are numerous'), is senseless when applied to particular members of the species ('This horse is numerous'). If this be so, then since singular predictions are an indispensable element in science, the Frequency Theory fails as the comprehensive account of probability that Reichenbach and others have claimed for it. We can best convey the critics' unease with some examples of single-case inductive probability remarks:

1. The probability of rain tomorrow given present meteorological information is about 0.80.
2. Given all the available evidence, the special theory of relativity is highly probable.

In each of these, the inductive probability value—or "weight" value—is in the Frequency Theory simply a long-run frequency. Therefore the frequentist must regard (1) as saying something like "In an infinite sequence of days following days that are meteorologically like today, it rains about 80 percent of the time." For many critics, to interpret (1) in this way strains common sense and distorts common usage; we are not talking about the set of all days (past, present, and future) following those that are in some sense "like" today, we are simply talking about *tomorrow*. To be sure, the frequency with which rain has occurred in the past on days following days like today is *evidence* concerning the chance of rain tomorrow, but to say this is to miss the point. The statement "The probability of rain tomorrow given that in the past it has rained about 80 percent of the time on days following days like today is about 0.80" is just another inductive probability statement on a par with (1). It is not a frequentist *analysis* of (1) but rather something equally in need of analysis. A frequentist analysis must of necessity be an assertion about a *sequence* of events having a limit, not about a single event like tomorrow.

Similarly, (2) would have to say something like "Theories of the same type as the special theory, supported by the kind of evidence presently available, turn out to be true far more often than they turn out to be false." But theories of *what* type? How are we to delineate the class of such theories? And what kind of sequence of theories of that type exists? And as before, are we even saying anything about all such theories? Are we not simply talking about the special theory?

6. The pragmatic justification poses problems as well. Frequency theorists perhaps would not object to some of the consequences outlined here—indeed they have already been mentioned. The point in raising them again is that even if the pragmatic justification is otherwise without fault, it still remains a very weak (and to many critics, inconsequential) justification. Frequentists maintain that re-peated use of the Straight Rule will *eventually* lead to predictive success *if* success is at all possible. The italicized words 'eventually' and 'if' are where the troubles lie.

First, "will eventually lead to success" is to be understood rather narrowly; viz., "will correctly determine long-run limiting frequencies." This might "eventually" happen by repeated correction of projected frequencies, but perhaps it will take 1 million or 10 million years. So even if success comes, it may come "too late" for us or even for all humankind.

Second, "if success is possible" is intended to remind us of Hume's result. The pragmatic justification provides no *assurance* that any of our predictions are correct or even probably correct. Frequentists admit that there is no reason to believe categorically that success will in fact come sometime. Nor is the resort to a "practical limit" of any help in these cases. There is no assurance of this sort of limit either, and even if it exists its discovery also might come too late or else be detectable earlier by the use of another method.

More generally, the pragmatic justification does not come to grips with the problem of vindicating short-run frequencies. An insurance company is interested in the frequency with which U.S. men over age 50 die of heart disease in the next fifteen or twenty years, but it is not interested in what a frequentist would regard as a "long-run" frequency. Moreover, the frequentist must allow that over the short run another method may be more successful than use of the Straight Rule, and the upshot is that we cannot be sure, for any given *finite* sequence, that if anything will work the Straight Rule will.

To follow up a bit, there are alternatives to the Straight Rule whose use exhibits the same self-corrective feature. Predictions made on the basis of such rules will converge toward a limit over the long run if such a limit exists (e.g., instead of x/y, predict that $\mathrm{fr}(F/G) = (x + j)/(y + k)$, where j and k are numerical constants). As such, and contrary to what Reichenbach indicated, the pragmatic justification vindicates not just use of the Straight Rule but use of these other rules as well, since if the limit exists repeated use of them will eventually find it. Now as an observed sequence gets longer and longer, predictions made by these rules will vary less and less from one another and from the Straight Rule (notice that as y keeps increasing, the value $(x + j)/(y + k)$ will get closer and closer to the Straight Rule's prediction of x/y since the constants k and j will have a diminishing influence on the ratio). So over the long haul, predictions made by these rules will be very close to those made by the Straight Rule, but over the *short* run the predictions we make could vary a great deal depending on which rule we choose (for relatively small y, the difference between $(x + j)/(y + k)$ and x/y could be quite significant). Since on the pragmatic justification there is no decisive reason for choosing between these rules, significantly different predictive values are equally justified, and our choice of value is almost arbitrary.

For example, suppose the limiting frequency of *F* given *G* is ⅗ and that the observed frequency after, say, 1000 observations is ⅔. There is a vindicated rule on the pragmatic justification that will predict a limiting frequency of ⅗, *not* the Straight Rule of course since it will predict ⅔ at this point. This other rule, if it were used in this instance, would actually be superior to the Straight Rule in that we could achieve success earlier through its use. But the trouble of course is that we do not know in advance what the long-run frequency is (we do not know that it is in fact ⅗), and hence we do not know which rule to use—one is as good as the other as far as the pragmatic justification is concerned. Thus we have no basis for knowing what predictions to make.

Section 3. The Logical Theory _____

Frequency theorists hold that inductive probability is just a subspecies of frequency probability, but logical theorists maintain that inductive probability—and hence degree of confirmation—is an *irreducibly logical concept.*[7] They acknowledge the concept of frequency probability and grant that it provides a good analysis of what were termed "descriptive" probability statements back in Chapter Four. But they further hold that the concept of degree of confirmation cannot be analyzed in frequentist terms.

Instead, logical theorists maintain that *degree of confirmation is an objective, logical relation* holding between a pair of statements. The relation is objective in that it exists independent of our thought about it; it is something we can discover, not something we create. Just as the relation of validity holds objectively between premise and conclusion in deductive inference, so likewise that *x* is the correct value to which *p* is confirmed by *q* (i.e., that 'Pr(*p/q*) = *x*' expresses a truth) is an objective matter in inductive logic. Of course, in the Frequency Theory inductive probability is an objective concept too, but a mathematical one. For the logical theorist though, degree of confirmation is a purely logical relation essentially linked to the notion of inference, and the calculus of inductive probability is to be formulated in terms of statements rather than—as the frequentist would have it—properties.

But there is more. Whereas inductive probability statements are empirical in the Frequency Theory, the Logical Theory holds that they are *logically true-or-false.* Just as determining that *q* validly follows from ~*p* and '*p* v *q*' is an a priori matter involving no appeal to observation, so likewise verifying that *x* is the value to which *q* confirms p is a matter that requires only logical techniques and a grasp of the meanings of the two statements. And just as the corresponding conditional '$[(p \lor q) \& \sim p] \supset q$' is logically true, so is the inductive probability statement '$\Pr(p/q) = x$'. Of course in the typical case p and q are themselves factual (just as the components of a tautology often are) but that one confirms the other to a particular degree is not an empirical matter. In the Logical Theory, inductive probability statements are accorded the same philosophical status as mathematical claims.

There is one more element in the Logical Theory, and it is tied to the claim that inductive probability statements are true or false on objective, logical grounds. *True inductive probability statements constitute a standard of rational behavior under conditions of uncertainty.* If it is true that $\Pr(p/q) = x$, then x is the degree to which a person is rationally entitled to believe p on the basis of the evidence in q. If a person S has determined that '$\Pr(p/q) = x$' is true, then

    i. x is a fair betting quotient for S with respect to a bet on p given q (at least for small stakes relative to S's total wealth).[8]

    ii. x is the factor by which the value or worth of the circumstance described by p must be multiplied to yield a rational expected value for S of the course of action under consideration.

Thus a "reasonable" person will believe a tautology to the degree 1, and that a spade will be drawn from a full bridge deck to the degree ¼. Moreover, a bet on the latter statement would be accepted only at odds of 3 to 1 or more.

The first major logical theorist was the well-known economist, mathematician, and philosopher John Maynard Keynes. In his classic *A Treatise on Probability*,[9] Keynes argues eloquently and persuasively for all of the theses just described. However, the most complete and sophisticated version of the Logical Theory has been developed by the philosopher Rudolf Carnap, and we shall focus on his theory. Unlike Keynes, Carnap holds that inductive probability is partly definable and that quantitative probability values are obtainable, in principle at least, for any pair of statements.

Carnap begins with the subjective degree of belief a person S has in a statement p at a time t. It is possible to determine what S's degree of belief is, say, by observing S's betting behavior, and Carnap takes the subjective degree with which S believes in p at t to be the highest betting quotient with which S is willing to bet on p (for small stakes) at t.

Of course the degree of belief a person has in a statement usually depends, at least in part, on the information available to him or her at the time. Let q be the observational knowledge S has at t, and let us consider just the influence of this factor on degree of belief. The *credibility* of p given q—for short, $Cred(p/q)$—is the degree of belief S would have in p if q were S's total body of evidence. People of course will often differ in the credibility values they assign to p given q, and hence will exhibit different "Cred-functions." Whereas S's actual degree of belief is relativized to periods of time, the Cred-function implicitly employed is to be thought of as a more or less lasting character trait, specifically as S's dispositions for forming beliefs on the basis of his or her observations. Although credibility is a more remote and abstract concept than actual degree of belief, Carnap feels that only for it can we find a sufficient number of rationality requirements that will serve as a basis for constructing an adequate system of inductive logic.

Presumably most adult human beings will exhibit some sort of Cred-function, but it may not be a *rational* one (as with a paranoic to take an extreme case). Such functions are irrational in that when used in evaluating a course of action, they lead to unreasonable decisions (such as accepting a bet at what would normally be considered outrageous odds). For Carnap, inductive logic is to be developed in terms of a Cred-function whose employment would lead to rational behavior under conditions of uncertainty; that is, *inductive probability is a rational Cred-function*. At one time,[10] Carnap held that there was just one such function, but in later writings he allows that several Cred-functions can serve as equally good analyses of inductive probability; two reasonable individuals might display different, though no doubt similar, Cred-functions.

But this is just a first step, for the notion of a Cred-function is a quasi-psychological concept insofar as it concerns what a person would believe under certain conditions. The Logical Theory, however, holds that degree of confirmation is a logical relation independent of the subjective degree of belief a person has or would have. Let us abbreviate the expression, 'the degree to which q confirms p' as '$c(p/q)$'. For a given pair of statements, p and q, we may imagine many different "c-values," some rational and some not. We thus have a set of confirmation functions—or *c-functions* as they are called—and in the Logical Theory they are objective, logical relations. Where c is a particular confirmation function, if x is the correct value for $c(p/q)$, this is a matter that can be determined on purely logical, a priori grounds—much like determining the validity of an argument in deductive logic. The value a c-function assigns to a pair of statements depends only on the logical and semantical properties of those statements, and hence such functions are specifiable without reference to human beings and their beliefs.

However it should not be thought that Cred-functions and c-functions are distinct entities. The difference is rather like that of a rock considered simply as a physical object and as a tool that may be used for a specific purpose; to specify it as a tool requires stating its relation to human endeavors. A rock may serve as someone's tool, and similarly a given c-function may serve as someone's Cred-function; and just as the rock exists even if no one uses it, so will the c-function. The link between these two notions is forged as follows: An *inductively adequate* c-function is one such that if people were to use it as their Cred-function, it would lead them to make rational decisions. So the explication of inductive probability as a rational Cred-function in no way turns it into a "subjective" concept.

Moreover, Carnap's explication has in his view an important advantage over the approach of Keynes and earlier theorists in that it leads to a numerical scale of probability values. That is, each c-function represents a *quantitative inductive method;* if S has chosen a particular c-function, then "inductive reasoning" by S about p on the basis of q is aimed at determining the value of $c(p/q)$. We have already noted that such a c-value depends only on purely logical considerations, and we will now spell out more fully what this means.

The technique for calculating c-values has in fact already been outlined in our discussion of alternative inductive logics back in the last section of Chapter Five. To make explicit what was there implicit, each of three logics described is representable as a c-function: Carnap uses '$c^*(p/q)$' to express the value assigned by what we called SIL to p given q and '$c^\dagger(p/q)$' for that assigned by RIL. So we have already seen how to determine c-values; to define a c-function (an inductive logic or method), we first assign values to state descriptions of a language such that they sum to 1. Using some principles of the calculus we can then determine the unconditional value of any statement and also its conditional value relative to another statement.

Each c-function thus defines for a given language and domain an inductive logic, and the determination of c-values is a purely logical task employing the principles of the calculus and the semantical characteristics of the formal language. Our earlier specification of inductive logics is a simplification of Carnap's actual procedure, but the end results and underlying concepts are his and we may thus carry over our characterizations of SIL and RIL (while CIL is representable as a c-function too, it is a somewhat different case from those Carnap defines and we shall put off coverage of it for now). For SIL, $c^*(p/q)$ is calculated using the theorems of the calculus (mentioned in Chapter Five) from the probability assignments to state descriptions dictated by what was called the "Principle of Scientific Logic"; for RIL, $c^\dagger(p/q)$ is determined from those theorems together with the assignments made by the "Principle of Random Logic."[11]

It should be apparent by now that there are in theory infinitely many distinct c-functions—and hence inductive logics—though many differ only slightly from c*. It is c* and these similar functions that Carnap regards as inductively adequate for use as a Cred-function. We have seen that c* (or SIL) assigns higher unconditional values to state descriptions describing "uniform" worlds, and Carnap has laid out an elegant and ingenious method for arranging all inductive logics of this kind on a continuum according to how quickly or slowly they enable us, so to speak, to "learn from experience"—that is, according to how large an increase in c-value occurs between a statement like 'c(Gb/Fa & Ga & Fb)' and the initial statement 'c(Gb/Fb)'. For all the c-functions of the continuum, the c-value that object b is white given both that it is a swan and that the already observed object a is a white swan will exceed the c-value that b is white given just that it is a swan, but the c-functions differ in the degree to which the former value exceeds the latter. "Learning from experience" for a given c-function means how it shapes our expectations of the future from the evidence that constitutes our relevant experience.

[The next four paragraphs could be skipped on a first reading.]

To see how this continuum is developed, let k be the number of Q-properties of a domain; in the simple domain D of Chapter Five, $k = 4$. Now any basic property of the domain can be expressed by a disjunction of Q-properties. Thus the property F in D is represented by the disjunction '(Fx & Gx) v (Fx & $\sim Gx$)'. Where w is the number of disjuncts (two in the present case), the *relative width* of F is the ratio w/k; for F in D it is ½. However, Carnap does not employ small domains like D, but instead develops his apparatus for domains with infinitely many individuals and any finite number of properties. For such domains, Carnap's *continuum of inductive methods* may be specified by the following rules; where a_i is any arbitrary individual and F any property:

I. $c(Fa_i) = \dfrac{w}{k}$ (for $i = 1, 2, 3, \ldots$)

II. $c[Fa_i/\mathrm{fr}_n(F) = s/n] = \left(\dfrac{s}{n}\right)\left(\dfrac{n}{n+\lambda}\right) + \left(\dfrac{w}{k}\right)\left(\dfrac{\lambda}{n+\lambda}\right)$ for $i > n$

(As before, '$\mathrm{fr}_n(F) = s/n$' means "the relative frequency with which the property F has occurred in n trials is s/n"; i.e., out of n observations s of them have been F). In (II) λ is a parameter such that when it is fixed as a particular nonnegative real number, the result is that (I) and (II) define a specific inductive logic or method. These logics of the continuum are ordered by the roles played by empirical data and the initial c-values given by (I).[12] More fully, the righthand side of (II) is a sum of two factors: an empirically observable frequency, s/n, and the relative width, w/k, each influenced by a ratio involving n and λ. Since s/n can be determined only by observation, it is called *the empirical factor*, whereas w/k is based on the logical structure of the domain and language and is fixed in advance of observation—it is *the logical factor*.

Before observation, $c(Fa_i) = w/k$. As the number of observed instances, n, increases, $c[Fa_i/fr_n(F) = s/n]$ moves from w/k toward s/n. So the c-functions under consideration (except $c\dagger$) fulfill the following condition:

III. $\underset{n\to\infty}{\text{Limit}}\ \ c\,[Fa_i\,/fr_n\,(F) = s/n] = \dfrac{s}{n}, \qquad$ for $i > n$

For example, suppose we observe 100 objects 60 of which are swans; then later 1000 objects 500 of which are swans. Condition (III) tells us that the long-run tendency is for a c-value like $c[Fa_{1001}/fr_{1000}(F) = \frac{1}{2}]$ to be closer to $\frac{1}{2}$ than $c[Fa_{101}/fr_{100}(F) = \frac{3}{5}]$ is to $\frac{3}{5}$. And this is just what we should expect; as our experience grows (as n gets larger and larger) the predictive values provided by the c-function should approach the observed frequency, s/n. Whatever differences the inductive logics may exhibit, it is reasonable to expect them to behave in this way given that all are such that their c-values reflect "learning from experience" to one degree or another. Note that (I) and (II) are very similar to a simple enumeration rule for whatever inductive logic we obtain once λ has been fixed. The major difference is that only one property is mentioned instead of two. An enumeration rule stated with respect to one property is a special case of (I) and (II), viz., where there are no counterinstances and $s = n$.

Let us now consider some of the inductive logics we may obtain. Keeping n fixed, let us set $\lambda = k$; that is, λ is simply the number of Q-properties. With this choice of λ, (II) becomes

$$c[Fa_i/fr_n(F) = s/n] = \frac{sn}{n^2 + nk} + \frac{wk}{kn + k^2} = \frac{s + w}{n + k}$$

Note that if n increases, $(s + w)/(n + k)$ approaches s/n since w and k, being fixed, have less and less influence on the ratio. More important, it can be shown that $(s + w)/(n + k)$ approaches s/n in a fashion that accords roughly with our own probabilistic intuitions. That is, when $\lambda = k$, the result is c^* and hence SIL. The preceding formulation can be shown equivalent to the Principle of Scientific Logic.

The remarkable result of Carnap's continuum is this: As λ *increases* from k the logical factor becomes more and more important in determining c-values like $c[Fa_i/\text{fr}_n(F) = s/n]$, and as λ *decreases* from k the empirical factor becomes more dominant. Moreover, as λ approaches infinity, (II) approaches the values for c†; that is, the c-values approach w/k, which is what RIL predicts (imagine larger and larger numbers for λ in (II)). Thus RIL, in which no learning from experience occurs, is a limiting case of the continuum. On the other hand, as λ decreases toward 0, the empirical factor takes precedence since $w/k[\lambda/(n + \lambda)]$ in (II) approaches 0. So when $\lambda = 0$, we obtain an inductive logic very similar to the frequency theorist's self-corrective rule since (II) in such a case simply projects the observed frequency s/n as the c-value. Hence, as λ increases (decreases), we obtain inductive logics in which the logical (empirical) factor becomes more influential in determining a new c-value upon the discovery of another item of evidence.

Inductive probability has been explicated as a rational Cred-function, or in other words, a c-function that is "inductively adequate." It remains however to spell out more fully just what inductive adequacy is, and to this end Carnap has proposed a system of inductive logic in which the rationality requirements that make for an inductively adequate c-function are stated in the form of axioms. Each axiom lays down a condition that a c-function must satisfy in order to serve as a rational Cred-function. That is, the axioms are intended to select from the continuum those c-functions on which the inductive probability concept may be based.

The axioms state purely logical properties of c-functions; the theory of c-functions is thus a part of logic and inductive probability is the objective, logical concept leading to the rational decision making that the Logical Theory requires. Some of the axioms that follow pertain to formal languages that are a bit more complex than those considered in so far that they appeal to "families" of predicates. Such a family is a set of predicates representing mutually exclusive and jointly exhaustive properties (e.g., colors), and hence such languages more closely approximate natural languages than the one in Chapter Five, in which all basic properties are logically independent. Even so, they remain simple devices, and further axioms would be required for more sophisticated symbolisms involving, for example, relations.

Axioms 1–5: These are the standard axioms of the calculus (with 'c' in place of 'Pr').

Axiom 6: In a language for a domain with a finite number of possible worlds, if $c(p/q) = 1$, then $q \rightarrow p$.

Note that Axiom 6 is the converse of Axiom 3 restricted to finite domains, and was briefly discussed earlier in connection with the notion of a partial book. A c-function is said to be *regular* if and only if the values it assigns state descriptions sums to 1 and obeys the principles of the calculus in determining conditional values like $c(p/q)$. Regular c-functions are precisely those that satisfy Axioms 1–6 (restricted to finite languages), and c^* and $c\dagger$ are of course regular. An irregular c-function cannot serve as an inductively adequate Cred-function.

The next five axioms are termed *axioms of invariance,* and they represent what Carnap takes to be the kernel of truth in the Principle of Indifference. Any c-function satisfying Axiom 7 assigns equal values to *isomorphic* state descriptions and is said to be *symmetrical* (again, c^* and $c\dagger$ are examples).

> ***Axiom 7:*** The value of $c(p/q)$ remains unchanged under any finite permutation of objects.

> ***Axiom 8:*** The value of $c(p/q)$ remains unchanged under any permutation of predicates of any family.

> ***Axiom 9:*** The value of $c(p/q)$ remains unchanged under any permutation of families with the same number of predicates.

> ***Axiom 10:*** The value of $c(p/q)$ remains unchanged if the domain of objects is enlarged (where p and q are any truth-functional sentences).

> ***Axiom 11:*** The value of $c(p/q)$ remains unchanged if further families of predicates are added to the language.

By virtue of Axiom 10 it suffices to employ infinite languages when studying inductive logics, which was the procedure we used in examining the continuum. The upshot of Axiom 11 is that c-value depends upon only those predicates occurring in p and q, and not as in Carnap's earlier version of the theory on the total number of predicates in the formal language.[13]

> ***Axiom 12:*** $c[Fa_i/\mathrm{fr}_n(F) = s/n \ \& \ Fa_{i+1}] > c[Fa_i/\mathrm{fr}_n(F) = s/n]$, for $i > n$.

Axiom 12 reflects "learning from experience" and is crucial in the derivation of various inductive rules of inference as theorems.[14] In addition, a version of Principle (III) is included as an axiom as well.

The function $c\dagger$ violates Axiom 12, and hence RIL is not inductively adequate. Moreover, the c-function corresponding to the Frequency Theorist's Straight Rule violates Axiom 6 and hence is also inadequate.[15]

Even though these principles are stated as axioms, it still seems reasonable to demand that some sort of grounds be given for them. Since the c-functions satisfying all of the axioms are those that may serve as rational Cred-functions, Carnap takes the problem of justifying induction to be that of giving reasons for accepting the axioms. To this end, an associate of Carnap's, John Kemeny, has offered "conditions of adequacy" to provide them with intuitive support.[16] Since the axioms themselves are intended as rationality requirements underlying our use of inductive probability, these adequacy conditions must presumably reflect our deep-seated intuitions on what is rational from both a deductive and inductive standpoint. The conditions include

CA1: A c-function must not define a betting system in which a Dutch Book or partial book can be made.

CA2: $c(p/q)$ is to depend only on the statements p and q.

CA3: Proper names that are logically alike must be treated a priori alike (e.g., prior to any evidence, $c(Fa) = c(Fb)$).

CA4: The definition of c must take into account learning from experience.

(Further conditions are needed for formal languages more complex than those we have studied.) Axioms 1–6 are to be supported by CA1, axioms 7–9 by CA3, axioms 10 and 11 by CA2, and axiom 12 and principle (III) by CA4.

Kemeny's reasons for accepting Carnap's axioms have, according to both writers, this characteristic: They are based on our intuitive judgments concerning inductive strength and hence concerning the inductive rationality of practical decisions like bets. One consequence of this, it is claimed, is that the reasons are purely a priori; they are independent both of factual principles about the world (e.g., uniformity of nature) and of specific past experiences (e.g., the success rate of bets based on a c-function that satisfies the axioms). Of course the value of $c(p/q)$ depends on the factual statement q containing the available empirical evidence, but the acceptability of the axioms by means of which $c(p/q)$ is determined—and by means of which restrictions are placed on what counts as an admissible c-function—is an a priori matter and independent of such evidence. In fact, Carnap agrees fully with Hume's claim that any attempt to justify induction on the basis of a factual, empirical principle is bound to be question begging, while nonetheless maintaining that his axioms can be given an a priori justification. Though Hume showed that no rational justification could be supplied for SIL on factual and empirical grounds, Carnap maintains that his reconstruction of SIL (in the form of c* and the axiom system) is rationally justified on purely a priori considerations.

Carnap draws another consequence from Hume. Inductive reasoning, he says, is usually misconstrued inasmuch as it is regarded as an *inference* from known statements to a new statement, and when a high probability is ascribed to the latter the result is the *acceptance* of that statement. But Carnap contends that accepting the statement flies in the face of Hume's result; it would then be impossible to answer the Humean charge that induction has no rational grounds. That is, to accept a predictive statement, *p,* as conclusion of an inductive inference is to accept a factual statement that possibly will turn out to be false and whose justification ultimately rests on an unsatisfactory principle like the uniformity of nature. But to accept a statement like '$c(p/q) = x$' is to accept one that, being logically true, can never turn out to be false and whose justification does not rest on any factual principle. Rather, the grounds for assigning x to p given q are a priori. Instead, then, of a person S asserting the conclusion of an inductive inference, *p,* S should rather assert something like the following: at the present time my total evidence is *q,* and $\text{Cred}_s(p/q) = 0.85$. Instead of asserting *p,* S asserts '$\text{Cred}_s(p/q) = 0.85$', for it is the result of inductive reasoning. Hume's thesis does not apply since S can give a priori grounds for adopting it. Because it is derivable from '$c(p/q) = 0.85$', it is a logical truth based upon the definition of 'c'. And since S's choice of c was guided by the axioms, c is a rational Cred-function which leads to S's actual degree of belief in *p.*

Many philosophers have claimed that we need the acceptance of a factual, predictive statement like *p* as a basis for action. And if, as Carnap holds, inductive reasoning results merely in statements devoid of factual content like '$\text{Cred}(p/q) = 0.85$', how can inductive logic fulfill its purpose of guiding our practical decisions? Carnap replies that S has a factual basis in the evidence statement *q,* and to come to a rational decision acceptance of *p* is not needed. The subjective degree of belief that ensues from the Cred statement is sufficient for determining a rational expected value and hence for making a rational choice. He nicely sums up his views on justification:

> On the one hand we see that inductive reasoning is used by the scientist and the man in the street every day without apparent scruples; and we have the feeling it is valid and indispensable. On the other hand, once Hume awakens our intellectual conscience, we find no answer to his objection. Who is right, the man of common sense or the critical philosopher? Hume's criticism of the customary forms of induction was correct. But still the basic idea of common sense thinking is vindicated: induction, if properly reformulated, can be shown to be valid by rational criteria.[17]

Some Objections to the Logical Theory:

1. For Carnap's system, the following—and rather disconcerting—result holds: In any domain with infinitely many objects, the initial probability or c-value of a universal generalization like 'All F are G' will be 0 regardless of which c-function is used, and it will remain 0 regardless of how much confirming evidence is available (e.g., evidence like that provided by Fa & Ga and Fb & Gb). Moreover, in any "large" finite domain—one with many more objects than domain D of Chapter Five—the initial probability of the generalization will be very close to 0, and even a vast amount of confirming evidence will produce only a minute increase in value. Why close to 0? 'All F are G' is more fully expressed as 'For every object x, $Fx \supset Gx$'. Its initial probability will equal that of the conjunction of all singular instance statements—one statement for each object in the domain:

$$(Fa \supset Ga) \ \& \ (Fb \supset Gb) \ \& \ (Fc \supset Gc) \ \& \ . . .$$

So there will be as many conjuncts as there are objects. But we know that the probability of a conjunction is determined by multiplying those of its conjuncts. Since these are ratios between 0 and 1, the more conjuncts there are, the closer the product is to 0.

Some critics find these consequences so counterintuitive as to warrant rejection of the entire system. For his part, Carnap claims he does not find this result "entirely implausible" and maintains that, for the purpose of guiding our practical decisions, "instance confirmation" is enough. By this he means determining, relative to a body of evidence, the c-value of a statement like, 'The next F observed will be G', as opposed to "generality confirmation" where the confirmed statement is 'All F are G'. On the practical level, we are more concerned with knowing the probability that the *next* instance observed will be like those in the past than in knowing the chance that *all* instances whatever are of that character. This result, he claims, holds even for more theoretical pursuits; a chemist is more concerned with whether the next sodium salt to be tested burns with a yellow flame than with whether all of them do—though here his reply seems less plausible (scientists are concerned with discovering laws, and of course such statements are universal).

In any case, the consequences concerning generalizations are discomforting enough to have led some (including Carnap) to attempt to develop systems of induction in which well-confirmed generalizations can attain respectable probability values. In recent years systems have been devised that do this, but they are more complex and unwieldy than the one examined in this chapter.[18]

Only time will tell whether a system that is both fair to generalizations and free of the complications found in present-day versions can be developed. So perhaps the problem of generalizations will turn out to be just an example of the growing pains of a new discipline rather than a ground for rejection. But even if this is achieved, it must still be kept in mind that the Logical Theory has been developed only for relatively simple formal languages that do not capture the full complexity of scientific discourse. Again, only time will tell whether it can be extended to more sophisticated languages.

2. Has Carnap provided a rational justification for SIL and similar methods on purely a priori grounds? Axiom 12 is a basic principle of Carnap's system that reflects learning from experience and is justified by CA4. It is satisfied by SIL but not by RIL. The a priori rejection of RIL seems reasonable. A hypothetical person with our a priori knowledge of logic and mathematics but with no actual experience of the real world might at first suppose (perhaps using the Principle of Indifference) that possible worlds are equally likely—an assignment of course that yields RIL. But as he makes his a priori calculations in the RIL system he quickly realizes that once he is placed in the actual world this logic does not enable him to revise his expectations of the future in light of the evidence he obtains. So in advance of any experience of the world he rejects RIL.

However, let us reconsider Counterinductive Logic. Like the others it can be expressed by a c-function that is both regular and symmetrical, but of course it would be rejected by Carnap since it fails to satisfy Axiom 12. Indeed, it is so different from those considered thus far that it does not appear on the continuum. The continuum functions enable us to one degree or another to learn "positively" from experience; for example, $c^*(Gb/Fa \ \& \ Ga \ \& \ Fb) > c^*(Gb/Fb)$. Unlike RIL though, the CIL function enables us to learn from experience but "negatively"—the value it assigns Gb given $Fa \ \& \ Ga \ \& \ Fb$ is less than the initial value. Now CA4 says only that the c-function we choose must facilitate learning from experience; it does not specify how we are to learn. As such, it supports not only Axiom 12 but an opposite version that justifies CIL and rejects SIL; viz., the version obtained by replacing '>' in Carnap's axiom with '<'. But of course this would be intolerable. CA4 would justify a system of induction diametrically opposed to c^* and its relatives, so the a priori justification of the latter inductive logics would fail.

Perhaps then what Carnap and Kemeny meant by CA4 is this: The chosen c-function should enable us to learn *postively* from experience. But the trouble now is that this revised CA4 does not appear to be an a priori condition, and we would not be able to reject CIL in the same way as RIL. What a priori grounds are there for preferring Axiom 12 to its CIL counterpart? In advance of experience we may know that we will want to revise our beliefs as new evidence comes in, but do we know whether to revise them up or down? Whereas there may be a priori grounds for not assigning equal probability values to possible worlds, there seems to be no such reason for biasing our assignments in favor of one type of world rather than another. Whichever way it is done, we have a logic in which we "learn" in some way from experience.

If CA4 is allowed to stand unrevised, then it fails to justify the a priori choice of SIL over CIL. And if it is revised, we no longer have an a priori justification of SIL. Of course if the revised CA4 is empirical, the ghost of Hume returns to haunt us.[19]

3. The Logical Theory maintains that inductive probability statements are, if true, logically true, and are thus like tautologies and other a priori statements. Now suppose person S wishes to determine the probability that the Sox will win their next game, say to make a rational bet. Where 'W' represents the statement that the Sox win, S considers the following statements (the 's' superscript again indicates probability in the SIL sense and hence that S used c* or a close relative in determining that x, y, and z are the correct values to assign):

   a. $Pr^s(W/E) = x$ **b.** $Pr^s(W/E \ \& \ F) = y$ **c.** $Pr^s(W/G) = z$

Let E express some relevant evidence such as the strengths and weaknesses of the Sox and their opponent. Let F express the more recent information that two of the Sox's best hitters are injured and will not play. Let G express the claim that the Sox are racked with dissension and loss of morale. Suppose S knows E and F to be true and knows G to be false (or at least has no grounds for thinking it true). Moreover, S has no further evidence on which to base a decision. Which of the inductive probability statements should S select in determining what sort of bet to make? Common sense would dictate (b); statement (a) contains some but not all of the relevant evidence available and (c) contains false or at least unverified information. Only (b) gives S all the available, reliable evidence.

But in the Logical Theory each statement is a logical truth, and hence x, y, and z are all "correct" values as determined by c*. Each merely says that an event W will happen with a certain probability relative to a particular body of evidence; since (a), (b) and (c) are logically on a par with one another (as a set of three tautologies would be), what sense can be made of the claim that the value y in (b) is somehow superior to or more "correct" than the others?

The answer, according to Carnap, lies in a principle governing the application of inductive probability statements to practical situations (and which are briefly mentioned in Chapter One):

> **Rule of Total Evidence:** In the application of inductive logic to a given knowledge situation, the total evidence available must be taken as a basis for determining the degree of confirmation.[20]

This seeming truism thus plays a vital role in the Logical Theory, for without it S would have no basis for selecting (b) over (a) and (c) in determining what bet to accept. The rule would seem to have both a practical and a moral point. S would be wrong from a practical standpoint to use (a), and a jury would be wrong morally if in determining the probability of guilt it purposely disregarded certain relevant facts brought up during the trial.

However, one critic, A. J. Ayer, argues that appealing to the total evidence rule will not solve the logical theorist's problem. Using all the available evidence, he says, accords with common sense, but it cannot be justified on Carnap's principles.

> The [predicted event] will occur or it will not. To say that there is a probability, of a given degree, and that it will occur is to say only that the hypothesis that it will occur is confirmed to that degree by such and such evidence. If this proposition is true, it is necessarily true: but so are all the other true propositions which, on the basis of greater, or less, or partly, or wholly different evidence, assign to the hypothesis a different degree of confirmation. There is no sense therefore in which the proposition which brings in all the available evidence can be superior to any of the others as a measure of probability. And this being so, there can be no practical reason why we should take it as a guide.[21]

Ayer appears to be saying that a commonsense appeal to the rule is not available to logical theorists precisely because they must hold that a true inductive probability statement that is not based on the total evidence is just as much a necessary truth as one that does satisfy the rule.

It should be noted that one of Carnap's defenders, Carl Hempel,[22] has replied that the total evidence rule is not, as Ayer seems to think, a rule of inductive logic proper, but rather—as Carnap himself claims—of the logic of empirical inquiry. As such, the rule specifies a necessary condition for the rationality of inductive beliefs, and its justification lies in that alone: It expresses one of the conditions governing rational belief and choice. If S had acted on (a) rather than (b), S would not have acted rationally, nor would the jury that deliberately ignored some relevant evidence.

Whatever the outcome of this dispute, there are problems with the Rule of Total Evidence itself. One is that the total evidence that any adult human being has is so vast and complex that it cannot be fully schematized in any of the rules of inductive logic that Carnap has managed to derive as theorems of his present system. On this Carnap only says that a theorem of inductive logic "can nevertheless be applied indirectly, provided the additional knowledge is at least approximately irrelevant for the hypothesis in question."[23]

4. On the contention that inductive probability statements are logically true-or-false, Carnap says:

> The function c* has been defined in a purely logical way. Therefore . . . the true elementary statements of c* are accepted by all irrespective of their inductive methods. On the other hand . . . to propose Pr^s as an explicatum for [inductive probability] means to propose Pr^s as a Cred-function for the determination of practical decisions. . . . I claim that Pr^s is a good explicatum which means that the use of Pr^s (or what amounts to the same thing, c*) as a Cred-function leads to rational decisions. A statement of the form (1)"$Pr^s(h/e) = x$" can therefore in my opinion be analyzed as containing two cognitive components: (2)"$c*(h, e) = x$," and (3)"Pr^s (and hence c*) is a rational Cred-function." In contrast, what is expressed by the non-cognitive, purely volitional decision statement (4)"Let us henceforth use the function Pr^s as a Cred-function" is . . . not part of the meaning of (1). . . . I regard (1) as [logically true-or-false] because according to my conception no factual knowledge is relevant for the question of the truth of (2) or of (3).[24]

Logically true statements are true regardless of which possible world is in fact the actual one and hence say nothing about how the facts are (or are not); they are, as we have been putting it, devoid of factual content. The question now is whether an ordinary, true probability statement of the form

A. The probability of *h* given *e* is x/y

is adequately analyzed (or explicated) as Carnap's logically true statement:

1. $Pr^s(h/e) = x/y$

Statement (1) abbreviates the conjunction of statements (2) $c*(h/e) = x/y$, and (3) Pr^s is a rational Cred-function. Now there can be no doubt that 2 is a logical truth. We know that determining x/y to be the value assigned by c* is a purely logical task akin to constructing a truth table in deductive logic, and as Carnap points out it is accepted by all, including those who use a different c-function. Even a hypothetical user of Counterinductive Logic would have no quarrel with (2) since holding it does not *commit* one to using a particular inductive logic. Moreover, (3) can be verified on logical grounds simply by checking c^* with Carnap's axioms; since it satisfies all of them, it provides us with a rational Cred-function. So (1) is a logical truth since both of its conjuncts are.

But is (1) a satisfactory analysis of (A)? Does it capture the critical elements of (A)'s meaning as we intuitively understand it? In asserting (1), all that is being said is that a certain rational Cred-function assigns the value x/y to h given e, and in saying this no commitment is expressed to actually using that function. But one who asserts (A) would seem to be saying far more than this; one is claiming x/y to *be* in fact the correct value for h given e, and would reject the suggestion that it is some other value w/z, and indeed would consider a bet on h given e fair at odds $y - x$ to x rather than at $z - w$ to w. Unlike (1), in asserting (A) one does express a commitment to a particular inductive logic. To put the matter another way, it is very natural to suppose that (A) logically implies or validly yields a statement like:

B. The correct odds for a fair bet on h given e are $y - x$ to x.

But though (A) implies (B), (1) does not. For (1) is a logical truth and therefore only logical truths follow from it (no nontautology for example validly follows from a tautology), and (B) hardly seems to be a logical truth. A person who has adopted a different c-function satisfying Carnap's axioms would nonetheless hold (1) to be true since he can calculate what c^* assigns h given e just as easily as anyone else, and in addition he can check c^* against the axioms and readily determine that it provides us with a rational Cred-function. But while he would uphold a logical truth like (1) he would rationally reject (B) since his own c-function would dictate a different set of odds. Since on Carnap's own principles he must rationally believe (1) but can rationally reject (B), the latter does not follow from (1) and is not a logical truth. Thus although (A) surely would seem to imply (B), (1) does not, and this means that (1) does not fully capture the meaning of (A).

To escape this problem, the logical theorist could deny at the outset that (A) logically implies (B)—and Carnap appears to say this at times—but it surely seems a violation of sound common sense to deny it. What this points up is that everyday probability statements like (A) carry with them as part of their meaning certain commitments concerning belief and action that statements like (1)—being logical truths—do not. At the outset Carnap denied that the "noncognitive decision statement" (4), viz., 'Let us henceforth use Pr^s as a Cred-function', was part of the meaning of (1); and of course he had to deny this since otherwise (1) would not be logically true. The foregoing comments would appear to indicate that something like (4) is an element in the meaning of statements like (A), and to that extent (1) does not satisfactorily explicate (A), or at best gives only a partial analysis of it.

Section 4. The Subjective Theory _____

Despite vast differences, the Logical and Frequency Theories agree on a very basic point: There are objectively "correct" probability values. If ¼ is the correct value to assign the statement that a spade will be drawn from a bridge deck given the standard information, it is either because ¼ has been determined to be the limit of a particular empirical sequence of frequencies or because it is the value assigned by the rational Cred-function we have adopted.

In contrast, the Subjective Theory (also called the "Bayesian" or "Personalist" Theory) maintains that *probabilities are to be construed as actual, subjective degrees of belief,* and since people obviously differ on the degree to which they believe a given statement no degree of belief can be uniquely determined as the "rational" one. If Smith carefully examines p given q and decides that p is likely to the degree x, whereas Jones after doing the same assigns another value y, there is no saying as to which value is more accurate or correct. The probability value a person assigns simply expresses his or her commitment to behave in a certain way under certain conditions (such as what sort of bet would be considered fair in a given situation). Subjective probabilities should not be confused with inductive ones; later, we will see how inductive probabilities are handled on the subjectivist approach.

However, not all degrees of belief in a set of statements are acceptable in the Subjective Theory. Some as we know from Chapter Four are such that a Dutch Book can be made against the agent. So there is an objective constraint on our probability assignments, one that specifies a rationality requirement for any subject: *Our degrees of belief must satisfy the axioms of the probability calculus.* Smith and Jones may be "free" to assign different values to a set of statements, but neither would be considered a rational agent if they did so in such a way as to create Dutch Book situations. So the Subjective Theory is not simply a description of how people do in fact assign degrees of belief; if it were, it would merely be a psychological theory of partial belief. Rather, as a probability theory it proposes a standard of rational behavior: We ought to assign probabilities in accordance with the rules of the calculus. In this respect it resembles the Logical Theory, but for the subjectivist there are no conditions to be imposed on our partial beliefs beyond those of the calculus. Logical theorists, as we have seen, go much further, delimiting a class of inductive logics (including of course SIL) as the rationally acceptable ones, and to this end Carnap proposed his "invariance" and "learning from experience" axioms to single out such systems. For the subjectivist there is no preferred set of inductive methods; any method is allowed as long as the Dutch Book requirement is met. In other words, the subjectivist adopts Carnap's first six axioms but none of the rest, and thus "rational degree of belief" is a much broader (and weaker) notion than for a logical theorist.

We saw that the Dutch Book Theorem lays down a consistency requirement of sorts for our degrees of belief. One who violates the calculus in making probability assignments displays an inductive inconsistency that emerges in the form of a "no-win–always-lose" betting system, a situation that parallels the notion of logical inconsistency in deductive logic (as when, for example, both p and 'if p then q' are affirmed but q is denied). The importance of the Dutch Book was first recognized by the early subjectivist Frank Ramsey and developed more fully by another, L. J. Savage.[25] For both, the calculus may be looked on as a complex criterion of inductive consistency; a precise account of our partial beliefs, they argue, shows that the principles of the calculus are laws of consistency in this sense.

A theory of probability should tell us how to determine probability values, and for a subjectivist this means determining what a person's subjective degrees of belief are. One simple way, if it is available, is to consider the agent's hypothetical betting behavior; if one regards a bet on the Cubs winning their next game fair at odds of 3 to 1 against, then the subjective degree of belief in a Cubs victory is ¼. However, other techniques have been developed by Ramsey, Savage, and more recently Richard Jeffrey[26] in which a statement's probability may be determined by a preference ranking by the subject of various alternative acts that involve the statement. In fact techniques for determining consequence values of the acts have been devised too. Many of these methods are very sophisticated and beyond our scope; they properly belong to the rapidly growing discipline of decision theory, and subjectivists were among the earliest pioneers in this field. But it will be helpful to examine a simple case. Suppose we know the values a person attributes to the consequences of two alternative acts under consideration and also that our subject is indifferent between them (likes them equally). In such a case we can often determine what probabilities this person assigns to the relevant statements. Suppose Johnson travels often to Baltimore from New York; she dislikes driving because of the expressway traffic, and the bus is cramped and uncomfortable. That leaves the plane or Amtrak (which we will suppose are about equal in terms of cost and safety). It takes Amtrak about two and one-half hours to make the trip, whereas the plane takes one and one-half hours (including the trips to and from the airport). However, it is winter and the airport sometimes experiences weather problems, and in such cases the plane trip takes about four and one-half hours on average. We thus have

A_1(plane): 4.5 hours if bad weather; 1.5 hours otherwise.
A_2(train): 2.5 hours regardless of weather.

It seems reasonable to use the negatives of the trip times as our consequence values; thus –4.5, –1.5, and –2.5.

We now want to determine the probability, x, that Johnson attributes to the statement, W, that the airport is experiencing bad weather. If in fact she is indifferent between the two acts, determining this value just takes some arithmetic. To make calculation easier, we will add 4.5 to each consequence getting 0, 3, and 2, respectively. Where $Pr(W) = x$ and $Pr(\sim W) = 1 - x$, we have

$$EVal(A_1) = 0x + 3(1 - x) = 3 - 3x \qquad EVal(A_2) = 2x + 2(1 - x) = 2$$

Since Johnson is indifferent, we know that these expected values are equal. Hence we solve for x in $3 - 3x = 2$, and see that for her (whether she is explicitly aware of it or not) $Pr(W) = \frac{1}{3}$.

Along with these techniques, Ramsey began and Savage completed an axiomatic system of subjective probability and expected value based on the relation of preference between acts. The axioms take the form of "self-evident" rules of choice, for example that our preferences should be transitive (i.e., if A_1 is preferred to A_2 and A_2 to A_3, then A_1 is to be preferred to A_3). The idea is that in any choice situation, we should make our decisions using these rules and those derivable from them. Savage was then able to prove an important theorem that roughly stated says that choices made according to the rules both maximize expected value and satisfy the probability calculus. When we make our decisions according to this "calculus of choice," we are at least implicitly abiding by the RMV and meeting the Dutch Book requirement. There is thus a normative element in the Subjective Theory beyond that of avoiding a Dutch Book: subjectivistic decision theory provides a set of norms for human decision making. Moreover, by means of the preceding theorem, Savage's system (along with others developed more recently) provides a justification for using RMV, as well as a clear, pragmatic analysis of the terms 'expected value' and 'probable'. Neither of these ends is achieved on the more standard approach to expected value (as in Chapter Three) where these concepts are simply assumed.

For the subjectivist, subjective probabilities are to be distinguished from the inductive probabilities that are our main concern, for the former are construed as unconditional probabilities (Johnson's belief about the airport was rendered simply '$Pr(W) = \frac{1}{3}$'). Degree of belief statements of the form, '$Pr(p) = x$', are basic for the subjectivist since they are the statements on which our rational decisions are to be based. No doubt in many cases evidence for p is relevant to determining the value x, but this is not made explicit, for the point of such statements is not to measure the strength of an inductive argument but rather to measure a person's partial belief in a given statement. Inductive probability statements of course are conditional statements that express an assessment of an inductive argument, and for logical theorists they are the most fundamental form. They could accomodate degree of belief statements too, since the "rational" degree of belief value of a statement can be identified with its inductive probability given all relevant information in our body of knowledge; that is, $Pr(p) = Pr(p/q)$, where q expresses the known information. But the subjectivist will not proceed this way, and we must now examine how inductive probability and inductive inference are to be characterized in the subjectivist scheme.

If two different persons can have different degrees of belief in the same set of statements—two different "belief functions"—the same individual at different times can also have distinct belief functions. And this is what we should expect of course, for as more knowledge is acquired we will want to revise many of our beliefs in light of the new evidence. As our lives unfold, our experience is constantly providing us with new information; suppose then at a given time a subject's belief function is Pr_n and later observations provide the subject with a new piece of knowledge, q. **The Rule of Conditionalization** (or RC) characterizes the move from a belief function Pr_n to a "new" belief function, Pr_{n+1}, where q is taken into account in the reassessment of a statement p:

RC: For any statement p, $Pr_{n+1}(p) = Pr_n(p/q)$.

That is, the new subjective probability of p is its old one conditional on the just acquired information q. The conditional value, $Pr_n(p/q)$, is itself regarded as simply a ratio of two unconditional values since we know by Theorem 13 that $Pr_n(p/q) = Pr_n(p \& q)/Pr_n(q)$.

Let $q_1, \ldots, q_n$ express the new items that are successively added to our body of knowledge through observation. Where p is any statement (but most important a nonobservation statement such as a prediction or generalization) we have a continuing sequence of belief functions generated by the use of RC: $Pr_n(p) = Pr_{n-1}(p/q_{n-1})$, $Pr_{n+1}(p) = Pr_n(p/q_n)$, and so on. However, by Theorem 13,

$$Pr_{n+1}(p) = Pr_n(p/q_n) = \frac{Pr_n(p \ \& \ q_n)}{Pr_n(q_n)}$$

By RC on both numerator and denominator of the righthand expression, we have

$$= \frac{Pr_{n-1}(p \ \& \ q_n/q_{n-1})}{Pr_{n-1}(q_n/q_{n-1})}$$

Applying Theorem 13 to the top and bottom of the fraction, and eliminating the common denominator in both, we get

$$= \frac{Pr_{n-1}(p \ \& \ q_n \ \& \ q_{n-1})}{Pr_{n-1}(q_n \ \& \ q_{n-1})}$$

Applying Theorem 13 once again (but in the other direction) we finally have

$$Pr_{n+1}(p) = Pr_n(p/q_n) = Pr_{n-1}(p/q_n \ \& \ q_{n-1})$$

Clearly this maneuvering can be extended to any $n > 1$. Generalizing, then, we may say that the degree of belief value, $Pr_{n+1}(p)$, which was arrived at by repeated use of RC on the q is the very same value that we would obtain by applying RC just once to the conjunction of all the qs; in other words, $Pr_{n+1}(p) = Pr_1(p/q_1 \ \& \ \ldots \ \& \ q_n)$. Now the "embryonic" belief function, Pr_1, was not arrived at by using RC, and so it does not depend on what the actual contents of our body of knowledge are. This means that the quantity $Pr_1(p/q_1 \ \& \ \ldots \ \& \ q_n)$ measures the support $q_1 \ \& \ \ldots \ \& \ q_n$ *would* provide for p regardless of whether any or all of the qs were in fact part of our existing knowledge. For this reason, $Pr_1(p/q_1 \ \& \ \ldots \ \& \ q_n)$ may be taken as an inductive probability value—it measures the strength of the argument from the conjunction of the qs as premise to the conclusion p for the individual in question. For the subjectivist then, inductive inference provides a model by which "new" degrees of belief are generated from "old" ones, and more generally by which our beliefs in nonobservational statements emerge from the statements reporting our direct experience of the world. Insofar as inductive probability may be characterized in terms of Pr_1, it has been given a subjectivist analysis.

The foregoing should make clear that determining conditional values like $Pr_n(p/q_n)$ is an important task for the subjectivist, and perhaps the most important principle in this regard (and in fact for induction and statistical inference generally) is Bayes' Theorem. Suppose Smith's degree of belief in the statement (H) that the Bears will win their next game is only 0.2, and his belief in the statement (E) that their starting quarterback has recovered from injury is but 0.3. However the chance that he has recovered if the Bears win is high, say 0.75. Using Bayes' Theorem, we can now calculate the conditional probability that the Bears will win given a recovery (note that the denominator, $Pr_n(E)$, by Theorem 11 is a shorthand way of expressing the denominator of Bayes' Theorem in Chapter Three):

$$Pr_n(H/E) = \frac{Pr_n(H)Pr_n(E/H)}{Pr_n(E)} = \frac{(0.2)(0.75)}{0.3} = 0.5$$

So if Smith should discover before game time that E is true, then he should assign a probability of ½ to a Bears victory. Of course by RC it is tempting here to say that $Pr_{n+1}(H)$ *ought* to be ½ for Smith (and a logical theorist no doubt would say just that). But for the subjectivist one belief function is as good as another as long as they satisfy the Dutch Book requirement, and the subjectivist is thus limited to saying something like "if you desire that your beliefs be consistent over time, you will find some useful counsel in RC."

One advantage of Bayes' Theorem for the Subjective Theory is that highly subjective *prior* probabilities that are fed into the theorem often will have a diminishing influence as more and more evidence is collected. Two investigators might have wildly different initial degrees of belief in a set of hypotheses, but as testing goes on their posterior probabilities will tend to be very similar—the evidence in effect swamps the subjective estimates that were used to begin the research. Thus the final results in many instances are not influenced in a measurably significant way by the prior probabilities, and the element of arbitrariness that many find disturbing about the Subjective Theory is minimized.

In our conditionalization rule RC it is assumed that the statement q, which effects the belief change from $Pr_n(p)$ to $Pr_{n+1}(p)$, has become an item in our corpus of *knowledge*—that our observations have made us certain of its truth to the point of assigning it a probability of 1. Since $Pr_{n+1}(p) = Pr_n(p/q)$ by RC, the Pr_{n+1} function was generated by "conditionalizing" on the evidence statement q; hence for q itself $Pr_{n+1}(q) = Pr_n(q/q) = 1$. Thus for example if we see with our own eyes that an unknown substance burns with a yellow flame, that increases the probability that it is a sodium salt, and the observation statement reporting what we saw is now regarded as a certainty. But many observation statements are not like this; you saw something move in the shadowy darkness of your cellar and it looked very much like a mouse, but you are not certain that it was—it *might* have been something else. Here, the statement reporting the mouse sighting would be assigned a high probability but not a value of 1, and RC is not set up to handle such cases.

Furthermore, many philosophers have argued that we are *never* justified in assigning a probability of 1 to a factual statement (only logical truths warrant that value). We have already seen one reason for this: the partial book. If you hold that $Pr(p) = 1$, then you must consider a bet on p fair at 0 to 1 odds. Hence if you are truly willing to put your money where your mouth is, you should be agreeable to a "bet" where you lose everything if p turns out to be false and win nothing if it turns out true. There are other reasons for this attitude as well, though a discussion of them more properly belongs to the theory of knowledge rather than inductive logic. Suffice to say that, while our senses are a generally reliable instrument, they are not such as to make us absolutely certain of the phenomena we experience; even in a seemingly straightforward case like the yellow flame, you could have been hallucinating without knowing it, the lighting conditions might have been deceptive, or you could have developed a sudden case of color blindness. Although these are highly unlikely they are not impossible, and hence a probability value of perhaps 0.98 is more appropriate than unity. For philosophers who take this approach, the RC model is inadequate (this is a problem for logical theorists too, since they generally assume that in the inductive probability statements to be used in practical decisions the evidence statement is a bona fide item of our body of knowledge).

As a result, some philosophers have felt it desirable to replace RC with a rule for moving from $Pr_n(p)$ to $Pr_{n+1}(p)$, where the evidence statement q bringing about the change is not rendered a certainty. A workable rule to this end has been offered by Richard Jeffrey.[27]

> **Rule of Uncertain Evidence** (RUE): Where a change in degree of belief for a statement q occurs from $Pr_n(q)$ to $Pr_{n+1}(q)$, then for any statement p, $Pr_{n+1}(p) = [Pr_{n+1}(q) \times Pr_n(p/q)] + [Pr_{n+1}(\sim q) \times Pr_n(p/\sim q)]$.

Note that where '$Pr_{n+1}(q) = 1$', the RUE formula collapses into that for RC.

While RUE is of great value as a "fallibility" mechanism for a change of belief, the relation between subjective and inductive probability becomes obscure. Unlike the RC approach, we no longer work

from a set of certainties, $q_1, \ldots, q_n$, but from a set of basic, unconditional probabilities, $Pr_0(q_1), \ldots, Pr_0(q_n)$—unconditional since they are
not the result of inductive reasoning from a set of premises but instead
are the direct result of our observational experience. It does not seem
that RUE can be applied in such a way that it will lead us to the
results obtainable through repeated use of RC.[28]

More generally, relating degrees of belief to inductive probabilities
is a complex matter on the sort of fallibility approach implicit in RUE.
Since our body of evidence can no longer be characterized as a set of
certainties, determining a degree of belief for a nonobservational
statement p depends not just on the inductive probability of an
argument like $q_1, \ldots, q_n \therefore p$, but—inasmuch as there is some chance
for each q being false—on further arguments expressing the various
possible mistakes, such as $q_1, \ldots, \sim q_n \therefore p$. It is not at all clear as to
how a subjective probability is to be distilled from a set of inductive
ones such as these.

Some Objections to the Subjective Theory

1. Perhaps the most obvious objection is this: It is going too far to
claim that, as long as the calculus is obeyed, any assignment of probability values to a set of statements is legitimate and indeed "rational."
For the subjectivist, two reasonable persons confronted with the same
evidence can have different degrees of belief in the same statement, and
there is no "objective" way of settling such a dispute—as there is over
questions like whether 5283 is a prime number or whether the atomic
weight of neon is 26. However, as we saw in the previous chapter, if p
and q are logically independent, *no* statement of the form '$Pr(p/q) = x$'
is provable from the calculus alone nor is its negation. Hence any value
for x is allowable on the Subjective Theory. Where D_1 represents the
statement that a die falls deuce on a given toss and E abbreviates the
usual information, any value assigned to '$Pr(D_1/E)$' between 0 and 1
inclusive is "reasonable" as long as it is inductively consistent with the
agent's other probability assignments. But do we really wish to say that
a person who seriously claims that $Pr(D_1/E) = 0.98$ or that $Pr(D_1/E) = 0.00001$ is being reasonable? Most people would say that the "correct" value is $\frac{1}{6}$ or something very near it, and this is an assertion both
a logical theorist and a frequentist could uphold. But subjectivists
cannot quarrel with an assignment like 0.98; their advice is limited to
saying that if people who believe such things agree to wagers at the
corresponding odds, they might eventually come to feel that such an
assignment should be revised (but still, they were acting "rationally" in
making those assignments to begin with).

While most of us are willing to allow for relatively minor differences in probability estimates, we are unwilling to consider *all* belief

functions as reasonable simply because the calculus is not violated. Is a religious opponent of evolutionary theory being reasonable in ascribing a very high probability to the earth's being only 12,000 years old and in dismissing out of hand all of the geological evidence that points to a much greater age? Is a gambler who bets on fifteen at the roulette table being reasonable if he claims to be certain that he will win and yet can provide no concrete grounds to dissuade the rest of us from supposing that the odds are 37 to 1 against him?

We have seen that subjectivists try to soften the impact of these considerations by claiming that repeated use of Bayes' Theorem will in many instances tend to minimize radical differences in opinion that are reflected in initial probability values (though often a *very* long sequence is needed). But even here there is a problem: Initial probabilities of 0 and 1 are permissible on the Subjective Theory and the subsequent or posterior probabilities in such cases will be the same, thus precluding any eventual agreement.

Subjectivists hold that we are expecting too much if we maintain that two people with the same body of evidence should always, or even usually, agree on a probability value. Perhaps the logical theorist is wrong in supposing that it is possible to devise a set of rules that will resolve differences of probabilistic opinion; and perhaps it is not possible to give a more substantial account of inductively rational belief than mere conformity with the calculus. But the subjectivist has not shown that these tasks are impossible, and as the previous examples show the vast majority of us use terms like 'rational' and 'reasonable' in a much more restrictive fashion.

2. We saw in the previous chapter that alternative logics like SIL, CIL and RIL each constitute a standard or norm of inductive rationality. Rational action is associated with inductively strong inferences, though of course the three logics differ sharply on just which inferences are to be counted as inductively strong. But it should now be clear that the subjectivist rejects the linkage between rationality and inductive strength. The *only* such standard is conformity with the calculus, and since that is a feature common to all three logics, a hypothetical subject who uses CIL or RIL is just as rational as the rest of us who employ SIL. Moreover, the appeal to Bayes' Theorem as a mechanism that over time brings two agents' probability estimates closer together will not work here. For one who uses CIL assignments to state descriptions, the use of rules like Bayes' Theorem will on the contrary tend to make such estimates diverge even more from those of the rest of us.

Nor are things any better with RIL, which as we have seen precludes learning from experience. It can be easily shown that if RIL assigns a statement like Ga a probability of, say, ½, the value will remain ½ regardless of how many times rules for changing belief functions like RC and RUE are applied to it (e.g., $Pr_r(Ga) = Pr_r(Ga/Gb) = Pr_r(Ga/Fa \& Fb \& Gb)$. Thus the only way we would be able to change our original estimate for Ga would be to observe directly (if we were fortunate enough) the fact of a being G (or not being G, whichever is the case). It would be pointless on the RIL scheme to draw *inferences* about Ga on the basis of newly acquired observation statements, since the probability estimate given such evidence is no different from the original one. RIL thus constitutes an inductive dead end, and yet its employment is no less rational for a subjectivist than is the use of SIL.

3. The Subjective Theory also runs into trouble over well-confirmed generalizations like 'All ravens are black'. Here, the statement concerns an indefinitely large class of objects (ravens), thus making it implausible to suppose that it will be decisively confirmed in a finite period of time. Where 'A' represents the generalization about ravens, how is the subjectivist to analyze a statement like 'Pr(A) = 0.9'? Presumably an agent who believes this statement would be willing to wager $9 to win $1, but how could we ever determine whether such a bet has been won? Regardless of how many observations we make of black ravens, it still remains possible that the next observation will falsify A and hence it is possible for the wager to be lost. No finite sequence—however large—of observations, $Ra_1 \& Ba_1$, $Ra_2 \& Ba_2$, $Ra_3 \& Ba_3$, and so forth will ever bring it about that the wagerer should be paid the $1 winnings. Indeed, why should we prefer to bet on 'Pr(A) = 0.9' rather than, say, on the chance that a coin will come up heads in three straight tosses? Even though the likelihood of winning is slim in the latter case, we at least stand a chance of collecting. The subjectivist analysis of probability statements in terms of our willingness to bet seems to founder over statements like A whose truth cannot be definitively settled over a finite time span.

To make matters worse, suppose we are confident of the truth of A to the degree 0.9, and suppose also we are confronted with the following choice:

1. Betting that A will be falsified through the observation of a nonblack raven within the next five years
2. Betting that a single, well-balanced die will show a six in twenty straight tosses

We might very well prefer (1) to (2), and thus we would have no reluctance to bet on A being false in many situations like the preceding. Previously we were reluctant to bet on A being true—preferring instead the wager on three consecutive heads. Yet through all of this we are supposedly very confident of A's truth, making it difficult to see how such a high degree of belief can be explained on the subjectivist's scheme.[29]

Notes _____

1. For this chapter, it is essential that the reader be familiar with the materials in Chapter Five, especially Sections 3 and 6.

2. Perhaps the most prominent advocate of the Classical View was the astronomer Pierre Simon de La Place in *A Philosophical Essay on Probabilities,* (reprint, New York: Dover Publications, 1951).

3. For more criticism of the Principle of Indifference, see Henry Kyburg, *Probability and Inductive Logic* (New York: Macmillan, 1970), Chapter 3. The second objection to the principle discussed here was proposed by Rudolf Carnap in *Logical Foundations of Probability* (Chicago: University of Chicago Press, 1951), see Section 110.

4. This discussion presupposes a familiarity with Section 3 of Chapter Four.

5. See Reichenbach, *Theory of Probability* (Berkeley: University of California Press, 1949).

6. Ibid., p. 482. For more on the self-corrective method and the pragmatic justification, see the last half of Chapter 11.

7. For this section, the reader should be familiar with the last section of Chapter Five.

8. Why the qualification about small stakes? Would you accept a slightly favorable bet if a millionaire opponent demands that you put up *all* your money?

9. J. M. Keynes, *A Treatise on Probability* (London: Macmillan, 1921).

10. *Logical Foundations* is an example of the earlier view. For the later one see *The Continuum of Inductive Methods* (Chicago: University of Chicago Press, 1952).

11. To simplify the exposition at this point, the notion of a c-function as presented here is an amalgam of two distinct concepts in Carnap's work: a c-function and an m-function ("measure function"). Little is lost in doing this, and the reader has one less technical term to remember.

12. Since (I) and (II) are of interest only where F is an empirically observable property (swanhood, whiteness), w/k is restricted to values between but not including 0 and 1. Nonempirical properties such as Fx v $\sim Fx$ and Fx & $\sim Fx$ have relative widths of 1 and 0, respectively.

13. The axioms presented here—and much of the surrounding exposition— are from "Replies and Expositions," in *The Philosophy of Rudolf Carnap,* ed. P. A. Schilpp (LaSalle, Ill.: Open Court, 1963). It must be noted that Carnap's procedure in this work for determining c-values is different in several key respects from the method outlined earlier in this section and in Chapter Five. The emphasis now is on predicate families and the number of predicates in such a family rather than on the number of independent predicates and Q-properties. However, an exposition of this more recent approach is beyond our scope; suffice to say that Carnap's underlying philosophical position is unchanged. One of the advantages of the newer approach is that it permits adoption of John Kemeny's second Condition of Adequacy (to be discussed shortly) by means of which Axioms 10 and 11 are justified. That condition (viz., that the value $c(p/q)$ is to be depend solely on p and q) did not hold for the earlier system since c-values

were partly determined by the number of independent, basic properties of the domain (thus precluding Carnap's system from being a "Logical Theory" in the fullest sense) and by the number of primitive predicates of the formal language for expressing those properties (with the unfortunate consequence of tying c-values to the "richness" of the language being used).

14. Carnap actually formulates this axiom in a different but equivalent form.

15. The function $c\dagger$ is obtained when λ approaches infinity. When 'λ' is replaced with '∞' in (II), the righthand side reduces to w/k, which is the initial value in (I); hence no "learning from experience." Also, when $\lambda = 0$, the c-function obtained is in effect the Straight Rule. It tells us that if all observed swans are white, then since the relative frequency = 1, the c-value of the next swan being white is also 1 even though being a swan does not logically imply being white. So this function violates Axiom 6.

16. John Kemeny, "Carnap's Theory of Probability," in Schilpp, *The Philosophy of Rudolf Carnap*.

17. From "The Aim of Inductive Logic," in *Logic, Methodology and Philosophy of Science,* ed. E. Nagel et al. (Palo Alto, Calif.: Stanford University Press, 1965).

18. J. Hintikka, "A Two-Dimensional Continuum of Inductive Methods," in *Aspects of Inductive Logic,* ed. J. Hintikka and P. Suppes (Amsterdam: North-Holland, 1966), pp. 113–132.

19. Actually, Carnap has a response at this point because it can be shown (but won't here) that CIL and similar logics violate Axiom 10, thus allowing him still to reject CIL on a priori grounds. However, there are problems pertaining to the Condition of Adequacy on which that axiom rests. Space does not permit any further exploration of these matters, and it should be abundantly clear by now that the objections and rejoinders considered thus far do not settle definitively the questions that have been raised. See the references at the end of this chapter for more information.

20. See Carnap, *Logical Foundations,* p. 211. The principle has also been formulated in terms of using all of the *relevant* evidence available to us, but this is really no different from Carnap's statement since the irrelevant portion of the "total evidence available" is by definition that portion whose inclusion or exclusion from q in $\Pr(p/q) = x$ does not change the value x.

21. A. J. Ayer, "The Conception of Probability as a Logical Relation," in *Observation and Interpretation,* ed. S. Korner (New York: Proceedings of the Ninth Symposium of the Colston Research Society, 1957).

22. Carl Hempel, "Inductive Inconsistencies," in *Aspects of Scientific Explanation* (New York: The Free Press, 1962).

23. R. Carnap, "On the Application of Inductive Logic," *Philosophy and Phenomenological Research* 8: 133–148.

24. From "Replies and Expositions," *Logical Foundations.* For uniformity, Carnap's sign 'P*' has been replaced throughout with our 'Pr^s'. In place of 'logically true-or-false', Carnap uses the phrase 'L-determinate'.

25. Frank P. Ramsey, *The Foundations of Mathematics,* ed. R. Braithwaite (London: Routledge and Kegan Paul, 1950). See also Leonard J. Savage, *The Foundations of Statistical Inference* (New York: John Wiley and Sons, 1962).

26. Richard C. Jeffrey, *The Logic of Decision* (New York: McGraw-Hill, 1965).

27. *Ibid.,* Chapter 11. The formula is easily established with the help of Axiom 1, Theorem 5, and some truth-table considerations.
28. For a more complete account of changing beliefs, see Brian Skyrms's fine discussion in *Choice and Chance,* 2nd ed. (Encino, Calif.: Dickenson, 1975), Chapter 6. For more advanced coverage, see Jeffrey, *Logic of Decision.*
29. For a subjectivistic attempt at resolving this problem, see Jeffrey, *ibid.,* Chapter 12, Section 4.

Further Reading

Expositions and Defenses of the Frequency Theory

Feigl, Herbert. "De Principiis Non Disputandum . . . ?" In S. Luckenbach, ed., *Probabilities, Problems and Paradoxes.* Encino, Calif.: Dickenson, 1972.

von Mises, Richard. *Probability, Statistics and Truth.* New York: Macmillan, 1957.

Reichenbach, Hans. *Theory of Probability,* trans. E. Hutten and M. Reichenbach, 2nd ed. Berkeley: University of California Press, 1949.

Salmon, Wesley. "Vindication of Induction." In H. Feigl and G. Maxwell, eds. *Current Issues in the Philosophy of Science.* New York: Holt, Reinhardt and Winston, 1961.

_____. "The Justification of Inductive Rules of Inference." In I. Lakatos, ed., *The Problem of Inductive Logic.* Amsterdam: North Holland, 1968.

_____. "On Vindicating Induction." In S. Luckenbach, *Probabilities, Problems and Paradoxes.* Encino, Calif.: Dickenson, 1972.

Some Critical Essays on the Theory

Barker, S. F. "Comments on Salmon's 'Vindication of Induction'." In H. Feigl and G. Maxwell, eds., *Current Issues in the Philosophy of Science.* New York: Holt, Rinehart and Winston, 1961.

Black, Max. "Can Induction be Vindicated?" *Philosophical Studies* 10 (1959).

Burks, Arthur. "Reichenbach's Theory of Probability and Induction." *Review of Metaphysics* 4 (1951).

Lenz, John. "Problems for the Practicalist's Justification of Induction." *Philosophical Studies* 9 (1958).

Lenz, John. "The Frequency Theory of Probability." In E. Madden, ed., *The Structure of Science.* Boston: Houghton Mifflin, 1959.

Kyburg, Henry. *Probability and the Logic of Rational Belief,* Chapter 2. Middletown, Conn.: Wesleyan University Press, 1961.

Expositions and Defenses of the Logical Theory

Carnap, R. "On Inductive Logic." *Philosophy of Science* 12 (1945).

_____. "The Two Concepts of Probability." In H. Feigl and W. Sellars, *Readings in Philosophical Analysis.* New York: Appleton-Century-Crofts, 1949.

———. *The Continuum of Inductive Methods.* Chicago: University of Chicago Press, 1952.

———. *The Logical Foundations of Probability,* 2nd ed. Chicago: University of Chicago Press, 1962.

———. "Replies and Systematic Expositions." In P. Schilpp, ed., *The Philosophy of Rudolf Carnap,* pps. 966–998. La Salle, Ill.: Open Court Press, 1963.

———. "The Aim of Inductive Logic," in E. Nagel at al., eds., *Logic, Methodology and Philosophy of Science.* Palo Alto, Calif.: Stanford University Press, 1962.

———. *Studies in Inductive Logic and Probability* (with R. Jeffrey). Berkeley: University of California Press, 1971.

Hempel, Carl. "Inductive Inconsistencies." In *Aspects of Scientific Explanation.* New York: The Free Press, 1965.

Kemeny, John. "Carnap's Theory of Probability and Induction." In P. Schilpp, ed., *The Philosophy of Rudolf Carnap,* La Salle, Ill.: Open Court Press, 1963.

Keynes, J. M. *A Treatise on Probability.* London: Macmillan, 1952.

For essays critical of the Logical Theory, see first those by Arthur Burks, Hilary Putnam, and Ernest Nagel in the P. Schilpp, ed., *The Philosophy of Rudolf Carnap* (La Salle, Ill.: Open Court Press, 1963). See also Carnap's replies to them. For more, see the following.

Ayer, A. J. "The Conception of Probability as a Logical Relation." In S. Korner, ed., *The Colston Papers,* vol. 9, pps. 12–17. 1957.

Kyburg, Henry. *Probability and the Logic of Rational Belief.* Middletown, Conn.: Wesleyan University Press, 1961.

Lenz, John. "Carnap on Defining 'Degrees of Confirmation'." *Philosophy of Science* 23 (1956): 230–236.

Expositions and Defenses of the Subjective Theory

de Finetti, Bruno. "Foresight: Its Logical Laws and Its Subjective Sources," In H. Kyburg and H. Smokler, eds., *Studies in Subjective Probability.* New York: Wiley and Sons, 1964.

Jeffrey, Richard. *The Logic of Decision.* New York: McGraw-Hill, 1965.

Kyburg, H., and Smokler, H., eds., *Studies in Subjective Probability.* New York: Wiley and Sons, 1964.

Ramsey, Frank. *The Foundations of Mathematics,* ed. R. Braithwaite. London: Routledge and Kegan Paul, 1950. See the essay "Truth and Probability."

Savage, Leonard. *Foundations of Statistics.* New York: Wiley and Sons, 1954.

Skyrms, Brian. *Choice and Chance,* Chapter 6, 3rd ed. Encino, Calif.: Dickenson, 1975,

Criticism of the Subjective Theory

Burks, Arthur. *Cause, Chance and Reason,* Chapter 5. Chicago: University of Chicago Press, 1977.

Kyburg, Henry, *Probability and the Logic of Rational Belief,* Chapter 3, Middletown, Conn.: Wesleyan University Press, 1961.

Some Problems In Decision Theory

We now take a brief look at some philosophical issues in decision theory and some of the problems that arise for the expected value concept. In many cases the probabilities involved are not inductive ones but rather subjective or personal probability estimates of the kind discussed in Chapter Seven. In these cases, the term 'expected utility' would be more appropriate than 'expected value', but for uniformity we shall continue to use the latter term as well as the abbreviation 'EVal'.

Our expected value calculations for many of the wagers discussed in Chapter Three were carried out in terms of dollars, and in any game offered by a casino (except, under some difficult to attain conditions, blackjack) the expected value, so calculated, will obviously be negative for the player. We saw for example that placing a dollar on the field bet at a craps table has an expected value of –\$0.055. However, if the enjoyment derived from gambling was worth ten cents a play, the expected value would be positive to the wagerer.

Yet there is something artificial about figuring expected value in these terms, and not just because a monetary value is assigned to the "pleasurable" aspect of an activity. To appreciate this, let us first remind ourselves of the **Principle of Expected Value** (EVP):

> **EVP:** If $p_1, \ldots, p_n$ are mutually exclusive and jointly exhaustive on condition q, and c_i is a consequence of act **a** that occurs if p_i is true, then

$$\text{EVAL}\,(\mathbf{a}/q) = \sum_{i=1}^{n} [\Pr(p_i/\mathbf{a}\ \&\ q) \times \text{Val}(\mathbf{c}_i)]$$

Clearly the principle requires that the values of each of an act's consequences be determined individually, but the pleasure of gambling appears to be associated with the entire system of consequences rather than with the outcomes taken separately. The gambler derives enjoyment from the knowledge that while none of the outcomes is certain to occur, all have a chance—and some are of considerable value.

This last point raises a general problem concerning the concept of expected value and the rule of maximizing expected value. For there seem to be several kinds of cases where the value associated with a course of action cannot be neatly parceled out among its various possible outcomes. As an illustration, we will consider a version of the "Allais Paradox" (sometimes called the "Sure Thing Paradox"). Suppose we have 100 three-by-five cards numbered consecutively from one to one hundred. They are shuffled and one card is drawn. Let P_1, P_2, and P_3 be as follows:

> P_1: One of the cards numbered 1 to 89 is drawn
> P_2: The card numbered 90 is drawn
> P_3: One of the cards numbered 91 to 100 is drawn

Now consider the acts

> A_1: You receive \$10 million if P_3, otherwise nothing
> A_2: You receive \$1 million if P_2 or P_3, otherwise nothing

Most people would choose A_1 over A_2 on the grounds that success is improbable in either case (0.1 for A_1 and 0.11 for A_2), and A_1 has the larger prize. And even those who disagree would have to grant that preferring A_1 was at least a reasoned decision. Now let us consider two more acts:

> A_3: A gift of \$1 million
> A_4: \$1 million if P_1, nothing if P_2, \$10 million if P_3

Here, many people (at least many nonmillionaires) would choose A_3, and with good reason again. On A_3 you are certain to become a millionaire, whereas in A_4 there is a small chance that you will end up with nothing. So A_3 is a sure thing but A_4 is not; and anyone inclined to opt for A_4 would still have to admit that there was nothing foolish about choosing A_3. After all, a bird in the hand is worth two (or even ten) in the bush. So far, then, we have two sober, rational choices:

> **1.** A_1 is to be chosen over A_2
> **2.** A_3 is to be chosen over A_4

But how do these choices look from the standpoint of expected value? For present purposes, it does not matter whether the values placed on the three consequences are expressed in dollars or in utiles defined in terms of a utility function that accords with the Diminishing Value of Money principle. The following results will hold regardless of whether $10 million is valued at ten times $1 million or at a ratio as low as only twice $1 million. Hence we shall use just 'x' and 'y'.

First, we examine the expected values of $\mathbf{A}_1$ and $\mathbf{A}_2$:

3. $\text{EVal}(\mathbf{A}_1) = \Pr(P_1)0 + \Pr(P_2)0 + \Pr(P_3)x$

4. $\text{EVal}(\mathbf{A}_2) = \Pr(P_1)0 + \Pr(P_2)y + \Pr(P_3)y$

Now EVP dictates that we make the choice stated in (1), for within the range of values for x and y the calculation shows that $\text{EVal}(\mathbf{A}_1) > \text{Eval}(\mathbf{A}_2)$; that is,

5. $\Pr(P_2)0 + \Pr(P_3)x > \Pr(P_2)y + \Pr(P_3)y$

If we now add $\Pr(P_1)y$ to both sides of (5), we obtain

6. $\Pr(P_1)y + \Pr(P_2)0 + \Pr(P_3)x > \Pr(P_1)y + \Pr(P_2)y + \Pr(P_3)y$

However, the lefthand side of (6) is identical with $\text{EVal}(\mathbf{A}_4)$ and the righthand side of (6) is identical with $\text{EVal}(\mathbf{A}_3)$. It follows that $\text{EVal}(\mathbf{A}_4) > \text{EVal}(\mathbf{A}_3)$, which means by the **Rule of Maximizing Expected Value** (or RMV) that $\mathbf{A}_4$ is to be chosen over $\mathbf{A}_3$, just the opposite of what we are told by (2).

This is the Allais Paradox. On the one hand, eminently rational grounds were given for *both* (1) and (2), but on the other RMV tells us that if we decide according to (1) we cannot also conform with (2); in other words (1) and (2) express *inconsistent* choices using EVP.

The source of the problem appears to lie in the reason given for choosing $\mathbf{A}_3$—we are certain to succeed, absolutely no risk is present. The preference of $\mathbf{A}_1$ over $\mathbf{A}_2$, as we have seen, logically requires that no matter what quantity is added to both sides of (5), we must prefer the left side to the right side. The trouble is that when we add the particular quantity, $\Pr(P_1)y$, we obtain a sure thing that did not exist before. We have seen that we often place a premium on certainty, but the concept of expected value does not allow for any special consideration to be placed on the fact that I am *certain* to receive something of great value on one alternative whereas on the other there is a chance I will get nothing whatever.

What is worse, the paradox provides a counterexample to a basic theorem of the decision theories mentioned in our discussion of the Subjective Theory back in Chapter Seven. The **Sure Thing Principle** states that if two acts have the same consequence for a given p_i, then the subject's preference between the two acts should be independent of what exactly that consequence is. For example, A_1 and A_2 have the same outcome for P_1 (viz., receiving nothing), and so if P_1 occurs, it would not matter which of the two acts were chosen. Hence the principle tells us that our decision between the two should focus on the consequences for P_2 and for P_3.

This seems reasonable enough, but notice that A_3 and A_4 also have the same consequence for P_1 (viz., receiving \$1 million), so again the decision should be based on an examination of the outcomes for P_2 and P_3. We may set out the two decision situations as follows (for simplicity, stating the consequences in monetary units):

Act	P_1	P_2	P_3
A_1	0	0	\$10 million
A_2	0	\$1 million	\$ 1 million
A_3	\$1 million	\$1 million	\$ 1 million
A_4	\$1 million	0	\$10 million

This table makes clear that the first pair of acts have the same consequence for P_1 and similarly for the second pair. So by the Sure Thing Principle, our decisions should focus on conditions P_2 and P_3. But now notice that the consequences of acts A_1 and A_4 are the same for P_2 and P_3, and similarly, the consequences of acts A_2 and A_3 are the same for those two conditions. Hence, the two decision situations are identical as regards P_2 and P_3. Therefore, if we choose A_1 over A_2, we must also choose A_4 over A_3 (and similarly, if A_4 is chosen, A_1 should be too). In other words, it validly follows from the Sure Thing Principle that

A_1 should be preferred to A_2 if and only if A_4 is preferred to A_3

Yet we have already seen that it seems quite rational to choose A_3 while also choosing A_1. Moreover, empirical studies tend to bear this out. In one of them, corporate executives were confronted with the two choice situations, and 40 percent of them chose both A_3 and A_1.[1]

Does the Allais Paradox show that we must reject the Sure Thing Principle? In general, decision theorists are loathe to give up the principle; in some cases it is a valid consequence of the axioms of their theories, in others it is an axiom itself. Hence some have continued to argue that despite appearances the choice of both A_3 and A_1 is irrational behavior (a violation of a sound decision principle), while others have maintained that the principle becomes a sound one when certain restrictions are placed on its application. Still others hold that no violation of the principle occurs—when the outcomes are more fully specified (such as the anticipated "regret" one might feel if P_2 should occur given the choice of act $\mathbf{A}_4$) the choice of both $\mathbf{A}_3$ and $\mathbf{A}_1$ is sanctioned by the principle. We cannot explore the matter any further here, but an extensive literature has grown up around both the principle and the paradox.[2]

The Allais Paradox suggests that perhaps security and risk are properties of the act as a whole. The overall worth of an act is not always equal to the sum of the values and probabilities of its parts—in the foregoing example the worth of $\mathbf{A}_3$ exceeds its expected value. Similarly, a gambler as we saw gains satisfaction from certain kinds of risk taking and insecurity per se. But one who feels that gambling is morally objectionable or who is just highly conservative in financial matters obtains no such satisfaction and would no doubt find gambling to be a distinctly unpleasant activity even where the expected value is positive.

However, the Sure Thing Principle is not the only decision-thoeretic dogma that runs into trouble; the **Dominance Principle** does too. At first sight, it seems quite obvious. If one act "dominates" another in the sense that the values of the consequences of the first all exceed the corresponding values of those consequences for the second, then the subject should choose the first act. If you are given a choice between

$\mathbf{A}_1$: Receive \$5 if a coin shows heads, pay \$5 if it shows tails

$\mathbf{A}_2$: Receive \$4 if a coin shows heads, pay \$6 if it shows tails

you would obviously choose $\mathbf{A}_1$ since it dominates $\mathbf{A}_2$; it has the more valuable consequence if the coin comes up heads (\$5 vs. \$4) and the more valuable consequence if tails appears instead (−\$5 vs. −\$6). So regardless of whether the coin comes up heads or tails, you are better off choosing the first act. The Dominance Principle thus tells us to choose $\mathbf{A}_1$, and of course a calculation using EVP and then invoking RMV would give us the very same advice.

The Dominance Principle was a staple of early decision theories, but it eventually came to be seen as untenable—at least in the simple form just stated. To see why, let us consider an example adapted from Richard Jeffrey.[3] Bert is a heavy smoker who sees only two alternatives: continuing to smoke at the rate of at least two packs a day (call this $\mathbf{A}_1$) and quitting altogether ($\mathbf{A}_2$). Alternatives like cutting down to less than a pack a day or switching to pipes and cigars are not viable options for him. Bert is a 35-year-old American man, and he has seen an American Cancer Society study according to which 23 percent of all 35-year-old American men who are nonsmokers can be expected to die before age 65 whereas 41 percent of such men who smoke two or more packs a day can be expected to die before that age. Bert sees as the relevant statements for his decision:

P_1: I die before age 65
P_2: I live to age 65 or more

and based on the Cancer Society's statistics, his probabilities are

$$Pr(P_1/A_1) = 0.41 \qquad Pr(P_2/A_1) = 0.59$$
$$Pr(P_1/A_2) = 0.23 \qquad Pr(P_2/A_2) = 0.77$$

Where C_1 is the consequence of dying before 65 and C_2 that of living to 65 or beyond, we suppose Bert evaluates these consequences taking into account the pleasure derived from smoking and the pain of going cold turkey. Thus, using utiles specified in some appropriate way, his valuations are

If A_1 is chosen: $Val(C_1) = 0 \qquad Val(C_2) = 100$
If A_2 is chosen: $Val(C_1) = -5 \qquad Val(C_2) = 95$

Note that A_1 dominates A_2 and thus the Dominance Principle tells Bert that he should opt for continuing to smoke. Its advice here is that a rational person who obtains pleasure from smoking should go ahead and smoke.

But this is bad advice if Bert, like most of us nowadays, believes that there is a *causal* connection between continuing to smoke two packs a day and dying before age 65. That is, performing act A_1 causally contributes to the occurrence of death before 65 (in effect, to P_1 being true). This choice situation differs from the coin situation described earlier; there, the choice of an act had no bearing on whether the coin would show heads or tails. But here the choice of an act has a causal influence on which of P_1 or P_2 will be true. The Dominance Principle fails in choice situations where the acts under consideration are believed by the agent to be causally linked to the various conditions (described by statements, $p_1, \ldots, p_n$) that must be weighed in making the decision.

But if we simply use EVP to determine our choice, we obtain

$$EVal(A_1) = (0.41)(0) + (0.59)(100) = 59$$
$$EVal(A_2) = (0.23)(-5) + (0.77)(95) = 72$$

So by RMV Bert should choose A_2. It is an advantage of EVP that it specifies the probabilities of conditions P_1 and P_2 as *conditional* on the acts under consideration and hence unlike the Dominance Principle can take into account the possible influence of the acts themselves in determining relevant probability values.[4]

Fortunately, the Dominance Principle is easily amended to bring it in line with typical EVP calculations:

> **Revised Dominance Principle:** If act **a** dominates all alternative acts in a choice situation involving conditions $p_1, \ldots, p_n$, then the agent should choose act **a** *provided that* he/she believes that which act is performed has no causal influence on which of $p_1, \ldots, p_n$ is true.

This revised principle is widely accepted by decision theorists nowadays as accurately prescribing rational behavior. Of course applicability is another matter; there are not many practical decision-making contexts where one act in fact dominates all of its competitors. Nonetheless, the principle gives us sound, commonsense advice in those cases where it does apply and seems to be immune to counterexamples. On the other hand, EVP and RMV are supposed to be applicable to *all* decision-making contexts that involve a set of mutually exclusive and jointly exhaustive conditions, $p_1, \ldots, p_n$. So the EVP/RMV combination is the more important of the two, but it is equally important that it agree with the commonsense prescriptions of the revised principle in all those contexts where the latter does in fact apply.

Unfortunately, they do not always agree. In recent years, a number of interesting and provocative counterexamples have been proposed wherein the Revised Dominance Principle (and common sense) tell us one thing but EVP/RMV another. That is, in these decision situations the latter prescribes the wrong advice. All of the examples share a common feature: while the acts under consideration by the decision maker are believed to be *causally* independent of the relevant conditions, $p_1, \ldots, p_n$, they are not *probabilistically* independent of them. In other words, while the agent believes that which act is chosen has no causal influence on which of $p_1, \ldots, p_n$ is true, the probability estimates he or she gives for $p_1, \ldots, p_n$ *are* influenced by the acts under consideration. There will be one set of probability values given act a_1, another for a_2, and so forth, just as in the heavy smoker case—except there the different sets of values were the result of the agent's belief concerning a causal connection, whereas in the examples to be given here it is for a different reason. Thus, since there is a lack of belief in a causal relation, the Revised Dominance Principle applies to the counterexamples, and it gives us good advice whereas EVP/RMV does not. Let us look at one of the counterexamples that has been proposed.

The Eccentric Smoker. It was once suggested that the statistical correlation between heavy prolonged smoking and lung cancer is to be explained not by smoking being a cause of lung cancer but rather by smoking and the susceptibility to cancer *both* being effects of a common cause, specifically a genetic predisposition stemming from a defective gene. A person having the defective gene is more likely to contract lung cancer *and* more likely to choose to smoke than a person who does not have it, but prolonged smoking raises the probability of developing cancer not because it is a causal agent, but rather because it is a symptom of the defective gene. So if the gene is defective, cancer is more likely regardless of whether you smoke or abstain; (and if the gene is not defective, your chance of cancer is not affected by whether you smoke). Suppose Betty seriously believes this hypothesis and has some rational basis for it (perhaps some tentative studies have suggested it). Let us also suppose that she has tried smoking on several occasions and found it a pleasurable and satisfying experience. Given her belief in the hypothesis, should she smoke?[5]

It must be emphasized here that Betty's hypothesis does *not* say that the defective gene promotes an uncontrollable desire to smoke. The issue is not compulsive behavior but rational choice. Thus, the hypothesis claims that those who have the bad gene are more likely to choose to smoke than those who do not have it. It must also be stressed that whether the hypothesis is true is not at issue here; the relevant point is that Betty firmly believes it to be true.

Now surely the answer to the question of whether she should smoke is *yes,* if she genuinely believes the hypothesis. If she has the defective gene, then given the present state of medical science, nothing can be done about it. And if she has it, her chances of getting lung cancer are above the norm, but again there is nothing she can do about it. Given the hypothesis she believes, smoking will not further raise her chances since it is only a symptom of having the bad gene, not a potential cause of lung cancer. So why not go ahead and smoke if she finds it enjoyable?

Moreover, the Revised Dominance Principle prescribes smoking as the rational choice. Since Betty does not believe that the act of smoking has any causal influence on contracting lung cancer, the principle is applicable here, and smoking is clearly the dominant act; because of the enjoyment derived, she prefers the combination smoking-and-developing-cancer to abstaining-and-developing-cancer, and equally of course smoking-without-cancer is preferred to abstaining-without-cancer. So the revised principle and common sense agree here; smoking is the better choice under the (admittedly unusual) circumstances.

But let us now look at what EVP/RMV prescribes. Let A_1 be the act of taking up smoking and A_2 that of abstaining. The relevant conditions are

P_1: She develops lung cancer
P_2: She does not develop lung cancer

Given the defective-gene hypothesis and the attendant circumstances, the following probability estimates seem to be reasonable, and we will suppose that they are values Betty assigns (in any case, $Pr(P_1/A_1)$, for example, could be reduced to less than 0.4 or raised to 0.99 without affecting the point under discussion):

$$Pr(P_1/A_1) = 0.6 \qquad Pr(P_2/A_1) = 0.4$$
$$Pr(P_1/A_2) = 0.1 \qquad Pr(P_2/A_2) = 0.9$$

Note that $Pr(P_1/A_1)$ is much higher than $Pr(P_1/A_2)$, so A_1 (smoking) raises the chance of P_1 (lung cancer). But again, on Betty's hypothesis this is not because A_1 is a causal agent of cancer, but because it is symptomatic of the real cause, the bad gene. So while there is a probabilistic dependence here, there is no causal dependence between performing the act and developing cancer.

Using a utility scale to reflect the relative worth she attaches to the consequences, and again taking into account the pleasure she derives from smoking and the discomfort of refraining from it, her valuations are

If A_1 is chosen: $Val(C_1) = -8 \qquad Val(C_2) = 12$
If A_2 is chosen: $Val(C_1) = -10 \qquad Val(C_2) = 8$

A_1 is the dominant act and so by the revised principle should be chosen. But by EVP we have

$$EVal(A_1) = (0.6)(-8) + (0.4)(12) = -4.8 + 4.8 = 0$$
$$EVal(A_2) = (0.1)(-10) + (0.9)(8) = -1 + 7.2 = 6.2$$

Hence by RMV Betty should choose A_2, which just seems wrong. It would be a hopeless attempt to elude a cause of lung cancer; all it does is remove a symptom (and an enjoyable one at that).

Defenders of EVP have argued that, with appropriate clarifications and additions, EVP can be made to give the right advice.[6] Others, however, claim that EVP must be rejected and replaced by a quite different formula. For them, examples like Betty's situation show that

EVP is not sensitive enough to certain kinds of causal beliefs relevant to the agent's deliberations, and hence that causal concepts must be incorporated into the determination of expected value.[7]

There has been extensive and detailed debate on this issue, and we cannot even begin to explore it here. But we can note the consequences for two of the most puzzling and fascinating decision problems that have ever been raised: the Prisoners' Dilemma and the Newcomb Paradox. For those not already familiar with these problems, here they are.

The Prisoners' Dilemma. Two men are arrested for robbery. The police are convinced they did it but do not have all the evidence necessary for conviction. So they tell the suspects: "In a moment we will put you in different cells where you cannot communicate with each other, and each of you has one hour to decide whether you will confess. If one of you agrees to confess but the other does not, the confessor will go free but the other will be sentenced to ten years in prison (it has already been arranged with the judge). If both of you decide to confess, however, each of you will be sentenced to only four years. If neither of you decides to confess, we can still imprison both of you for one year on other charges (resisting arrest, vagrancy)." Assuming that each suspect thinks there is a high probability that his colleague will make the same decision one way or the other, should they confess?

The Newcomb Problem. A multibillionaire for whatever reason has taken a special interest in you, observing your actions over the years and making predictions about what you would decide to do (he might, for example, have predicted which college you would decide to attend). While he has not been infallible, his predictions about you have been right far more often than they have been wrong. On a Friday afternoon he tells you, "When you enter the bank Monday to do your usual business, I will be there and will offer you $1500. Over the weekend I will have made a prediction as to whether or not you will accept it, but of course you will not know what this prediction is. If I predict that you will refuse the $1500, I will deposit $1 million in your checking account before you enter the bank. If I predict that you will accept it, I will not." Sure enough, when you enter the bank on Monday, the billionaire is there and promptly offers you $1500. Should you accept?[8]

Many theorists who have considered these cases hold that the answers to our questions are "yes" and "yes." Those answers are endorsed by the Revised Dominance Principle since the dominant acts are respectively: choosing to confess and accepting the $1500. That the principle applies in both instances is evident from the fact that it would be ridiculous for the agents in question to suppose there is any causal connection between the act chosen and which of the relevant conditions will turn out to be true. Whether one of the prisoners confesses or not has no causal influence on what the other prisoner decides to do. Accepting or refusing the $1500 has no causal bearing on what prediction the billionaire makes (indeed the prediction is made well before the offer is presented to you). So the revised principle applies here and provides sound counsel, according to many writers. But as we will now see, EVP/RMV give the answers "no" and "no." However, unlike the case of the smoker who believes the defective-gene hypothesis, EVP here provides what some theorists consider the right answer.

The Prisoner's Dilemma Again: Let A_1 be the act of confessing and A_2 that of not confessing. The conditions are

P_1: The other prisoner confesses
P_2: The other prisoner does not confess

One of the fascinating aspects of this problem is that each prisoner must assess the probability that the other prisoner will think along the same lines and make the same decision. So let us suppose that one of the prisoners, Sam, figures that it is highly likely his compatriot will come to the same decision—specifically an 80 percent chance that they both decide to confess or decide not to confess. Thus Sam's probabilities are

$$Pr(P_1/A_1) = 0.8 \qquad Pr(P_2/A_1) = 0.2$$
$$Pr(P_1/A_2) = 0.2 \qquad Pr(P_2/A_2) = 0.8$$

Where C_1 is the consequence of the other prisoner's choice to confess and C_2 that of her choice not to do so, Sam uses the negatives of the various prison terms as his values:

If A_1 is chosen: $Val(C_1) = -4 \qquad Val(C_2) = 0$
If A_2 is chosen: $Val(C_1) = -10 \qquad Val(C_2) = -1$

Hence A_1 is the dominant act and by the Revised Dominance Principle (and no doubt by the thinking of the clever police officials) it should be chosen. But what does EVP tell us?

$$EVal(A_1) = (0.8)(-4) + (0.2)0 = -3.2$$
$$EVal(A_2) = (0.2)(-10) + (0.8)(-1) = -2.8$$

Thus RMV tells Sam that he should choose A_2, that is, don't confess. More generally, the same advice will be given by RMV if the probability that the other prisoner will decide as Sam does is greater than

0.77. The probabilities of the other prisoner confessing if Sam does and of not confessing if Sam does not need not be the same (as they are in the example), but if both exceed 0.77, RMV will prescribe not confessing. Yet in choosing not to confess, Sam risks ten years in prison whereas the worst he can get if he decides to confess is only four years and there is also the chance of going scot free.

The Newcomb Problem Again: Let A_1 be the act of accepting the $1500 and A_2 that of refusing it. If the billionaire has a track record of being correct in his predictions about you of roughly 90 percent, the conditions and probabilities are

P_1: The billionaire predicts that you will accept the money
P_2: The billionaire predicts that you will refuse the money

$$\Pr(P_1/A_1) = 0.9 \qquad \Pr(P_2/A_1) = 0.1$$
$$\Pr(P_1/A_2) = 0.1 \qquad \Pr(P_2/A_2) = 0.9$$

So if you accept the $1500, and the billionaire correctly predicts that you will accept it, there is a 0.9 chance you end up with just that and no more, but a 0.1 chance you will have a grand total of $1,001,500 if the prediction is incorrect (i.e., he predicted that you would refuse the $1500). If you refuse the money and the billionaire correctly predicts that you will refuse it, there is a 0.9 chance that you will end up with $1 million, and a 0.1 chance that you will get nothing at all if the prediction is wrong (i.e., he predicted that you would accept the $1500). Where C_1 is the consequence for each act of the prediction that you will accept and C_2 that of your refusing, the values are (again, for simplicity using dollars)

If A_1 is chosen: $\text{Val}(C_1) = 1500 \qquad \text{Val}(C_2) = 1,001,500$
If A_2 is chosen: $\text{Val}(C_1) = 0 \qquad \text{Val}(C_2) = 1,000,000$

thus showing that A_1 is the dominant act and hence by the revised principle should be chosen. But now let us look at the EVP calculations:

$\text{EVal}(A_1) = (0.9)(1500) + (0.1)(1,001,500) = 1350 + 100,150 = 101,500$
$\text{EVal}(A_2) = (0.1)0 + (0.9)(1,000,000) = 900,000$

Thus by RMV we are counseled to refuse the money, which conflicts with what we are told by the revised principle and, for many people at least, plain common sense. Notice that in one respect the Newcomb Problem resembles the Allais Paradox: by accepting the $1500 you are certain to come away with something whereas if it is refused there is an outside chance you will get nothing.

It has been convincingly demonstrated that The Prisoner's Dilemma is just a double-barreled version of the Newcomb Problem, albeit a more down-to-earth one.[9] As Richard Jeffrey has aptly put it, the latter is "a prisoner's dilemma for space cadets." Just as Sam must weigh the chance that his partner will decide to perform the same act that he (Sam) will perform, so in the Newcomb Problem you must weigh the chance that the billionaire will predict the same act as the one you will perform. Moreover, in each case the choice is between an act offering what under the circumstances is a large chance at a small good (only four years in prison, $1500) versus a small chance at a large good (going free, $1,001,500), and on the other hand, an act offering a large chance at an almost-as-large a good (only a year in prison, $1,000,000) versus a small chance at an evil (ten years in prison, no monetary reward). Because of the parallel reasoning, we will focus hereafter on the Newcomb Problem.

So who is right? Should you accept the $1500 or not? The question has been extensively debated by philosophers, decision theorists, and social scientists with one result: deadlock. While no poll is available, it is probably true that most opt for accepting the $1500, but opinions remain firm on both sides. We will now explore some of the reasons that have been offered by each of the parties to the dispute.

First, let us consider those who say: don't take the $1500. One reason should be pretty obvious by now. If you refuse the $1500, there is a 0.9 chance that the billionaire predicted this and hence that you would find $1 million in your checking account; but if you accept the $1500, there is a 0.9 chance the billionaire predicted *that* and hence that you would have only the $1500. A 0.9 chance at $1,000,000 is better than a 0.1 chance at $1,001,500 even though it carries with it a small, 0.1 chance of winding up with nothing. Moreover, suppose the billionaire has made the same offer to hundreds of other people, and suppose also that his powers of prediction with respect to them are as accurate as they have been with you: viz., a 0.9 probability that he will correctly predict what they decide. Then if probabilities and frequencies are even roughly the same, about 90 percent of the refusers have walked away with $1 million while only about 10 percent of the accepters have. So the best choice in this situation is to refuse the offer.

Now let us look at the other side. One argument is based on the Revised Dominance Principle and applies even if the predictive accuracy exceeds 90 percent. By the time you enter the bank on Monday, the billionaire has already made his prediction, and depending on what was predicted, either $1 million already has been deposited in your account or it has not. At this point, the money's being there—or its not being there—is a fait accompli and cannot be changed by anything you do or decide to do. Regardless of which act you choose, you now possess all the money in your account, but if you accept the billionaire's offer you will possess an additional $1500. No matter what amount of money is now in your checking account (and again, whether the million is there is beyond your control), you are better off with that sum plus the $1500 than without it. In other words, you should take the $1500 regardless of how accurate the billionaire's predictions are, for you thereby get $1500 more than you would if you declined, and you would receive—or not receive—the $1 million regardless of whether you accepted the $1500.

To reinforce this argument, imagine that a good friend of yours, Alice, is a teller at the bank; and she is the sort of person who would look out for your best interests. You have told her of the millionaire's offer, and when you enter the bank on Monday, she knows whether or not the $1 million has been deposited in your account. However, she cannot communicate with you because she is busy with customers, and the billionaire demands that you accept or refuse the $1500 immediately. Even though Alice cannot help you out here, it will be very useful for you to imagine what she *would* advise if she could. If the $1 million has been deposited, she would advise you to accept the $1500, since you would then have both amounts. If the $1 million was not deposited, she would again advise you to accept the $1500, since you would at least be $1500 better off than you are now. So in any case, you should take the $1500. If a helpful friend, who possesses more information about the situation than you, would advise you to take the money, then you should take it.[10]

There is a further reason for accepting the $1500. It is argued that the case of the Eccentric Smoker and the Newcomb Problem are structurally very similar in terms of the kind of probability assessments and consequence values the agent arrives at, and even in his or her beliefs about the presence (or absence) of various causal factors. Everyone—or nearly everyone—seems to agree that in the smoking example the dominant act of smoking should be chosen under the circumstances. But if so, they should opt for the dominant act of accepting the $1500 in the Newcomb Problem. Not to do so would be inconsistent given the formal similarity of the two decision situations. We will briefly look at the reasoning involved here.

First, of course, there is a dominant act in both situations, but beyond that they are parallel in terms of how probabilities and values are assigned. If you choose the dominant act (smoking, accepting the billionaire's offer), you obtain a small good (the pleasure of smoking, the $1500) at the expense of a low probability of obtaining a much greater one (avoiding lung cancer, receiving the million dollars). If you choose the other act (abstention, refusing the offer), there is a high probability of obtaining the larger good at the expense of a small probability of "the worst of all possible worlds" occurring (abstaining but developing cancer, receiving neither the $1 million nor the $1500).

Moreover, the agent does not believe that there is any causal connection between performing the acts under consideration and the relevant conditions obtaining, but nevertheless there is a probabilistic connection. Betty does not believe that smoking causes cancer, but her hypothesis nonetheless dictates that cancer is more likely if she smokes than if she does not. Similarly, in the Newcomb case you do not believe that which act you decide to perform has any causal influence on what the billionaire will predict (nor that what he predicts has any causal bearing on which act you will choose), but even so missing out on the $1 million is more likely if you accept the $1500 than if you refuse it. In each situation, the conditions are probabilistically connected with the acts but not causally so.

In addition, in each situation whether or not the conditions actually obtain are beyond the agent's control. On Betty's hypothesis, neither smoking nor refraining has any bearing on whether or not she develops lung cancer. In the Newcomb case, nothing you do has any bearing on whether or not the $1 million will be in your account when you enter the bank on Monday.

The difference between the two situations—at least as they have been described thus far—is that in the smoker example there is a common cause of both cancer and the choice to smoke, the defective gene. But, so the argument goes, does not the Newcomb Problem cry out for a common cause too? Given the very strong statistical correlation between the acts you have performed in the past and what the billionaire predicted you would do, is it not farfetched to suppose that this was just a matter of luck on the billionaire's part? Assuming that you have been aware through the course of your life that the billionaire was making these predictions and had been correct so often, surely you would have formed the hypothesis that there was some causal basis for the correlation, even though you may be unsure of what it is (much as Betty does not know the exact process by which the bad gene produces its effects). The acts do not cause the predictions, and unless you are prepared to accept some strange form of mental telepathy, the predictions do not cause the acts. So it is more likely that there is a common cause of both, perhaps reflected in a predictive method used by the billionaire (though it need not be a conscious one) and developed through past observations and experiences. To the extent that "you" as the protagonist in the Newcomb case have such a causal belief, the situation almost exactly parallels Betty's. So if smoking is the most rational choice in her case, accepting the $1500 is the most rational in yours.

So the Eccentric Smoker case sheds some light on the kind of deliberation involved in the Newcomb Problem and the Prisoner's Dilemma. But as we noted earlier, its chief importance here pertains to EVP and RMV—as does the Allais Paradox. The general problem raised in our discussion is this: let us suppose that any rational person who must choose among alternative courses of action in uncertain conditions assigns a certain "worth," positive or negative, to each act. Let us also suppose (though it is arguable on philosophical grounds) that each such "worth" may be given quantitative expression; that is, by a real number in utiles suitably defined (though again one might have qualms about the existence of such a definition). Finally we will suppose that it is always best to choose an act whose worth is not exceeded by any of its alternatives. The question then is this: should we identify this intuitive "worth" of an act with the expected value of that act as defined by EVP? The Allais Paradox and the Eccentric Smoker example suggest that for some acts, their "worth" might well differ from their expected value.

Notes _____

1. See K. R. MacCrimmon, "Descriptive and Normative Implications of the Decision-Theory Postulates," in *Risk and Uncertainty,* ed. K. Borch (New York: St. Martin's Press, 1968), pp. 3–23.
2. The Sure Thing Principle was first formulated by the noted decision theorist L. J. Savage. See his *The Foundations of Statistics* (New York: Wiley and Sons, 1954), especially pp. 101–103. For a different response to the paradox, see Richard Jeffrey, *The Logic of Decision,* 2nd ed. (Chicago: University of Chicago Press, 1983), Chapter 1. An excellent general discussion of the problem, along with many references for further reading, may be found in Ellery Eells, *Rational Decision and Causality* (Cambridge: Cambridge University Press, 1982), see Chapter 1.
3. Jeffrey, ibid., Chapter 1.
4. Earlier decision theorists like Savage used unconditional probabilities when calculating expected utilities and required that the probabilities for the conditions under consideration be the same for all acts in the decision situation (like our earlier coin example). Despite his commitment to the Dominance Principle, Savage could obtain the same result in his system as we (and Jeffrey) have here (that A_2 is the better choice) but it is a more complex and unintuitive calculation.
5. This example was suggested by the statistician Ronald Fischer. Very similar examples have been proposed by Brian Skyrms, and by Alan Gibbard and William Harper.
6. See especially Jeffrey, *The Logic of Decision,* Chapter 1; and Eells, *Rational Decision,* Chapters 6 and 7.

7. Three examples of such "causal" theories may be found in David Lewis, "Causal Decision Theory," *Australasian Journal of Philosophy* 59 (March 1981); Brian Skyrms, "The Role of Causal Factors in Rational Decision," in *Causal Necessity* (New Haven, Conn.: Yale University Press, 1980); and Alan Gibbard and William Harper, "Counterfactuals and Two Kinds of Expected Utility," in *Foundations and Applications of Decision Theory,* vol. 1 (Dordrecht: D Reidel, 1978).

8. This version of the Newcomb Problem is used by Jeffrey, *The Logic of Decision,* who attributes it to Howard Sobel. The problem gained wide attention upon the publication of Robert Nozick's "Newcomb's Problem and Two Principles of Choice," in *Essays in Honor of Carl G. Hempel,* ed. N. Rescher et al. (Dordrecht: D. Reidel Publishing Co., 1969). Nozick there attributed the problem to William Newcomb. Originally the millionaire's offer was $1000, but given the ravages of inflation since 1969, $1500 (or an even greater sum) seems more appropriate now.

9. David Lewis, "Prisoner's Dilemma Is a Newcomb Problem," *Philosophy and Public Affairs* 8 (1981), pp. 235–240.

10. This sort of argument has been proposed by G. Schlesinger; see his "The Unpredictability of Free Choices," *The British Journal for the Philosophy of Science* 25 (1974).

Index